Global Approaches
to the Holocaust

Contemporary Holocaust Studies

SERIES EDITORS

Ari Kohen
Gerald J. Steinacher

Global Approaches to the Holocaust

Memory, History, and Representation

EDITED BY MARK CELINSCAK AND MEHNAZ AFRIDI

University of Nebraska Press
LINCOLN

© 2025 by the Board of Regents of the University of Nebraska

All rights reserved

The University of Nebraska Press is part of a land-grant institution with campuses and programs on the past, present, and future homelands of the Pawnee, Ponca, Otoe-Missouria, Omaha, Dakota, Lakota, Kaw, Cheyenne, and Arapaho Peoples, as well as those of the relocated Ho-Chunk, Sac and Fox, and Iowa Peoples.

Publication of this volume was assisted by the University of Nebraska at Omaha Department of History's Charles W. and Mary Caldwell Martin Fund.

For customers in the EU with safety/GPSR concerns, contact:
gpsr@mare-nostrum.co.uk
Mare Nostrum Group BV
Mauritskade 21D
1091 GC Amsterdam
The Netherlands

Library of Congress Control Number: 2025000620

Designed and set in Minion Pro by A. Shahan.

Contents

Acknowledgments   ix

Introduction: Series of Concentric Circles   1
MARK CELINSCAK AND MEHNAZ AFRIDI

Part 1. Memory

1. Holocaust Memory in South Africa   17
SHIRLI GILBERT

2. Remembering the Holocaust in Mauritius: Legacies of Slavery, Colonial Violence, and Jewish Displacement   29
RONI MIKEL-ARIELI

3. Japan and the Holocaust: Domesticating Others' Horror   45
ROTEM KOWNER AND RAN ZWIGENBERG

4. Holocaust Memory: Temporalities, Actors, and Practices in Two National Cases, Argentina and Mexico   59
EMMANUEL KAHAN AND YAEL SIMAN

5. Resonances of the Holocaust in the Memory of Nazi Victims and Survivors Living in Chile   73
NANCY NICHOLLS LOPEANDÍA

Part 2. History

6. From Ominous to Miracle Poems: North African Musical Prophecies and Histories of the Holocaust   89
AOMAR BOUM

7. Open Doors and Open Hearts: President Manuel
   Quezon's Holocaust Sanctuary in the Philippines   105
   BONNIE M. HARRIS

8. Fort Ontario and American Debates over
   Refugee Admission   117
   REBECCA L. ERBELDING

9. Limiting the Undesirables: Jewish Refugee
   Migration to Australia in 1938 and 1939   131
   PAUL R. BARTROP

10. Reviewing the Past, Re-Viewing the Nation:
    Early Canadian Responses to Abella and Troper's
    None Is Too Many   145
    RICHARD MENKIS

11. Mexico and the Holocaust: The Contradictions of
    Postrevolutionary Immigration Policy   165
    DANIELA GLEIZER

Part 3. Representation

12. Holocaust Education in South Asia: The
    Much-Needed Response to Holocaust Denial,
    Trivialization, and Inversion   179
    NAVRAS J. AAFREEDI

13. Approaches to Holocaust Education in the
    Arab World: Obstacles and Solutions   193
    MOHAMMED S. DAJANI DAOUDI AND ZEINA M. BARAKAT

14. "When This Happens, Whoever Can Write":
    The Testimonial Representation of the Holocaust
    in Colombia   207
    LORENA CARDONA GONZÁLEZ

15. Holocaust Education in Australia: History,
    Importance, and Challenges   221
    SUZANNE D. RUTLAND

16. Aotearoa New Zealand   233
    ANN BEAGLEHOLE

17. Representing the Holocaust in a Museum Setting
    in Post-Apartheid South Africa and Africa   249
    TALI NATES

    Conclusion   263
    MARK CELINSCAK AND MEHNAZ AFRIDI

    Epilogue   267
    MARK CELINSCAK, MEHNAZ AFRIDI, AND ILAN STAVANS

    Contributors   281
    Index   289

Acknowledgments

The editors of this volume first met in January 2011 at the United States Holocaust Memorial Museum when they attended the Jack and Anita Hess Seminar for Faculty led by Hank Greenspan and Wendy Lower. Sessions focused on how to incorporate eyewitness testimony, including interviews and memoirs, in teaching about the Holocaust. One of the themes that emerged from the seminar was how testimonies can challenge and complicate our understanding of the past. At the time, Mehnaz was working on the role of Muslims in the Holocaust, a subject not yet well understood. Her research not only discussed antisemitism in the Arab world but also revealed how Muslims both helped Jews and were sometimes victimized alongside them in Arab countries under the Vichy government. Meanwhile, Mark was investigating how British and Canadian forces became involved in the liberation of a Nazi concentration camp. Both projects relied on eyewitness testimony and ultimately explored connections to the Holocaust outside continental Europe. Nearly ten years later, as editors we proposed a volume to bring together a range of scholars who demonstrate the global dimensions of the Holocaust.

Global Approaches to the Holocaust is part of the University of Nebraska Press's Contemporary Holocaust Studies series. We thank series editors Ari Kohen and Gerald Steinacher for their support, guidance, and encouragement. Established in 2019, the series focuses on contemporary issues connected to the study of the Holocaust, such as antisemitism, racism, political extremism, and ethno-nationalism. It aims to make academic research findings accessible and to foster dialogue between researchers, educators, and the broader public.

The first volume in the series, *Unlikely Heroes: The Place of Holocaust Rescuers in Research and Teaching* (2019), edited by Kohen and Steinacher, examines a wide range of activities that aided Jews during their persecution by the Nazi regime. The book reveals the challenges rescuers faced in assisting Jews during the war. The second volume in the series, *Antisemitism on the Rise: The 1930s and Today* (2021), also edited by Kohen and Steinacher, analyzes antisemitism during the 1930s and 1940s, and it draws parallels to today. The book considers how antisemitism progressed over time.

We are honored to edit the third volume in this series, *Global Approaches to the Holocaust: Memory, History, and Representation*. We would like to thank Ari and Gerald for their invitation to edit the third volume in the series; we appreciate their partnership. We are also grateful to Bridget Barry, editor-in-chief of the University of Nebraska Press, for her support. We thank acquisitions editor Courtney Ochsner for her time and effort working on this volume.

We are so very appreciative of the twenty-one scholars who contributed to this volume. Although their geographic specialties span different parts of the globe, their dedication to studying and better understanding the Holocaust is an objective they all share. *Global Approaches to the Holocaust* was conceptualized during a global pandemic, which created unexpected delays. We appreciate everyone's patience, kindness, and consideration as we worked to put this book together. Each scholar featured in the volume has made important contributions to the field of Holocaust studies. We are honored to feature their research in this book.

Lastly, the editors would like to thank their respective partners and children for their love, patience, and support as they navigated this challenging yet rewarding project.

Global Approaches
to the Holocaust

Introduction

Series of Concentric Circles

MARK CELINSCAK AND MEHNAZ AFRIDI

Most of European Jewry was murdered [in the Holocaust],
and the murderers were European Gentiles.
—Alvin Rosenfeld

The Holocaust no longer belongs only to Israel and the
Jews. Today, it belongs to the whole world.
—Tom Segev

Can an event defined by many people as a watershed in European
history . . . be remembered outside the ethnic and national boundaries
of the Jewish victims and the German perpetrators?
—Daniel Levy and Natan Sznaider

This volume takes as its starting point the global dimensions of the Holocaust, including the killing of Jews outside continental Europe.[1] It brings together memory, history, and representation, sometimes in the most unlikely places. Japan, for example, memorializes Chiune Sugihara, who served as vice-consul in Lithuania during the Second World War and issued thousands of transit visas to refugees attempting to flee Europe. He provided documents to Jews to permit their travel through Japan to the Dutch island of Curaçao in the Caribbean Sea. For his efforts during the Holocaust, the state of Israel declared Sugihara "Righteous Among the Nations." His work during the war, along with the history of the Holocaust, is detailed at the Chiune Sugihara Memorial Hall in Gifu, Japan. There are several sites of Holocaust remembrance and education in Japan that note Sugihara's efforts, including the Holocaust Education Center in Hiroshima, the Holocaust Education Resource Center in Tokyo, and the Auschwitz Peace Museum in Fukushima.

Why are there museums, memorials, and education centers in Japan about the genocide of European Jews, a crime that occurred nearly ten thousand kilometers away on another continent and that did not, in any major way, involve the country's citizens? Do the efforts of Chiune Sugihara make the Holocaust, in some small manner, a part of Japanese history? Why do the stories of Sugihara, Anne Frank, and the Holocaust in general concern the Japanese people? Rotem Kowner and Ran Zwigenberg's essay in this volume explores how the Holocaust is remembered in Japan, including responses to the diary of Anne Frank.

As a non-European country, Japan is certainly not alone in memorializing the Holocaust and teaching about it. *Global Approaches to the Holocaust* highlights that there are countless sites of Holocaust remembrance and education around the world. The Shanghai Jewish Refugees Museum commemorates the Jewish exiles who fled Europe and were forced to live in the city's ghetto during the Holocaust. The Hong Kong Holocaust and Tolerance Centre is devoted to Holocaust education in China. Quezon City in the Philippines features the Philippine–Israel Friendship Park, located within the Quezon Memorial Circle, which commemorates President Manuel L. Quezon's efforts to accept a thousand Jewish refugees into the country. The Holocaust Museum in Buenos Aires documents the Holocaust as well as the history of Argentina's Jews. Likewise, the Holocaust and Genocide Centre in Johannesburg raises awareness about the Holocaust as well as the Rwandan genocide, while the Cape Town Holocaust Centre teaches the Holocaust alongside many other genocides. There are also major Holocaust museums and centers in Australia, Canada, Mexico, New Zealand, and the United States. Countries around the world mark, remember, commemorate, and teach about the Holocaust.

This volume considers the Holocaust as a global event that reverberated far beyond Europe. It presents a diverse range of voices that add to the historical, memorial, and representational reach of the subject. This volume asks: What happens when scholars shift their focus from an exclusively European perspective and adopt a more global approach? What new insights are gained from exploring the impact of the Holocaust from outside the European milieu? How do countries that were not directly impacted by Nazi policies of occupation and extermination remember the Holocaust? What consequences does an expansive approach to the Holocaust entail? From essays about North and South Africa, Mauritius, Japan, Argentina, Mexico, Chile, the Philippines, the United States, Australia, Canada, India, Pakistan, Palestine, Colombia, New Zealand, and more, *Global Approaches to the Holocaust* seeks to create a critical voice in Holocaust studies that is not exclusively about Europe but also about Asia, Africa, South and North America, and the Middle East.

As a subject of historical study and as a crime that has been memorialized, the Holocaust has global significance and implications, whether cultural, social, political, artistic, geographic, or economic.[2] A crime perpetrated by Nazi Germany and its collaborators against Jews extends far beyond continental Europe. Alvin H. Rosenfeld explains that there have been serious "shifts of both definition and priority" in how the Holocaust has been understood over time.[3] From the earliest research into the subject, scrutinizing the experiences of those directly involved in the Holocaust was the primary concern of researchers.[4] For many scholars, these became the central categories of participants involved in the Holocaust. However, as the field expanded, so too did the subjects under investigation.[5]

Contemporary study of the Holocaust now explores individuals such as liberators and survivors, resisters and rescuers, alongside "Nazi hunters" and absconding war criminals, as well as those who profited during the Holocaust.[6] The range of topics has also swelled to include life in the displaced persons camps, postwar trials, Holocaust denial, and the like. These topics call into question both the geographical and chronological scope of the Holocaust. For example, should connections to the Holocaust by countries such as Canada and the United States, however tentative, be viewed as part of the history and study of the subject? Indeed, there are several links to the genocide for both countries, such as their restrictive immigration policies before, during, and after the war, refusal to accept Jewish refugees aboard the MS *St. Louis*—in which hundreds were later killed in the Holocaust—along with efforts as liberators of Nazi camps, involvement in postwar trials, assistance in the displaced persons camps, and the permitting of perpetrators to settle in their respective countries. Does the study of such topics from the point of view of these two countries enhance our understanding of the Holocaust? *Global Approaches to the Holocaust* answers these questions in the affirmative.

Likewise, is the chronological history of the Holocaust exclusively from 1941 to 1945, when most of the large-scale killings occurred? How does expanding the chronological scope change or challenge our understanding of the Holocaust? Does the history of the Holocaust extend to both the prewar period, including the establishment of the Dachau concentration camp (1933)—the first built by the National Socialists—the Nuremberg Laws (1935), and Kristallnacht (1938), and the postwar period, including the International Military Tribunal (1945–46), the Kielce pogrom (1946), and the displaced persons camps (1945–52)? Again, *Global Approaches to the Holocaust* answers in the affirmative.

In addition to its history, this volume explores how the Holocaust is remembered and how this memory has been debated in different countries. In previous studies, such as *The Holocaust and Memory in the Global Age*—one of the first comprehensive studies of the Holocaust as "global memory"—Daniel Levy and Natan Sznaider explore how the subject transcends both time and space. They argue that the "abstract nature of 'good and evil' that symbolizes the Holocaust . . . contributes to the *extraterritorial* quality of cosmopolitan memory."[7] Similarly, in *Marking Evil: Holocaust Memory in the Global Age*, Amos Goldberg contends that for some the "Holocaust has become an event of international political and cultural importance . . . [that] has undergone a form of globalization and that its memory has become a supreme ethical imperative for many societies in the world."[8] To an extent universalization has turned the Holocaust into a "foundational event," as Alon Confino suggests, thus becoming a moral benchmark for our time.[9]

Much like the example of Chiune Sugihara, *Global Approaches to the Holocaust* is illustrative of this transnational turn in Holocaust remembrance. Sugihara's efforts have been widely recognized around the world, especially by Israel (for saving Jews), Lithuania (where his wartime work occurred), and Japan (his home country). One of our volume contributors, Rotem Kowner, reveals that the "commemoration of Sugihara contributes to our understanding of how the universalization of the Holocaust has taken place and of how transnational memory functions."[10] These three countries—Israel, Lithuania, and Japan—along with others, have helped spread awareness of Sugihara globally.[11] He is never presented in the same manner, as each country promotes different aspects of his story to fit their needs. Each nation carefully navigates how to present the memory of Sugihara yet must also contend with how he has been characterized elsewhere in the world. Similarly, *Global Approaches to the Holocaust* explores how the memory of the genocide has been traversed and shaped not only in Japan but in South Africa, Mauritius, Chile, Argentina, and Mexico.

As the field of Holocaust studies expands and incorporates a greater range of topics, Rosenfeld asks, "Will the overwhelmingly destructive history of the Holocaust be accurately remembered and still at the center of concern?"[12] In short, as scholars investigate issues further removed from the murder of European Jews, will the field lose its fundamental focus? Or does the exploring of subjects such as resistance, rescue, liberation, displacement, and immigration enhance our understanding of this genocide? A. Dirk Moses notes the various anxieties scholars have about "diminishing the Holocaust" through comparisons with other genocides or by expanding the study beyond Europe.[13]

This volume makes it clear that there are global dimensions to the Holocaust, whether they are historical—however tenuous—memorial, or representational. How might scholars proceed in terms of the global dimensions of the Holocaust? Peter Novick suggests that "Holocaust memory" can be understood as a series of "concentric circles."[14] While he doubts its memory will ever become truly "global," his concept of "concentric circles" underscores some of the tensions concerning the historical, memorial, and representational aspects of the subject. According to Novick:

> In the innermost circle are Israel, a country whose population—or much of it—has a special relationship to the victims of the crime, and Germany, the country of the criminals and their descendants. The next circle is made up of the countries of Europe that were occupied by Germany during World War II, which were the scene of the deportation to death (or the actual murder) of their Jewish citizens. Once we leave Europe we move to countries without any such "organic" connection to the Holocaust.... [If] what is at issue is the division between those with "organic" ties to the protagonists and those with no such ties, one should discuss, alongside Germans, both Jews in Israel and Jews in the Diaspora. But it seems to me manifestly the case that the sort of relationship to the great crime that is shared by Jews and Germans makes their sense of connection to the Holocaust so much greater than that of others as to constitute a difference in kind, rather than just one of degree.[15]

Americans as liberators of Nazi camps offer the country a connection to the Holocaust, yet their relationship to the subject will be different in context, intensity, and scope when compared to Germany. In terms of Novick's concept of "concentric circles," we must also be mindful that, while initiated by Nazi Germany, more than 90 percent of Jews killed in the Holocaust were killed outside of prewar German borders. Conquest and occupation were key elements in the killing process. Moreover, the research of scholars such as Jan Tomasz Gross, Jan Grabowski, and Barbara Engelking has revealed, for example, Polish complicity in the Holocaust.[16] Likewise, the Holocaust in North Africa has long been overlooked. During the war Morocco and Algeria fell under the pro-Nazi Vichy regime, while Tunisia and Libya suffered under German and Italian occupation. Jews in North Africa saw antisemitic policies imposed on them, including the expropriation of property, internment, and forced labor. Moreover, Maghrebi Jews were deported to Nazi extermination camps from North Africa.[17] This volume explores the historical connections to the Holocaust, largely, although not exclusively, through the topic of immigration in the United States, Canada, Australia, Mexico, Morocco, and the Philippines.

In many ways the Holocaust was a particular event that has become universalized. Dan Diner suggests that the Holocaust is a "universal crime [that] was perpetrated against humanity in the medium of the extinction of a particular group, namely the Jews."[18] The Second World War was a global affair of which the Holocaust was a significant part. The historical, memorial, and representational linkages between the two subjects have established a correlation in many countries around the world, some stronger than others.

While the merits and demerits of the study and representation of the global impact of the Holocaust can be debated, its reality simply cannot be ignored. As chapters in *Global Approaches to the Holocaust* demonstrate, the Holocaust reverberates on virtually every continent and in a broad range of countries. Aleida Assmann notes: "As a universal reference and a global icon, it is understood in countries all over the world. Through representations such as images, films, books, events, and discourses, the Holocaust has spread to become a universal symbol with a global resonance."[19] Engaging with these histories, representations, and symbols is one of the aims of this volume. In the following chapters broad historical connections to the genocide are elucidated, the contours of its memory are delineated, and how both are represented in various ways are clarified, all the while being mindful of the subject's distortion. "[The] Holocaust has become a volatile area," Rosenfeld warns, "of contending images, interpretations, historical claims and counter-claims."[20] How have these claims and counterclaims, along with the expanding chronology and the changing geographic scope, impacted the study of the Holocaust?

In the past, Holocaust studies have typically been approached from an exclusively, albeit understandably, European perspective and often by historians. Indeed, as a watershed event in history, scholars focused primarily on the dynamic between male perpetrators and victims in German-occupied Europe. Over time Holocaust studies expanded to include the experiences of women—both victims and perpetrators—Sinti and Roma, gay men, the disabled, refugees, and other minority groups. Consequently, the field began to encompass a larger geographic identity. As researchers have come to better understand the scope of the Holocaust, it has become more complex with emergent scholarship from diverse perspectives and geographic areas. Indeed, some of the most recent and fascinating areas of research on the Holocaust often come from such previously understudied countries such as Morocco, India, Argentina, Mexico, China, and Algeria.

The last decade has seen an increase in research that explores the Holocaust by adopting a global perspective. These approaches do not detach themselves from European history; rather, they incorporate perspectives and voices not always considered in more traditional studies of the Holocaust. For example, Aomar Boum and Sarah Abrevaya Stein's *The Holocaust and North Africa* is the first English-language study to explore how the Holocaust was viewed in North Africa. Likewise, Michael Rothberg's *Multidirectional Memory: Remembering the Holocaust in the Age of Decolonization* is one of the first to bring together Holocaust and postcolonial studies. These vibrant, innovative works push the boundaries of Holocaust studies in exciting, original directions.

This volume concerns how the Holocaust was and continues to become a global event. It does not explore the Holocaust and other genocides comparatively. Instead, it examines the various linkages between the Holocaust as a subject—historical, memorial, and representational—in countries around the world. As A. Dirk Moses offers, approaching the Holocaust from a global frame of reference brings us toward a "genuine interest in all civilizations and cultures facing the challenge of imposing and resisting hegemony in a competitive system of nation- and empire-states."[21] *Global Approaches to the Holocaust* strives to connect all of us as a global human community through stories about birth, death, immigration, and survival.

Keeping in mind the debates about the Holocaust as a European or universal catastrophe, this volume demonstrates the deepening of these questions and presents the reader with a multitude of approaches to decipher where and when the impact of the Holocaust begins and ends. From the historical perspective to the memorialization and representational value of the Holocaust, this book presents a rarified lens into the expanding research into the imprints, effects, and need for further study of the subject. Research continues to show that people today have little or no knowledge of the Holocaust.[22] This volume acts as a conduit to see how this lack of awareness has impacted different geographic ranges, races, and immigration history.

Global Approaches to the Holocaust is organized into three key sections. The first, "Memory," explores how the Holocaust has been both remembered and memorialized around the world. How do various countries publicly recall the Holocaust? The worldwide reach of the subject is clear in this chapter. From Latin America to South Africa to Mauritius and Japan, countries around the world reflect on the crimes and injustices of the Holocaust in a variety of ways. The authors in this section reveal the kind of impact the subject can make on a nation's history alongside contemporary issues such as antisemitism, racism, and bigotry.

In "Holocaust Memory in South Africa," Shirli Gilbert discusses the tensions of remembering the Holocaust before, during, and after apartheid, as well as the deep memories of colonial resistance by Jews and non-Jews. How the memory of the Holocaust in South Africa has evolved over time is a central focus of the chapter. In its transition to a democratic form of governance, Gilbert reveals how the Holocaust became a "benchmark" in South Africa as it continues to come to terms with its own painful past.

In "Holocaust Memory: Temporalities, Actors, and Practices in Two National Cases, Argentina and Mexico," Emmanuel Kahan and Yael Siman investigate how the memory of the Holocaust was expressed in two Latin American countries. This comparative approach allows the authors to demonstrate how the remembrance of the Holocaust differs in the two cases, as well as how national contexts and local interpretations cast doubt over the notion of a fixed global memory of the Holocaust. Likewise, in "Japan and the Holocaust: Domesticating Others' Horror," Rotem Kowner and Ran Zwigenberg explore a series of questions about the Holocaust in the Japanese context. The chapter examines the country's knowledge of the Holocaust from the 1950s to the present. The authors explore the wartime wounds of the Japanese, especially the atomic bombings of Nagasaki and Hiroshima, which became a reference point in their understanding of the Holocaust. Kowner and Zwigenberg discuss how the Holocaust and other atrocities have impacted Japanese intellectual life and remembrance of the Second World War. The authors highlight Japanese appropriation of the Holocaust, which is used for its healing and denial of certain painful memories.

The contours of memory differentiate in other essays, such as "Remembering the Holocaust in Mauritius: Legacies of Slavery, Colonial Violence, and Jewish Displacement" by Roni Mikel-Arieli. The author seeks to discover how Holocaust memory in Mauritius relates to Jewish deportation to the island during the war. An important aspect of this essay discusses how Jews were deported to Mauritius and had already experienced the rise of Nazism, antisemitism, and racial persecution. In "Resonances of the Holocaust in the Memory of Nazi Victims and Survivors Living in Chile," Nancy Nicholls Lopeandía considers the oral narratives of European Jews who found sanctuary in Chile, before, during, and after the Second World

War. The essay details the history of Chile and how European Jews immigrated to a country in the Global South. Lopeandía asks readers to consider the hardships Holocaust survivors faced while living under a military dictatorship (1973–90) in another part of the world. It is an example of what Michael Rothberg has termed "multidirectional memory," a process that features "ongoing negotiation, cross-referencing, and borrowing."[23] Lopeandía concludes that for the Holocaust survivors who settled in Chile after the war, their memories were influenced by the distinct framework of the Global South.

The second section, "History," explores the Holocaust largely from the perspective of immigration and national politics. The authors in this section provide a closer look into the overarching issues of national policies about Jews as well as antisemitism in the context of each country. These essays examine how one might read Holocaust history in terms of antisemitism and xenophobia that are evidenced in the discussions on immigration policies and actions against Jews. The genocide itself did not necessarily occur in many of these countries, but the resentment of immigrants, antisemitism, and racist attitudes kept Jews out at times. There are also overlooked histories of rescue and accommodation analyzed in this section.

Bonnie M. Harris's essay, "Open Doors and Open Hearts: President Manuel Quezon's Holocaust Sanctuary in the Philippines," examines a country where Jews were welcomed during the war. The author explores how Manuel Luis Quezon y Molina, the central figure in the Philippine evolution from a Spanish colony to an independent republic, helped shape the nation's response toward the oppressed of the world, especially Jewish refugees. The organized programs established in the Philippines, which were empowered by Quezon, were hospitable and allowed for resettlement.

Another rare example is illustrated in Aomar Boum's chapter, "From Ominous to Miracle Poems: North African Musical Prophecies and Histories of the Holocaust." The author demonstrates the deep-rooted influences of the Holocaust in Morocco by exploring how music became a tool of resistance. The essay provides a short history of the early 1930s when North African Jews were warning about the rise of Adolf Hitler. As Boum notes, some even wrote and published poems before the war about the "Nazi omen." His essay brings to the reader the rich songs, poems, and words that served as a prewar warning of the destructive ideology of Nazism.

This section also highlights important turning points in the history of the United States. For example, "Fort Ontario and American Debates over Refugee Admission" by Rebecca L. Erbelding illustrates the complex and at times problematic immigration policies of the United States. In this essay, the author focuses on Fort Ontario in Oswego, New York, the only refugee camp established in the United States during the Second World War. The 982 people, mainly Jews, who arrived in August 1944 were the only Holocaust-era refugees to enter the United States outside of the immigration system. Erbelding argues that the experiences of these refugees and their hardships have been left out of the history in the United States. The essay also expounds on how the flawed actions of the U.S. government in trying to deal with refugees have been repeated over the subsequent decades. Likewise, in "Limiting the Undesirables: Jewish Refugee Migration to Australia in 1938 and 1939," Paul R. Bartrop reveals that approximately 90 percent of qualified Jews were rejected from Australia because they were Jews. Many of these issues continue to resonate in the world today.

Moreover, as Richard Menkis notes in his essay, "Reviewing the Past, Re-Viewing the Nation: Early Canadian Responses to Abella and Troper's *None Is Too Many*," debates in Canada over the immigration of Jews in the 1930s and 1940s raise questions not only about the past but also about policies being proposed and implemented in the present. In "Mexico and the Holocaust: The Contradictions of Post-Revolutionary Immigration Policy," Daniela Gleizer explains, "The Mexican experience shows how one specific administration could simultaneously adopt contrary positions on different groups of refugees seeking asylum." The range of these historical essays brings us to the question of the expansiveness of Holocaust history and how one understands the geographic boundaries if we employ such a multidimensional lens.

The third and final section of this volume, "Representation," explores the Holocaust through education, testimonial literature, and museum settings. The International Holocaust Remembrance Alliance (IHRA)—founded in 1998 as the Task Force for International Cooperation on Holocaust Education, Remembrance, and Research (ITF)—was established to unite governments worldwide to promote Holocaust education.[24] Indeed, Holocaust scholars and centers have conducted numerous data analyses of how much students or society know about the genocide. How can Holocaust education make a difference in a nation's curriculum? What do local communities need to do to make Holocaust studies a part of international curriculums?

In this section we have included Palestine and India to demonstrate the amount of work that needs to be done to stop antisemitism and Holocaust denial. For example, in "Holocaust Education in South Asia: The Much-Needed Response to Holocaust Denial, Trivialization, and Inversion," Navras

J. Aafreedi explores the landscape of South Asia and the challenges of Holocaust denial and trivialization. He makes the case for the value of Holocaust education in India and, by extension, around the world. This essay is also a study about the absence of Holocaust education in South Asia. Aafreedi examines several newspapers and religious and propaganda journals that highlight the antisemitic attitudes prevalent in South Asia. An explicit and deeply important topic that has been discussed by many Israeli educators is how to introduce Holocaust education into the Palestinian curriculum. In "Approaches to Holocaust Education in the Arab World: Obstacles and Solutions," Mohammed S. Dajani Daoudi and Zeina M. Barakat investigate the many challenges and barriers to Holocaust education in the Arab context, especially in Palestine. They provide an overview of the crucial need for Holocaust education in not only Palestine but also the Arab and the Muslim worlds. The authors focus on the importance of teaching about the experience of suffering and discuss how it can impact feelings of empathy for the "other" and, in the Palestinian context, Israelis and Jews. From history of the roots of antisemitism in the Arab world to case studies and education curricula, the essay examines Holocaust denial and distortion. Dajani and Barakat expand the field of Holocaust studies through recognition of one another's pain and acknowledging the truth of Jewish and Palestinian suffering at different but important points in history.

In "'When This Happens, Whoever Can Write': The Testimonial Representation of the Holocaust in Colombia," Lorena Cardona González relays a deepening of the testimony of Jews whose lives were impacted and shattered by the Holocaust. These painful works of testimonial literature reflect on the identity of the survivor. The author also expands on how we might think of the Holocaust and Jewish immigration during periods of war and violence in Colombia. Was the trauma of persecution, dehumanizing mistreatment, and death revived through these works of representation?

This section also highlights the work of Holocaust education. In "Holocaust Education in Australia: History, Importance, and Challenges," Suzanne D. Rutland discusses the history of Holocaust education that developed with the opening of museums in Melbourne in 1984 and Sydney in 1992. The author shows the differences in Holocaust education for the public and how the Jewish communities in Melbourne and Sydney developed different outreach programs over the last two decades.

In "Representing the Holocaust in a Museum Setting in Post-Apartheid South Africa and Africa" and "Aotearoa New Zealand," Tali Nates and Ann Beaglehole, respectively, raise important questions about Holocaust education in countries with their neglected communities. They both argue that education can remain relevant to future generations by using the Holocaust to combat intolerance and racism. Each nation adopts its technique for Holocaust education, and the authors note how important it is to have approaches to teaching the subject so that it can reach audiences in South Asia, Africa, and elsewhere.

In the volume's conclusion we explore some historical narratives that exemplify the complexity of the Holocaust and its global reach. *Global Approaches to the Holocaust* closes with two vignettes concerning the worldwide dimensions of the Holocaust, told through the lives of individuals. Both essays characterize the range of Jewish survivor experiences from the viewpoint of persecution, immigration, loss, and memory. The first essay explores the life of Charles K. Bliss, who was interned at both the Dachau and Buchenwald concentration camps. His flight from persecution led Bliss to six countries over four continents and to countless cities. His life story demonstrates how the global war both directly and indirectly impacted the lives of so many victims during the genocide. In the second essay of the epilogue, Ilan Stavans demonstrates the power of stories to articulate that which is difficult to grasp: the pain of others. Stavans combines fiction, family autobiography, and history to retell the imagined story of Guita Blumenthal, one of the 937 passengers aboard the MS *St. Louis*. The account is told through the perspective of Abel Eisenberg, her twenty-nine-year-old boyfriend and Stavans's great-uncle, who had reached Cuba three years earlier and had helped arrange Blumenthal's ticket from Hamburg, Germany. The overarching theme of the essay is the intermingling of the wider world with the calamity of the Holocaust. The author leaves us with the silences and complexities of the human story. "The *St. Louis* returned to Hamburg," Stavans tells us, "without passengers."

Global Approaches to the Holocaust critically engages with the Holocaust through history, memory, and representation. It also demonstrates that the study of the Holocaust in Africa, the Middle East, South Asia, South Africa, Australia, Latin America, and North America raises important questions about the policies and politics of each nation. The scholars in this volume bring new, innovative approaches to the study of the Holocaust and reflect on how it has impacted the global community with its actors both near and far.

Notes

First epigraph: Alvin H. Rosenfeld, *A Double Dying: Reflections on Holocaust Literature* (Bloomington: Indiana University Press, 1980), 160.

Second epigraph: Original: "Der Holocaust gehört nicht mehr nur Israel oder den Juden, er gehört heute der ganzen Welt." Tom Segev in an interview with *Wiener Zeitung*, May 27, 2006.

Third epigraph: Daniel Levy and Natan Sznaider, *The Holocaust and Memory in the Global Age*, trans. Assenka Oksiloff (Philadelphia: Temple University Press, 2006), 4.

1. Christopher R. Browning, *The Origins of the Final Solution: The Evolution of Nazi Jewish Policy, September 1939–March 1942* (Lincoln: University of Nebraska Press, 2004), 1. As Browning notes, "In a brief two years between the autumn of 1939 and the autumn of 1941, Nazi Jewish policy escalated rapidly from the prewar policy of forced emigration to the Final Solution as it is now understood—the systematic attempt to murder every last Jew *within the German grasp*" (italics added). This includes outside continental Europe, such as North Africa, the Channel Islands, and elsewhere. For example, Aomar Boum's essay in this volume explores the Holocaust in German-occupied North Africa.
2. For example, see Jan Eckel and Claudia Moisel, *Universalisierung des Holocaust? Erinnerungskultur und Geschichtspolitik in internationaler Perspektive* (Göttingen, Germany: Wallstein Verlag, 2008).
3. Alvin H. Rosenfeld, *The End of the Holocaust* (Bloomington: Indiana University Press, 2011), 6.
4. For example, Raul Hilberg, first in his pioneering *The Destruction of the European Jews* and in subsequent works, presented a triad of agents in the Holocaust known as the perpetrator, the victim, and the bystander. Raul Hilberg, *The Destruction of the European Jews* (Chicago: Quadrangle Books, 1961), and *Perpetrators, Victims, Bystanders: The Jewish Catastrophe, 1933–1945* (New York: HarperPerennial, 1993).
5. Those who are called "rescuers" or "helpers" have also become a focal point in contemporary Holocaust studies. In both scholarly research and popular media, rescuers have been elevated in public consciousness. Individuals such as Chiune Sugihara and Aristedes de Sousa Mendes fall into this category. For example, see Ari Kohen and Gerald J. Steinacher, eds., *Unlikely Heroes: The Place of Holocaust Rescuers in Research and Teaching* (Lincoln: University of Nebraska Press, 2019).
6. For example, see Mehnaz Afridi, *Shoah through Muslim Eyes* (Brighton, UK: Academic Studies Press, 2017); Mark Celinscak, *Kingdom of Night: Witnesses to the Holocaust* (Toronto: University of Toronto Press, 2022); Wolf Gruner, *Resisters: How Ordinary Jews Fought Persecution in Hitler's Germany* (New Haven CT: Yale University Press, 2022); Gerald Steinacher, *Nazis on the Run: How Hitler's Henchmen Fled Justice* (Oxford: Oxford University Press, 2011); David de Jong, *Nazi Billionaires: The Dark History of Germany's Wealthiest Dynasties* (Boston: Mariner Books, 2022).
7. Levy and Sznaider, *Holocaust and Memory*, 4 (italics added).
8. Amos Goldberg, "Ethics, Identity, and Antifundamental Fundamentalism: Holocaust Memory in the Global Age (a Cultural-Political Introduction)," in *Marking Evil: Holocaust Memory in the Global Age*, ed. Amos Goldberg and Haim Hazan (Oxford: Berghahn Books, 2015), 4.
9. Alon Confino, "The Holocaust as a Symbolic Manual: The French Revolution, the Holocaust, and Global Memories," in Goldberg and Hazan, *Marking Evil*, 59.

10. Rotem Kowner, "A Holocaust Paragon of Virtue's Rise to Fame: The Transnational Commemoration of the Japanese Diplomat Sugihara Chiune and Its Divergent National Motives," *American Historical Review* 128, no. 1 (March 2023): 62.
11. Kowner, "Holocaust Paragon," 47–48.
12. Rosenfeld, *End of the Holocaust*, 247.
13. A. Dirk Moses, "Anxieties in Holocaust and Genocide Studies," in *Probing the Ethics of Holocaust Culture*, ed. Claudio Fogu, Wulf Kansteiner, and Todd Presner (Cambridge MA: Harvard University Press), 332–35.
14. Peter Novick, "The Holocaust Is Not—and Is Not Likely to Become—a Global Memory," in Goldberg and Hazan, *Marking Evil*, 48.
15. Novick, "Holocaust Is Not," 48–49.
16. For example, see Jan Tomasz Gross, *Neighbors: The Destruction of the Jewish Community in Jedwabne, Poland* (Princeton NJ: Princeton University Press, 2012); Jan Grabowski and Barbara Engelking, eds., *Night without End: The Fate of Jews in German-Occupied Poland* (Bloomington: Indiana University Press, 2022).
17. Aomar Boum and Sarah Abrevaya Stein, introduction to *The Holocaust and North Africa*, ed. Aomar Boum and Sarah Abrevaya Stein (Stanford CA: Stanford University Press, 2019), 7.
18. As quoted in Aleida Assmann, "The Holocaust—a Global Memory? Extensions and Limits of a New Memory Community," in *Memory in a Global Age: Discourses, Practices and Trajectories*, ed. Aleida Assmann and Sebastian Conrad (London: Palgrave Macmillan, 2010), 106.
19. Assmann, "The Holocaust," 114.
20. Rosenfeld, *End of the Holocaust*, 7.
21. A. Dirk Moses, "The Holocaust and World History: Raphael Lemkin and Comparative Methodology," in *The Holocaust and Historical Methodology*, ed. Dan Stone (New York: Berghahn Books, 2012), 286.
22. "New Survey by Claims Conference Finds Significant Lack of Holocaust Knowledge in the United States," Conference on Jewish Material Claims Against Germany, March 2018, https://www.claimscon.org/study/.
23. Michael Rothberg, *Multidirectional Memory: Remembering the Holocaust in the Age of Decolonization* (Stanford CA: Stanford University Press, 2009), 3.
24. See Larissa Allwork, *Holocaust Remembrance between the National and the Transnational: The Stockholm International Forum and the First Decade of the International Task Force* (London: Bloomsbury Academic, 2015).

Part 1
Memory

1

Holocaust Memory in South Africa

SHIRLI GILBERT

This chapter surveys how the Holocaust featured in public discourse in South Africa before, during, and after apartheid. Memory of Nazism was regularly invoked during the apartheid years (1948–94) by Jews as well as non-Jews across the political spectrum. Where some saw obvious parallels between the two systems, others however drew starkly different conclusions. Some sought to downplay the connections, though for disparate reasons; others overstated them, challenging the apartheid state with the most morally potent language they could muster. Both mainstream and leftist Jewish responses were nourished by Holocaust memory, but in each case that memory had widely divergent implications and forms. During the transition to democracy in the early 1990s, the Nazi past was perceived as an obvious and potent historical benchmark for understanding what had happened in South Africa, for envisioning justice and reconciliation, and for thinking about how apartheid might be historicized and commemorated.

Despite the pervasiveness of Nazism in South African public discourse, there has been little scholarly discussion of Holocaust memory as it developed and shifted over the course of more than seven decades, an absence that is conspicuous not least because of South Africa's identity as the quintessential racial state after World War II. This brief synopsis outlines the broad contours of this complex history, identifying some of the key events and trends, and emphasizing the shifting and sometimes unexpected ways in which the Nazi past has informed engagement with the apartheid past and the postapartheid present.

Nazi Influences (1933–45)

The impact of Nazism in South Africa has been the subject of some debate, much of it political rather than scholarly. The relationship between Nazi ideology and Afrikaner nationalism—the broad political movement from which apartheid ultimately emerged—has been an issue of especially intense contestation, and it is sometimes difficult to distinguish historiography from writing that itself participates in the process of shaping memory and discourse on the subject.

For apartheid's opponents, establishing local connections with wartime fascism was one way to explain the nature of the racist regime and the struggle against it. Several quasi-scholarly texts advancing this thesis were produced during the apartheid era, their titles asserting clear political standpoints.[1] The regime's defenders, by contrast, downplayed the Nazi influence as a passing flirtation with foreign ideologies. In the postapartheid period, commentators across the political spectrum have variously minimized the historical links, gently disparaged the "hyperbole" employed by activists during the apartheid era, and stressed the continuing relevance of the analogy to South Africa's ongoing efforts to confront its past.[2]

Distinct from these often polemical writings, work by Milton Shain and Patrick Furlong reveals that although apartheid South Africa was always quite distinct from Hitler's Germany, Afrikaner nationalist politics were indeed influenced by ideas derived from Europe, particularly Nazi Germany, in the 1930s and 1940s. In particular, while antisemitism had not been absent from South African life before this period, the 1930s saw increasing manifestations of explicitly political anti-Jewish behavior in a Nazi mold. In October 1933, just months after Hitler's accession to power, the South African Gentile National Socialist Movement, better known as the Greyshirt Movement, was established under the leadership of Louis T. Weichardt. The most prominent and successful of a number of radical right "shirt" movements to arise at this time, it was openly pro-Nazi and drew on a distinctively European antisemitism. By 1933 the Nazi party had already established local branches in South Africa and had begun to distribute substantial amounts of propaganda material. The popular Nazi-inspired Ossewabrandwag (Oxwagon Sentinel), an Afrikaner paramilitary movement, was established in 1938, and in 1940 Oswald Pirow founded the avowedly pro-fascist Nuwe Orde (New Order) party.[3]

While these were radical right-wing organizations, their ideas resonated well into the mainstream. The Quota Act of 1930, which targeted Jewish immigration from Eastern Europe, was premised on the notion of Jews' "unassimilability"—a concern expressed by Minister of the Interior D. F. Malan and echoed across party and linguistic lines.[4] Jewish immigration from Germany between 1934 and 1936 fueled increasing radicalization in the Gesuiwerde (Purified) National Party (NP), the Afrikaner opposition to the ruling United Party coalition, and by the 1938 election antisemitism had become an integral aspect of its platform.[5] In 1937 the Aliens Bill was introduced, largely to stem the influx of German Jewish refugees.[6] Nationalist newspapers minimized or refuted Germany's actions, including its aggressive expansionist policies and violent anti-Jewish attacks, and the NP opposed the decision to enter the war against Germany in 1939; Parliament ultimately supported Prime Minister Jan Smuts' effort only by a very narrow majority of 80 to 67.[7]

While Afrikaner nationalism absorbed the influence of Nazi ideas, it is worth emphasizing that Nazism was never appropriated wholesale or without qualification, and that apartheid, when implemented in 1948, became in fundamental ways a distinct ideological and political system. To begin with, it was a system of exploitation rather than of genocide. In addition, although race was the key organizing principle for all areas of life, according to the sociologist Deborah Posel, apartheid ideologues "eschewed a science of race, explicitly recognising race as a construct with cultural, social and economic dimensions."[8] While the precise meaning of apartheid was disputed from the outset, in Nationalist rhetoric it was justified not on the basis of white racial superiority but rather in terms of "separate development."

Whatever the precise nature of Afrikaner nationalism's link with Nazi Germany, the Jewish community certainly perceived a profound threat and in attempting to mobilize support consistently reiterated that antisemitism had "found a footing here through direct Nazi stimulus."[9]

Apartheid (1948-94)

Under Malan's leadership the National Party won an unexpected election victory in May 1948. Popularly dubbed the "Malanazis," many of the party's leaders were known Nazi sympathizers.[10] They came to power on a platform of apartheid ("apartness"), a system of political and social organization intended to push existing segregation even further in order to—in Malan's euphemistic terms—"give the various races the opportunity of uplifting themselves on the basis of what is their own."[11]

Antiracist activists in South Africa had long pointed to connections between Nazism and the scourge they were fighting at home. In its "Declaration to the Nations of the World" drafted in July 1945, for example, the Non-European Unity Movement declared, "The peoples of the world who were horrified by the inhuman record of Nazism may be unaware of the fact that the Non-Europeans [non-whites] of South Africa live and suffer under a tyranny very little different from Nazidom."[12] The Nazi analogy became even more potent after the advent of apartheid, and activists frequently made reference to the links between the Nazis and the "Nats."[13] In

1957 the young firebrand Nelson Mandela wrote: "The Nationalist Government have frequently denied that they are a fascist Government inspired by the theories of the National-Socialist Party of Hitlerite Germany. Yet the declaration [sic] they make, the laws they pass and the entire policy they pursue clearly confirm this point."[14] There are numerous similar examples of activists (in South Africa and in exile) as well as solidarity movements making reference to the Nazi past during the apartheid period. The analogy was often invoked in deliberately polemical ways: if the anti-apartheid struggle was to be understood as "the most important moral battle in the world since the defeat of Nazism,"[15] international audiences would need to be presented with a clear historical parallel between Nazi ideology and its echoes in the present. Frequent comparisons were made between discriminatory legislation in South Africa and Nazi Germany, and the genocide was invoked as a warning of what apartheid might become if left unchallenged.[16]

Comparisons between Nazism and apartheid were not only directed toward external audiences. The South African Indian activist Ahmed Kathrada, to give one prominent example, emphasized that his thinking about racism in South Africa had been formatively shaped by visits in 1951 to the sites of Auschwitz and the Warsaw Ghetto, as well as his engagement during his long imprisonment on Robben Island with Anne Frank's *Diary* and other Holocaust texts.[17]

Jews were disproportionately represented among the ranks of antiracist activists, and some echoed these comparisons.[18] In his memoir *Into Exile*, for example, Ronald Segal, editor of the influential journal *Africa South*, referred to apartheid's "spiritual predecessor, the Germany of the Nazis," and drew numerous parallels between the two systems.[19] The educationist Franz Auerbach, a refugee from Nazi Germany, repeatedly pointed to the "similarities between some present features of life in South Africa and life under Hitler."[20] The discourse of South African Jewish activists is replete with similar examples, although it should be stressed that some rejected the contention that their activism was in any way motivated by Jewish history or identity.

The mainstream Jewish community increasingly avoided such explicit comparisons, however. In the early postwar decades, the community still unambiguously framed its battle against antisemitism as inextricably linked to the broader struggle against racist, antidemocratic forces in South Africa, seen against the background of Nazi racism. While this stance was driven in part by community interests, it also shows Jews' recognition that their historical experience of persecution might inform their responses to racism in the wider world.[21] Nonetheless, comparisons between Nazism and apartheid declined in mainstream Jewish discourse from the late 1950s as the community sought to secure its relationship with the government, to distance itself from Jewish activists who might threaten that security, and to assert its sense of commitment and belonging to South Africa. Holocaust memorialization and education during the apartheid period were almost exclusively initiated by Jews. The first commemorative gatherings were held as early as 1942, and in subsequent years Holocaust memorial ceremonies were a regular item on the communal agenda. By 1960 the South African Jewish Board of Deputies (SAJBD) could proudly report that "in South Africa the occasion is better observed than in many other countries."[22]

South African Jews also put notable effort into memorial building in the immediate postwar period, in contrast to other Jewish communities outside Europe. Discussions about a communal monument began as early as 1946 around the Hungarian Jewish immigrant Hermann Wald's colossal statue *Kria* (1946), and the first communal memorial dedicated to the six million victims was consecrated in Cape Town in October 1954. More significantly, in May 1959 the immense *Six Million* (also sculpted by Wald) was unveiled at West Park Cemetery in Johannesburg, with extensive cross-communal support.[23]

Jewish memory narratives from early on made little if any reference to the local political context and were underpinned by the idea of the Holocaust's uniqueness. Perhaps the most significant emphasis of commemorative narratives was the reborn "new Jew" of Israel, who relied on their own strength and defenses in preserving the Jewish future. The Holocaust and Zionism were closely connected throughout the apartheid years, coming to constitute the two "central pillar[s] of South African Jewry's civil religion."[24] In remembering the Holocaust, Jewish leaders warned repeatedly of the antisemitic dangers that Jews faced in the post-Nazi era, and emphasized that the obvious lesson to be learned from the genocide was that only defiant self-reliance, particularly in the form of Israel, could ensure Jewish existence.[25]

The Nazi past surfaced periodically in mainstream South African public discourse, though links to apartheid were again seldom made. The stage play *The Diary of Anne Frank* enjoyed enormous success with white audiences in the 1950s, and it was revived several times in subsequent decades. Diverging from the American script, however, local productions foregrounded Anne's Jewishness, emphasizing the story's particularity and thus deflecting from any connections that might have been drawn with the local context.[26] Nazi Germany was a consistent subject on school history syllabi, compulsory from at least 1964, though connections with apartheid were hardly in evidence.[27] Where the subject of Nazi Germany arose in public conversation, as during the capture and trial of Adolf Eichmann in 1960–61, the Jewish communal leadership emphasized the dangers of antisemitism and the Holocaust's uniqueness.[28] The fierce debate surrounding the screening of the "Genocide" episode of *The World at War* in 1976 reflected the growth of Holocaust denial in this period, seen also in the Jewish community's legal battle that same year against Richard Harwood's book *Did Six Million Really Die?* Denialism remained the preserve of a far-right fringe, however, perhaps as a result of growing relations between the South African and Israeli governments from the 1970s.[29]

In sum, although some South African activists invoked the Nazi past in order to protest apartheid's injustices, when it came to Jewish as well as broader South African public discourse, few links were identified with the local context. The gradual rapprochement between Jews and Afrikaners was facilitated in part by this willful amnesia about the Nazi period.[30] If one of the challenges for American Jews in the postwar period was preserving minority group consciousness while also integrating into the larger society, as Eric L. Goldstein has suggested, the South African case did not present a similar dilemma.[31] In fact, apartheid's emphasis on "separate development" was conducive to a narrowing focus on Jewish life and welfare, as Gustav Saron recognized: "the general cultural and political climate in South Africa, which emphasizes the separateness of the various racial and cultural groups of the population, favours the perpetuation of a Jewish group existence."[32]

After Apartheid (1994–)

While the divisive political context of apartheid South Africa gave rise to several distinct, conflicting narratives relating to the Nazi past, during the transition period in the 1990s growing efforts began to construct more consensual memory cultures as part of the shift toward democracy. Scholarship on memory in post-apartheid South Africa has emphasized the conscious centrality of history to the new government's project of reconciliation and nation building and the concomitant investment in memory narratives that promoted unity and avoided jeopardizing the fragile political situation.[33]

The Holocaust featured regularly in the public sphere as part of these broader narratives. Its prominence can be attributed somewhat to the global ascendancy of Holocaust memory in this period and to Jewish support, but these are only partial explanations. The country's transition provided particularly fertile soil for the growth of distinct memory narratives; indeed, the

Holocaust was considered one of the most obvious yardsticks for thinking about South Africa's recent past.[34]

Anti-apartheid rhetoric persisted well into the 1990s, particularly in the controversial book *Reconciliation through Truth*, in which cabinet minister Kader Asmal and his coauthors characterized apartheid as a crime against humanity through a comparison with Nazism.[35] Alongside this trend was an increasing tendency to highlight the differences as well as the similarities between Nazism and apartheid and to emphasize how memory not only of the Nazi regime but specifically of the genocide could inform the process of nation building. The Holocaust featured substantially in discussions about memorializing apartheid, particularly in the vigorous debate about plans for Robben Island, the location of the infamous prison for Black male political opponents of the regime.[36]

The Holocaust also surfaced regularly in discussions around the Truth and Reconciliation Commission (TRC), which began its work in April 1996. To begin with, the decision to pursue the path of a truth commission rather than criminal trials was justified explicitly with reference to the Nuremberg Trials.[37] The commission's investigation of the antecedents and causes of gross human rights violations, and the "motives and perspectives" of the perpetrators, also drew substantially on Holocaust research.[38] The Holocaust was a pervasive presence in discussions around reconciliation and rehabilitation and was frequently invoked by individuals as they recounted their experiences at TRC hearings.[39]

Another key moment in the development of Holocaust memory narratives after apartheid was the high-profile exhibition "Anne Frank in Our World," which opened on the eve of the first democratic elections in March 1994. The keynote address at the Johannesburg opening was given by Nelson Mandela, one of his first public acts as president. The exhibition firmly established the connection between apartheid and the Holocaust in the crucial period when memory narratives were beginning to be formed. Anne's story was a powerful vehicle for promoting the aims of national unity, not least because it allowed for a generalized focus on human rights without requiring audiences to confront the complexities of their past.[40]

Paradoxically, the Holocaust became a key means for the Jewish community to assert its identification with and commitment to the new democracy. This entailed a corresponding modification of memory narratives. Increasingly, the focus on particularist concerns that had characterized community memorialization under apartheid expanded to encompass a universalized language that by that time had also begun to dominate globally.[41]

The unparalleled public response to the "Anne Frank in Our World" exhibition led to the establishment in 1999 of the Cape Town Holocaust Centre (since renamed the Cape Town Holocaust and Genocide Centre, CTHGC), the first of its kind in Africa. Like the exhibition, the CTHGC was established, and is strongly supported, by the Jewish community, but it also has many non-Jewish patrons and financial backers.[42] Echoing the universalized language of twenty-first-century Holocaust remembrance, the CTHGC describes its mission as "creating a more caring and just society in which human rights and diversity are respected and valued."[43]

In 2007 an umbrella body, the South African Holocaust and Genocide Foundation (SAHGF), was established in response to the Department of Education's introduction of the Holocaust into the national curriculum, which resulted in massively increased demand from schools and teachers across the country. The CTHGC could not answer this demand alone, and two further independent centers were opened to cope with the need for education and teacher training. The Durban Holocaust Centre (since renamed the Durban Holocaust and Genocide Centre), founded in 2008 by Mary Kluk, chronicles the history of the Holocaust with a particular focus on the story of Anne Frank, concluding with a display on rescuers in twentieth-century genocides, including the Holocaust, Rwanda, Bosnia, and Cambodia.[44] The Johannesburg Holocaust and Genocide Centre began operating in 2008 under the direction of Tali Nates and in September 2015 moved into an iconic new building in the heart of the city. The center's work is focused primarily on the Holocaust and the 1994 genocide in Rwanda, and its educational initiatives explore the connections between genocide and contemporary human rights issues.[45]

The Holocaust remains a prominent feature of the postapartheid landscape. Books, films, TV programs, and theatrical productions dealing with the Holocaust are widely accessible. The three Holocaust centers welcome approximately fifty thousand visitors each year, most of them South Africans rather than foreign tourists, and deliver extensive educational training and resources throughout South Africa. Nates maintains that the Holocaust has served as an "excellent entry point" for tolerance education because it is "removed from the local experience" and is thus "less emotionally charged." The Holocaust allows an opportunity to discuss local racism more openly because it is less immediate.[46]

During the transition from apartheid, the Holocaust was a means for the new government to establish its commitment to human rights and thereby restore South Africa's image on the international stage. The larger question of why it was this history in particular—as opposed, for example, to violent colonial pasts or racism in the American South—that featured so prominently in attempts to understand apartheid, however, requires much fuller exploration.[47] It also remains to be seen to what extent contemporary anti-Zionism and the Israel-apartheid analogy, which dominates public discourse on the subject of the Israeli-Palestinian conflict, will shape the development of Holocaust memory narratives in South Africa in years to come.

Notes

1. Brian Bunting, *The Rise of the South African Reich* (Middlesex, UK: Penguin, 1964); Sipo E. Mzimela, *Apartheid: South African Naziism* (Nairobi, Kenya: Evangel, 1983).
2. Hermann Giliomee, "The Making of the Apartheid Plan, 1929–1948," *Journal of Southern African Studies* 29, no. 2 (2003): 373–92; Heribert Adam, "Anti-Semitism and Anti-Black Racism: Nazi Germany and Apartheid South Africa," in *The Holocaust's Ghost: Writings on Art, Politics, Law and Education*, ed. F. C. DeCoste and Bernard Schwartz (Edmonton: University of Alberta Press, 2000), 244–59; Kader Asmal, Louise Asmal, and Ronald Suresh Roberts, eds., *Reconciliation through Truth: A Reckoning of Apartheid's Criminal Governance* (Cape Town, South Africa: David Philip, 1996).
3. Patrick J. Furlong, *Between Crown and Swastika: The Impact of the Radical Right on the Afrikaner Nationalist Movement in the Fascist Era* (Middletown CT: Wesleyan University Press, 1991); Milton Shain, *A Perfect Storm: Antisemitism in South Africa, 1930–1948* (Johannesburg, South Africa: Jonathan Ball, 2015); Christoph Marx, *Oxwagon Sentinel: Radical Afrikaner Nationalism and the History of the Ossewabrandwag* (Pretoria, South Africa: Unisa Press, 2008).
4. Shain, *Perfect Storm*, 12–17.
5. Furlong, *Between Crown and Swastika*, 61–69.
6. Richard Mendelsohn and Milton Shain, *The Jews in South Africa: An Illustrated History* (Johannesburg, South Africa: Jonathan Ball, 2008), 106–11. For more on German Jewish refugees in South Africa, see Lotta M. Stone, "Seeking Asylum: German Jewish Refugees in South Africa, 1933–1948" (PhD diss., Clark University, 2010); Shirli Gilbert, *From Things Lost: Forgotten Letters and the Legacy of the Holocaust* (Detroit: Wayne State University Press, 2017).
7. Milton Shain, "South Africa," in *The World Reacts to the Holocaust*, ed. David S Wyman (Baltimore: Johns Hopkins University Press, 1996), 670–89, here 675–76.
8. Deborah Posel, "What's in a Name? Racial Categorisations under Apartheid and Their Afterlife," *Transformation* 47 (2001): 50–74, here 53.
9. Shirli Gilbert, "Jews and the Racial State: Legacies of the Holocaust in Apartheid South Africa, 1945–60," *Jewish Social Studies* 16, no. 3 (2010): 32–64, here 37.
10. Furlong, *Between Crown and Swastika*, 77–82; Michael A Green, "South African Jewish Responses to the Holocaust, 1941–1948" (master's thesis, University of South Africa, 1987), 181–83.
11. Saul Dubow, *Apartheid, 1948–1994* (Oxford: Oxford University Press, 2014), 10–11.

12. Thomas Karis and Gwendolen M. Carter, eds., *From Protest to Challenge: A Documentary History of African Politics in South Africa, 1882–1964*, vol. 2, *Hope and Challenge, 1935–1952*, by Thomas Karns (Stanford CA: Hoover Institution Press, 1972), 358.
13. See, for example, "Are Nats Nazis?" *Black Sash* 1, no. 7 (July 1956): 1; "Judgment on Herrenvolk," *Fighting Talk* 16, no. 2 (March 1962): 11.
14. Nelson Mandela, "Bantu Education Goes to University," *Liberation*, June 1957.
15. Mark Gevisser, *Thabo Mbeki: The Dream Deferred* (Johannesburg, South Africa: Jonathan Ball, 2007), 397.
16. Shirli Gilbert, "Anne Frank in South Africa: Remembering the Holocaust during and after Apartheid," *Holocaust and Genocide Studies* 26, no. 3 (2012): 366–93, here 368; Joanna R. Schacter, "World War Two and the Holocaust in Black South African Discourse: 1938–1987" (master's thesis, McGill University, 2018). On the use of anti-fascist and anti-Nazi rhetoric by anti-apartheid activists, see Asher Lubotzky and Roni Mikel Arieli, "'The Great Trek towards Nazism': Anti-Fascism and the Radical Left in South Africa during the Early Apartheid Era," *South African Historical Journal* 74, no. 1 (2021): 135–59.
17. Roni Mikel Arieli, "Ahmed Kathrada in Postwar Europe: Holocaust Memory and Apartheid South Africa (1951–1952)," *African Identities* 17, no. 1 (2019): 1–17. See also Roni Mikel Arieli, "Between Apartheid, the Holocaust and the Nakba: Archbishop Desmond Tutu's Pilgrimage to Israel-Palestine (1989) and the Emergence of an Analogical Lexicon," *Journal of Genocide Research* 22, no. 3 (2020): 334–53; Roni Mikel Arieli, "Reading *The Diary of Anne Frank* on Robben Island: On the Role of Holocaust Memory in Ahmed Kathrada's Struggle against Apartheid," *Journal of Jewish Identities* 12, no. 2 (2019): 175–95.
18. On Jewish activists in the anti-apartheid struggle, see Gideon Shimoni, *Community and Conscience: The Jews in Apartheid South Africa* (Hanover NH: Brandeis University Press, 2003); Immanuel Suttner, ed., *Cutting through the Mountain: Interviews with South African Jewish Activists* (Johannesburg, South Africa: Viking Penguin, 1997).
19. Ronald Segal, *Into Exile* (London: Jonathan Cape, 1963), 34, 308.
20. Franz Auerbach, "Our Responsibility," *Etz Chayim News* 2, no. 6 (September 1960): 33–37, here 34.
21. At this time sectors of the mainstream Jewish community also engaged in a range of welfare activities directed at non-whites; see Gilbert, "Jews and the Racial State."
22. *Report of the Executive Council of the South African Jewish Board of Deputies, April 1958 to August 1960* (Johannesburg: South African Jewish Board of Deputies, 1960), 33.
23. Gilbert, "Jews and the Racial State"; Roni Mikel Arieli, *Remembering the Holocaust in a Racial State: Holocaust Memory in South Africa from Apartheid to Democracy (1948–1994)* (Berlin: De Gruyter Oldenbourg, 2022), chap. 2.
24. Mendelsohn and Shain, *Jews in South Africa*, 190–91.
25. Gilbert, "Jews and the Racial State."
26. Gilbert, "Anne Frank in South Africa," 366–93.
27. Shirli Gilbert, "Nazism and Racism in South African Textbooks," in *Holocaust Memory and Racism in the Postwar World*, ed. Shirli Gilbert and Avril Alba (Detroit: Wayne State University Press, 2019), 350–85.

28. Mikel Arieli, *Remembering the Holocaust*, chap. 3.
29. See Mikel Arieli, *Remembering the Holocaust*, chap. 4; Milton Shain and Andrew Lamprecht, "A Past That Must Not Go Away: Holocaust Denial in South Africa," in *Remembering for the Future: The Holocaust in an Age of Genocide*, ed. John K Roth and Elisabeth Maxwell (New York: Palgrave, 2001), 1:858–69, here 862.
30. Claudia Bathsheba Braude, ed., *Contemporary Jewish Writing in South Africa: An Anthology* (Cape Town, South Africa: David Philip, 2001), xii.
31. Eric L. Goldstein, *The Price of Whiteness: Jews, Race, and American Identity* (Princeton NJ: Princeton University Press, 2006).
32. Gustav Saron and Louis Hotz, "Epilogue, 1910–1955," in *The Jews in South Africa: A History*, ed. Gustav Saron and Louis Hotz (Cape Town, South Africa: Oxford University Press, 1955), 398.
33. Patrick Harries, "From Public History to Private Enterprise: The Politics of Memory in the New South Africa," in *Historical Memory in Africa*, ed. Mamadou Diawara, Bernard Lategan, and Jorn Rusen (New York: Berghahn Books, 2010), 121–43.
34. In addition to texts cited below, see Jonathan D. Jansen, *Knowledge in the Blood: Confronting Race and the Apartheid Past* (Stanford CA: Stanford University Press, 2009).
35. Asmal, Asmal, and Roberts, *Reconciliation through Truth*.
36. Annie E. Coombes, *History after Apartheid: Visual Culture and Public Memory in a Democratic South Africa* (Durham NC: Duke University Press, 2003), 69, 84.
37. Susan De Villiers, ed., *Truth and Reconciliation Commission of South Africa Report* (Basingstoke, UK: Macmillan Reference, 1998), 97–98, 122.
38. De Villiers, *TRC Report*, 271, 284, 294.
39. See Reparation and Rehabilitation Committee transcripts, accessed June 26, 2014, http://www.justice.gov.za/Trc/reparations/index.htm; De Villiers, *TRC Report*, 5–6, 97–98, 122.
40. Gilbert, "Anne Frank in South Africa."
41. On the place of Holocaust memory in contemporary South African Jewish identity, see Shirli Gilbert and Deborah Posel, "The Holocaust, Apartheid, and South African Jewish Perspectives on Victimhood," *Journal of Jewish Identities* 14, no. 2 (2021): 155–70.
42. Personal communication with Richard Freedman, director of South African Holocaust and Genocide Foundation, January 20, 2011.
43. Cape Town Holocaust and Genocide Centre, "About Us," accessed January 27, 2022, https://ctholocaust.co.za/about/. See also Oren Baruch Stier, "South Africa's Jewish Complex," *Jewish Social Studies*, n.d., 123–42.
44. Durban Holocaust and Genocide Centre, "About Us," accessed April 2, 2020, https://dbnholocaust.co.za/.
45. Tali Nates and Shirli Gilbert, "The Development of the Johannesburg Holocaust and Genocide Centre," in *Holocaust and Human Rights Museums*, ed. Jennifer Barrett, Avril Alba, and Dirk Moses (University of Pennsylvania Press, forthcoming).
46. Tali Nates, "'But, Apartheid Was Also Genocide . . . What about Our Suffering?' Teaching the Holocaust in South Africa—Opportunities and Challenges," *Intercultural Education* 21, no. S1 (2010): S17–26, here S19–20. On teaching the Holocaust in

postapartheid South Africa, see also Tracey Petersen, "Teaching Humanity: Placing the Cape Town Holocaust Centre in a Post-Apartheid State" (PhD, University of the Western Cape, 2015).

47. Shirli Gilbert, "Remembering the Racial State: Holocaust Memory in Post-Apartheid South Africa," in *Holocaust Memory in a Globalizing World*, ed. Jacob S. Eder, Philipp Gassert, and Alan E. Steinweis (Göttingen, Germany: Wallstein, 2017), 199–214.

2

Remembering the Holocaust in Mauritius
Legacies of Slavery, Colonial Violence, and Jewish Displacement

RONI MIKEL-ARIELI

There were 1,600 of them, crowded side by side in the passage between the two ships which were going to dock at the harbour of Port Louis. Men, women, and children exhausted, with tired eyes and pain-filled looks. . . . On the early morning of December 26, 1940, Port Louis barely awakened from the day after Christmas. Delcourt was on platform D to which the refugees were to arrive. He came, like hundreds of Mauritians, to see these foreigners who had fled their homelands.
—Alain Gordon-Gentil, *Le Voyage de Delcourt*

On December 9, 1940, 1,581 Jewish refugees fleeing Nazi-controlled Europe, and surviving a long journey to British Mandated Palestine, were deported to the British colony of Mauritius. The refugees spent almost five years in the Beau-Bassin prison before leaving the island in August 1945. With their departure, the site and the story all but disappeared from collective memory. Despite some commemorative efforts since the 1990s, the Jewish deportation to Mauritius has largely been neglected from most accounts of the Second World War and the Holocaust, and, until recently, it has been also on the periphery of Mauritian collective memory.[1]

Located off the eastern coast of Africa, Mauritius, an island with no Indigenous population, has a complicated colonial history. The first Creoles (Afro-Mauritians) were brought in as slaves during the Dutch occupation in the seventeenth century and the French occupation in the eighteenth century mostly from East African Mozambique and Madagascar, with a few non-African slaves arriving from India, Indonesia, and Malaysia.[2] A small number of Chinese (Sino-Mauritians) were also brought to the island, first as indentured laborers during the Dutch occupation, and later under French and British rule, as free merchants.[3] Moreover, after the British gained control of the island in 1810, the French settlers maintained their economic and cultural status. Following the abolition of slavery in 1835, the British brought in indentured laborers from India.[4] The Indo-Mauritians soon became the majority ethnic group and had the capacity to compete economically with the European elites, facing a relatively accommodating colonial government that supported the preservation of traditional Hindu customs.[5] Consequently, while the Creoles had no unified identity due to their varying slave origins, the other ethnic groups had developed somewhat of a collective identity.[6]

Mauritius gained independence on March 12, 1968, becoming a polyglot society with small but economically powerful Franco-Mauritian and Chinese elites and a strong Indo-Mauritian and Creole presence. Nowadays, the island also has a small Jewish community of forty-three members who are not related to the wartime refugees.[7] Therefore, as Srilata Ravi argues, "In Mauritius, the notion of a shared past is difficult to forge."[8]

According to the 2018 Global Peace Index (GPI), Mauritius is ranked in the top twenty of the world's most peaceful countries.[9] However, anthropologist Thomas Hylland Eriksen argues that since Mauritius gained independence, "peace is maintained on the crowded, culturally heterogeneous island only because there is a precarious numerical equilibrium and functioning politics of compromise between the ethnic groups. Any 'upsetting of this balance' would ostensibly threaten the peace."[10] This pitfall of multiculturalism is a direct expression of the national slogan "unity in diversity," which involves a careful distribution of cultural capital in the country to maintain social cohesion. Nevertheless, the decision to create Mauritian national unity tends to preclude the distinctiveness of the collective identities of the groups, which, in turn, avoid dwelling on their past.[11]

Recently, however, through the work of activists, poets, and authors, the local histories of slavery and colonialism have regained some resonance.[12] In this context, over the last two decades the Jewish deportation becomes central as a somewhat nonconflictual history to engage within this multiethnic society. This chapter explores the modes of Holocaust remembrance in Mauritius from the departure of the detainees in August 1945 to the present, by focusing on the local commemoration efforts of this episode of Jewish displacement, which directly connects Mauritius to the Holocaust. It provides an in-depth description of the local mnemonic practices of the Jewish deportation at the site of the St. Martin Jewish cemetery—the only physical trace left on the island after August 1945. Furthermore, in a very different modality, the chapter moves to investigate the Jewish deportation as an entry point for local authors to engage with Mauritius's legacies of slavery and colonial violence.

The Deportation: A History

The Jewish deportation to Mauritius began when three ships—*Pacific*, *Milos*, and *Atlantic*—set sail from Tulcea, Romania, to Haifa Harbor in the British Mandate of Palestine, carrying 3,500 Jewish refugees. These ships were chartered on September 4, 1940, by the Committee for Jewish Overseas Transports, under the leadership of Austrian Jewish financial adviser Berthold Storfer and with the consent and cooperation of Nazi German authorities.[13]

The *Milos* and *Pacific* arrived in Haifa in early November. However, because of the 1939 British White Paper and the strict immigration quota for Jews entering Palestine, the refugees were transferred to the ship *Patria* to be deported to Mauritius.[14] When the *Atlantic* passengers arrived in Palestine on November 24, their transfer to the *Patria* began as well. However, in retaliation to the deportation plan, the Haganah, the underground military organization of the Yishuv, decided to plant a bomb on the *Patria* to disable it and prevent it from leaving Haifa. It exploded on November 25, at 9 a.m., causing the tragic death of approximately 260 Jewish refugees.[15] The British authorities permitted the survivors of the *Patria* to remain in Palestine, transferring them to the Atlit detention camp.[16] However, the *Atlantic* passengers who had not yet been transferred to the *Patria* were kept in a separate section of the camp.[17] Two weeks later, on December 9, 1940, they were forcibly removed from Atlit and loaded on two ships to be deported to Mauritius.

After traveling in the deportation ships for seventeen days, the refugees arrived in Port Louis, Mauritius and were transferred to the Beau-Bassin prison, which was converted into a detention camp.[18] They were defined by the local colonial authorities as "European Detainees," and "ordinances" were established to legalize their detention and status, as well as to prevent contact between them and the local population.[19] The high walls of the principal compound of the camp ensured separation between the men, who were kept in the prison cells, and the women and children, who were in huts in a separate compound.[20] Not until July 1942, after the detainees protested vehemently, did a new order permit the wives to visit the men's camp at certain daytime hours.[21] Indeed, the two main hardships of the detainees' internment was the lack of freedom and the impossibility of leading a normal family and sex life. In addition, many of the refugees arrived on the island in poor physical health. Therefore, soon after their arrival on the island, the local authorities established a hospital and allocated an area outside a local Christian cemetery to establish a Jewish cemetery for the dead.[22]

Despite the harsh conditions, the detainees maintained a rich cultural and social life. There were two active synagogues, schools, adult education centers, youth movements, theater groups, a Zionist association, a library, a camp newspaper, coffee shops, and a soccer team.[23] Workshops were established in the camp where the detainees manufactured toys, bags, recycled papers, and wooden items.[24] These activities were made possible mainly through the material aid provided by the South African Jewish Board of Deputies (SAJBD) and other Jewish organizations.[25] Additionally, in late 1941 some of the skilled detainees received temporary permits to work outside the camp in electricity and telephone services, the local manufacture of cosmetics and toys, and as music, art, and language teachers at local primary schools.[26]

On February 21, 1945, Sir Bede Clifford, the governor of Mauritius, informed the detainees' leadership that the British authorities had decided to allow the Jewish refugees to enter Palestine. However, it took another six months before the refugees left the island.[27] The only evidence left of the Jewish presence on the island was the St. Martin Jewish cemetery, where 126 refugees who died during their detention are buried.[28]

Local Efforts of Commemoration: The South African Connection

On July 27, 1944, more than a year before the detainees left the island, the Jewish Cemetery Committee of the Beau-Bassin camp turned to the area commandant with a request to transfer the property of the Jewish cemetery to the SAJBD. Louis Gradmann, a German Jewish refugee who was in charge of all religious affairs at the camp, including the care of the cemetery, wrote to the area commandant: "Thus the Jewish cemetery will be an eternal memorial of the generosity of the Mauritius Government which gave asylum to Jewish refugees during the second world war, maybe also a sightseeing spot to visitors on this island."[29] Furthermore, before their departure, Gradmann asked Archbishop Otter-Barry, the bishop of Mauritius, to look after the Jewish cemetery.[30] Throughout the years the SAJBD, which received ownership of the Jewish cemetery on the island in 1946, relied on reports from local Mauritians about the condition of the cemetery. In 1956 Pierre de Comarmond, manager of the Mauritian-based Medene Sugar Estate Company (MSEC), reported on the deterioration of the cemetery and offered his help in supervising its reconstruction. Despite de Comarmond's death in February 1968, MSEC continued to look after the cemetery until May 1981.³¹

In 1977 Mauritian architect Jacques Desmarais reported to the SAJBD that many tombstones, erected during the war from a porous volcanic stone, had weathered badly.³² The SAJBD decided to cover the costs of the restoration and replacement of tombstones, and on August 14, 1988, a ceremony was held in Mauritius marking this restoration and the unveiling of two plaques in tribute to Desmarais and the MSEC for their contribution to the preservation of the cemetery. Among the guests were seven former detainees, the retired deputy commander of the camp, and several Mauritians who used to work there.³³

It is important to note that at the time of the deportation, the only Jew on the island was a businessman named Isia Birger. When the Mauritian Sub-Committee of the Council for Refugee Settlement was established under the SAJBD, Birger became the liaison officer between the detainees and the committee and after the war was involved in maintaining the Jewish cemetery together with de Comarmond. In 1981 he took over the responsibility for the completion of the above-mentioned reconstruction work at the cemetery in which he is now buried.³⁴

In November 1998 Rabbi Silberhaft, the spiritual leader and CEO of the African Jewish Congress (AJC), which represents the Jewish communities on the African continent, visited the Jewish cemetery. He soon discovered that the replaced tombstones also did not withstand the local weather and that in some cases the inscriptions had become illegible. Rabbi Silberhaft arranged for new, smaller plaques to be made in South Africa and brought to Mauritius to be constructed on the base of the graves.³⁵

In late April 1999 a memorial service was organized at the Jewish cemetery with fifty former detainees and their families. At the ceremony, former detainee Aaron Zwergbaum, who served as the detainees' representative during their detention, stated: "One can readily say that the South African Jews took better care of us than we really deserved.... If all Jews had done their duty as the Jews of South Africa had then the situation of the Jewish people would have been a different one."³⁶ Organized by the Friends of Israel in Mauritius (L'Amicale Maurice-Israel), the event was attended by numerous local and foreign dignitaries, including the president of Mauritius, Anjini Chettiar, and Israel's honorary consul-general for Mauritius, Naphtali Regev, Zwergbaum's son, who was one of the children born in detention on the island.³⁷

Although Mauritian officials were present at these events, the Jewish deportation remained unknown to most Mauritians. Moreover, in 2006 a graffiti reading "Al-Queda" appeared on the Amicale Maurice Centre building, heightening fears of antisemitism on the island. Responding to this antisemitic manifestation, Sir Anerood Jugnauth, president of the Republic of Mauritius, strongly stressed the need to combat extremism and foster religious tolerance in Mauritius society and declared that "his government would take all steps necessary to prevent racist or anti-Semitic activities."[38] Following these developments, a decision has been made to establish a permanent exhibition in Mauritius to explore the story of the deportation. The driving force behind this initiative was South African Jewish leader Mervyn Smith, president of the AJC at that time, together with Rabbi Silberhaft and Owen Griffiths, the chairman of the Island Hebrew Congregation.[39] In late 2014 the Beau-Bassin Jewish Detainees Memorial & Information Centre (BBJDMIC) was officially opened inside a memorial chapel at the Jewish cemetery's garden.[40]

During my first visit to Mauritius in May 2019, I contributed to the formation of a collaborative partnership between the Johannesburg Holocaust & Genocide Centre (JHGC), the Rosa Luxemburg Stiftung–Southern Africa, and the BBJDMIC. The visit received significant media attention, showcasing the public interest in revisiting this episode.[41] A second visit followed in January 2020, where a committee was established to advance the memory of the deportation in Mauritius, and I became actively involved in local commemoration efforts. The committee launched a video testimony project, focusing on local Mauritians who had personal recollections of the detainees. It also started planning the seventy-fifth commemorative ceremony marking the liberation of the detainees from Mauritius. However, a month later, the COVID-19 pandemic changed all those plans when globally all aspects of memorialization had to move to the digital space.

On July 31, 2020, almost eighty years after the deportation, a letter written by Lord (Tariq) Ahmad of Wimbledon, minister of state for South Asia and the Commonwealth and the prime minister's special representative on preventing sexual violence in conflict, was delivered to Griffiths, chairman of the BBJDMIC. This letter recognized the suffering endured by European Jews who fled persecution in Nazi-occupied Europe and paid tribute to the important work of the BBJDMIC. The letter was vaguely worded and fell short of an apology, stating that "there are open questions about whether things could have been done differently, such as the 1939 White Paper, which capped the number of visas issued to Jews wanting to go to the British mandate of Palestine."[42] The 1939 White Paper was meant to provide a solution for the increased flow of European Jews into Palestine following the worsening situation of Jews in the growing Nazi Reich and as a direct reaction to the Arab revolt of 1936–39.[43] This vague statement serves as a contemporary indication of Britain's avoidance of taking responsibility for the consequences of its immigration policy during the Second World War.

Although it was not an official apology, the letter was unprecedented. It was delivered ahead of the seventy-fifth commemorative ceremony, which eventually took place online on August 12, 2020. The commemoration event was attended by 194 guests, more than half of them former detainees and relatives. Many Mauritians attended, as well as the ambassador of Germany and the high commissioner of Great Britain.[44] On December 2, 2020, an event marking the eightieth anniversary of the *Patria* disaster and the Jewish deportation to Mauritius was held online. Hosted by the BBJDMIC, the JHGC, and Tel Aviv University, this event included academic lectures and a conversation with former detainee Oscar Langsam, who was deported to Mauritius with his mother when he was ten years old.[45] At the event the BBJDMIC launched its new official website in English and French, which covers the educational work of the memorial, the history of the deportation, interviews, press coverage, and archival material.[46] Since 2020, the commemorations marking the deportation in December and the liberation in August—became annual online gatherings, where the BBJDMIC and the JHGC are collaborating with various organizations to remember the Jewish deportation to Mauritius.

The BBJDMIC strengthened its international resonance when it joined the #TogetherWeRemember Coalition in April 2020. This coalition of leading Holocaust, genocide, and human rights organizations held an annual virtual twenty-four-hour global vigil to conclude Genocide Awareness Month. The April 2020 BBJDMIC program included interviews with former detainees; a conversation with Vanessa Calou, education officer of the Memorial; and a virtual visit to the cemetery.[47]

In the April 2021 vigil, the BBJDMIC collaborated with the South African Holocaust & Genocide Foundation and focused on the experiences of those displaced because of genocide, mass atrocities, and identity-based violence.[48] As part of the program, students of Université des Mascareignes (Mauritius) read from the private diaries of thirteen-year-old, Danzig-born Arie Leopold Keller, who was deported to Mauritius with his mother. Keller's diaries, which describe his escape from Danzig, the journey to Palestine, and his detention in Mauritius, were donated to the Ghetto Fighters House Archives in January 2019.⁴⁹ The students reflected on the relevance of his writing to their local context. One of them stated: "When reading this (the diary) I understand that there are many things that happened in our country that we don't really know, especially what happened at Beau-Bassin. I did know that there was a Jewish cemetery at St. Martin, but I did not know this story and it is quite shocking to see that there are such things that happened in the past. . . . We should be aware of it, and it should teach us a lesson for the future. It must be taught in schools as part of the history of Mauritius."⁵⁰ History is taught in Mauritius in primary and secondary schools as part of social studies, alongside geography and sociology. However, the curriculum is limited to superficially focusing on the country's colonial past with modern history barely taught.⁵¹ Although the BBJDMIC holds educational visits for local high school students where they learn about the history of the Holocaust, the subject is not part of the national curriculum, and therefore its inclusion depends on the initiative of individual teachers. Nevertheless, since the late 1990s, the Jewish deportation became more visible through the work of local Mauritian writers who utilized this history as a new way of understanding local legacies of colonial violence.

Jewish Displacement, Legacies of Slavery, and Colonial Violence

Ravi argues that literature as a medium of remembrance "challenges the ethicized memorial registers that have contributed to the communalization of Mauritian society by mitigating, demystifying, creolizing and even deliberately effecting these manipulated pasts of free and forced labour in the postcolonial and post-national present of Mauritian modernity."⁵² Indeed, while the history of the Jewish deportation to Mauritius is relatively unknown to most Mauritians, since the late 1990s several local authors explored this episode in their writing. In 1998 Geneviève Pitot, a French Mauritian residing in Germany, provided the first comprehensive account of the Jewish deportation to many Mauritians in her book *The Mauritian Shekel*. Growing up in Mauritius, Pitot had been introduced to this history by her teacher, Anna Frank Klein, a German detainee and an established painter who worked for a year as an art teacher in Pitot's high school.⁵³

In 2007 a novel, *Le dernier frère* (*The Last Brother*), was published by Mauritian author Nathacha Appanah, focusing on a fictional friendship between a descendant of indentured laborers and a Jewish refugee from Czechoslovakia. Appanah's novel creates moments of intersection between the local legacies of slavery and colonialism and the story of the Jewish deportation.⁵⁴ These intersections were the source of several studies. It was positioned by

Françoise Lionnet as "the first text that actually strives to capture the voice and perspective of a native Mauritian as he lives through, and later in life recollects, the unusual events of his childhood"; and by Krik Sides as a text that allows "for an intricately entangled and multi-directional narrative of both Jewish and colonial displacements on the island."[55]

Appanah's novel was not the first to capture these entanglements. In 2001 Mauritian author Alain Gordon-Gentil wrote a novel, *Le Voyage de Delcourt*, focusing on the life experiences of a young Creole man and his romantic relationship with a Jewish refugee from Danzig.[56] While Appanah's novel focuses on the encounters between the local population and the Jewish detainees as a space for local repressed histories, Gordon-Gentil had a different objective in mind. In an interview he stated: "The Creole society has very difficult relations with its roots, because contrary to Indians, Chinese or White people, they don't know their roots."[57] As is explained below, his novel points to the pitfalls of multiculturalism and exposes the painful silence of local histories in Mauritius and its devastating consequences on local identities.

The first part of the novel describes Delcourt's studies in Europe and reveals his complex identity as a Creole. While in London, he lives with his Indo-Mauritian friend, Kewal, who is a keen activist in the Indian independence struggle. Delcourt is rootless; he represents the Creoles as "people without history, located in a geopolitical space that conjures up a tabula rasa or the utopias associated with desert islands."[58] While Kewal dreams of returning to Mauritius after his studies to become a local politician, Delcourt wants to be "a nomad, without ties, without roots."[59] These two characters represent the fragile relations between Creoles and Indo-Mauritians in Mauritius society and reflect the abysmal difference between the two groups' identities.

The second part of the novel continues to shed light on the effects of colonialism on Mauritian group identities. However, it complicates this mixture of local identities by observing Delcourt's encounter with the Jewish refugees detained on the island. Chapter 8 describes their arrival in Port Louis and the warm reception they received from the island's population. Delcourt stood with hundreds of Mauritians on platform D when the refugees arrived. This is where he saw Marika for the first time: "The last bus had passed by and Delcourt waved his hand. Through the window, a young girl smiled at him. She had a gentle face that seemed to come out of a world that did not know any pain. He had remained frozen, unable to take his eyes off this young girl who continued to smile."[60] Delcourt received a permit to enter the camp and deliver his cargo of potatoes and cassava but was not allowed to speak to Marika as *ordinances* prevented contact between the refugees and the local population. His friend Kewal, who became an active politician in Mauritius, helped him eventually obtain permission from Governor Clifford to visit Marika in the camp.[61] Kewal's close political ties with the colonial authorities, which reflect the relative mobility of the Indo-Mauritians compared to the Creoles in British colonial society, eventually enabled him to obtain papers authorizing Marika to leave the camp and live on the island as a free woman.[62]

When Delcourt arrived in the camp in order to release Marika, he met Rabbi Bieler, who was the chief rabbi of the Danzig Jewish community. When Marika introduced Rabbi Bieler to Delcourt, the rabbi turned to him saying: "I wanted you to know that we will be returning soon to our Promised Land. Here, we all love Marika, and we are sad to know that she will not be with us when we will touch this earth that we have been waiting for so long. You have a homeland; you surely understand what I mean."[63] Delcourt's answer reflects his detachment from his country. He proclaimed, "Sir, I don't know what you mean when you speak about a homeland. I never had a homeland. My homeland is not an earth. It is a woman. It is Marika. I also waited for a long time to find her."[64]

After living together throughout wartime, in August 1945 Marika told Delcourt that her fellow detainees received permission to return to Palestine and that she decided to join them. "I miss them! They are in distress, and I know I can comfort them. They are waiting for me, they need me. You are rich, I have nothing to offer you that you don't already have."[65] Delcourt's obsessive love toward Marika is positioned against her Zionist tendencies and her longing for the Promised Land. He cannot understand Zionism and is unable to come to terms with the fact that Marika prefers her love for a land over loving him. The story ends with the two standing at platform D again, almost five years after they first saw each other.[66]

Gordon-Gentil's novel points to entangled histories through the literary representation of the complicated multiethnic nature of Mauritian society during the Second World War. Through the specificity of the Jewish history of persecution, statelessness, and detention, he points to the constraints of Mauritian society as the direct and indirect outcome of historical colonial violence. A particular focus is given in the novel to the marginalization of the unrooted Creole identity on the island: first, it is positioned against the Indo-Mauritian rich identity and its nationalistic ties to India, and then against the detainees' Jewish identity and Zionist tendencies.

Conclusion

Holocaust memory in Mauritius is directly related to the Jewish deportation to the island during the war and to the concrete site of the St. Martin Jewish cemetery. The Jews deported to Mauritius had experienced the rise of Nazism, German occupation, and racial persecution. However, because they were fortunate enough to escape antisemitic persecution and murder, their stories remain at the margins of most accounts of the Holocaust. Yet, these refugees eventually became victims of another form of violence—colonial persecution—imprisoned in a detention camp on a remote outpost of the British Empire in the Indian Ocean. While at the margins of Holocaust history, the deportation reveals the entanglement between wartime Europe and the colonial world. It connects the island to the grand processes and events related to the persecution and genocide of European Jewry while positioning Mauritius as a space of ongoing colonial violence.

This chapter demonstrates the modes of remembrance of the Holocaust in Mauritius by exploring the evolving local mnemonic practices of the Jewish deportation on the site of the Jewish cemetery from August 1945 to the present. Many of these practices were driven by the South African Jewish community. As demonstrated, South African Jewry continues to serve as an important force in the processes of remembrance of the deportation on the island and beyond it. However, since the 1990s there is a growing interest in the Jewish deportation in the Mauritian literary sphere, and this episode serves as a new way to understand the local legacies of colonial violence. Interestingly, while Mauritian society has a very complicated history of slavery and colonial occupations, the national tendency is to avoid dwelling on the past. However, it is through the Jewish deportation that the multicultural society not only reclaims its place in the history of the Holocaust but also provides space for other local histories to gain resonance.

Notes

This work was made possible thanks to the author's tenure as a Phyllis Greenberg Heideman and Richard D. Heideman Fellow at the Jack, Joseph and Morton Mandel Center for Advanced Holocaust Studies, United States Holocaust Memorial Museum; a Rosa Luxemburg Research Fellow at the Johannesburg Holocaust & Genocide Centre; and a Research Fellow of the Fondation pour la Mémoire de la Shoah at the Institute of Contemporary Jewry, The Hebrew University of Jerusalem. Epigraph: Alain Gordon Gentil, *Le Voyage de Delcourt* (Paris: Julliard, 2001), 107 [French]. Translated by the author.

1. Significant research on the deportation to Mauritius appeared in the book *The Mauritian Shekel: The Story of the Jewish Detainees in Mauritius, 1940–1945* (Port Louis, Mauritius: VIZAVI, 1998), written by Mauritian French author Geneviève Pitot; a traveling exhibition titled "Boarding Pass to Paradise" was curated by Israeli art-exhibition curator Elena Makarova and toured several European and Israeli venues between the years 2005 and 2008; a documentary titled *The Atlantic Drift* (2002) was made by the Austrian producer Michel Daëron, and another titled *In the Shadows of Beau Bassin* (2007) was produced by the South African independent filmmaker Kevin Harris; an archival collection was deposited in the Ghetto Fighters House Archives in 2008; in 2014 Pitot's book was translated into Hebrew, and during that year a memorial center and exhibition, housed in the Mauritian Jewish cemetery garden, was established by the African Jewish Congress to commemorate the Mauritian story.
2. Richard B. Allen, *Slaves, Freedmen, and Indentured Laborers in Colonial Mauritius* (Cambridge: Cambridge University Press, 1999), 9–32; William F. S. Miles, "The Creole Malaise in Mauritius," *African Affairs* 98 (1999): 213–14.
3. Federic Guccini and Migyuan Zhang, "'Being Chinese' in Mauritius and Madagascar: Comparing Chinese Diasporic Communities in the Western Indian Ocean," *Journal of Indian Ocean World Studies* 4, no. 2 (2021): 91–117.
4. Srilata Ravi, "Multiple Memories: Slavery and Indenture in Mauritian Literature in French," in *At the Limits of Memory: Legacies of Slavery in the Francophone World*, ed. Nicola Frith and Kate Hodgsoy (Liverpool: Liverpool University Press, 2015), 154.
5. Gretchen Heuberger, "Transnational Belonging: The Effect of the Independence and Partition of India on the Indo-African Diaspora," *Columbia Undergraduate Journal of South Asian Studies* 1, no. 2 (2010).
6. Françoise Lionnet, "'Dire exactement': Remembering the Interwoven Lives of Jewish Deportees and Coolie Descendants in 1940s Mauritius," *Yale French Studies* 118/119 (2010): 111–35, here 112.
7. For further information on the Jewish community in Mauritius, see Island Hebrew Congregation Website, accessed November 16, 2021, https://www.mauritiusjewishcommunity.com/.
8. Ravi, "Multiple Memories," 155.
9. Institute for Economics & Peace, Global Peace Index 2018: Measuring Peace in a Complex World, Sydney, June 2018, http://visionofhumanity.org/reports.
10. Thomas Hylland Eriksen, *Common Denominators: Ethnicity, Nation-Building and Compromise in Mauritius* (New York: Routledge, 1998), 48.
11. Thomas Hylland Eriksen, "Nationalism, Mauritian Style: Cultural Unity and Ethnic Diversity," *Comparative Studies in Society and History* 36, no. 3 (1994): 549–74, here 558.
12. Richard B. Allen, *Slaves, Freedmen, and Indentured Laborers in Colonial Mauritius* (Cambridge: Cambridge University Press, 1999); Anne Eichmann, "The Heritage of Slavery and Nation Building: A Comparison of South Africa and Mauritius," in *Slavery, Memory and Identity, National Representations and Global Legacies*, ed. Douglas Hamilton, Kate Hodgson, and Joel Quirk (New York: Routledge, 2012), 66.

13. To read about Storfer's operation, see Dalia Ofer, "The Rescue of European Jewry and Illegal Immigration to Palestine in 1940—Prospects and Reality: Berthold Storfer and the Mossad Lealiyah Bet," *Modern Judaism* 4, no. 2 (May 1984): 159–81, here 165.
14. Lauren Elise Apter, "Disorderly Decolonization: The White Paper of 1939 and the End of British Rule in Palestine" (PhD diss., University of Texas, 2008), 136.
15. Dalia Ofer, *Escaping the Holocaust* (Oxford: Oxford University Press, 1990), 31–32; Arieh J. Kochavi, *Displaced Persons and International Politics* (Tel Aviv: Am Oved, 1992), 8, 42.
16. Ofer, *Escaping the Holocaust*, 36.
17. Aaron Zwergbaum, "Exile in Mauritius," *Yad Vashem Studies* 4 (1960): 191–257; Zwergbaum, "Exile in Mauritius," 203.
18. Zwergbaum, "Exile in Mauritius," 205–8.
19. "The European Detainees (Control) Ordinance, 1940—Boundaries of Detainment Camp," *Mauritius Gazette*, 1940, Mauritius National Archive.
20. "The European Detainees (Organization and Administration) Regulations, 1941," Government Notice no. 15, *Mauritius Gazette*, February 1, 1941; "The European Detainees (Performance of Detainment Area duties) Regulations, 1941," Government Notice no. 26, *Mauritius Gazette*, February 8, 1941; "The European Detainees (Discipline) Regulations, 1941," Government Notice no. 26, *Mauritius Gazette*, February 8, 1941, all in Mauritius National Archive.
21. Aaron Zwergbaum, *The Second Year on Mauritius* (N.p., 2000), 5–9; Zwergbaum, "Exile in Mauritius," 222.
22. On the establishment of St. Martin Jewish Cemetery, see Shula Parush, *The Story of the Jewish Cemetery in Mauritius* (Jerusalem: self-published, 2021) [Hebrew].
23. Pitot, *Mauritian Shekel*, 161, 165–67.
24. Mauritius Sub-Committee meeting, Johannesburg, South Africa, February 16, 1942, Rochlin Archive; two dolls, a pencil case, and a tin star, all manufactured by Kitty Drill-Schrott in the detention camp in Mauritius, Mauritius Exile Collection, Catalog No. 907, Ghetto Fighters House Archives.
25. On the establishment of the SAJBD's special committee on Mauritius, see G. Osrin, "Note on Refugee Funds Raised in the Union: Austrian & Polish Jewish Relief Fund," 6–7, Austrian and Polish Jewish Relief Fund 1938–1941, SAJBD Collection, Holocaust-Related Records, United States Holocaust Memorial Museum (USHMM) Archive.
26. "Des experts," *Le Mauricien*, February 2, 1942. On the British colonial perception of the Jewish detainees, see Roni Mikel Arieli, "The Jewish Question in the British Colonial Imagination: The Case of the Deportation to Mauritius (1940–1945)," *Jewish Social Studies* 27, no. 3 (2023): 58–87.
27. Pitot, *Mauritian Shekel*, 224–27.
28. The monthly reports issued by the Mauritius Government House to the Secretary of State for the Colonies during the years of detention, which contained lists of detainees who died in detention, reveal that in most cases the cause of death was typhoid, malaria, or, later, polio. However, while it does not appear in these reports, there was at least one case of suicide. For the reports, see, for example, Letter No. 28 from the Governor of Mauritius to Secretary of State for the Colonies, February 10, 1941; Letter No. 92 from the Governor of Mauritius to Secretary of State for the

Colonies, May 2, 1941, both in Out Correspondence Colonial Section, Mauritius National Archive.

29. Letter from Louis Gradmann to Area Commandant, Detainment Camp, July 27, 1944, quoted in Parush, *Story of the Jewish Cemetery*, 70.
30. Pitot, *Mauritian Shekel*, 228.
31. "M. Jacques Desmarais & Pierre De Comarmond & Maxime Series," in St. Martin's Ceremony: Mauritian Exiles, April 21, 1988, 130A Mauritius, 1, Rochlin Archive.
32. Letter from Abramowitch, Schneider, Sacks & Associates to the SAJBD, "Jewish Cemetery—Mauritius," March 31, 1971, 30A, Rochlin Archive.
33. "Mauritius," African Jewish Congress, November 11–16, 1996, 130A Mauritius, 1, Rochlin Archive.
34. "M. Jacques Desmarais & Pierre De Comarmond & Maxime Series," in St. Martin's Ceremony: Mauritian Exiles, April 21, 1988, 130A Mauritius, 1–2, 11–16, Rochlin Archive.
35. "Mauritian Jewish Cemetery—Part of the Jewish Mosaic," *African Jewish Chronicle*, November 1998.
36. "High Praise for SA Jewry at Mauritius Reunion," *Jewish Report*, May 7, 1999.
37. "British Detainees Return to Mauritius for Reunion," *South African Jewish Chronicle*, May 1, 1999, 8.
38. "New Documentary to Explore Story of Mauritius Jewry," *SA-SIG Newsletter* 8, no. 1 (September 2007): 6–7.
39. The Island Hebrew Congregation was established in 2007 as the Jewish community's representative body in the religious, cultural, and civil rights spheres in Mauritius. See Island Hebrew Congregation, https://www.mauritiusjewishcommunity.com/.
40. Krik B. Sides, "Holocaust and the Indian Ocean: Jewish Detention in Mauritius (1940–1945)," *Quest: Issues in Contemporary Jewish History* 19 (2021): 131.
41. For media coverage of the project in Mauritius, see "Le Journal Télévisé—Juin 02, 2019," MBC, http://mbc.intnet.mu/article/le-journal-t%C3%A9l%C3%A9vis%C3%A9-juin-02-2019.
42. Letter from Lord (Tariq) Ahmad of Wimbledon, Minister of State for South Asia and the Commonwealth and Prime Minister's Special Representative on Preventing Sexual Violence in Conflict, to Owen Griffiths, Chairman of the BBJDMIC, July 31, 2020, cited in "The British Government's Official Acknowledgement of the Detainees' Suffering," Beau Basin Jewish Detainees Memorial & Information Centre, July 31, 2020, https://jewishdetaineesmauritius.com/the-british-governments-official-acknowledgement-of-the-detainees-suffering/.
43. Lauren Elise Apter, "Disorderly Decolonization: The White Paper of 1939 and the End of British Rule in Palestine" (PhD diss., University of Texas at Austin, 2008), 136.
44. For the recording of the Virtual Commemoration Ceremony for the 75th Anniversary of the Release of the Jewish Detainees from the Beau-Bassin Prison, see "75th Anniversary Commemoration in Mauritius," https://www.youtube.com/watch?v=E7c6eRkTM0A.
45. For the recording of the Virtual Commemoration Ceremony for the 80th Anniversary of the Deportation to Mauritius, see "Commemoration of the *Patria* Disaster and

the Deportation to Mauritius," December 2, 2020, https://jewishdetaineesmauritius
.com/commemoration-of-the-patria-disaster-and-the-deportation-to-mauritius/.
46. BBJDMIC, https://jewishdetaineesmauritius.com/.
47. For the recording of the Together We Remember Virtual Global Vigil, April 30, 2020, see "The Jewish Deportation to Mauritius, 1940–1945, Global Vigil, April 2020," https://youtu.be/4StRu12Vjog.
48. The South African Holocaust & Genocide Foundation is the association of the three Holocaust & Genocide Centres in Cape Town, Durban, and Johannesburg. For the recording of the Together We Remember Virtual Global Vigil, April 29, 2021, see "Displaced Voices in Southern Africa: Seeking a Safe Haven," April 29, 2021, https://www.youtube.com/watch?v=NX68z3NZfWA&list=PLp_5wNJ3gfJoOFCj98KAp8a29Rg5liJRY&index=9.
49. Arie Leopold Keller Diaries, file 40284, Mauritius Exiles' Collection, Ghetto Fighters House Archives.
50. "Displaced Voices in Southern Africa."
51. Seema Goburdhun, "Teaching History in Primary Schools in Mauritius: Reflections on History Teachers' Pedagogical Practices," *Yesterday & Today*, no. 28 (2022): 83–96.
52. Ravi, "Multiple Memories," 170.
53. Pitot, *Mauritian Shekel*, 1.
54. The novel was translated into English and Hebrew and has been part of the French literature curriculum in Mauritius public high schools since 2016.
55. Lionnet, "'Dire exactement,'" 113; Sides, "Holocaust and the Indian Ocean," 118.
56. Gordon-Gentil, *Le Voyage de Delcourt*.
57. Alain Gordon-Gentil, personal communication with the author, November 9, 2021.
58. Françoise Lionnet, "Cosmopolitan or Creole Lives? Globalized Oceans and Insular Identities," *Profession*, 2011, 23–43, 26.
59. Gordon-Gentil, *Le Voyage de Delcourt*, 32, 23.
60. Gordon-Gentil, *Le Voyage de Delcourt*, 109.
61. Gordon-Gentil, *Le Voyage de Delcourt*, 137.
62. Gordon-Gentil, *Le Voyage de Delcourt*, 165.
63. Gordon-Gentil, *Le Voyage de Delcourt*, 168.
64. Gordon-Gentil, *Le Voyage de Delcourt*, 168.
65. Gordon-Gentil, *Le Voyage de Delcourt*, 189.
66. Gordon-Gentil, *Le Voyage de Delcourt*, 193.

3

Japan and the Holocaust
Domesticating Others' Horror

ROTEM KOWNER AND RAN ZWIGENBERG

During the course of the past seven decades, Japanese society has developed a consuming interest in the Holocaust and invoked its name on many occasions. This interest is rather curious given than Japan was not one of the Holocaust's perpetrators, nor was it involved in any kind of collective violence toward Jews in any other period. Similarly curious is the fact that Japan has never hosted any substantial Jewish community in its home islands, and its encounter with Jews began as late as the nineteenth century. This interest in the Holocaust, we argue, is associated with the Japanese fascination with Jews, with the perceived utility of the Jewish experience for domestic purposes, and with a concern for the image Japan wishes to project internationally. To understand this phenomenon, our chapter explores the evolution of the Japanese knowledge of the Holocaust, the ways it has been invoked in Japan and overseas, and the motives for its use.

The Evolution of Knowledge about the Holocaust

The Japanese public's first substantial acquaintance with the Holocaust occurred with the publication of the translation of Anne Frank's *Diary of a Young Girl* into Japanese in December 1952. Published a mere year after its first appeared in Europe, the book became an instant bestseller in Japan and topped the lists in 1953. Since then, more than four million copies of the Japanese translation of the diary were sold, and it became a symbol of the misery of war or of persecution in general rather than a source of identification with the Jews.[1] Accordingly, the figure of Anne Frank was often tied to that of Sadako Sasaki (1943–55), a young victim of atomic bombing of Hiroshima, which was also conceptualized as a victim of an abstract "bomb" and war.[2] In addition, Frank's story has also been told in popular manga and anime formats, especially of the *shōjo* manga (comics aimed at a teen female readership) variety, where the focus was also on her experience as an adolescent girl.[3] To this very day Anne Frank has remained the most prominent Jewish figure the Japanese associate with the Holocaust.

Decades after her book's first appearance in Japan, she became the fulcrum of exhibitions and even an educational center and constitutes a source of avid interest. In 2014 copies of Anne Frank's *Diary* and other Holocaust-related books were vandalized at public libraries in Greater Tokyo, and the story became a major news item, both domestically and beyond Japan.[4] Eventually, the thirty-six-year-old Japanese man arrested for vandalizing the books was not charged after he was found to be mentally incompetent. Ten days after the arrest, however, Prime Minister Abe Shinzō visited the Anne Frank Museum in Amsterdam. Abe noted the "deep connection" between Japan and the Anne Frank diary, as well as the fact that many Japanese take the time to visit the museum when they are in Amsterdam.[5]

During the 1950s the Japanese public was also introduced to the murderous German persecution of the Jews through various publications. One particularly influential work in this respect was Viktor Frankl's *Man's Search for Meaning*, examined below, which was translated into Japanese in 1956 under the title *Yoru to kiri*—or "Night and Fog" in English (the same title as Alain Resnais's film, which was released in the same year and had no relation to Frankl's book).[6] Similar intellectual works on the Holocaust, such as Jean Paul Sartre's *The Jew and the Anti-Semite* and Eli Cohen's *Human Behavior in the Concentration Camps*, were translated in 1957, alongside the release of several related films, such as the aforementioned *Night and Fog* and the German film *Thirteen Steps*. To many Japanese, however, a genuine understanding of the Holocaust only came during the Adolf Eichmann trial in the early 1960s. The trial brought several Japanese journalists to Jerusalem, and their dispatches were accompanied with detailed reports on Jewish history and wartime persecution.[7] Both the trial and the works cited above gave rise to an understanding of the Holocaust by the Japanese intelligentsia and popular media that construed it as a crime specifically committed against the Jews, but also as a part of a larger conversation about the meaning and legacy of totalitarianism.[8]

The Holocaust was thus not seen as a separate phenomenon but was subsumed under the rubric of Nazi crimes. For instance, an April 1961 editorial in the *Yomiuri Shinbun*, a leading right-of-center daily, argued Eichmann's actions were the product of totalitarianism and conformism: "[One] can find Eichmann-like fanaticism in other dictatorships. . . . This is the result of the same kind of group thinking when one person thinks like ten thousand."[9] Left-wing commentators alternated between critique of Stalinism and Nazism and critique of Japan's militarism and sense of victimization. Author Takeyama Michio, for example, wrote "Khrushchev answered [Eichmann's] complaint (in his speech denouncing Stalin). . . . First, one says 'I was just following orders' . . . [then] he claims the nation was deceived."[10] In both these statements, and many others, it is hard to find any mention whatsoever of antisemitism, racism, or genocide.

In the following decades, the Holocaust penetrated the Japanese imaginary and intellectual discourse. During twenty years alone (1965–84), about fifteen works of Holocaust literature were translated into Japanese, including books by Elie Wiesel, Primo Levi, and Paul Celan.[11] The Auschwitz Museum, in collaboration with Japanese institutions and of its own accord, also sent a number of traveling exhibitions to Japan, culminating in the exhibit "Auschwitz Is Etched in Our Heart," which traveled around Japan in 1989.[12] There are presently several museums in Japan that present the Holocaust as either their primary or secondary theme. The most relevant among these is the Holocaust Education Center, which was established in 1995 in the town of Fukuyama, Hiroshima Prefecture. Otsuka Makoto, the founder and current director of the center, is the pastor of a local church. This church is a branch of the Holy Ecclesia of Jesus, an independent Japanese Church and a movement founded in 1946 with a view to recovering apostolic Christianity and entrusted with a special mission regarding the nation of Israel. Otsuka had met Otto Frank, Anne Frank's father, and consequently decided to display the belongings of those who died in concentration camps as well as photographs of victims among other items collected from Holocaust survivors. Several other museums are devoted to the actions of the Japanese diplomat Sugihara Chiune and the visas he issued to Jewish refugees in 1940, and in this context, they present various aspects of the Holocaust. These include the Chiune Sugihara Memorial Hall in Yaotsu, Gifu (opened in 2000); the Port of Humanity Tsuruga Museum, Tsuruga, Fukui Prefecture (opened in 2008); and the Chiune Sugihara Sempo Museum, Tokyo (active 2018–21). In addition, there are small Holocaust exhibits, including artifacts from the camps, in various peace museums across Japan including Fukushima and Ritsumeikan University in Kyoto.[13]

In terms of the number of visitors, however, the most influential event has been a large Holocaust exhibition that began touring the country in 1994. Organized by Tokyo's Soka University and the Simon Wiesenthal Center in Los Angeles, this traveling exhibition attracted more than two million visitors during the thirteen years of its first tour.[14] Launched again in Tokyo in 2015 as part of the events marking the seventieth anniversary of the end of the war, it has been presented in twenty-three Japanese cities, including Osaka, Nagoya, Kobe, and Yokohama.[15]

The Holocaust and the Fate of Hiroshima and Nagasaki

Postwar Japan had its own grand sites of calamity: the cities of Hiroshima and Nagasaki. Commemoration of the bombings was influenced by and entangled with commemoration of the Holocaust, especially in later years.[16] Current estimates suggest that about four hundred thousand people lost their lives in Hiroshima and Nagasaki in the years after the United States had dropped an atomic bomb on each city. With time, and especially after the end of the Allied occupation in 1952, the American bombing of these two cities became a national symbol of Japanese victimization. Following the Eichmann trial, many Japanese began to associate Hiroshima and Nagasaki with the Holocaust. Most of them, argues historian Gavan McCormack, historically perceived the atomic bombing "as a crime of such magnitude as to warrant analogy with Auschwitz."[17] Several Japanese writers and artists have also made a vivid association with Auschwitz. The Japanese poet and peace activist Kurihara Sadako, for example, has likened Hiroshima to Auschwitz in her poetical work since the 1960s.[18] "Of the world's two great holocausts," she wrote, "Auschwitz was a major atrocity carried out by the enemies of the victorious Allies; Hiroshima/Nagasaki was a major atrocity carried out by the Allies."[19] Likewise, the husband and wife artists Maruki Iri and Maruki Toshi, who attained international fame for their depiction of the suffering of Hiroshima's victims, dedicated a second mural to Auschwitz and its victims in 1977.[20]

The most notable endeavor that connected the atomic bomb and the Holocaust was most likely the decades-long effort to create a Hiroshima-Auschwitz Museum in Hiroshima. The beginning of this initiative was in 1962, the year Eichmann was hanged and the year in which the world stood on the brink of nuclear war with the Cuban missile crisis. These twin events convinced a group of Japanese activists of the need to reach out to Auschwitz survivors and work together to prevent both another Hiroshima and another Auschwitz. However, the activists did not reach out to Jewish survivors but rather to Polish prisoners' organizations and to the Auschwitz Museum (then controlled by Poland's communist government). The activists, among whom was a Buddhist priest, also made a pilgrimage to Auschwitz and participated in the anniversary ceremony of its liberation by the Red Army. This episode was the beginning of extensive exchanges, among which were the aforementioned Auschwitz museum exhibits, that led to the museum plan. The plan failed eventually for both political and financial reasons, but Buddhist priests and others continue such pilgrimages for peace to Auschwitz, and a number of small memorials and museums contain some of the objects and remains brought back by the initial peace group.[21]

Hiroshima and Nagasaki also clarified, for many, the differences between Japanese and German wartime conduct. Not only did, the argument went, Imperial Japan not persecute any people in the systematic way adopted by Nazi Germany, but Japan itself was the victim of the first atomic attack in history. Thus, the death of hundreds of thousands of innocent Japanese civilians served to balance feelings of guilt toward Asia, and the linkages made with Jewish victimization became a further means of attracting attention to Japanese misery.[22] Nevertheless, associating Hiroshima with Auschwitz hid the tragedies' dissimilarities in scale and background. Kurihara Sadako, for example, believed that—for the survivors—the legacy of Hiroshima was worse than that of the Holocaust. In a 1984 review of Lawrence Langer's *The Holocaust and the Literary Imagination*, for example, Kurihara wrote that "Auschwitz ended, but the survivors of Hiroshima/Nagasaki still have lived with the hell of terror of invisible radioactivity inside their bodies."[23] In other words, Kurihara argued, the atomic bombings were not only comparable to the Holocaust but also had even more pernicious effects.[24]

Holocaust Psychology, the A-bomb, and the Problem of Totalitarianism

The comparison between the Holocaust and atomic bombings of Hiroshima and Nagasaki has proved to have additional ramifications initially unforeseen. In 1985 psychiatrist and activist Nakazawa Masao complained that *hibakusha* (Japanese A-bomb survivors) "did not have [their] Frankl to handle those problems."[25] Indeed, the works of Viktor Frankl and other psychologists dealing with the Holocaust had been well known in Japan for decades but not for their psychological insights into A-bomb trauma. For their part Japanese psychologists and intellectuals did not form a clear association between the bomb and the camps. Instead, most of them perceived the experience in the Nazi concentration camps through the lens of their own victimization by their compatriot "militarists" and then the Americans (via the A-bomb) and connected this experience to the problem of authoritarianism. Psychologist Kido Kōtarō, for example, made this connection explicit in a 1955 essay that examined Bruno Bettelheim's 1943 article "Individual and Mass Behavior in Extreme Situations." In his essay, Kido mentioned Bettelheim's Jewish origin only in passing. He was far more interested in Bettelheim's status as a thinker and as a "subjective individual" who "used himself as a guinea pig . . . [and] analyzed the psychological mechanism of 'soul murder,' but saved his own soul." Kido further argued that Bettelheim did so by "splitting his ego into 'observing ego,' and 'real ego.'"[26]

Kido focused on the loss of humanity and "the process of personality disintegration in the camps . . . where human dignity is shredded like a piece of paper, and tortured labor turns people into slaves more obedient than bass [fish]."[27] Kido also emphasized regression, as "[prisoners] regressed to the childish belief that the Gestapo is righteous and kind, which they have received as an image of the Almighty Father."[28] Kido further highlighted the coercive power of the group on the individual prisoner and the ingenuity of the Gestapo, such that by "throwing the individual into . . . the group, they have, by both external and internal pressure, regressed the individual to a childlike mode of behavior and blind obedience to the will of the leader."[29] Kido also made this coded reference to Japanese fascism explicit when he wrote that Bettelheim's work "reminds us of the Japanese military." Wartime Japan was a "concentration camp [organized] by the ruling class to deprive the people of their critical spirit and instill a spirit of obedience." Referring to a concept of a "vacuum zone" of non-thought developed by writer Noma Hiroshi, Kido argued that "the vicious cycle of adaptation and regression was extended to the entire nation, turning the whole of Japan into a 'vacuum zone' and a concentration camp."[30] Another psychologist, Shimizu Ikutarō, connected Bettelheim's images of broken prisoners, "who were treated as subhuman," to the outbreak of the Korea War at that time and to the reemerging images of bombed and starving Asians on the newsreels. In expressing his concern that Japan will be next, Shimizu warned, "We live in a world where [Bettelheim's] work is still not out of date."[31]

Psychologist Shimoyama Tokuji, who translated Viktor Frankl's *Man's Search for Meaning*, offered a more nuanced treatment. In his introduction to this book, Shimoyama, unlike Kido, compared the experience of Auschwitz to the "Nanking Incident of 1937, in which Japanese troops, after occupying Nanking, shot, burned, tortured, raped, and murdered an estimated 200,000 innocent civilians." Auschwitz and Nanking, they wrote, "make one ashamed to be human. These events occurred in relation to the war, but not in the war itself, but rather in [connection to] the internal politics of the nation and its people."[32] Shimoyama's sense of guilt was thus rather limited (he was ashamed to be human, not Japanese). He was far more concerned with the issues of mechanized mass killing. As he wrote, "this was not the result of primitive impulses or temporary excitement, but rather of organization, efficiency, and circumscription based on calm and careful planning... where 'modern mass-production industries were mobilized to reduce man from a vertical walking animal to a kilogram of ash.'"[33] For Shimoyama, Hiroshima and Nagasaki served as a grim warning for "the unfolding possibility of a new tragedy" and an example of the "correlation between technology and politics in the new machine age."[34] Thus, for him, Hiroshima was a more appropriate equivalent to Auschwitz and the horrors of the new age, while Nanking was conjured to be the more "primitive" impulse (and, by implication, a thing of the past that the new Japan left behind). Moreover, the A-bomb and the Holocaust were seen as abstract experiences rather than as an experience that impacted real people in need of treatment. In 1950s Japan, it was thus the "authoritarian personality" rather than "A-bomb neurosis" that was connected to the experience of the camps. This was not unique to Japan. Holocaust victims in the 1950s were for the most part similarly neglected in the West, and the entire event was not even known as the Holocaust at the time. Yet in Japan, Holocaust scholarship, ironically, also served to highlight Japan's own victimization.[35]

Holocaust Denial

The emergence of Holocaust denial writings in Japan may seem peculiar at first. After all, Japan was not involved directly in the Holocaust, either in the systematic extermination of Jews for being Jews or in the saving of Jews once systematic mass killing began in June 1941. Similarly, Japanese antisemitism did not evolve from an encounter with Jews, and it does not have deep historical roots or religious origins. Antisemitism in Japan has also never gained wholehearted governmental support, nor did it develop due to a significant conflict between Israel and Japan. In fact, Japanese antisemitism has appeared almost exclusively in written form and has never sunk to the level of damage to property or to physical attacks on Jews. It is for these reasons that Japan seems to occupy a special place in research on attitudes toward Jews in modern times.[36] Nonetheless, Holocaust denial in Japan did not emerge in a vacuum. Although the country lacks most of the features that characterize antisemitic societies, the first outburst of anti-Jewish race hatred in Japan occurred with the outbreak of the Pacific War (1941–45). The latter half of the 1980s also witnessed a resurrection of negative Jewish images as a new wave of antisemitic writings swept Japan. During this literary "renaissance," the Christian pastor Uno Masami emerged as the most influential author of antisemitic material. In 1986 alone, two of his books sold a combined total of 1.1 million copies.[37] Uno was certainly the most successful promulgator of antisemitism in modern Japan, but he was obviously not alone. By 1987 nearly a hundred books that carried the word "Jew" in their titles were in circulation, and many large bookstores displayed them in a special "Jewish corner."

The most well-known example of Holocaust denial in the Japanese media took place in 1995. That year *Marco Polo*, a weekly magazine with a circulation of over two hundred thousand, carried an article that denied the systematic gassing of Jews and claimed that Hitler did not intend to exterminate the Jewish people.[38] Within weeks of its publication, a campaign by international Jewish groups caused major advertisers to abandon the magazine, and both the international and the domestic press condemned the article. In response *Bungei Shunjū*, the magazine that was the publisher of *Marco Polo*, published an apology and shut down the magazine.[39] In the wake of the incident there was a growing awareness of the Holocaust in Japan and increased sympathy for the Jewish people. It also acted as a warning to other producers of antisemitic material—signaling that their activities were not only being monitored but were also no longer being tolerated. Moreover, a February 1999 Tokyo District Court ruled that Nazi Germany had murdered many Jews by poison gas in its concentration camps, echoing the findings established by the international tribunal for war crimes at Nuremberg. By confirming the basic facts of the Holocaust, the Japanese judicial system ended more than three years of confusion regarding the status of the Holocaust and the legitimacy of its denial in Japan.[40]

The Appropriation of the Holocaust

The first formal recognition of Japanese helping the Jews during the Holocaust occurred in 1984. During that year Yad Vashem granted the Japanese ex-diplomat Sugihara Chiune (1900–1986) the title of "Righteous Among the Nations." Between 1939 and 1940, Sugihara had served as a vice consul in Kaunas, then Lithuania's capital, and in this capacity granted transit visas to a few thousand Jews who were able to leave the country for East Asia shortly after the Soviet Union had annexed the country.[41] About two thousand of them reached Japan, from which more than half continued to other destinations, and the rest, who could not find a further safe haven, were deported to Shanghai in summer 1941. Yad Vashem's recognition exerted very little impact at first, and Sugihara passed away two years later with hardly any media attention. Nonetheless, this recognition was pivotal in the long run since it prompted further commemoration and imbued Sugihara with an aura of official legitimacy. Once this official recognition had been secured, additional organizations and individuals in Japan joined forces in introducing Sugihara's name to a larger audience. Among other things, they adapted his story into TV docudramas, a musical, and eventually, in 2015, a full-length feature.[42]

At present, the commemoration of Sugihara in books, films, and other tokens of tangible memory has grown to such a scale that it seems to mask and at times displace the memory of the Holocaust. The recent relaunching of the Holocaust exhibition is a case in point. Whereas the exhibition initially focused on the image of Anne Frank, its second tour focused on Sugihara too. The juxtaposed portrayal of the two may seem self-evident to the contemporary Japanese audience: the world's ultimate victim alongside her ultimate savior in a confusing proximity that almost suggests that Sugihara saved Frank. With the rising recognition of Sugihara as a savior of wartime Jews, other figures came to the fore with supporters applying to Yad Vashem and requesting that these figures should also be similarly recognized. The first among these is Kotsuji Setsuzō (1899–1973), a scholar of Semitic languages and adviser on Jewish affairs to Harbin's governor in the 1930s. Kotsuji assisted Jewish refugees during their stay in Kobe during 1941 and converted to Judaism himself two decades later. The second figure among these is the Imperial Japanese Army officer Lieutenant General Higuchi Kiichirō (1888–1970), who served in Manchuria in early 1938. In his 1971 autobiography, Higuchi claimed that he personally allowed twenty thousand Jews fleeing persecution in Nazi Germany to enter and find safe haven in Manchuria during the winter of early 1938.[43] Although this claim lacks historical base or supporting testimony, Higuchi has recently gained considerable recognition and admiration.[44] Multiple articles in the Japanese media have lauded his accomplishments, and to honor his achievements, a statue was erected in his hometown of Hyogo Prefecture in 2022.[45]

The commemoration of Sugihara and other aspiring rescuers has not been a spontaneous phenomenon. And yet, while it often began as a family enterprise, it did not take long for this commemoration to be embraced by Japan's conservative right wing. During the early 2000s, revisionist books denying the Nanjing massacre began to use Sugihara's name to show that wartime Japan did not resemble Nazi Germany.[46] The comparison with this Axis ally was effective, since it turned the media spotlight toward this remote diplomatic act of benevolence and away from Japan's innumerable wartime atrocities in Asia. In this context the identity of Sugihara's visa recipients gradually assumed a considerable degree of importance since it linked the Japanese wartime experience with the Jews and the Holocaust.

Indeed, from that point onward, official Japan could cast itself in the role of a "good" country that helped the Jews rather than that of an Axis villain.[47]

One of the main venues that is presently promoting the cause of the Holocaust in Japan is Nihon Bunka Channel Sakura (Japanese Culture Channel Sakura), an internet website and channel founded in 2004. With leading nationalist conservatives among its supporters and contributors and thousands of videos uploaded, the topics on which this channel focuses cover Japanese modern history and, in particular, the country's role in the Second World War. The Holocaust receives a considerable degree of attention in the programs aired by the channel, but always in a Japanese context. Thus, the epic saga of Chiune Sugihara has been presented and discussed in various forms, as have been the stories of Higuchi, Norihiro Yasue, and Koreshige Inuzuka, as well as those of other figures related to the prewar Japanese policy toward Jews. Unsurprisingly, all these figures are invariably presented as rescuers of Jews from the Holocaust.[48] When seen in this light, Jeffrey Hall has recently concluded, Channel Sakura invokes the Holocaust solely for domestic causes. It exploits it "to celebrate Japanese who were credited with saving Jews during the Second World War and to paint Japan as a victim of 'lies' that sought to compare Imperial Japan's wartime conduct [notably the Nanjing massacre and the forced use of women as sexual slaves by the Imperial Japanese Army] as something similar to the Holocaust."[49]

Conclusions: The Motives for Invoking the Holocaust in Japan

Altogether the Holocaust occupies a curious and unforeseen place in the Japanese intellectual life and the memory of the Second World War. The initial encounter with sporadic testimonies of the Holocaust in the 1950s has transformed over time into an intimate acquaintance with this event. Although Japan was an axis power and incarcerated about half of the Jews living in its wartime empire, the Japanese public has evinced a consuming and guiltless interest in the Holocaust and largely identified with Jewish suffering and victimhood. This interest was neither abstract nor accidental as the Holocaust has been invoked to stress the nation's own wartime victimhood, notably the unprecedented dropping of the two atom bombs on Hiroshima and Nagasaki. With the passage of time, Japanese officials associated with assisting Jews during the initial stages of the Holocaust have also received particular degree of attention. Furthermore, their commemoration is presently used to underscore the nation's wartime humanitarianism and thus serves to counterbalance accusations against the atrocities committed in the emperor's name. In this sense, and in a global perspective, Japan is a prominent case of using and misusing the memory of Holocaust for domestic ends that are completely detached from either the Jews or their European destruction.

Notes

1. David G. Goodman and Masanori Miyazawa, *Jews in the Japanese Mind: The History and Uses of a Cultural Stereotype* (New York: Free Press, 1995), 67–72; Rotem Kowner, "The Imitation Game? Japanese Attitudes towards Jews in Modern Times," in *The Medieval Roots of Antisemitism*, ed. Jonathan Adams and Cordelia Heß (London: Routledge, 2017), 83–84.
2. Roni Sarig, "Sadako Sasaki and Anne Frank: Myths in the Japanese and Israeli Memory of the Second World War," in *War and Militarism in Modern Japan: Issues of History and Identity*, ed. Guy Podoler (Folkestone, UK: Global Oriental, 2009), 172; Eric Margolis, "Anne Frank and Sadako Sasaki: Two Girls That Symbolize the Horrors of War," *Japan Times*, December 20, 2020.
3. Ben Whaley, "When Anne Frank Met Astro Boy: Drawing the Holocaust through Manga," *positions: asia critique* 28, no. 4 (November 2020): 729–55.
4. See, for example, Ardien Dier, "Japan Mystery: Anne Frank's Diary Torn Apart," *USA Today*, February 21, 2014.
5. BBC, "Japan PM Shinzo Abe Visits Amsterdam's Anne Frank Museum," March 24, 2014.
6. Viktor E. Frankl, *Yoru to kiri: Doitsu kyōsei shūyōsho no taiken kiroku*, trans. Shimoyama Tokuji (Tokyo: Misuzu Shobō, 1956).
7. See, for example, Kaikō Takeshi, *Koe no Karyūdo* (Tokyo: Iwanami, 1962).
8. Ran Zwigenberg, *Hiroshima: The Origins of Global Memory Culture* (Cambridge: Cambridge University Press, 2014), 176–207.
9. *Yomiuri Shinbun* editorial, cited in Zwigenberg, *Hiroshima*, 184.
10. Takeyama Michio, cited in Zwigenberg, *Hiroshima*, 184.
11. UNESCO Index Translation, cited in Kurihara Sadako, "The Literature of Auschwitz and Hiroshima," *Holocaust and Genocide Studies* 7 (1993): 77–106.
12. Zwigenberg, *Hiroshima*, 290.
13. See Katō Ariko, "Nihon ni okeru horokōsuto no juyō to dainiji sekai taisen no kioku–'Hiroshima Aushuvittsu' no heiwashugi gensetsu," in *Horokōsuto to Hiroshima: Porando to Nihon ni okeru dainiji sekai taisen no kioku*, ed. Katō Ariko and Jacek Leociak (Tokyo: Misuzu Shobō, 2021), 222–76.
14. See, for example, "Holocaust Exhibition in Hiroshima," *Soka Gakkai International Quarterly Magazine*, October 1995, 8–9.
15. "The Holocaust: Yūki no shōgen—horokōsuto-ten Anne Furanku to Sugihara Chiune no sentaku," Soka University, https://www.soka.ac.jp/assets/static/special/holocaust/.
16. See Ran Zwigenberg, "Modern Relics: The Sanctification of A-Bomb Objects in the Hiroshima Museum," *Journal of Holocaust and Genocide Studies* 35 (2021): 44–62.
17. Gavan McCormack, *Emptiness of Japanese Affluence* (Armonk NY: M. E. Sharpe, 1996), 242.

18. Sadako Kurihara, *When We Say Hiroshima: Selected Poems* (Ann Arbor: Center for Japanese Studies, University of Michigan, 1999).
19. Kurihara, "Literature of Auschwitz and Hiroshima," 86.
20. See John W. Dower and John Junkerman, eds., *The Hiroshima Murals: The Art of Iri Maruki and Toshi Maruki* (New York: Kodansha International, 1985).
21. See Zwigenberg, *Hiroshima*, 208–96.
22. Mick Broderick, ed., *Hibakusha Cinema: Hiroshima, Nagasaki and the Nuclear Image in Japanese Film* (London: Kegan Paul, 1996); Michael J. Hogan, ed., *Hiroshima in History and Memory* (Cambridge: Cambridge University Press, 1996).
23. Kurihara, "Literature of Auschwitz and Hiroshima," 90.
24. Kurihara was not alone in this sentiment. See Zwigenberg, *Hiroshima*, 188.
25. Nakazawa Masao, cited in Ran Zwigenberg, *Nuclear Minds: Cold War Psychological Science and the Bombings of Hiroshima and Nagasaki* (Chicago: University of Chicago Press, 2023), 176.
26. Kido Kōtarō, "Tamashī no satsujin ichi ichi kyōsei shūyōsho to ningen," *Gendai shinrigaku 6, seiji to keizai no shinrigaku* (1955), 59.
27. Kido, "Tamashī no satsujin." 59.
28. Kido, "Tamashī no satsujin." 64.
29. Kido, "Tamashī no satsujin." 64
30. Kido, "Tamashī no satsujin," 65.
31. Shimizu Ikutarō, "Jinkaku no Kuzure jō ni kō shite ichi ichi Nachisu shūchū shūyōsho no hitobito," *Nihon hyōron* 25, no. 12 (1950): 34.
32. Shimoyama wrote the introduction with his (unnamed) publisher. See Shimoyama Tokuji, introduction to Viktor E. Frankl, *Yoru to kiri: Doitsu kyōsei shūyōsho no taiken kiroku* (Tokyo: Misuzu Shobō, 1956), 2.
33. Shimoyama, introduction to Frankl, *Yoru to kiri*, 3.
34. Shimoyama, introduction to Frankl, *Yoru to kiri*, 4.
35. For extensive treatment of this issue, see Zwigenberg, *Nuclear Minds*.
36. See, for example, Rotem Kowner, *On Ignorance, Respect, and Suspicion: Current Japanese Attitudes towards Jews* (Jerusalem: Vidal Sassoon International Center for the Study of Antisemitism, 1997).
37. Uno Masami, *Yudaya ga wakaru to Nihon ga mietekuru* (Tokyo: Tokuma Shoten, 1986); Uno Masami, *Yudaya ga wakaru to seikai ga mietekuru—1990-nen "shūmatsu keizai sensō" eno shinario* (Tokyo: Tokuma Shoten, 1986).
38. Nishioka Masanori, "Nazi gasu shitsu ga nakkata," *Marco Polo*, February 1995, 170–79.
39. Rotem Kowner, "Tokyo Recognizes Auschwitz: The Rise and Fall of Holocaust-Denial in Japan, 1989–1999," *Journal of Genocide Research* 3 (2001): 269–70; Rotem Kowner, "The Strange Case of Japanese 'Revisionism,'" in *Holocaust Denial: The Politics of Perfidy*, ed. Robert Wistrich (Berlin: De Gruyter, 2012), 186–89.
40. Kajimura Taichirō, *Jānarizumu to rekishi ninshiki: Horokōsuto o dō tsutaeru ka* (Tokyo: Gaifūsha, 1999).
41. For recent explorations of this 1940 affair, see Kanno Kenji, *"Inochi no biza" gensetsu no kyokō* (Tokyo: Kyōwakoku, 2021); Rotem Kowner, "The Mir Yeshiva's Holocaust Experience: Ultra-Orthodox Perspectives on Japanese Wartime Attitudes towards Jewish Refugee," *Holocaust and Genocide Studies* 36 (2022): 295–314; Rotem Kowner,

"The Puzzle of Rescue and Its Memory: Sugihara Chiune and the 1940 Exodus of Jewish Refugees from Lithuania Redux," *Journal of World History* 35, no. 2 (2024).

42. For Sugihara's commemoration, see Eldad Nakar, "Sugihara Chiune and the Visas to Save Lives," *Japan Focus* 6 (January 1, 2008); Rotem Kowner, "A Holocaust Paragon of Virtue's Rise to Fame: The Transnational Commemoration of the Japanese Diplomat Sugihara Chiune and Its Divergent National Motives," *American Historical Review* 128 (2023): 31–63.
43. Higuchi Kiichirō, *Attsu-Kisuka-gun-shireikan no kaisōroku* (Tokyo: Fuyō Shobō, 1971), 351–58.
44. For Higuchi's claim for fame and its motives, see Rotem Kowner and Joshua Fogel, "Questionable Heroism," *Number 1 Shimbun*, December 2022.
45. See, for example, Noburu Okabe, "Finally, a Statue for General Higuchi Who Saved Thousands of Jews from Nazi Persecution," *Japan Forward*, May 18, 2018.
46. Takemoto Tadao and Ōhara Yasuo, *Saishin "Nankin daigyakusatsu": Sekai ni uttaeru Nihon no enzai* (Tokyo: Meiseisha, 2000), 134; Tanaka Masaaki, *What Really Happened in Nanking: The Refutation of a Common Myth* (Tokyo: Sekai Shuppan, 2000), 129.
47. For the motives of Sugihara's commemoration, see Nakar, "Sugihara Chiune"; Kowner, "Holocaust Paragon."
48. See Jeffrey J. Hall, "The Uses of the Holocaust in Japanese Conservative Internet Media," *Journal of Asia-Pacific Studies* (Waseda University) 26 (2016): 254–56.
49. Hall, "Uses of the Holocaust," 257.

4

Holocaust Memory
Temporalities, Actors, and Practices in Two National Cases, Argentina and Mexico

EMMANUEL KAHAN AND YAEL SIMAN

While Europe was the Holocaust's epicenter, its consequences were global. The resulting debates about the Jewish refugees during the Evian Conference in 1938 showed the responsibility of a broad set of countries in their refusal to provide a safe haven to the victims of Nazism. Various Latin American countries shared a policy of prohibition to the entry of Jewish refugees, unrelated to their political regimes.[1] Additionally, the refugee question led to significant debates, although with specific characteristics in every Latin American context. Furthermore, early on a series of strategies developed to denounce, mourn, and remember the extermination of the Jews.

This chapter examines the moments and ways in which the memory of the Holocaust was expressed in two Latin American countries: Argentina and Mexico. The selection of the two cases is based on their differences, rather than their shared traits. Argentina has historically been a receiving country of large waves of European immigrants while Mexico has received one of the lowest percentages of immigrants in the region. In spite of restrictive migratory policies in both countries, about 25,000–35,000 Jewish refugees went to Argentina between 1933 and 1945, but only 1,800–2,200 went to Mexico.[2] The two countries had a very different political history in the twentieth century: military dictatorships in Argentina and an authoritarian regime in Mexico, although both experienced transitions to democracy in the last decades. While various international events impacted them, the processes of Holocaust remembrance varied greatly. It is precisely this strong contrast between the two cases that allows us to examine how international phenomena interacted with national processes, leading to different memory contents and practices. A comparative approach reveals not only the plurality of Holocaust memory in the region but also the particular role of the national context, the local adaptations and interpretations, thus questioning the widely shared view of a global Holocaust memory.[3]

Memory is not a single or clear-cut phenomenon, while Holocaust memory is a fusion of old and contemporary religious and cultural practices.[4] As a tragic event, the Holocaust cried out for commemorations that were readily developed.[5] Although the voices of survivors had a central place in this memory, it was not immediate or the sole place. Instead, Holocaust memory in Argentina and Mexico engaged multiple actors—survivors, Jewish leaders, intellectuals, artists, public functionaries—and institutions such as Jewish agencies, museums, and research commissions, among others.[6]

This chapter examines the various memory narratives and practices in a broad temporary spectrum. It focuses on three historical moments: early Holocaust memories (mourning and commemoration), plural memories (the victim-witness or activist, old and new narratives, the expansion of commemoration), and recent memories (testimony and public usage of the Holocaust). Similar to other parts of the world, since the mid-1940s, an early Holocaust memory began to develop in Latin America. Initially it denounced the Nazi crimes and mourned for the enormous loss. Over time the actors diversified while the purposes and the meanings changed.

Early Holocaust Memories

Survivors carried with them the memory of the Holocaust, but many were reluctant to talk about their afflictions. Hasia R. Diner's research shows that in the United States, communities, synagogues, and other Jewish venues were in constant mourning.[7] These were small and scattered efforts and did not have the mass exposure of later events and Holocaust museums. Similarly, in Israel the earliest commemorative efforts were in small clusters of communities. A parallel phenomenon took place in Latin America.

During the first postwar years, a series of initiatives was carried out in Argentina. First, local interpretations of Nazism allowed the denunciation of the fascist character of Juan Domingo Perón's regime (1946–55). The committees formed by socialists and communists, the Radical Civic Union and two commissions of the Parliament—the Research Commission of Anti-Argentinean Activities (1943) and the Libertadora—represented Peronism as similar to European fascism. Although recent investigations have shown that the government of Perón was not antisemitic, this idea prevailed and has recurred in public debates.[8] Second, a series of editorial projects was part of an early Holocaust memory at the national level. As stated by Alejandro Dujovne, following the triumph of German troops in Poland, the cultural editorial Yiddish center in Warsaw fell.[9] This event led to the emergence of a Jewish cultural metropolis successor: Buenos Aires—given the low production cost, the large number of editorial presses, and the presence of

Yiddish-speaking Jewish editors who knew Polish, German, and Hebrew. From 1946 until the mid-1960s, Holocaust survivor testimonies were published as part of the collection *Dos Poylishe Ydntum*, under the direction of Marc Turkow, member of the Union of Polish Jews.

This editorial initiative in Argentina was developed together with commemorative practices, given the scope of the tragedy and the difficulty of talking about it through other means.[10] In both Argentina and Mexico, monuments were built in Jewish cemeteries in 1947: La Tablada cemetery in Buenos Aires and the Ashkenazi cemetery in Mexico City.[11] Although the genre was different, Mexico also had early traces of Holocaust memory in literary works, such as the novel of German Jewish intellectual Anna Seghers, and the work of Alberto Halabe, a Jewish Syrian immigrant.[12] All of them denounced the Nazi crimes.

Although the first commemorations in Mexico took place in the cemetery's monument, they were organized in public spaces in Argentina (e.g., the Luna Park stadium).[13] In both countries the main symbolic referents (although not the only ones) came from Israel: Yom Hashoah and the heroic Warsaw Ghetto Uprising. On April 8, 1956, for instance, the *Israelite Press* in Mexico announced that the Jewish Sports Centre joined the community's efforts to commemorate the "Uprising of the Warsaw Ghetto and the Tragic Death of Six Million Israelite Victims of Nazism."[14] While the local Jewish Agency organized yearly commemorations that called for the participation of all the ethno-national Jewish groups, in the first postwar year, the Ashkenazi narrative excluded the Jews of the Balkans, Greece, and the Middle East from the Holocaust's experience of victimhood.[15] Furthermore, Holocaust commemorations were closed to the outside. In both countries, survivors did not yet emerge as a coherent group.[16]

Early Holocaust memory initiatives engaged a broad set of subjects and institutions in the two countries. While some had a clear commemorative intention, others sought to intervene in public debates. Although they were part of a symbolic repertoire throughout the twentieth century, there was no social global demand for the memory of this history.[17]

Plural Memories

In the 1960s and 1970s several international events ignited new debates and narratives around the Holocaust in Argentina and Mexico: the Eichmann trial (1961), the 1967 Arab-Israeli War, and the UN resolution declaring Zionism as "a form of racism" (1975). In Argentina, Eichmann's capture reintroduced the Holocaust into the national public debate.[18] As Rein (2001) has shown, the resulting diplomatic frictions between Israel and Argentina revealed the two countries' differing interpretations of this episode. While Argentina claimed the violation of its sovereignty, Israel requested comprehension given Eichmann's criminal responsibility.[19]

The Eichmann case revived old local narratives regarding the Holocaust. This is exemplified by a book written by Silvano Santander, a leader of the Radical Civic Union who participated in the first investigative commission of anti-Argentine (Nazi) activities. Santander includes descriptions of the trial (which he witnessed), fragments of testimonies, and a prologue that identifies Perón's government with Nazism.[20] This was the last attempt to closely connect Peronism and Nazism. In that historic moment, new narratives of the Holocaust emerged: right-wing nationalist organizations claimed that Jews had dual loyalty to both Argentina and Israel. Furthermore, Jews were represented as not loyal to Argentina. In this context organizations such as Tacuara or the Nationalist Restorative Guard launched accusations and attacks against Jewish institutions and individuals. This campaign escalated in a national context of great political violence.[21] In Mexico, the trial was widely covered by the Mexican press.[22] Nevertheless, unlike Argentina, it did not lead to a divisive or violent environment against local Jews.[23]

Before and after the trial, survivors formed associations: Sherit Hapleitah (Surviving Remnants) was founded in Argentina in the 1950s, and the Unión de Miembros de la Resistencia, Deportados y Víctimas de la Segunda Guerra Mundial in Mexico in 1965 (Union of Members of the Resistance, Deported and Victims of World War II).[24] They met regularly to listen to each other's stories as "implicated listeners."[25] In Mexico, survivors gave testimony in the radio, press, schools, and universities. They also communicated and published their critical position toward policies of discrimination and human rights abuses in other countries.[26] In Mexico, survivors gave testimony in the radio, press, schools, and universities. They also communicated and published their position toward various audiences.[27] Additionally, they supported the first Holocaust Museum in Mexico, founded in 1970.[28] A similar museum in Argentina was created several years later and is discussed in the next section. In Argentina, survivors not only shared their stories; they also became activists and political subjects.

The political radicalization in Argentina led to the reconfiguration of Holocaust narratives in the 1960s. In particular, Jewish youth movements—Zionists and organizations linked to the national Left—established connections between the Warsaw Ghetto Uprising and the revolutionary struggles in Latin America against military regimes or governments that were considered pro-imperialist.[29] Since the 1967 Arab-Israeli War, left-wing organizations represented Israel as a satellite of Western imperialism in the Middle East.[30] These discourses were in tension with the narrative of the Holocaust's singularity, largely promoted by the Jewish leadership. Holocaust survivors expressed their opposition through marching on the streets of Buenos Aires, warning the public against the risk of another extermination of the Jews. Thus, in 1967 Sherit Hapleita mobilized as a legitimate bearer of an extreme experience.[31] The responses were very unfortunate: the police repressed the protestors, the national press mocked them, and the right-wing nationalist organizations called them "out of place, transferring their unjustified hatred to Argentina."[32]

Holocaust commemorations expanded in both countries: they involved the participation of many individuals and institutions, although with different meanings for each. In Argentina, the political usages of the Holocaust no longer questioned Peronism but, instead, denounced the dangers faced by Israel or, as previously mentioned, elaborated connections with the revolutionary change in Latin America. In Mexico, commemorations were organized by both Ashekanzi and Sephardic communities.[33] Survivor-witnesses acquired a more active role in such events. Ida Benadón, born in Salonika and a survivor of Auschwitz and Bergen-Belsen, remembers that during Yom Hashoah in the Sephardic synagogue, she was asked to light the first of six candles.[34] In 1958, in a commemoration organized by the Ashkenazi community (Kehilah) in a local theater (Teatro Artes), Rabbi Yaacov Avigdor, a Polish Holocaust survivor, talked about his experiences in the concentration camps.

A profound change took place between Israel and Latin America in 1973, given the economic impact of the Arab oil embargo and the centrality of the Palestinian question. Specifically, new power relations and Israel's conquest and occupation of territories led to the consolidation of prejudice against Israel as the perpetrator, no longer the victim. This growing distance between Israel and the region was expressed in the General Assembly United Nations (UN) Resolution 3379, which equated Zionism with racism in 1975. Mexico voted in favor.[35] While Mexico's position toward the UN resolution led to the questioning of the Jewish community's legitimate presence in Mexico, Holocaust survivors did not mobilize politically against it. The visit of President Luis Echeverría to Yad Vashem in Jerusalem, following Mexico's UN vote, provoked the renewal of a narrative of open doors toward Jewish refugees, although the reality had been very different.

Between the 1960s and the 1980s, an important shift came with witness testimony. Some of the first memoirs were written in Argentina as early as 1946.[36] This type of literary witnessing began in Mexico several years later, perhaps because of the larger number of Holocaust survivors that arrived in Argentina, the older local Jewish community, and the existence of publishing houses interested in this topic.[37] More survivors wrote their memoirs in the 1980s and 1990s. Neftali Frankel, Auschwitz survivor, shared his testimony in the Mexican press and published two books.[38] Survivors were hopeful that their testimony would help preserve the memory of the Holocaust and prevent future massacres, exemplified by the universal message of "never again." Additionally, in Mexico, an oral history project was developed at the end of the 1980s by the Hebrew University of Jerusalem, through its Institute of Contemporary Judaism, and Mexico's Friends Association of Hebrew University.[39]

Contemporary Memories

In the 1990s Holocaust memory was expressed in testimony projects, museums, and commemorations leading to a "golden age" of remembrance and public sentiment. Furthermore, Holocaust post-memory addressed what was no longer survivor memory or direct archival historical research, but the proposition that such memory was now born by a new set of individuals such as children of survivors or even their grandchildren.[40] Narratives of uniqueness coexisted with universal memory cultures, often in tension with each other. Furthermore, in the twenty-first century the memory of the Holocaust entered a comparative stage with respect to other genocides.[41] This has been particularly evident in Argentina, where alluding to the Nazi extermination of the Jews has functioned as a way to denounce the crimes of the last military dictatorship (1976–83).

The military regime used state terrorism extensively, committing systematic human rights' violations and leading to a gruesome outcome: thirty thousand disappeared persons, five hundred kidnapped children, and a high number of political prisoners and exiles. The criminal character of the Argentinean dictatorship was criticized internationally, underscoring the persecution of Jewish political militants.[42] Parliament commissions in the United States, international organizations that issued reports (Amnesty International and the Interamerican Commission of Human Rights), and public statements by intellectuals (such as Marek Halter in France) emphasized the "special treatment" (torture) of Jews in clandestine detention centers, followed by their assassination or disappearance. When the democratic process began, such reports were complemented by a series of initiatives of human rights organizations and journalists that referred to the Holocaust as analogous to the experience of the dictatorship's victims.[43]

Since the 1980s, Holocaust memory became a key national referent to denounce the dictatorship's criminal acts, as well as to justify the intervention of human rights organizations and the judicial strategies against the perpetrators. But the political use of the Holocaust analogy acquired greater importance and complexity in the 1990s when two terrorist attacks were carried out against Jewish institutions: the Israeli Embassy in Buenos Aires (1992) and the AMIA (Asociación Mutual Israelita de la República Argentina, 1994).[44] Although the judicial investigations failed, the state promoted Holocaust memory to make public opinion sensitive toward discrimination and the need for a plural citizenship. This policy materialized in a series of initiatives that called for Holocaust reflection, remembrance, and research: in 1997 the National Commission for Truth Clarification of Nazi Activities in Argentina (CEANA) was created, and in 2000 Argentina adhered to the Stockholm Declaration, which led to establishment of the International Holocaust Remembrance Alliance (IHRA).[45]

The institutionalization of Holocaust memory is observed in the state's educational policy. Resolution 80 (2009) promoted a "Holocaust Teaching Plan" that incorporates this historical event and other genocides of the twentieth century in the curriculum.[46] The public relevance of Holocaust memory has been complemented by the educational work of multiple programs and institutions: the Holocaust Museum in Buenos Aires, the Anne Frank Center–Argentina, the Program Morei-Morim of the Bama Foundation, and the Raphael Lemkin seminar for the prevention of genocides, organized by the Auschwitz Institute for the Prevention of Genocide and Mass Atrocities. These initiatives resulted from both the national context and global dynamics: the impact of the collection of Holocaust testimony by the Survivors of the Shoah Visual History Foundation (created by filmmaker Steven Spielberg) in the mid-1990s, the participation of youngsters in the March of the Living, and the participation of educators in courses at Yad Vashem. The state's memory policy has been sustained throughout time, independently of the political party in power. Today, a collective Holocaust memory in Argentina is also expressed in numerous monuments and plaques across the country.

As in Argentina, Holocaust memory in Mexico was impacted by a series of global initiatives: the United Nations mandate (2005) to commemorate the Holocaust annually on January 27; the UNESCO Latin American network of Holocaust education; the promotion of oral history projects (such as the University of Southern California Shoah Foundation); and educational initiatives by Yad Vashem, Facing History and Ourselves, and the United States Holocaust Memorial Museum, among others. But in contrast to Argentina, the Mexican state did not frame a memory policy that integrated the Holocaust. Nevertheless, since 2010 the Museum of Memory and Tolerance has become a central referent that to some extent fills this void.[47] Its narrative is both singular and universal: it establishes the Holocaust as a paradigmatic genocide in the twentieth century, but it connects it to other historic genocides and "intolerable" contemporary situations: discrimination, human rights violations, femicides, disappearances, and torture, among others. The museum has simultaneously become a site for education and civic encounters between government, citizenship, victims, and NGOs.[48] Additionally, Holocaust commemorations are a yearly practice, reaching diverse audiences and actors in Mexican society.[49] Various memory initiatives—testimony, education, museums, memorials, and commemorations—have informed the cultural production that focuses on the Holocaust and that has simultaneously impacted academic research, although at a much greater scale in Argentina.[50]

Final Comparative Reflections

This chapter shows that Holocaust memories in Argentina and Mexico have some common characteristics but also significant differences. The global memory of the Holocaust has been adapted, interpreted, used, and given meaning based on singular national processes, narratives, actors, and practices. In both countries Holocaust memory began to develop early on, but it did not interact with national political conflicts in the same way, and it did not acquire the same level of institutionalization.

In Argentina, this memory alluded to local political scenarios and was expressed by multiple actors since the postwar years, while in Mexico it developed in more restricted sectors of the Jewish community and was disconnected from episodes of national political violence. Thus, one might say that a collective Holocaust memory developed in Argentina while only a segmented one in Mexico. This can be seen in the different roles of survivors in each country. In Argentina, the survivor became a political subject capable of denouncing and questioning the dangers against Israel or the crimes of the military dictatorship. In Mexico, despite state repression and violence in the 1960s and 1970s, survivors remained nonpolitical witnesses. The role of the survivors in the two countries may be explained by the distinct scale of antisemitism and political violence in each country.

Thus, survivors in Mexico might not have felt their survival threatened, in contrast to Argentina.

Socio-demographic specificities also explain these different processes in the region. Argentina had considerable Jewish immigration since the end of the nineteenth century that produced an early public debate on the so-called Jewish question. This led Jewish organizations to develop strategies to combat antisemitism and affirm their legitimate place in the Argentinean nation. Furthermore, Argentina received a large number of survivors who, given particular situations—the Arab-Israeli wars and the terrorist attacks of the 1990s—represented a sensitive presence in the public sphere. In Mexico, by contrast, Jews and Jewish survivors remained a tiny minority, not representing a critical mass in the country. But the survivors' more limited participation in the Mexican public sphere might also be related to the pattern adopted by the local Jewish leadership not to publicly question state policy.

Finally, this study shows that national contexts may have a great influence on Holocaust memory. Thus, the notion of a global memory of the Holocaust becomes problematic in regions such as Latin America. Although some of the components of such memory are the same—the criminal character of Nazism, the recognition of the Jews as singular victims of extermination, the recognition of the survivor-witness, and the importance of testimony— the modes of expression are not identical to the ones found in Europe, the United States, or Israel. As stated by Maurice Halbwachs, *les cadres sociaux de la mémoire* (the social frameworks of memory) have a determinant weight when trying to comprehend the ways in which our societies connect, elaborate, or give meaning to their past.[51]

Notes

1. Argentina, Bolivia, Brazil, Colombia, Costa Rica, Cuba, Chile, Guatemala, Haiti, Honduras, Mexico, Nicaragua, Panama, Paraguay, Peru, Dominican Republic, Uruguay, and Venezuela participated at the Evian Conference. Exceptional cases include Bolivia (Leo Spitzer, *Hotel Bolivia: The Culture of Memory in a Refuge from Nazism* [New York: Hill and Wang, 1998]) and Dominican Republic (Allen Wells, *Tropical Zion: General Trujillo, FDR, and the Jews of Sosúa* [Durham NC: Duke University Press, 2009]), given their willingness to receive a large number of Jewish refugees. Avraham Milgram, ed., *Entre la aceptación y el rechazo: América Latina y los refugiados judíos del nazismo* (Jerusalem: Yad Vashem, 2003).
2. Haim Avni, *The Role of Latin America in Immigration and Rescue during the Nazi Era (1933–1945): A General Approach and Mexico Case Study* (Washington DC: Woodrow Wilson International Center for Scholars, 1986).

3. Andreas Huyseen, *En busca del futuro perdido: Cultura y memoria en tiempos de globalización* (México: Fondo de Cultura Económica, 2002).
4. Susannah Radstone and Bill Schwarz refer to memory as the site of many intersecting issues: temporal imaginings of the past, present, and future; subjectivity and identification; the passage from the inner life to the outer world; and the politics of being in the world and of recognition. Susannah Radstone and Bill Schwarz, eds., *Memory: Histories, Theories, Debates* (New York: Fordham University Press, 2010).
5. Gabriel Mayer, "Polity and Changing of Holocaust Memory," *International Journal of Advances in Social Sciences and Humanities* 7, no. 3 (March 2019).
6. Following Elizabeth Jelin's conceptual framework, we observe how the Holocaust was remembered and represented by different "memory entrepreneurs" depending on the specific national context and historical moment. Elizabeth Jelin, *Los trabajos de la memoria* (Madrid: Sigloo veintiuno de España editores, 2002).
7. Hasia R. Diner, *We Remember with Reverence and Love: American Jews and the Myth of Silence after the Holocaust, 1945–1962* (New York: New York University Press, 2009).
8. See more in Raanan Rein, *Argentina, Israel y los judíos: Encuentros y desencuentros, mitos y realidades* (Buenos Aires: Lumière, 2001); Raanan Rein, *Los muchachos peronistas judíos: Los argentinos judíos y el apoyo al Justicialismo* (Buenos Aires: Sudamericana Castellano Editorial, 2015).
9. Alejandro Dujovne, *Una historia del libro judío* (Buenos Aires: Siglo XXI, 2014).
10. Malena Chinsky, "Memorias olvidadas: Los judíos y la recordación de la Shoá en Buenos Aires" (PhD diss., Universidad Nacional de General Sarmiento-Ides, 2017); Mayer, "Polity and Changing of Holocaust Memory."
11. Yonia Fain, originally from Kamyanets, Russia, and a survivor of the Holocaust, was responsible for the painting of the monument's chapel. Fain emigrated to Mexico City in 1946 but left for New York in 1953. He had a close relationship with Mexican muralists such as Diego Rivera and Rufino Tamayo. In the monument's chapel, Fain painted Ezequiel's vision: a juxtaposition of killing, death, and rebirth.
12. Between 1941 and 1942, Anna Seghers wrote *Transit*, a novel that describes her flight from Nazi Europe. The first edition was published in German: Anna Seghers, *Transit* (Frankfurt: Verlag der Autoren, 1944). Other editions followed in English (trans. James Austin Galston [Boston: Little, Brown, 1944]), Spanish (trans. Carlos Lorente [Barcelona: Editorial Seix Barral, 1947]), and French (trans. Lucienne Frappier [Paris: Éditions de Minuit, 1948]), all under the title *Transit*. Alberto Halabe wrote *A Sabbatical Night*, the story of a Jewish family that was captured by the Gestapo. It has been presented in theaters in Mexico City since 1941. It was published until 1973. Alberto Halabe, *Una noche sabatal* (Mexico City: Ediciones Era, 1973).
13. This collective memory also developed among survivors in other geographical locations who erected memorial cemeteries—cenotaphs with the engraved names of the victims. Such cenotaphs fostered a group memory, although a small one. Annette Wieviorka, *The Era of Witness*, trans. Jared Stark (New York: Cornell University Press, 2006), 51.
14. "Noticias del CDI," *Prensa Israelita*, April 7, 1956, Archive of the Jewish Documentation and Research Center of Mexico (CDIJUM).
15. *Prensa Israelita*, April 6, 1957, page 6-A, CDIJUM.

16. Anette Wieviorka describes how the first Jewish survivor associations were based on ties of sociality and mutual aid but only addressed those who shared the same experience. Only in a few places did their rare efforts to bring memory to public attention succeed. Wieviorka, *Era of Witness*.
17. Latin America was not exceptional in this regard. In 1947 the first stone for a Holocaust memorial was laid in New York City while the Center for Documentation of Contemporary Jewry (established in 1943) collected materials that were submitted to the French prosecution at the Nuremberg trials. In 1953 documents were combined with rituals as the first stone of a Paris memorial was laid. Until the early 1960s, it was the only memorial in the world located in a public space. Wieviorka, *Era of Witness*.
18. In 1960, according to Annette Wieviorka, the capture of Adolf Eichmann and his trial in Jerusalem marked a "pivotal moment" in the history of the memory of the genocide, and the "advent of the witness." Wieviorka, *Era of Witness*.
19. The diplomatic conflict was soon resolved through the exchange of ambassadors and the presentation of Argentina's complaint to the United Nations.
20. Santander had previously published the same assertion in two flyers. See Silvano Santander, *Técnica de una traición: Juan D. Perón y Eva Duarte, agentes del Nazismo en Argentina* (Buenos Aires: Edición Argentina, 1955); Silvano Santander, *Yo Acusé a la Dictadura* (Buenos Aires: Ediciones Gure, 1957).
21. Leonardo Senkman, *El antisemitismo en Argentina* (Buenos Aires: Lùmiere, 1989).
22. Carlos Denegri, a Mexican reporter of the newspaper *Excelsior*, was admitted to the trial.
23. Marianne Hirsch and Leo Spitzer refer to Shoshana Felman's conception of Hannah Arendt's *Eichmann in Jerusalem* and Claude Lanzmann's film *Shoah* as two fundamental works that provoked conceptual breakthroughs in our apprehension of the Holocaust during this second historical moment. Marianne Hirsch and Leo Spitzer, "The Witness in the Archive: Holocaust Studies/Memory Studies," *Memory Studies* 2, no. 2 (May 2009): 151–70; Hannah Arendt, *Eichmann in Jerusalem: A Report on the Banality of Evil* (New York: Viking Press, 1963); Claude Lanzmann, dir., *Shoah*, New Yorker Films, 1985, 566 min.
24. The Survivor Union in Mexico was initially led by Dunia Wassertrom, originally from Russia (Ukraine) and a survivor of Auschwitz. In Argentina an important figure and head of Sherit Hapleitah was José Moskovits, born in Hungary.
25. According to Natasha Zaretsky, an "implicated listener" is a listener who shares aspects of the same story. Natasha Zaretsky, "Child Survivors of the Shoa: Testimony, Citizenship, and Survival in Jewish Buenos Aires," in *The New Jewish Argentina: Facets of Jewish Experiences in the Southern Cone*, ed. Adriana Brodsky and Raanan Rein (Leiden: Brill, 2013).
26. Zaretsky, "Child Survivors of the Shoa."
27. On January 30, 1969, the Association of Holocaust Survivors in Mexico sent a telegram to the UN General Secretary U Thant to protest against the "genocide" of fourteen persons in Iraq.
28. The Holocaust museum was founded by Dr. Tuvie Maizel. It was located in a community (Ashkenazi) center: Nidjei Israel—Acapulco 70. The museum closed its doors following the earthquake in 2017.

29. Beatrice D. Gurwitz, *Argentine Jews in the Age of Revolt: Between the New World and the Third World* (Leiden: Brill, 2016).
30. Emmanuel Kahan, "Revaluando el sionismo y la causa palestina: Intelectuales argentinos frente al conflicto árabe-israelí. Recepción y debates durante la Guerra de los Seis Días (1967)," *Anuario de Historia de América Latina* 58 (2021).
31. Emmanuel Kahan, "Los sobrevivientes del Holocausto en Argentina frente a la guerra de los Seis Días (1967)," *Revista Historia y MEMORIA*, no. 18 (January–June 2019).
32. Anonymous, "Una nota al presidente," *La Razón*, June 6, 1967, 4.
33. One of the commemorations sought to remember the six million killed by the Nazis in Europe and Salonika, as well as other Sephardic communities. Among the participants were the Sephardic Union and the Sephardic Zionist Organization.
34. USC Shoah Foundation Institute, interview with Ida Benadon (VHA Interview, Venezuela, July 23, 1996).
35. This new position contrasts with the large support given by Latin American countries to the UN General Assembly's partition plan and the creation of a Jewish state. Judit Bokser and Yael Siman, "La histórica relación entre Israel y Latinoamérica. Holocausto y representaciones culturales," *Foreign Affairs Latinoamérica* 21, no.1 (January 2021).
36. One if these memoirs was written in Yiddish by Malka Owsiany (Buenos Aires, 1946). Simja Sneh also wrote his memoir a few years later (Buenos Aires and Mexico, 1952).
37. Masha Greenbaum, *Una ventana al infierno*, ed. Costa-Amic (Mexico City, 1962). Many years later Masha Greenbaum gave testimony to the Wiesenthal Center in Los Angeles in 1991 and to Yad Vashem in 2012. "Oral History Interview with Masha Greenbaum," United States Holocaust Memorial Museum, October 8, 1991, https://collections.ushmm.org/search/catalog/irn513295; "Entrevista a Masha Greenbaum," Centro Mundial de Commemoración de la Shoá, May–June 2012, https://www.yadvashem.org/es/education/educational-materials/articles/interview-with-masha-greenbaum.html. Dunia Wasserstrom wrote her testimony in 1974, and her memoir, *Nunca jamás . . . Memorias de un sobreviviente de Auschwitz*, was published in various editions starting in 1975. A few other memoirs were published between 1970 and the 1980s, and a greater number since the 1990s.
38. Frankel's testimony was published in the newspaper *Excelsior*. Neftali Frankel, *Auschwitz: Campo de exterminio; Prisionero no. 161040 (Sobreviviente)* (Mexico City: EDAMEX, 1986). He published a second book in 1990: *Yo he conocido el infierno: Testimonio de un sobreviviente en la Europa nazi* (EDAMEX); English ed.: *I Survived Hell: The Testimony of a Survivor of the Nazi Extermination Camp* (New York: Vantage Press, 1991). Frankel emigrated with his father to Mexico in 1946 but moved to El Paso, Texas, in 2003. See "Frankel, Neftali (ESP)," El Paso Holocaust Museum and Study Center, https://elpasoholocaustmuseum.org/frankel-neftali-esp/.
39. The oral history project conducted 152 interviews mainly between 1987 and 1989 with Jewish immigrants, including Holocaust survivors. This project sought to reconstruct the history of the Jewish community in Mexico and to recover its collective memory. The description of the methodology is found in *Testimonios de Historia*

Oral: Judíos en México. Institute of Contemporary Judaism, Hebrew University of Jerusalem, and Friends Association of the Hebrew University of Jerusalem in Mexico, Mexico, 1990.

40. Marianne Hirsch and Leo Spitzer, "The Witness in the Archive: Holocaust Studies/Memory Studies," *Memory Studies* 2, no. 2 (May 2009).
41. James E. Young, *The Texture of Memory: Holocaust Memorials and Meaning* (New Haven CT: Yale University Press, 1993).
42. Emmanuel Kahan, *Memories That Lie a Little: Jewish Experiences during the Argentine Dictatorship*, trans. David Foster (Leiden: Brill, 2019).
43. Emmanuel Kahan, "Los fantasmas de la dictadura y la agenda de los derechos humanos entre los actores de la comunidad judía argentina durante la recuperación democrática (1979–1984)," *Pasado y Memoria: Revista de Historia Contemporánea* 20 (2020).
44. Natasha Zaretsky, *Acts of Repair: Justice, Truth, and the Politics of Memory in Argentina* (New Brunswick NJ: Rutgers University Press, 2021).
45. Mexico is not a member of IHRA.
46. Celeste Adamoli and Emmanuel Kahan, "El abordaje del Holocausto desde la trama educativa: Consideraciones sobre la construcción de una política de educación y memoria," *Aletheia: Revista de la Maestría y Memoria de la FaHCE* 7, no. 14 (April 2017).
47. The origins of the Mexican museum can be traced to 1999, when it was founded as a not-for-profit association. There are no similar museums outside Mexico City and only a few memorials.
48. Yael Siman, telephone interview with Adán García, academic director, Museum of Memory and Tolerance (Mexico City, May 15, 2019).
49. Since the late 1990s, the Jewish Central Agency of Mexico has organized an event that brought together the different ethnic Jewish groups to commemorate Yom Hashoah. On the development of Holocaust commemorations in both countries, see Yael Siman and Emmanuel Kahan, "La memoria global del Holocausto en contextos nacionales: Prácticas commemorativas en Argentina y México," *Istor: Revista de Historia International* 82 (Autumn 2020): 79–109.
50. Ariana Huberman and Alejandro Meter, eds., *Memoria y representacion: Configuraciones culturales y literarias en el imaginario judio latinoamericano* (Rosario, Argentina: Beatriz Viterbro Editora, 2006); Leonardo Senkman and Sosnowski, *Fascismo y nazismo en las letras argentinas* (Buenos Aires: Lumière, 2009); Lyor Zylberman and Liliana Feierstein, *Narrativas del terror y la desaparición en América Latina* (Buenos Aires: Universidad Nacional de Tres de Febrero, 2016); Sabine Schlickers, *De Auschwitz a Argentina: Representaciones del nazismo en la literatura y cine, 2000–2020* (Buenos Aires: Biblos, 2021).
51. Maurice Hallwachs, *La mémoire collective* (Paris: Albin Michel, 1997).

5

Resonances of the Holocaust in the Memory of Nazi Victims and Survivors Living in Chile

NANCY NICHOLLS LOPEANDÍA

In this chapter I analyze the oral narratives of European Jews who found refuge in Chile before, during, and after World War II and the Holocaust; that is, the victims of the Nazi persecution that began in the first half of the 1930s and survivors of the Holocaust.[1] Their lives in Chile, and in other countries to which they emigrated, are situated in a broad spatial and temporal space, which raises many questions, especially when we speak of refuge in a country of the Global South, remote and unknown to many in Europe from the 1930s to the 1950s, as Chile was. We know that most of them adapted and rebuilt their lives in this country, formed families, and engaged in national life through business activities, and in some cases even at a political, social, and cultural level. A minority emigrated again because they did not feel at ease in a "less developed" country, or because they reunited with relatives in other countries, or because they simply sought a better quality of life on other horizons. Within this minority, there were several who emigrated in the face of the imminent arrival of a socialist government in the 1960s, or in 1973, as this possibility materialized when Salvador Allende, an avowed Marxist, triumphed in the presidential election. What place does the memory of the Holocaust have in this decision? After decades of relative tranquility and political stability in the country, did they fear a devastating leftist totalitarianism? Was the trauma of the experiences of persecution, dehumanizing mistreatment, and death revived? And in the face of the Pinochet dictatorship, did the memory of the Holocaust resonate?

This study is based on the analysis of thirty-one testimonies of Nazi victims and Holocaust survivors (eighteen men and thirteen women) who found refuge in Chile. The interviews are found in two collections of testimonies: Voces de la Shoá of the Corporación Memoria Viva and Visual History Archive of the USC Shoah Foundation.[2]

Testimonies: A Window into the Subjectivity of Experiences

The Holocaust testimonies discussed in this chapter are valuable and complex pieces in terms of the memory of those who express them. They undoubtedly shed light on the lives of European Jews who were victims of Nazism in its various stages. They also tell us about the post-Holocaust period.[3] However, there are considerable differences; some testimonies may elaborate on what happened "after," while others barely mention this period of their lives.[4] In the latter cases a biographical gap is generated between the moment in which the narration is concentrated—World War II, persecution, and Holocaust—and the moment in which the speaker gives testimony. For example, with some exceptions, we know little about how the victims who escaped before the war and the victims of the Holocaust adapted to life in Chile, how they managed to make a living, what they thought of the country when they arrived and then over time, and, most importantly for this study, what consequences the experiences in Nazi Germany and countries occupied by Hitler, and especially those of the Holocaust, had on their lives. Although in some testimonies there is discussion about the permanence of the trauma expressed in the sensory memory, or recurrent nightmares, there is no explicit mention of the trauma. Nor is there any mention of the continuity of the traumatic experiences or of therapeutic support; on the contrary, many of them report not having told their family or friends about what they had lived through, the moment of the interview being the first time they had given testimony.

This last type of silence occurs because the memory is precisely traumatic or very painful, significant, and disturbing; the victim does not want to bring the memory to the present, does not want it to be relived. In these cases it would not necessarily be a matter of forgetting, but possibly of experiences loaded with meanings, alive in the memory even if in an unconscious way, but disturbing and difficult, so that the preference is for it to be kept "locked away."

What happens after the Holocaust is fundamental to understanding how an extreme event, considered both a trope of memory and a prism through which other events of a similar nature are studied, generated trauma in the victims and survivors, in their descendants, and to a certain extent in the whole of the society in which they were inserted.[5] Testimonies, in this sense, are appropriate devices for representing the past since they narrate it from the subjectivity of the speaker, involving the emotional level, giving meaning to and interpreting the experience. They do so from the present in which the testimony is produced, thus incorporating the set of experiences up to that moment, as well as the multiple representations made by others about the events narrated, which slip into the memory and become their own. When analyzing oral testimonies, the subjective element is even more evident if we consider that the way in which the past is narrated, what is highlighted and what is omitted, what is forgotten and what remains, is the result of the process of personal recollection that unfolds over time. Dominik LaCapra argues, "Testimonies are significant in the attempt to understand experience and its aftermath, including the role of memory and its lapses, in coming to terms with—or denying and repressing—the past."[6]

Arrival and the First Time in a Country at the End of the World

Chile—in the memory of the testimonies—was a country that was reached out of necessity; no one chose it as a desired destination for migration or refuge, as was the case of the United States and, in Latin America, Argentina. Very few knew about Chile. Some had relatives already living in the country, which acted as a factor in the migration, and others arrived because these were the only visas available when it was practically impossible to emigrate to other places. The experience of arrival varied according to several factors, with place of origin, age, and time of arrival (before or after the war and the Holocaust) being some of the most relevant in the characteristics acquired. The majority of the witnesses were children, adolescents, or young people when they arrived in Chile. They came with their parents and siblings; therefore, when they testify they refer to what they experienced, but they also narrate what in their eyes was what their parents or other adults experienced. In this way we gain access to the child and adult experience through the testimony of these children who recall in their own adulthood their childhood perceptions.[7]

Arrival was, in most cases, difficult, a cultural shock, especially when coming from the more developed European capitals such as Berlin. Santiago and other Chilean cities were growing rapidly in the 1940s and 1950s but were still relatively underdeveloped, where flashes of modernity coexisted with remnants of older, traditional life.[8] In spite of this, Chile was in the memory of the victims and survivors the country that saved them from the Holocaust, or that gave them a possibility to restart their stories after their experiences in the concentration and extermination camps.

There is very little mention of how the experience in the new country affects them and how they deal with a traumatic past, and therefore it seems that this narrative section is somewhat disconnected from that of the Holocaust experience, as if the new beginning in Chile had erased the past and with it the horror and pain. Fortunately, we have a few reflections that demonstrate otherwise. Marion Mostny remembers the first years in Chile when the Jewish holidays were celebrated, especially Yom Kippur. "Holidays were terrible," she remembers. "Why?" the interviewer asks.

> Oh because everybody was always crying and crying and crying, you know, there were memorials.... When you have memorials on Yom Kippur the custom was that children who have both parents alive did not stay for that service, so we are always sent out ... and then this was in 1939, and then 40 ... and then when came to 42, and 43 they said we're going to pray for the ones who are prisoners or whatever so that was new added to the book, and then after 45 when one knew what had happened ... it was changed to what they said that there isn't a single family who doesn't have somebody who perished, and the children whether your parents are alive you can stay, for your grandparents.[9]

The loss of family members was particularly painful during religious holidays.

The Survivors: Getting on with Life in the Best Way Possible

Leo de Jong, a Dutch Jew who had returned from the Bergen-Belsen concentration camp to Amsterdam, his hometown, reentered school and remembers that "everyone wanted to get back to life and not think too much about what had happened."[10] We come across brief references of this kind in the survivors' testimonies, which aim at resuming "normalcy," work or school activity, or earning a living again after having lost family and friends, most of their capital and assets, and the entire prewar Jewish cultural horizon, without paying too much attention to emotional recovery. The arrival in Chile—far from the scenes of the genocide—may have represented some kind of processing of the trauma. Kurt Herdan, a Romanian Jew sent to Soviet forced labor camps, narrates openly that after his liberation he had "abandoned the thought of living," but in Chile he met his future wife, and she "taught him to live again."[11] Others concentrate their narrative about Chile on their work, on how they gradually got ahead. However, the traumatic experience creeps in through interstices beyond conscious control.

La Capra argues: "In traumatic memory the event somehow registers and may actually be relived in the present, at times in a compulsively repetitive manner. It may not be subject to controlled, conscious recall. But it returns in nightmares, flashbacks, anxiety attacks, and other forms of intrusively repetitive behavior characteristic of an all-compelling frame."[12] Alice Himmel, a Hungarian Jew, survived the Holocaust in an orphanage in Budapest. At one point she was taken to the banks of the Danube to be executed, but in an instinctive act she threw herself into the river and saved herself from death. If the memory of this extreme event that Alice Himmel experienced is blocked, and the images are fading with the passage of time, the nightmare unfolds, evidencing its latency, its actuality, its traumatic nature. As LaCapra explains, "Something of the past always remains, if only as a haunting presence or symptomatic revenant."[13] Echoing the distinction made by this author between absence and loss, the former situated on a transhistorical level devoid of time and the latter historically located,[14] we can affirm that the past in its traumatic expressions appears uninvited in the timeless realm par excellence, that of dreams.

Alice reminisces:

> Lately I wake up with fewer nightmares, but until recently my husband had to wake me up many times because I was screaming. . . . One that comes back many times, the buildings were interconnected in the subway where we went during the bombings and [pause] there was a space and the nightmare was that I could get through this . . . one square meter and my mom couldn't, my mom gets trapped, then she goes back to the other side and I'm alone again, then my grandma tries to get through and she can't either and I stay on the other side and the screams start, that's one, and the other one of facing the rifles trying to avoid the bullets, these are two that still come back.[15]

Alice's memories of her horrific past would return to her in various haunting dream sequences.

The images of what Klara Sternbach lived through in Auschwitz also reappear in recurrent nightmares, inserted into stories different from reality, modified, but maintaining the terrifying substrate of experience. Toward the end of the interview, the interviewer asks: "And is war something that you could leave behind, your experiences, or is it something that you still carry with you?" Klara responds:

> The concentration camp you can't leave behind, and the older you get, the more you don't feel it, the more you dream, and you have more "white nights" as I say, that you don't want to sleep because you don't want to keep dreaming because of all that I went through; and you won't believe me, and I felt that my children wouldn't understand what is persecution of religion and race, I didn't tell them that I was in Auschwitz, and neither

did my husband because he went through much worse still. . . . I don't know, no, no, no, I try sometimes at night when it is very difficult, to sit and be seated, do you understand? So as not to go on with the dream, it haunts you, it didn't leave us without a scar.[16]

For Klara and others, the pain of past experiences is something that remains, endures.

Political Stability and the Memory of Rewarded Effort

From the early 1930s, Chile lived through a period of political stability, which was not interrupted until the arrival of the Popular Unity to the government in 1970. The testimonies rarely mention the political situation of the country at the time of their arrival or in the following years, which changes when they refer to the Popular Unity (1970–73) and the dictatorship of Salvador Allende (1973–90). This silence, together with the fact that among those who narrate this period, the great majority refer to how they tried to earn a living, can be interpreted as an appreciation of a political and economic context that made it possible for them to work and prosper. Among the testimonies analyzed, dedication to commercial activity is one of the most recurrent among the victims and survivors of the Holocaust, although there are also artists and professionals among them.[17]

The narrative of labor insertion in the country is told by young men and women who were already of working age, but also by sons and daughters who remember how their parents looked for work for the first time or set up a small workshop at home, which eventually became a larger company. Beyond their particularities, the narratives have in common the fact that they can be interpreted as a process of constant effort, sacrifice, learning, and creativity, in which the person starts with practically nothing or very little and with time progresses until attaining a comfortable and even successful livelihood. As Irene Klein puts it, "The life narrative advances with the eagerness to legitimize itself as a story 'worth telling,' that is, as a story that can be understood and heeded, that is, accepted by the community of readers who listen to it."[18] The stories are arranged—with data emerging from reality—following a known plot anchored in tradition, in textual paradigms as Klein says, but also in models created by the community. Among these paradigms distinguished by Klein, there are three that can be applied to the narratives that were analyzed: the story of the poor and honest worker, a rising career, and the struggle of the immigrant.[19] These three plots are interwoven with the life experiences of Holocaust survivors and victims, giving meaning to their arrival and new life in Chile. The effects of the suffering or trauma, however, are obliterated in this part of the narrative. Like a chapter without continuity, the suffering in Europe is not evoked—except when it appears as ghostly—as an obstacle to the efforts made and rewarded. The narratives are effectively the resonance of how life was experienced and understood in those years, as the blank page of a new chapter that is written without looking at the previous one. As Kurt Herdan explains without preamble at the beginning of his interview: "I avoid looking back." However, just as Kurt adds, after a pause, "but of course it doesn't work for me,"[20] the imprint of the past in the memory loomed, uninvited.

The Mobilizing Memory

From the 1960s Chile, a country with considerable socioeconomic inequalities, underwent profound social and political reforms. In the presidential elections of 1964, the Christian Democrat Eduardo Frei triumphed, supported not only by the center but also by the right, which sought to avoid the ascent to power of the socialist Salvador Allende. However, in 1970 Allende won the presidential elections, becoming the first Marxist to come to power through democratic means. In the "thousand days" of the Popular Unity government, the "Chilean route to socialism" was launched; the Social Property Area of the state was created, made up of the key industries, services, and financial capital of the economy, which meant that many private companies were confiscated and passed into state control; the Agrarian Reform initiated in the previous government was deepened. The government of the Popular Unity was for many the opportunity for materializing the dream of a more egalitarian and just society. For the opponents it was the threat of a "new Cuba," of the loss of freedom and of private property. This threat and the fear that followed were shared by some of the Holocaust survivors and victims based in Chile.[21] Marion Mostny recounts:

> When the communists were coming to Chile or it looked as if they were, we decided . . . paranoia or threat or whatever that was, we said we are not going to wait until 1939, that was our expression, you know. . . . This is 1933, we see it's coming, we can sell our business, we can sell our house, we can take our children wherever we want to, the children were at an age where you took them, they didn't ask. . . . That was part of this feeling of, you know, we said we are not going to repeat the mistake they made.[22]

Marion Mostny's reflection is exceptional because it connects the two events with astonishing clarity. It is also one of the few testimonies among those analyzed that refers to how the Holocaust influenced the relevant decisions of her later life. Marion, her parents, and her brother managed to escape from Berlin just before the war broke out. She personally experienced prewar antisemitism as a child. However, in addition to her life being turned upside down when her family made the decision to flee to Chile, her mother's suffering at not being able to take her own mother with them is very present in her memory. After the end of the war, they learned of her death, and those of other relatives. This marked Marion's mother's life with deep sadness.

Viorica Silberstein, a Romanian Jew and survivor of Auschwitz, decided to go to Chile with her husband when communism appeared on her country's horizon. In Chile they resumed their lives and formed a family. "Everything was problem-free," she says, "until communism arrived, the[n] Allende, and we said to ourselves that there is nothing, nothing more precious in this world than freedom and getting away from war and getting away from communism, we couldn't stay here.... And then we decided that we have to go to Israel and again leave all our house, all our youth behind and we emigrated to Israel."[23] Viorica bases her decision to migrate with her family, abandoning what they had built in Chile, on a double experience: having survived Auschwitz and having fled the communist regime that was installed in Romania, her native country, in the postwar period. As she says, "Coming out of war and coming out of communism we cannot stay here, we simply cannot." She synthesizes the place that the memory of the two events occupies in the face of Allende's triumph. It would seem that the Holocaust acted as a mobilizing memory, a memory that warns that it is necessary to act in order not to fall back into what it projects as the jaws of totalitarianism. The Holocaust is, fundamentally, a foundational experience of evil, horror, and suffering that impels us to act in order not to repeat it.

Migration for Holocaust survivors who lived in Eastern European countries had the character of fleeing or flight. The narratives reveal the complexity and uncertainty of this flight, which was made with stopovers in a decimated Europe overcrowded with refugees. The momentary calm and a return to normality full of ghosts was interrupted again with this migration, this time in a context of peace. The fragments dedicated to flight reveal reckless actions in the midst of a context marked by the aftermath of devastation, in continuity with the extreme experiences of war. The fundamental difference is that, in this case, contrary to what happened in the Holocaust, the survivors made decisions, having regained their historical agency. Alice Himmel recalls the postwar period in Budapest, when she was reunited with her parents, also survivors:

> We tried to go back to . . . to our apartment which was also occupied but . . . with very decent people, former neighbors. We tried to resume a normal rhythm of our lives, let's think that it turned out, we were living a normal life, my parents were working, I was back to school [pause]. We had a good time, until the Russians started to tighten the belt little by little, and my dad said no again. And with our approval or with our opinion, my mum's and mine, shall we go? we left. And we left absolutely everything, an apartment . . . a good apartment, not a luxury one, newly furnished, a business, a good neighborhood, which is now a bank, with all the merchandise, and with a backpack each we left through the mined border, first to the former Czechoslovakia and from there to Austria, the three of us together. . . . We left on August 20th [19]49.[24]

Having survived the war, life in Hungary was no longer agreeable. The family had to embark on another difficult journey.

Paradoxical Memory

Viorica Silberstein and her family migrated to Israel, where they were reunited with the rest of their family who had survived the Holocaust, rebuilding their lives. But as she recalls: "Unfortunately the war of [19]73 came and I who thought I was the promoter of the whole, the emigration [sic] to Israel I said there is nothing worse than losing freedom, but there was something else worse, which is war, thinking that my three children are going to be taken together, even my husband, to war."[25] The feeling of losing family members forced a relocation. They decided to emigrate to Canada, where they had family, and where they lived for three and a half years:

> We felt welcomed again by my husband's family until one day I saw that my husband came every year here [Chile] because the business was still working and I saw that every time he came back he. . . . It was a nostalgia, a pain of not living in Chile, if our best years were here [in Chile], it was something that . . . as if we had been reborn here more than born because we knew other countries where it was not the same way of living, to be welcomed. . . . And he was 52 years old at the time and I said it can't be that he ruins his. . . . The children no longer need us, they are practically on their way . . . but he has to live his life and so we returned to Santiago in 1978 and we started again.[26]

Viorica Silberstein's memory, through her testimony, is paradoxical; the traumatic experience of the Holocaust prompted her to act in the face of political contexts that were threatening to her. However, in her narrative, the Pinochet dictatorship does not appear as a problematic regime. The dictatorship for many Chileans was a regime that saved the country from a massacre or civil war; moreover it saved the country from communism. As historian Steve Stern has pointed out, this vision corresponds to the "memory of salvation," in which the human rights violations committed by the regime were either the product of sporadic excesses or were a necessary social cost for the salvation of Chile.[27] It is possible that Viorica shared this memory, but it is also possible that her memory, as Portelli theorizes, was divided. That is to say, she condemned the Nazism that murdered her parents and siblings, that destroyed their way of life and plundered their property, and she also feared Soviet socialism and Allende's democratic socialism, but not the Pinochet dictatorship, because it did not persecute them as Jews, nor by virtue of their political ideas, nor did it even touch their daily lives.[28]

The silences of memory do not only correspond to forgetfulness; they are also related to contradictions, paradoxes, dissociations, or simply aspects that are not possible to enunciate because they are not allowed or would not be well received in the public sphere. For Portelli, these would be "problematic and unauthorized memories," which are relegated to the basement of oblivion.[29] The dictatorship left people dead, disappeared, and tortured, which is condemnable and disturbing, even for those who adhered to the memory of salvation. However, even if this part of history is obliterated in the discourse, or buried in oblivion, it is susceptible to reemerge, because memory is—as Portelli reminds us—only partially controllable, both in its content and in its functioning.[30] This is what happened when a Polish Jew survivor of the Warsaw Ghetto, recounts in his testimony: "I would like to talk here about Chile, that the left, the ultraleft [pause] was against me, and I was with Pinochet every day and worked in England for him, to extradite him to Chile.[31] . . . I went to greet Pinochet. . . . Is this coming out in this? Uuuuh [he covers his face with one hand and laughs], *I messed that up*."[32] Memories flood back and overwhelm the survivor.

Memory is not always unitary and coherent; it is full of contradictory areas, as shown by the testimonies that were analyzed. It is used in different ways by its bearers, who, faced with new and complex political situations, make decisions based on the traumatic weight of what they have lived through. The memory of some of the victims of the Nazi persecution and of the Holocaust who settled in Chile makes the dynamism that this memory contains more visible, as well as its constant reshaping in the context of a country of the Global South. It demonstrates what Michael Rothberg refers to as the multidirectionality of memory of the Holocaust.[33]

Notes

1. Although the origin (country, city or capital city, town, etc.) of the victims and survivors is a factor that, among others—such as social class, age, and gender—marks differences in the experiences of arrival and adaptation to Chile, in this chapter I only make a gross distinction when referring to the survivors who arrived in Chile from countries such as Hungary, Romania, Bulgaria, and Czechoslovakia (which after the war were under Soviet control). This is because their origin is relevant to the decisions that some of them made once in Chile.
2. I distinguish between two groups who arrived in Chile between the mid-1930s and the mid-1950s: victims of Nazi persecution (and their collaborators) in Germany and other European countries; and Holocaust survivors. The former arrived in the country between the mid-1930s to the end of 1939, once the war broke out. The latter arrived after the end of the war and, for a period of approximately ten years, between 1945 and 1955. Although the meaning of the concept of survivor has mutated over time, and there have been other definitions of the term—for example, refugee, displaced person, witness—in this chapter I use only the two concepts mentioned above, without entering into the conceptual debate, which is beyond the scope of this chapter. For this debate, see Alina Bothe and Markus Nesselrodt, "Survivor: Towards a Conceptual History," *Leo Baeck Institute Year Book* 61 (2016), https://doi.org/10.1093/leobaeck/ybw013.
3. The structure of the interviews conducted by the Shoah Foundation—and on which Fundación Memoria Viva based its own interviews—contemplated three time periods: life before Nazism and the war, followed by the war and the Holocaust, and ending with life after the Holocaust. Interviewers were advised to devote half an hour to the first period, one hour to the second, and half an hour to the third. Alejandro Baer, *El Testimonio Audiovisual: Imagen y memoria del Holocausto* (Madrid: Siglo XXI, 2005), 187. Nevertheless, in some of the interviews, the interviewer does not ask or asks very little about their life once in Chile.
4. This is largely due to how much the interviewer asks about this period.
5. Susan Rubin Suleiman, *La crisis de la memoria y la Segunda Guerra Mundial* (Madrid: Machados Libros, 2016), 14; Andreas Huyssen, *En busca del futuro perdido: Cultura y memoria en tiempos de globalización* (Buenos Aires: FCE, 2007), 17.
6. Dominik LaCapra, *Writing History, Writing Trauma* (Baltimore: Johns Hopkins University Press, 2001), 86–87.
7. In this sense these narratives speak to us of "experience as an uncontestable evidence." Joan W. Scott, "The Evidence of Experience," *Critical Inquiry* 17, no. 4 (Chicago: University of Chicago Press, 1991): 777.
8. For further details, see Yael Siman and Nancy Nicholls, "New Home and Transitional Spaces for Holocaust Survivors in Chile and Mexico," in *Beyond Camps and Forced Labour: The Holocaust and Its Contexts*, ed. S. Bardgett, C. Schmidt, and D. Stone (London: Palgrave Macmillan, Cham, 2020).

9. Marion Mostny, interviewed by VHA-USC Shoah Foundation, San Mateo, California, November 4, 1998, transcription by Nancy Nicholls.
10. Leo de Jong, interviewed by Voces de la Shoá Memoria Viva, Santiago, Chile, January 21, 2010, transcription and translation by Nancy Nicholls.
11. Kurt Herdan, interviewed by Voces de la Shoá Memoria Viva, Santiago, Chile, November 17, 2009, transcription and translation by Nancy Nicholls.
12. LaCapra, *Writing History*, 89.
13. LaCapra, *Writing History*, 49.
14. LaCapra, *Writing History*, 48 and 49.
15. Alice Himmel, interviewed by Voces de la Shoá Memoria Viva, Santiago, Chile, September 14, 2009, transcription and translation by Nancy Nicholls.
16. Klara Sternbach, interviewed by Voces de la Shoá Memoria Viva, Santiago, Chile, 2010, transcription and translation by Nancy Nicholls.
17. The existing Jewish family and organizational network in Chile was a relevant factor in the process of adaptation and survival during the first period after arrival. See Lorena Ávila, Nancy Nicholls, and Yael Siman, "Migration Narratives of Holocaust Survivors in Chile, Colombia and Mexico," *Lessons and Legacies* 14 (2021), http://dx.doi.org/10.2307/j.ctvl6t6nbt.11.
18. Irene Klein, *La ficción de la memoria: La narración de las historias de vida* (Buenos Aires: Prometeo, 2008), 69. Author's translation.
19. Klein, *La ficción de la memoria*, 22, 69.
20. Herdan, interview.
21. Among the testimonies analyzed, there are some of Nazi victims and Holocaust survivors who settled in Chile, and who then emigrated from Chile in 1970, but did not establish any relation with the Holocaust in their decision. This is the case of Harry Lewin, who happily settled in Chile and then migrated to England with his family. Harry Lewin, interviewed by VHA-USC Shoah Foundation, Bromley, England, September 14, 1997. There are also many cases of witnesses who did not migrate again when Allende came to power. One such case is Gunter Seelman, a socialist who supported the Popular Unity government and who would later be taken prisoner when the military carried out the coup d'état. Others make very brief and tangential references to the Allende period, generally about the economic situation, but without openly criticizing the government. Maxine Lowy conducted interviews with several Jews who had settled in Chile fleeing Nazism or who were victims of the Holocaust and had taken refuge in Chile. The interviews, conducted approximately between 2009 and 2014, reveal the fear in the face of the arrival of the Marxist left to power. For Raul Sohr, sociologist and international analyst interviewed by the author, this fear was a psychological rather than a real phenomenon and was based on previous anti-communism feelings that had nothing to do with Allende's Chilean path to socialism. Maxine Lowy, *Latent Memory: A Community Confronted by the Challenge of Human Rights in Chile* (Santiago: LOM, 2016), 57–64. In this chapter I focus on those who did make the decision to migrate in the face of a Marxist government.
22. Mostny, interview.
23. Silberstein, interview.

24. Himmel, interview.
25. Silberstein, interview.
26. Silberstein, interview.
27. Steve Stern, *De la memoria suelta a la memoria emblemática: Hacia el recordar y el olvidar como proceso histórico (Chile, 1973–1998)*, comp. M. Garcés et al. (Santiago: LOM, 2000), 15.
28. Alessandro Portelli, "El uso de la entrevista en la historia oral," *Historia, memoria y pasado reciente: Anuario Escuela de Historia UNR*, no. 20 (2003/2004): 41.
29. Alessandro Portelli, "Los usos de la memoria: Memoria-monumento, memoria involuntaria, memoria perturbadora," in *Historias orales: Narración, imaginación y diálogo*, ed. Alessandro Portelli (La Plata, Argentina: Prohistoria Ediciones, 2016), 481.
30. Portelli, "Los usos de la memoria," 475.
31. The survivor refers to the arrest of Pinochet in London between October 1998 and January 2000, when judge Baltazar Garzón had him arrested on charges of genocide. Finally, he was extradited to Chile.
32. David Feuerstein, interviewed by Voces de la Shoá Memoria Viva. Santiago, Chile, February 23, 2010, transcription and translation by Nancy Nicholls.
33. Michael Rothberg, *Multidirectional Memory: Remembering the Holocaust in the Age of Decolonization* (Stanford CA: Stanford University Press, 2009).

Part 2
History

6

From Ominous to Miracle Poems
North African Musical Prophecies and Histories of the Holocaust

AOMAR BOUM

Overture

For decades, scholars paid scant attention to the usefulness of popular culture, particularly poems and music, in their assessment of North Africa and World War II. The archival and historical significance of poetry and songs of the war have largely been ignored.[1] Given the dearth of information regarding popular thoughts and memories about Hitler and Nazi Germany, I argue that local North African music about World War II can help us fill this void and that songs are valuable sources. It should be noted that although only a few songs in recorded form survived the war, many continue to be heard in villages and towns throughout North Africa.

In this chapter I propose a sonic narrative of World War II in North Africa.[2] It is a sonic story that starts with musical notes and poems of Nazi forewarning, then goes through a high note of anxiety and fear of Marshal Pétain's and Hitler's bureaucracies of exclusionary anti-Jewish laws and forced labor as well death camps, and concludes with musical celebratory rhythms of triumph following the American and British landing on North African shores. I posit that these songs communicate feelings and emotions of the war interpreted through religious beliefs. I start this sonic account of the war with the voice of my father, a native Muslim villager of southern Morocco and his poetic account of the Allied landing in North Africa.

In early 1943 Faraji Boum, my father, was sent on a mission by the French military director of the Administrative Circle of Foum Zguid, southeastern Morocco, to deliver a letter to the military post of Ouarzazate. For years Faraji was an occasional *rqqāṣ* (courier).[3] Before the arrival of the French colonial administration to his home oasis in 1933, he intermittently delivered mail and news on behalf of the tribal lord of his region to other High Atlas chieftains, including Pasha Thami Glaoui. After the French control of the southern region of Draa and Tafilalet ended, Faraji was ordered to perform these same duties as part of a colonial system of forced labor locally known as *kulfa* or corvée (unpaid labor). Many hours of interviews between my father and me were conducted over a period of more than twelve years, extending from the late 1990s to early 2000s. Faraji, one of the oldest villagers today, reported how members of his own family sustained this abuse by asking him to perform these duties on behalf of his brothers or other members of the Boum clan. Faraji was doubly victimized—first by the colonial order and second by his own family members.

Faraji encountered the military deployment of Senegalese soldiers stationed in the south, also known as *tirailleurs*, upon his arrival at the military administrative bureau of Ouarzazate during World War II. He witnessed how the wives and children of these Senegalese soldiers bid them farewell as they mounted military trucks. For many of its military operations, the French colonial army relied on African soldiers, including the Senegalese, the Congolese, and the indigenous North Africans. Soldiers known as Goumiers were conscripted to serve in auxiliary military units of the French army of Africa.[4] For Faraji the mood of the war was already reflected through an indigenous song that circulated as early as November 1942 during the American landing near Casablanca. The song depicted the defeat of Vichy in Morocco, the end of its rule, and the new American administration of the Moroccan Protectorate. It pointed to the expectation that many communities had about the possibilities of German invasion of the region. The lyrics of the song are as follows:

> In the name of God, we start
> We waited for the arrival of Germans
> Instead, the Americans appeared
> The Germans erred and regretted
> The Americans now rule
> And if I am not mistaken
> It was Sunday when it started
> Casablanca is a warzone.
> Safi and Essaouira are full of pain.
> And by afternoon, France has a new government
> Did you see that Vichy put down its arms?
> For its own sake.[5]

The liberation of Morocco and Algeria by the Americans and their allies following the Allied landing in November 1942 was an occasion for indigenous Jews and Muslims to express their feelings and attitudes about the ongoing war. The poem begins with gratitude to God, which contextualizes the unfolding of the events. While the poem quoted above expressed largely a rural Muslim viewpoint about the conflict, Moroccan and North African Jews produced and performed, openly and secretly, songs and poems about the global conflict before, during, and after World War II. Unlike many popular Jewish poems that I discuss below, we do not have a record of Muslim songs about this period except a few cases like the one reported to me by Faraji or the famous song "Lmirikan" by Houcine Slaoui.

During the early 1930s, as I explain below, many North African Jews, such as Prosper Cohen and Isaac Knafo, took the political rise of Hitler seriously to the extent that some wrote and published poems before and during the war about what they described as the Nazi omen. Knafo and Prosper had access to writing, which partly explains why their texts and poems survived in the archives. Their words served as a prewar warning of the destructive ideology of Nazism. Some went to the extent of publishing poems cautioning Jews and non-Jews about the threat that the Third Reich posed for humanity. During the war, and especially after Operation Torch, North African Jews capitalized on the musical and folkloristic traditions of Purim and the Haggadah to express the religious tunes of triumph over Hitler and his supporters. In the following section I discuss these poetic and narrative musical texts from Morocco, highlighting their historical value as sonic texts that inform our understanding not only of the prewar period but also the global events of the war as they were heard through the music of Moroccan Jews. I argue that these sonic texts are important sources that should be added to the increasing archival forms of artistic Jewish resistance against Nazi art and music of hate against Jews.

Sonic Stories as Archives of Wartime North Africa

At the height of World War II, German military forces needed records to play in radio stations during its occupation of Europe, such as the Yugoslavia Belgrade Radio Station. The shortage of local music led Nazi authorities to rely on old records from Vienna, including "Lili Marlene," a song based on a poem written by Hans Leip in 1915. By coincidence "Lili Marlene" became a hit among German troops despite an early objection from Hitler's propaganda minister, Joseph Goebbels, on the grounds that its "nostalgic mood was bad for morale."[6] "Lili Marlene" became a leading Nazi propaganda song lifting soldiers' spirits in the battlefields of Europe and the southern Mediterranean. Hitler's propaganda machine inundated its airwaves in Europe with a collage of music and sound shaping the imagination of the German Army on many fronts. At home Germans witnessed live interpretations of the song in operas in Berlin. Yet as the German Forces Network relied on the song as a tool of morale building for months, the defeat of the Germany Army at Stalingrad in the Eastern European Front and Alamein in the Western Desert Campaign provided an opportunity for the British Command of the Eighth Army and the BBC to broadcast a new version of "Lili Marlene" as counterpropaganda. This is just one example of how music served the warring parties' multiple propagandistic and nationalistic purposes.

Outside the battlefields Nazi authorities and their Jewish victims relied on music for entirely oppositional goals. Nazi Germany used music and sound to build morale among its weary and extended troops, while European Jews drew on music to build spiritual strength to survive at all costs.[7] In the middle of hunger and death, Jews played and composed music. After the Holocaust many survivors described how their musical gifts saved them and other internees during the internment in death camps. Personal poems written in the camps provided a different understanding of the Holocaust. In her work on musical life in the camps and ghettoes of Germany and Poland, Shirli Gilbert details the role of sound as a means of resistance against the Nazi structures of violence and persecution.[8] Unlike songs such as "Lili Marlene," Gilbert puts the historical spotlight largely on the "music created, circulated, and performed on an informal basis by prisoners in various internment centers."[9]

In North Africa Jews produced their own genre of songs and poems in conversation with the context already examined in European Holocaust scholarship.[10] During the 1930s Moroccan Jews numbered around 250,000 and lived in rural and urban communities in the French and Spanish Protectorate. Unlike Algeria, where Jews were French citizens, Moroccan Jews retained their status as subjects of the sultan and continued to live among Arab and Amazigh communities.[11] In May 1940 Germany invaded France, and a month later Marshal Philippe Pétain, a World War I hero, signed the French-German armistice on June 22, 1940. The agreement placed southern France under a collaborationist regime in the city of Vichy. Under Pétain the Vichy authorities maintained their control over the protectorate of Morocco and all the Asian and African colonies. By early 1941 Xavier Vallat, the director of the Commissariat-General for Jewish Affairs, started writing Vichy's anti-Jewish legislation that would soon be implemented in France and its colonies, depending on the local and national political realities. On October 3, 1940, the first anti-Jewish law was introduced defining Jews living in France and French Algeria by race.[12] On October 7, 1940, Algerian Jewish citizenship was revoked following the abolition of the Crémieux Decree. In the protectorates of Morocco and Tunisia, local Jews were defined by their Islamic protected *dhimmi* status and therefore maintained their legal and social position as members of a religious community instead of racial group. By keeping their religious status, Moroccan and Tunisian Jews were able to maintain their social and economic positions in these countries, unlike in Algeria, which was part of France. After limiting Algerian Jewish access to any legal rights as citizens, another status was introduced on June 2, 1941, primarily to bar Jews from economic activities and limiting their access to finance and credit. Many Jews were prevented from owning businesses and working in the media. In the liberal sector, quotas (*numerus clausus*) limited the percentage of Jewish lawyers, doctors, architects, and notaries to 2 percent of the licenses allocated for these jobs. Jewish students were expelled from schools, but the community established a centralized system that absorbed the students and teachers who lost their spots and positions in the educational system as a result of the *numerus clausus*.[13]

In Morocco General Noguès oversaw the implementation of the racial laws of October 31, 1940, and June 2, 1941. Appointed as resident-general by the Popular Front administration of Léon Blum before the establishment of the Vichy government, Noguès oversaw a set of economic, educational, and administrative limitations and quotas on Moroccan Jews. While Moroccan Jews escaped the broad economic Aryanization of Jewish property as in Algeria, the anti-Jewish laws ordered many Jews to move back to the *mellah* (Jewish neighborhood), especially in cities such as Fez and Casablanca. As Vichy authorities expanded their anti-Jewish laws to different sectors of societies including the classrooms, pupils across Morocco were exposed to a new type of propaganda. With images of Marshal Pétain in every classroom, the few Jewish children who were allowed access to schooling were ordered to recite daily a poem honoring Pétain.[14] During an interview on April 3, 2019, David Bensimon described how the French authorities used the song "Maréchal, nous voilà" (Marshal, here we are) as part of the propaganda of sounds and music among children and the general public.[15]

Miracle Poems as History Writing

As the popular song conveyed by Faraji underscores, the Nazi and Vichy defeat in North Africa was attributed to a Heavenly Miracle, and Moroccan Jewish communities, like their ancestors before, codified its miraculous nature. Like many historical miracles that preceded Hitler's defeat, it is a Purim Katan (second and minor Purim), and therefore it deserves to be celebrated through singing and chanting. It is not a coincidence, therefore, that following Operation Torch on November 8–16, 1942, the Purim di Hitler was spontaneously announced not only by communal religious authorities but also ordinary Jews from different social classes as well. The poem inspired by Purim Katan is a historical text that outlines the event and its main characters. For example, in August 1578, King Dom Sebastian of Portugal was defeated in what would be known as the Battle of the Three Kings or Battle of Wadi al-Makhazin. Apart from the political ramification of this event on Moroccan and Iberian histories, Moroccan Jewish communities celebrated it as a Purim Katan. This is not difficult to understand in the context of the expulsion of Jews from Iberia in 1492. The Battle of the Three Kings became known as the Purim de los Christianos. The Jews of Tangier codified their own Purim Katan known as Purim de los Bombas following the Moroccan defeat by France at the Battle of Isly in 1844. In her historical analysis of this event and text of Purim de los Bombas, Susan Gilson Miller underscores the importance of Purim Katan of Tangier as local history: "Like most Moroccan cities, Tangier has its own body of written and oral tradition that makes up the distinctive cultural apparatus of the community, reinforcing a strong sense of local identity. . . . Local sources for the bombardment of 1844 demonstrate many of these traits. Indeed, the principle Jewish source—a Purim scroll—is not history in the conventional sense at all, but rather a ritual document retelling events according to a liturgical formula."[16] In this colonial wartime context of musical propaganda, North African Jews turned to their local musical traditions to pray for their safety and survival as early as 1940.[17] In response to Nazi and Vichy French propagandist deployment of music and poems such as "Lili Marlene" and "Maréchal, nous voilà," Moroccan and other North African Jews intuitively weaponized their local musical traditions as counter-soundscapes raising awareness about the danger of the Nazi regime and their French and Italian allies. Against the Nazi German and French denigration of Jewish music as a "degenerate" cultural form that threatened their national purity,[18] Moroccan Jewish poets and singers utilized their local musical traditions to spread awareness and alert their communities about the danger of the emerging fascism as early as the late 1930s.

In January 1940 *L'Avenir Illustre*, a Moroccan Jewish newspaper, published a few stanzas from the foreboding poem "Les Hitlériques" by Isaac D. Knafo. Hailing from a rabbinical and Maskilim family, Knafo, a playwright and poet, was born in Essaouira in 1912 and pursued his education in Paris before returning to his hometown.[19] His poem, which was drafted in pamphlet form just after the German occupation of Poland in the fall of 1939, depicts a world on the brink of destruction. So fearful was Knafo upon completing his poem that he walked the city of Essaouira collecting every copy for incineration. Little did Knafo know that his words had already appeared in print.[20] Written in the form of an "ode to Hitler," the poem predicted the defeat of Germany. It opens with a note to the reader:

> I have seen hatred flourish in the country of the Nazis,
> And a whole nation endures the caustic, corrosive acid
> Thrown at them like a cruel joke
> By the speeches of an insane, vulgar buffoon.
> This pernicious clown, seized by fury,
> Preaching denunciation, murder, and violence...
> Despite my indifference, I felt my face flush
> And turn bright red from shame and disgust.
> In my feeble hands, the whip of satire
> Is too clumsy to excoriate Hitler.
> At least it expresses my complete aversion.
> And that is why, reader, though I may displease you
> In order to release my sorrow and to cry out my anger
> I offer you this text filled indignation.[21]

Unlike Faraji's song that starts this chapter, Knafo narrates a different history that warns about what awaits Jews and the world. It is very clear from the content of the poem that Knafo was following the daily events in Europe and the rise of Hitler. In this long ode, Knafo details the racist and genocidal ideology of Nazism, highlights its destructive forces, and underscores the hell-like future that it will bring to Europe and the world.

A few years before Knafo, Prosper Cohen, writing in the Moroccan city of Meknes in 1934, resorted to historical precedents to describe Nazism. He compared the antisemitic language of the Nazi regime to attacks on Jews by the Persian Empire during the fourth century BCE in the form of a Megillah (text read during the Jewish holidays of Purim).[22] This parallel allowed Cohen to liken Hitler to Haman, the villain of the *Book of Esther*. "Everything that could be linked to Hitler's Germany, to misfortune, to anything or anyone that might cause material or moral harm, takes the name of Hitler, the Haman of the twentieth century," Cohen wrote. "Even children know this name and it's unfortunate reputation."[23]

We notice that Knafo's style was influenced by his secular and modern French education, while Cohen directly invokes Purim Katan. Therefore, and even though he is writing in the interwar period, Cohen is already seeing a similarity between Hitler and Haman, the vizier of the king of Persia, Ahasuerius, during the fifth century BCE.

As the war started, North Africans leaned on their religious musical tradition to manage the new realities of the war. The well-known Moroccan scroll *Megilla di Hitler* was written by Asher-Prosper Hassine (also known as Asher Hassin) (1918–95). A professor of Hebrew and a member of the Hebrew Association Magen Avraham in Casablanca during the war, Hassine also served in the Zionist Federation of Morocco.[24] In 1948 Hassine immigrated to Israel, where he served in the Knesset and founded the Union of North African Jews in Israel. He wrote and published in Casablanca before the end of the war. Written in seven chapters, this *Megillah* follows the style of the *Megillah Esther* in describing the rise of Hitler and his war against Jews before celebrating his defeat, as these sections from chapters 5 and 6 reveal:

> And it was in the third year of the war, and the Americans were garbed in vengeance and came to the help of Britain to fall upon the enemy together and destroy him, and to save humanity and to rescue the world, and to purge evil from the peoples' midst. And they set up weapons like the sand of the sea, and countless ships, mighty armies and many aircraft and gallant pilots. And they destroyed all the factories and ruined many of the places where they set up armaments, and the labor increased for the workers but they could not do it. And it was, when Hitler saw the powerful bombs that the Royal Air Force was dropping on him, his heart trembled and he grew filled with rage against the Jews. From my heart: After two years of war, the Germans and Italians were beaten and defeated and fled away morning with head covered. And they fled in terror and fear, and turned back, and the tumult grew in all the camp. And Hitler was full of anger against the Jews, and he wished to wipe out the Jews of Morocco and dwelling in Algeria, and to afflict them like their brethren....
>
> And the Americans came on the eighth of November and entered the cities on Wednesday the eleventh of November.... The Jews gathered in their cities and celebrated a festival of redemption, drinking and a holiday, and many of the Jews' pursuers in their cities acted as Jews, since the fear of the Allies had fallen upon them. And in each and every city where the Americans came, the laws of the Nazis and fascists were overturned, and the peoples rejoiced and were happy. And the Americans, French, and British pursued their enemies and forced them out of Africa, and did to them as they wanted.... Countless enemies fell,

and many armaments were found, and they did to their enemies as they wanted, and not a man stood against them, since the fear of the Allies had fallen upon them.[25]

In this excerpt and other sections of the *Megillat*, Hitler is described through terms and words that underscore the juxtaposition between evil and good. The narrative of Americans landing is framed through religious concepts where U.S. soldiers are described as agents of salvation and rescue.

In the aftermath of Operation Torch local Moroccan Jews composed and published a series of miracle poems (*qsidot*, sing. *qasida*) in Hebrew and Judeo-Arabic as a praise and "gratitude to God for sparing them the scourge of Hitler and his accomplices."[26] These Moroccan Jewish praise poems could be interpreted today as forms of social commentary that showcase the political and social attitudes of the community during the early stages of the war. David Guedj argues in his work that these poems follow a similar narrative structure that opens with the rise of Nazism in Germany and Hitler's conquest of mainland Europe, details the genocide of European Jews, and ends with the arrival of the Allied forces in North Africa and the sparing of local Jewish communities. Throughout these poems, the divine is invoked and the miracle is celebrated.

One such text is "Qasida di Hitler" (Qasida of Hitler) composed by Mattatiya (Matityah) Ben Simhon. A native of the coastal city of Essaouira (Mogador), Ben Simhon published one of the earliest praise poems about Hitler in the form of a *piyyut*—that is, a liturgical poem designed to be sung or recited during a religious service. Written in Judeo-Arabic following the piyyut style of and chilling praying pattern of "Mi El Kamokha," the *qasida* notes:

> In the days of Hitler
> the gangster enemy
> He and his friend
> the traitor Mussolini
> Connived to annihilate and destroy
> The people of God
> On November 11 He performed
> a merciful act for me
> By the beloved Allies
> Therefore, I will sing songs
> About the redemption
> of the people of God.[27]

From Ominous to Miracle Poems

Miracle poems like Ben Simhon's were drafted in real time—months or years after Hitler's rise to power. The text describes the rise of Hitler, how he and his consultants accused the Jews of trying to destroy him, and how he assembled a lot of weapons and began attacking neighboring countries. In the final stanza Ben Simhon offers a prayer for the sultan and the pasha of Marrakesh, Thami El Glaoui:

> God save our Master the Sultan
> grandson of Mulai El Hasan
> and may he always live in calm
> he and all his sons
> and our master el Galoui el Pasha
> whose table is always laid
> inside the garden and the orchard
> he and all his friends.[28]

The note about the *sultan* of Morocco highlights the ongoing debate about the sultan's professed role by members of the Jewish community in the protection and survival of Moroccan Jews.[29] Following a similar storyline and structure, Rabbi Avraham Halévi wrote the "Qasida di Hitler the Evil" in Hebrew. In the last section of this miracle poem, the author prays for the sultan:

> Let's Honor the French and His Majesty the King
> May He Save His Majesty
> We Pray for him
> For he cares about us
> Let's pray for his long life.

In addition to these poems with known authors, many praise songs are authorless; not all poems had known authors either. One of these authorless poems begins with the following lines with detailed descriptions of Hitler and his invasion of Europe:

> Listen my gentlemen,
> To the qsida of the bewitched Hitler,
> He wanted to destroy the whole world,
> Without compassion or pardon . . .

In general, the poems describe the different stages of the war from Hitler's rise to his defeat. The survival of these miracle poems in today's popular

North African Jewish memory highlights the broad reach of these texts that were produced by members from different social, cultural, and economic classes in Morocco. From a psychological perspective these poems reflect a state of mind of individuals as well as the general community that felt that the end of war was linked to the intervention of their Creator; therefore, we see the dominance of the liturgical aspect in these poems where mourning is absent and miracle celebration is the norm.

Musical Celebrations

The last sonic section of this musical narrative of the war is what I call "closing theme" songs that highlight the arrival of Allied soldiers and the ending of the anti-Jewish laws in Morocco. After Operation Torch, Nessim ben Shimon, also known as Simon the Hairdresser from Rabat, composed a song in Judeo-Arabic in the liturgical traditional style of the Haggadah (text read during the Jewish holidays of Passover). It was published with the approval of the Moroccan office of censorship to celebrate the American landing in Casablanca.[30] It echoes the linguistic style and narrative flow of the original text that narrates the Jewish exodus from Egypt. Ben Shimon's text is a rare native North African Jewish document that records the rise of Hitler, the menace of antisemitism, and the liberation of Morocco and North Africa:

> The Americans came in great haste
> That expression void of hope
> Which our fathers' frightened faces wore
> Due to Hitler
> The Hungry shall walk in fear
> The needy shall flee in fright.
> This year we are here
> Next year may we have peace and calm
> This year on the black market,
> Next year may we be free men in Palestine
> . . .
> Once upon a time, in the days of Mussolini the Great,
> Hitler and that bastard Göring,
> Ribbentrop and that Italian Ciano
> Came to plan and plot,
> In the course of that one night,
> Until the Angels of Destruction came

> And shook them, oh dear,
> And threw them into dawn's furnace.
> So spoke Roosevelt:
> For I am like a man who's hit seventy,
> Lucky enough to remember
> The ruin of Germany by air raids at night.
> Until Churchill came and taught,
> As it is written:
> "For ye shall remember
> What the Eighth Army did unto them
> On their way to Egypt."
> . . .
> Blessed is the All-present, blessed is He.
> Blessed for bringing the Brits
> And the Yanks, blessed is He.
> The Torah speaks of four sons:
> England, the wise one.
> Hitler, the wicked one.
> America, the good one.
> And Mussolini, who isn't worthy of our words.[31]

Unlike remote communities where my father Faraji depicted the American landing from a distance with limited or no encounter with American soldiers, urban Jews and Muslims in Casablanca, Safi, and other towns had a first-hand view of the operation. This moment of celebration is captured through a popular song titled "Lmirkan" by Houcine Slaoui that continues to live in the popular memory until today. In a humorous tone the songs portrayed the American soldiers in Morocco and their interactions with local population:

> Ayayayaya! New times are here.
> The Americans are here.
> People are empowered
> Women have rebelled
> Even the hags tore off their veils
> And filled their mouths with chew gum
> Married men waited in vain
> For their wives
> Handsome faces and green eyes
> Have spirited them away

And the girls parted their hair
And wore French skirts
The wanted to be with the Americans
And you heard was Okay okay! Bye bye!³²

Moroccan soundscapes of World War II on the tune of Slaoui highlights the joy of liberation and underscores a new era of social and economic changes that face Moroccan society with the arrival of news norms and food stuffs. For Moroccan Jews the American landing meant the beginning of a new era, especially after 1948, and the beginning of immigration abroad.

As sources of wartime North Africa, these poems illustrate how indigenous Jewish communities experienced the military conflict and survived its economic and political implications. In the absence of memoirs about the war written by North Africans during the conflict, we turn to these poems that provide a glimpse into the social implications of French anti-Jewish laws and German occupation of Tunisia.³³ Accordingly, through these muffled sounds of World War II we capture the political fears of North African Jews, their social anxieties about what awaited them, and the tribulations they faced after the arrival of American and British soldiers.

Notes

1. There is already an existing small literature about the Holocaust/Shoah in Middle Eastern and North African literature. See Robert Attal, "L'Allemagne nazie dans la poésie populaire des Juifs de Tunisie," in *Les Juifs d'Orient face au nazisme et à la Shoah (1930–1945)*, ed. Georges Bensoussan and Haïm Saadoun (Paris: Mémorial de la Shoah, 2016), 155–58. Lev Hakak, "The Holocaust in the Hebrew Poetry of Sephardism and Near Eastern Jews," *Shofar* 23, no. 2 (2005): 89–119; Joseph Chetrit, "Les Juifs de Mogador (Essaouira) pendant la Seconde Guerre Mondiale: La terreur de Vichy et sa gestion communautaire," in *Les Juifs d'Afrique du Nord face à l'Allemagne Nazie*, ed. Dan Michman and Haim Saadoun (Paris: Perrin, 2018), 147–76. Menash Anzi, "Le Second Guerre Mondiale et les Juifs du Yémen," *Revue d'Histoire de la Shoah* 205 (2016): 535–42.
2. Also see David Guedj, "Post–Second World War Praise Poetry, Lament and a Utopian Treatise in Morocco: Historical Literature on the Theme of the Second World War," *Journal of Modern Jewish Studies* 17, no. 4 (2018): 455–71; Aomar Boum and Sarah A. Stein, eds., *Wartime North Africa: A Documentary History, 1934–1950* (Stanford CA: Stanford University Press, 2022); Christopher Silver, *Recording History: Jews, Muslims and Music across Twentieth-Century North Africa* (Stanford CA: Stanford University Press, 2022).
3. Aomar Boum and Majdouline Boum-Mendoza, *The Last Rekkas: Chronicles of a Foot Courier in Southern Morocco* (Casablanca: Languages du Sud, 2024).

4. Driss Maghraoui, "The *Goumiers* in the Second World War: History and Colonial Representations," *Journal of North African Studies* 19, no. 4 (2014): 571–86.
5. Personal interview with Faraji Boum, Lamhamid, Foum Zguid, Tata, southern Morocco, April 12, 2004.
6. Hyatt King, "Lili Marlene," *British Museum Quarterly* 17, no. 3 (1952): 41–42.
7. Erik Levi, "The Aryanization of Music in Nazi Germany," *Musical Times* 131, no. 1763 (1990): 19–23; Pamela M. Potter, "Dismantling a Dystopia: On the Historiography of Music in the Third Reich," *Central European History* 40, no. 4 (2007): 623–51.
8. Shirli Gilbert, *Music in the Holocaust: Confronting Life in the Nazi Ghettos and Camps* (Oxford: Clarendon Press, 2005).
9. Gilbert, *Music in the Holocaust*, vii.
10. Aleksander Kulisiewiicz, "Polish Camp Songs, 1939–1945," *Modern Language Studies* 16, no. 1 (1986): 3–9; Bret Werb, "Fourteen Shoah Songbooks," *Musica Judaica* 20, no. 5774 (2013–14): 39–116.
11. Aomar Boum and Sarah A. Stein, *The Holocaust and North Africa* (Stanford CA: Stanford University Press, 2019).
12. Daniel Schroeter, "Vichy in Morocco: The Residency, Mohammed V, and His Indigenous Jewish Subjects," in *Colonialism and the Jews*, ed. Ethan Katz, Lisa Moses Leff, and Maud S. Mandel (Bloomington: Indiana University Press, 2017), 215–50.
13. Aomar Boum, "Re-drawing Holocaust Geographies: A Cartography of Vichy and Nazi Reach into North Africa," in *The Wiley Blackwell Companion to the Holocaust*, ed. Simone Gigliotti and Hilary Earl (Hoboken NJ: Wiley-Blackwell, 2020), 431–48.
14. Aomar Boum and Sarah A. Stein, eds., *Wartime North Africa: A Documentary History, 1934–1950* (Stanford CA: Stanford University Press, 2022), 56–57.
15. Boum and Stein, *Wartime North Africa*, 55–56. It should be noted that the song is a plagiarized version of the song "La Margoton du bataillou." The latter was written by Kazimierz Oberfeld, a Polish Jewish composer who was killed by the Nazis during the Holocaust.
16. Susan Gilson Miller, "Crisis and Community: The People of Tangier and the French Bombardment of 1844," *Middle Eastern Studies* 27, no. 4 (1991): 587. Also see Yogal S. Nizri, "Judeo-Moroccan Traditions and the Age of European Expansion in North Africa," in *The Sephardic Atlantic: Colonial Histories and Postcolonial Perspectives*, ed. Sina Rauschenbach and Jonathan Schorsch (London: Palgrave Macmillan, 2018), 333–60.
17. Zoë Jensiene Godfre, "Praise the Lord and Pass the Ammunition: Propaganda Music as a Governmental Marketing Tool during the WWII Era," in *Historians without Borders: New Studies in Multidisciplinary History*, ed. Lawrence Abrams and Kaleb Knoblauch (London: Routledge, 2019), 24–45.
18. Mark Lewis Singer, "Degenerate Music?! Musical Censorship in the Third Reich" (PhD diss., University of Maryland, 2011).
19. Isaac D. Knafo, "Les Hitlériques," in *L'Humour est l'enfant de poème: Poésies completes*, textes présentés et annotés par Asher Knafo (Jerusalem: Al-Shark Arab Press, 1997), 243–59.
20. Sarah A. Stein and Aomar Boum, "Praise Poems Depict North African Jewish Response to Events of World War II," *Jewish Journal*, July 12, 2022.

21. Rebecca Glasberg and Jessie Stoolman, trans., "A Fantastic, Anti-Hitler Poem Spared from Destruction," in *Wartime North Africa: A Documentary History, 1934–1950*, ed. Aomar Boum and Sarah A. Stein (Stanford CA: Stanford University Press, 2022), 30.
22. Yaron Tsur, "The Brief Career of Prosper Cohen: A Sectorial Analysis of the North African Jewish Leadership in the Early Years of Israeli Statehood," *Studies in Contemporary Jewry* 22 (2007): 66–99.
23. Rebecca Glasberg, trans., "Hitler as Haman," in Boum and Stein, *Wartime North Africa*, 23–25.
24. David Guedj, *The Hebrew Culture in Morocco, 1912–1956* (Jerusalem: Zalman Shazar Center, 2022) [Hebrew].
25. Asher P. Hassine, "Megilat Hitler—A Purim Sheni Scroll for French Armistice Day," Open Siddur Project, https://opensiddur.org/readings-and-sourcetexts/festival-and-fast-day-readings/jewish/purim-sheni-readings/megilat-hitler-by-prosper-hassine-casablanca-1944/.
26. Guedj, "Post-Second World War Praise Poetry," 457.
27. Mattatiya (Matityah) Ben Simhon, "Qasida of Hitler" (Casablanca) [Judeo-Arabic].
28. Ben Simhon, "Qasida di Hitler," quoted in Michal Saraf, *The Hitler Scroll of North Africa: Moroccan and Tunisian Jewish Literature on the Fall of the Nazis* (Lod, Israel: Habermann Institute for Literary Research, 1988) [Hebrew].
29. For more discussion on this issue, see Daniel Schroeter, "Vichy in Morocco: The Residency, Mohammed V, and His Indigenous Jewish Subjects," in *Colonialism and the Jews*, ed. Ethan Katz, Lisa Moses Leff, and Maud S. Mandel (Bloomington: Indiana University Press, 2017), 215–50; Joseph Chetrit, "Sultan Sidi Mohammed ben Youssef and the Jews of Morocco during the Second World War: New Discoveries," in *Jews and Muslims in Morocco: Their Intersecting Worlds*, ed. Joseph Chetrit, Jane S. Gerber, and Drora Arussy (Lanham MD: Lexington Books, 2021), 73–104.
30. Pinhas Cohen, *Langue et folklores des juifs marocains* (Rabat, Morocco: Éditions et Impressions Bouregreg, 2014).
31. Nissim ben Shimon, "The Hitler Haggadah" (Rabat, Morocco, 1943), translated from Judeo-Arabic by Adi and Schnytzer Jonnie Schnytzer, in *The Hitler Haggadah: A Moroccan Jewish Piece from World War II*, ed. Eppie Bat-Ilan and Roz Elmaleh (N.p.: Mineged, 2021).
32. Aomar Boum, trans., "Lmirikan," in Boum and Stein, *Wartime North Africa*, 281–83. Also see Christopher Silver, *Recording History: Jews, Muslims and Music across Twentieth-Century North Africa* (Stanford CA: Stanford University Press, 2022); Jamila Bargach, "Liberatory, Nationalising and Moralising by Ellipsis: Reading and Listening to Lhucein Slaoui's Song lmirikan," *Journal of North African Studies* 4, no. 4 (1999): 61–88.
33. There is an increasing number of memoirs written after the war in Israel and France. See David Guedj, "The Discourse in Israeli Theater Surrounding the Fate of North African Jewry during the Holocaust, 2017–2019," in *The Holocaust and Us in the Israeli Theater*, ed. David Guedj and Ofer Shiff (Sde-Boker, Israel: Ben-Gurion Research Institute, 2022), 256–75 [Hebrew].

7

Open Doors and Open Hearts
President Manuel Quezon's Holocaust Sanctuary in the Philippines

BONNIE M. HARRIS

Manuel Luis Quezon y Molina is a central figure in the early twentieth-century Philippine evolution from Spanish colony to independent republic. Between 1896 and 1902, he fought for his nation's independence in both the Philippine Revolution against Spain and the Philippine-American War. In 1907 he officially founded the Nacionalista Party, the oldest political party in the Philippines, as well as in all Southeast Asia. Emerging as the most important political individual in modern Philippine history at the time, Quezon represented his people in the U.S. Congress from 1909 to 1916 and served in the Philippine Senate continuously from 1916 until 1935 when he was elected the new Commonwealth's first president. He has been described by contemporaries and historians alike as a "master of political intrigue,"[1] a "skillful parliamentarian,"[2] an "uncompromising nationalist,"[3] "first and last, a politician,"[4] "the smartest Filipino of them all,"[5] "one of the greatest of all living statesmen,"[6] and the "greatest Filipino of his generation."[7] These and other descriptions of President Quezon portray a consummate civil servant who dedicated his life and energies to the betterment of political and economic security for his country and its people. But these sketches do not address the question at the heart of this treatise: namely, the actions of this world leader in risking his nationalist agenda and his international ambitions to rescue persecuted European refugee Jews from the terror of the Nazi Regime between 1937 and 1941. Perhaps Quezon's own words, spoken in June 1936, provide us a starting point: "All that is necessary, I think, to make a success in government is simply to act like a human being and decide questions as a human being."[8] In short, working for the welfare of others is the focus of good government. This chapter details how President Manuel Quezon shaped national responses of tolerance, social justice, and generosity toward the oppressed of the world, but especially toward those Jewish refugees whom he rescued from the uncertainties of a world on the brink of war when most other nations turned away.

On July 6, 1938, eighty delegates from thirty-two countries met in Evian,

France, to address the Jewish refugee crisis coming out of Hitler's Third Reich. The ten days of deliberation by the diplomats ultimately failed to perform the task of saving stateless Jews by increasing immigration thresholds or granting political asylum. It was one of the greatest humanitarian failures of the twentieth century. Nevertheless, as Western leaders lamented the persecution without offering solutions, the Asian island nation of the Philippines, led by President Manuel Quezon, already had rescue plans set into motion. Firmly recognized as the supreme "Filipino" leader, although duly respectful of the delicate relationship his office maintained with that of the U.S. high commissioner to the Philippines, Paul V. McNutt, Quezon responded in aiding Europe's refugee Jews as he assumed control of the immigration offices of his country at a time when the United States still held a controlling influence over his nation's future, illustrating his political skill and prowess.

U.S. immigration policies as they pertained to the Philippines at this time have a rather convoluted history. After decades of unrestricted flow of immigrants chasing after the promises of America's Industrial Revolution, the United States implemented obstructive laws and quotas designed to keep "undesirables" from reaching its coasts and, by extension, the coasts of its newly acquired territories. The U.S. Immigration Acts of 1917 and 1924, respectively, restricted millions of foreign aliens from entering the United States—initially based on their "quality" as future citizens and then subsequently based on numerical quota limits. Whereas the Immigration Act of 1917 outlined numerous physical and socioeconomic reasons why émigrés could be refused entry into the United States and, by legal extension, into the Philippines as a U.S.-held territory, the 1924 Immigration Act stipulated a quota system restricting immigration based on a numerical system of selection, which did not apply to the Philippines. It is extremely important to understand that no numerical restrictions on immigration into the Philippines existed during the years when Quezon and McNutt allowed Jewish refugees entrance into the archipelago, nor would such restrictions become law until the Philippine government passed their own immigration regulations in 1940.[9] The Immigration Act of 1924 also endowed the operation of U.S. consular offices abroad with power to either grant or refuse visas to foreign nationals seeking entrance into the United States, but this U.S. consular power did not apply to issuing visas to the Philippines. This became a diplomatic problem exacerbating an internal crisis in the Philippines that Quezon boldly remedied.

Paul V. McNutt arrived as U.S. high commissioner in 1937 and immediately recognized grave problems due to U.S. State Department directives to its consular offices abroad, which instructed "that they [consular officials] had no authority to refuse to issue visas for aliens desiring to proceed to the Philippines."[10] They were instead advised that the admission of persons into the territory was to be determined by immigration officers on site at Philippine ports upon their arrival. McNutt observed how Philippine immigration officers felt obligated to allow any and all foreign nationals entry into the country when they presented papers from U.S. consuls granting them passage to the Philippines. This amounted to unrestricted entrance of very "undesirable" people.[11] It was during this time that Quezon launched an investigation of his own into his nation's immigration departments after allegations of misconduct and corruption began to surface. His months-long probe resulted in the suspension of twenty-three officers, the prosecution of four, and the dismantling of the department. It was this fortuitous event in which Quezon brought the duties of the now defunct immigration division under his own personal purview that helped facilitate Jewish refugee rescue into the Philippines in a manner unprecedented in Jewish refugee history of the diaspora.

European Jews fleeing Nazi authority began arriving in Asian ports as early as 1933, following Hitler's ascent to power, with many sharing quarters on ships bound for Shanghai. In one year's time the refugee numbers in Shanghai went from 1,500 near the end of 1938 to nearly 17,000 by the end of 1939. Many jumped ship in ports of call along the sea lanes, disembarking in places such as Bombay, Singapore, Hong Kong, and Manila. However, the first significant influx of European Jews to arrive in Manila came from the German Jewish refugee community in Shanghai. When the Sino-Japanese War broke out on July 7, 1937, the Jewish Refugee Committee (JRC) in Manila received a telegram seeking assistance for Shanghai's refugees. The small Jewish community in Manila immediately raised $8,000, but the funds were held back when the Sephardic Jews of Shanghai assumed support for the needs of these refugees on their own. The JRC kept the funds in escrow for future needs, which happened sooner than expected.[12]

One month later the German government sent to Shanghai one of their luxury liners, the SS *Gneisenau*, tasked with evacuating all German nationals from the war zone, which included about thirty German Jewish refugee families. With Quezon's approval, the JRC in Manila took charge of the Jewish families at the request of the German consul in the Philippines, as the remainder of the German nationals completed their voyage back to Nazi Germany.[13] This spontaneous rescue of German Jews from Shanghai became the impetus for devised rescue plans that would bring over 1,300 refugee Jews to a safe haven in Manila.[14] The important players in that rescue, Philippine president Manual Quezon, U.S. high commissioner in the Philippines, Paul V. McNutt, the Frieder family of influential Jewish merchants, and members of the JRC in Manila, along with directors of various Jewish relief organizations in the world, successfully implemented selection and sponsorship programs to facilitate the rescue of European Jews—an act most nations of the world had deliberately evaded. After Quezon had generously allowed refugees from Shanghai a safe haven in the Philippines, McNutt used his discretionary powers to immediately put the necessary players together and begin the process of selective rescue.[15]

Once the decision to rescue had been made in accordance with Quezon's instructions that the rescue operation uphold the directives of the Immigration Act of 1917, McNutt requested that the JRC present to Quezon and himself "a list of those who might be absorbed" into the Philippine economy.[16] The JRC composed and sent to McNutt a list of needed professionals totaling about one hundred families who could readily assimilate into the economy and port city lifestyle of Manila. Once the JRC had completed its list and guaranteed that necessary funds for the refugees' initial three-months support were in escrow, they received approval from Quezon and McNutt and immediately shared the list with the Refugee Economic Corporation (REC) in New York City. The REC then forwarded the Quezon-McNutt list on June 1, 1938, to the Hilfsverein der Juden in Deutschland (Relief Association for Jews in Germany) in Berlin.[17] The list included physicians and dentists in various specialties, nurses, engineers, mechanics, accountants, dressmakers, barbers, cigar makers, and one conservative rabbi. Applications forwarded to the REC by the Hilfsverein in Berlin began arriving in July 1938. Meanwhile desperate refugees were disembarking in Manila in the summer months of 1938. Quezon's role in securing the life-saving visas necessary for the selected refugees' exodus from Nazi Germany cannot be overstated.

As the rescue plans materialized, Quezon's restructuring of his country's immigration policies and offices was also well underway, resulting in the unusual empowerment of the JRC in Manila with sole jurisdiction over immigrant selection for entrance into the Philippines. Quezon authorized this panel of Jewish businessmen to become the de facto immigration board for the entire country, as he had dismantled his immigration department following multiple criminal indictments. Thus, the processes for the approval of visas into the Philippines was placed squarely into the hands of the JRC, invested by President Quezon and approved by Paul

McNutt. This preempted any oversight by U.S. State Department officials and consular officers abroad in determining who received visas and who did not. U.S. visas to the Philippines still needed to be issued through U.S. State Department consular offices, but they had no power over selection.

After the Hilfsverein in Berlin received the Quezon-McNutt selection list in May 1938, they compiled applications from German Jewish candidates and forwarded them to the REC in New York, which then sent them to the JRC in the Philippines for their evaluation.[18] This committee then checked their prerequisites for immigration, including current passports, background information, former professional or other activities, available funds for temporary support, and the likelihood of eventual successful assimilation into local Philippine communities. When the JRC had the needed assurances, it prepared affidavits recommending the issuance of visas to the names and addresses of approved applicants, which were then presented to Quezon for his approval, since the newly reformed Philippine immigration board was under his direct authority. Once approved by Quezon, the lists were forwarded to McNutt, whose offices ensured that they were encoded for immediate wire transmission through the Bureau of Insular Affairs to the U.S. War Department. Once received there, the coded messages were deciphered by the War Department and delivered to State Department officials in Washington DC.

Through this process of communication McNutt directed that the State Department request "that appropriate consular officials be authorized to give visas" to the selected refugees.[19] The State Department followed McNutt's directives and notified consular officials throughout its European offices to contact the listed residents in their jurisdictions, advising them that a visa for their immediate immigration to the Philippines could be obtained at their nearest U.S. consulate. George Messersmith, assistant secretary of state, assured the high commissioner on November 30, 1938, that the names of the refugees "have been transmitted by mail to the consular officers in the respective districts of the aliens' residences.... The procedure of having the names of the refugees for whom the Philippine authorities have granted authorization for entry into the Philippine Island communicated through the War Department to the Department of State for transmission to the appropriate consular officers is considered to be satisfactory."[20]

The first selection list, composed on October 25, 1938, authorized visas for over one hundred German Jews—men, women, and children—along with six from Austria. The JRC augmented this list one month later with another forty-six names from Germany and two from Italy, totaling one hundred families in all. Through this method, the immigration of refugees into the Philippines came solely under the auspices of Commonwealth officials, Quezon and McNutt, and the members of the JRC. This Jewish immigration board had produced three different lists of approved immigrants before the end of 1938, always receiving more applications from desperate refugees than could possibly be funded and approved.[21] The JRC endorsed additional lists of immigrants every month of the first half of 1939, which became progressively shorter as fewer funds were available until rescue by selection faced suspension in June 1939. By this date 750 refugee Jews had arrived in the Philippines, and two-thirds had been successfully placed in positions of employment. The Jewish community of Manila raised $2,000 a month to support indigent refugees who could not assimilate economically. As 1939 wore on, the ability to procure employment for refugees declined, and the JRC devised proposals for an adjusted immigration program enabling rescue in the Philippines to continue.

The Quezon-McNutt selection plan morphed into a sponsorship program to further immigration to the Philippines in response to the escalating economic burden in sustaining an ever-increasing refugee population. The new program secured "substantial affidavit[s]" guaranteeing ample support for the applicants; a cash deposit in the committee trust fund to sustain every applicant for a minimum one year's support; and more careful scrutiny of applicants' qualifications ensuring their ability to become self-supporting.[22] Maintenance costs for a family of three for one year amounted to $1,800, plus an additional $100 per person was needed to be deposited for the administrative expenses of their rescue.[23] By October 1940 sponsorships enabled more refugees to find a haven in the Philippines, as funds were continually made available for rescue by the JDC in New York. Inquiries from leaders of the JDC to the REC in October 1941 sought more detailed information on the origins and operation of the rescue programs in the Philippines "and the applicability of the method used to the establishment of temporary havens elsewhere," thus demonstrating how rescue in the Philippines became a template for other sites of rescue being contemplated by these relief organizations.[24] But no other global site of refugee rescue saw its national leader offer both public lands and personal holdings for the benefit of destitute refugees as did the Philippine president, Manuel Quezon. Quezon's personal inclinations, partnered with his official pronouncements to offer sanctuary to the persecuted Jews of Europe, predate the Evian Conference and its offshoot, the Intergovernmental Committee on Refugees (IGCR), which floundered ineffectually in its mandate to "improve the present conditions of exodus and to replace them with conditions of orderly emigration."[25] The IGCR was tasked to "approach the governments of the countries of refuge with a view to developing opportunities for permanent settlement," while President Quezon offered up multiple sites in the Philippines to facilitate rescue through mass resettlement operations.[26]

Near the end of November 1938, one of the Frieder bothers, Morris Frieder, met with Joseph Hyman at the JDC offices in New York to discuss further funding for selection rescue already operating under Quezon's auspices in the Philippines. During this meeting Frieder stressed that the Philippines would be an ideal site for mass resettlement, provided refugee rescue through selection remained successful.[27] Quezon's support of such a venture stands unique among the leaders of the world at this time.[28] The Frieders approached President Quezon regarding a larger resettlement plan in the Philippines on the first day of December 1938 and recounted: "[Quezon said he] heartily approved our plan of resettling as many of the refugees as we cared to in Mindanao. He was willing to give them all the land that they wanted, build roads for them, and do everything in his power so that they could re-establish themselves. He intimated that Mindanao is big enough to support as many people as Luzon has, but he would be happy if we could settle a million refugees in Mindanao."[29] Philip Frieder's assessment of Quezon's offer for refugee resettlement in Mindanao described it as "a bigger project than Palestine. The land is more fertile than Palestine, there are more minerals, timber—as a matter of fact, it is the richest land in the Philippines—virgin soil. This is such an enormous proposition that one can hardly visualize the potentialities of same."[30] Quezon met with McNutt the next day to discuss it further. On December 2, 1938, McNutt radiogrammed a communiqué to U.S. Secretary of State Cordell Hull with his own assessment of President Quezon's intentions:

> President Quezon has indicated willingness to set aside virgin lands in Mindanao for larger groups of Jewish refugees. . . . Soil and climate conditions in Mindanao favorable to development of agricultural industries supplemental to Philippine agricultural economy. . . . The situation is now such that the larger program for the colonization of refugees in Mindanao can be successfully inaugurated if a message of approval is received from you. President Quezon is anxious that nothing be done which is not in accord with the policies of the United States. I urge your consideration of the suggestion and strongly recommend its approval if the proposal is in accord with established policies. McNutt.[31]

After years of negotiations, resettlement studies, and eventual U.S. State Department compliance for this massive relocation of European Jews into the Philippines, Quezon's resettlement plans, which would have provided safe haven for thousands of refugees, were cut short by the December 8, 1941, bombing of Manila by the Japanese and their subsequent invasion in January 1942. Its failure cannot dim the graciousness of Quezon's offer to provide a sanctuary planned for one million refugee families on the islands of Mindanao and Polillo.[32] Although this offer of thousands of hectares of land for mass resettlement never reached fruition, Quezon's gift of his own personally held lands to help further the fortunes of these destitute refugees provides ample witness to the humanity of this world leader.

In 1939 Quezon gifted his own personal property to the Jewish community in Manila as a resource for them to further the selection rescue plan by financing and constructing housing for refugee Jews on the site. The 7.5 acres of real estate in Mariquina was land adjoining his own house. He, in essence, embraced the Jewish refugees as his own neighbors. Four rented community houses were completed and in operation by February 1940, and a fifth was under construction when Alex Frieder commented that these were "situated on a conveniently located farm owned by President Quezon." Alex further recounted that the communal buildings "will house forty to fifty persons" who "will work on the farm and so provide themselves with fruits, vegetables, poultry, etc., so that their living costs will be reduced."[33] Named Mariquina Hall, the facility eventually accommodated forty refugee families in a farming co-op on a three-hectare farm in Quezon City—quite literally, a Jewish kibbutz in the middle of the Philippines on President Quezon's own land.[34] At the dedication of the site on April 24, 1940, Quezon gave an extemporaneous speech in the presence of several hundred settler Jews and Filipino dignitaries, politicians, and businessmen. His unguarded words declared:

> What a blessing to the Filipinos it should be if we learn from these few refugees who come to these Islands how to make even the rocky land of Mariquina produce enough quantities to support 40 persons. What a magnificent lesson we can get from that! That would simply mean that the Filipinos have no reason to fear; that if 40 people can raise enough to support them on four hectares, we with a population of 200 million people will be well off if we can learn to do just that. So, I think the Filipinos are going to realize that in allowing these few refugees to come to these islands, we are not only performing a humanitarian act, but

we are, in the end, going to profit from this humane act as is always the case. . . . It is my hope, and indeed my expectation, that the people of the Philippines will have in the future every reason to be glad that when the time of need came, their country was glad to extend to a persecuted people, a hand of welcome.[35]

As President Quezon's humanitarian inclinations to provide rescue opportunities for persecuted Jewish refugees took on this personal path, close associates and colleagues echoed his official positions. On March 14, 1939, Quezon's personal friend, Jorge Bocobo, president of the University of the Philippines and soon to be secretary of public instruction, addressed an audience of Filipinos and rescued refugees at a gathering of the Jewish Junior League:

> It is a most striking fact that the Philippines is probably the first country to make an offer for a planned, large-scale settlement of Jewish refugees from Germany. While other democratic nations have been willing to help the persecuted Jews of Germany, nevertheless their established national policies as expressed in their immigration laws do not permit them, for the present at least, to admit Jewish immigrants in large numbers. . . . But the situation calls for immediate action in order that the Jews in Germany may at once be delivered from the clutches of oppression. So, the Philippines has come forward to give an example to other democratic countries for a liberalization of immigration laws.[36]

Because of Manuel Quezon, uniquely devised selection and sponsorship programs in the Philippines accomplished what most other nations avoided: saving Jewish lives.

President Quezon's authorization of the JRC to oversee all immigration inquiries into the Philippines came during a favorable swing of fate when corruption had crippled its immigration offices, necessitating a complete revamping of the department with new immigration laws. The JRC's impartial, nonpartisan approach to selection between 1937 and 1940 guaranteed its ability to continue to offer refuge to Jews even after the newly constituted immigration laws of the Philippines went into effect in 1941. The rescue of refugees in Manila could not have happened had Manuel Quezon not been the president of the Philippines at that time. Even though U.S. High Commissioner Paul McNutt had jurisdiction over Philippine foreign affairs, Quezon could have declined to act if he had so wanted. But Quezon had many reasons to welcome Jewish refugees into his island nation, not least

Open Doors and Open Hearts

of all his own compassionate instincts. Even though U.S. State Department dealings, which exhibited anti-immigrant prejudices, effectively stalled Quezon's mass resettlement plans on Mindanao, it cannot extinguish the truth of his actions as the only head of state in the world at that time to openly welcome refugee Jews to his country's shores, and for that, thousands of today's descendants from the 1,300 he rescued will be forever grateful.

Notes

1. Michael Cullinane, "The Politics of Collaboration in Tayabas Province," in *Reappraising an Empire: New Perspectives on Philippine-American History*, ed. Peter W. Stanley (Cambridge MA: Harvard University, Committee on American–East Asian Relations of the Department of History and Council of East Asian Studies, 1984), 77.
2. Dean Kotlowski, "Independence of Not? Paul V. McNutt, Manuel L. Quezon, and the Re-examination of Philippine Independence, 1937–39," *International History Review* 32, no. 3 (September 2010): 506.
3. Sol H. Gwekoh, *Manuel L. Quezon: His Life and Career* (Manila: University Pub., 1948), 3.
4. Franklin D. Roosevelt, in Homer S. Cummings Diary, February 2, 1934, Homer S. Cummings Papers, Box 234, University of Virginia, Albert and Shirley Small Special Collections Library, Charlottesville.
5. David Bernstein, *The Philippine Story* (New York: Farrar, Strauss, 1947), 132.
6. General Douglas McArthur, introduction to Manuel L. Quezon, *The Good Fight: The Autobiography of Manuel L. Quezon* (New York City: W. Morgan Shuster, 1944), ii.
7. Gwekoh, *Manuel L. Quezon*, 188.
8. Manuel L. Quezon, "Speech of His Excellency Manuel L. Quezon, President of the Philippines, Before the Rotary Club of Manila, Delivered June 4, 1936," Official Gazette, https://www.officialgazette.gov.ph/1936/06/04/speech-of-president-quezon-before-the-rotary-club-of-manila/.
9. For further discussion on how the Immigration Laws of the Philippines, ratified in 1940 and enacted in 1941, affected rescue in the Philippines, see Bonnie M. Harris, *Philippine Sanctuary: A Holocaust Odyssey* (Madison: University of Wisconsin Press, 2020), chap. 4.
10. Paul V. McNutt, "Quarterly Report of the United States High Commissioner to the Philippine Islands to the President of the United States Quarter Ending Dec. 31, 1937," Indiana University Bloomington, Lilly Library Manuscript Collection, McNutt Mss., Box 9, 18.
11. McNutt, "Quarterly Report of the United States High Commissioner."
12. For greater details on the Philippine rescue of refugee Jews from Shanghai, see Harris, *Philippine Sanctuary*, 58–73.
13. "Memorandum of Conversation between Mr. Hyman and Morris Frieder of Cincinnati, Ohio on November 28th [1938] at 3:30 P.M.," American Jewish Joint Distribution Committee Archives, New York, JDC Collection 33/44, file #784.

14. Frank Ephraim, *Escape to Manila: From Nazi Tyranny to Japanese Terror* (Urbana: University of Illinois Press, 2003), 22. Frank Ephraim, a survivor of the Jewish refugee Community in Manila, presented a complete database of all the Jewish refugees who came to the Philippines to the JewishGen Family Genealogy website, in which he identified 1,301 names.
15. For greater details on how the inception for these rescued plans transpired, see Harris, *Philippine Sanctuary*, chap. 3.
16. Paul V. McNutt to Julius Weiss, May 19, 1938, American Jewish Joint Distribution Committee Archives, JDC Collection 33/44, file #784. See also "Memorandum of Conversation between Mr. Hyman and Morris Frieder."
17. "Memorandum of Conversation between Mr. Hyman and Morris Frieder."
18. Herbert Katzki, JDC Office meeting, June 23, 1939, American Jewish Joint Distribution Committee Archives, JDC Collection 33/44, file #784.
19. Katzki, JDC Office meeting.
20. Messersmith to McNutt, November 30, 1938, NARA II, Record Group 350, Records of the Bureau of Insular Affairs, General Classified Files 1898–1945, Entry 5, Box 1338, Folder #28943-16.
21. Correspondence between the Frieder brothers and officials of the JDC in New York City in October 1938 indicates that "hundreds of applications" of desirable refugees were being diverted to the JRC from various officials and agencies receiving inquiries from people wishing to immigrate to the Philippines, revealing that "200 to 300 families per month could come in if there were sufficient funds to provide for them." While we can never know just how many applications during these four years of organized rescue in the Philippines were received, we can reasonably conjecture that it could have been in the thousands, but the massive destruction Manila experienced at its repatriation from Japanese occupation at the end of the War in the Pacific destroyed the synagogue, social hall, homes, and offices of JRC members along with most of the records. See Harris, *Philippine Sanctuary*, 88–95.
22. Alex Frieder, "Jewish Refugee Committee," May 7, 1940, 19, American Jewish Joint Distribution Committee Archives, JDC Collection 33/44, file #784.
23. Emery Komlos, REC to James Becker, Chicago, July 3, 1940, American Jewish Joint Distribution Committee Archives, JDC Collection 33/44, file #784.
24. Emery Komlos to Robert Pilpel, October 17, 1941, attachment: "Refugee Immigration in the Philippines," American Jewish Joint Distribution Committee Archives, JDC Collection 33/44, file #784.
25. Department of State Press Release, "Text of Resolution Adopted July 14, 1938, by Intergovernmental Committee on Political Refugees at Evian, France," NARA II, Record Group 59, Intergovernmental Committee of Refugees, Country Files, "Philippines," Lot 52D408, Box 6.
26. Department of State Press Release, "Text of Resolution Adopted July 14, 1938."
27. "Memorandum of Conversation on November 28," American Jewish Joint Distribution Committee, JDC Collection 33/44, file #784.
28. At a reception held at the White House on October 17, 1939, FDR addressed about a dozen officers and representatives of the IGCR: "I take great pleasure in announcing today that active steps have been taken to begin work on the settlement projects

which have been made possible by the generous attitude of the Dominican Government and the Government of the Philippine Commonwealth." See FDR, "Statement of the President on Opening the Meeting of the Officers of the Intergovernmental Committee," October 17, 1939, Franklin D. Roosevelt Presidential Library & Museum, Master Speech File 1898–1945, Series 1: Master Speech File, Box 48, "Address to Officers of the Intergovernmental Committee" (speech file 1248).

29. Herbert Frieder to Bruno Schachner, December 8, 1938, American Jewish Joint Distribution Committee, JDC Collection 33/44, file #787a.
30. Frieder to Schachner, December 8, 1938.
31. Paul McNutt to Cordell Hull, "Translation of Radiogram in Code Received December 3, 1938," NARA II, Record Group 350, Records of the Bureau of Insular Affairs, General Classified Files 1898–1945, Entry 5, Box 1338, 1914–1945, file #28943-17.
32. For detailed historical treatment of the Mindanao Resettlement Plan, see Harris, *Philippine Sanctuary*, chap. 4.
33. Alex Frieder to Robert Pilpel, February 17, 1940, American Jewish Joint Distribution Committee, JDC Collection 33/44, file #784.
34. "Quezon's Policy on Jews," *Philippines Herald*, April 24, 1940, NARA II, Record Group 350, Records of the Bureau of Insular Affairs, General Classified Files, Box 1338, Entry 5, file #28943-23.
35. "Quezon's Policy on Jews," *Philippines Herald*.
36. Jorge Bocobo. "Jewish Settlement in Mindanao—Address by President Jorge Bocobo to the Jewish Junior League, Mar. 14, 1939," Bocobo Papers, University of the Philippines Main Library, Box 1, Folder 20.

8

Fort Ontario and American Debates over Refugee Admission

REBECCA L. ERBELDING

The Fort Ontario Emergency Refugee Shelter, in Oswego, New York, opened at 7:30 a.m. on Saturday, August 5, 1944, as the overnight train hugged the shores of Lake Ontario and pulled into the camp. Newsreel crews captured military police handing containers of milk up to the newly arrived refugees. Stretchers carried a few of the older passengers who had fallen ill on their two-week voyage from Europe on the *Henry Gibbins*, an army transport ship also carrying wounded American soldiers. The 982 refugees represented eighteen nationalities (although some were officially "stateless"). The youngest, Harry Maurer, had been born in an ambulance on the way to the dock in Naples two days before the *Henry Gibbins* sailed; the eldest, Isaac Cohen, had been born in Thessaloniki during the American Civil War. The only thing the refugees had in common was that they had all found themselves in Allied-liberated southern Italy in summer 1944, had expressed interest in the United States, and had signed paperwork acknowledging that they would repatriate to Europe after the war (although not everyone remembered having done so).

In the twelve years between 1933 and 1945, as years of persecution turned into a genocide in which 6 million European Jews were murdered, these 982 refugees were the only people brought to the United States outside of the immigration system as a response to the ongoing genocide. In January 1944 President Franklin Roosevelt announced a new policy of rescue and relief for those suffering under Nazi persecution. Public support grew in favor of bringing some of the victims to the United States, and in a period of six weeks in summer 1944, Allied aid workers chose nearly one thousand people and brought them to a country that had not thought through the implications of their arrival. The Fort Ontario refugees were surrounded by barbed wire for nineteen months, intended to be a visible sign of the country's stated commitment to help refugees, even as complications arose over their planned postwar repatriation.

The United States had no refugee policy in the 1930s and 1940s, nor a law to address the needs of migrants or asylum seekers. Although somewhere between 180,000 and 220,000 people fleeing Nazi persecution entered the United States between 1933 and 1945, they entered as immigrants. They were refugees in every sense of the word—and even referred to at the time as such—except under United States law, where they were subjected to the 1924 Johnson-Reed Immigration Act. That act set numerical limits on immigration from most of the world and instituted a racist quota system designed to provide more opportunities to countries with majority white Protestant populations than to countries in eastern Europe with large Jewish and Catholic populations. During debates over the 1921 Emergency Quota Act, Johnson-Reed's precursor, which set the first immigration quotas in U.S. history, the House of Representatives passed an amendment stipulating that people fleeing religious or political persecution would not be subjected to the quota limitations. The Senate voted it down, eliminating any refugee exemptions from the bill's final text.[1] When the quota system was rewritten and codified in the 1924 Johnson-Reed Act, there had been no precedent to honor, no law to reference during the refugee crisis of the late 1930s, and no appetite in the United States to liberalize immigration in any case.

The German quota remained unfilled for most of the 1930s, even Nazi Germany increasingly marginalized and victimized German Jews. By 1939 hundreds of thousands of Germans and Austrians, mostly Jews, had applied for the United States waiting list. Some had been imprisoned in concentration camps after Kristallnacht, allowed out only after signing documents promising to emigrate as soon as possible. Many had been stripped of their wealth, belongings, homes, and businesses, which made it difficult to provide the proof American diplomats demanded that potential immigrants would not become public charges upon arrival in the United States.

And yet, in 1939 and 1940, European Jews still represented more than half of all quota immigration to the United States, a fact both surprising and indicative of the stinginess of the immigration system in general.[2] After gathering extensive paperwork, submitting to an interview, and undergoing a medical exam, those approved received visas from State Department consular officers in their countries of residence. They arrived, mostly by ship, and mostly into New York harbor. These immigrants then spread throughout the country and started new lives. While they were subjected to some wartime restrictions and had to register with the government as noncitizen "aliens," in most cases Jewish refugees could blend into the population as much as their accents and personal experiences allowed. Unlike the Fort Ontario refugees in 1944, they were not interned upon arrival.

In November 1942 Operation Torch, the Allied invasion of North Africa, began. Immigration for most European Jews had already been impossible for over a year. Mass shootings in eastern Europe had been largely supplanted by stationary killing centers. Nearly 4.5 million Jews were murdered before the United States militarily engaged in the European Theater. Within weeks of the Allied invasion, American newspapers reported that Nazi Germany was planning to murder all the Jews of Europe. Throughout 1943 reports out of Europe were finally treated as credible, and pressure rose for the United States to do something to help the victims beyond the Roosevelt administration's stated priority of rescue through military victory.

In late 1943 Congress debated a "Rescue Resolution" calling on the president to establish a "commission of diplomatic, economic, and military experts to formulate and effectuate a plan of immediate action designed to save the surviving Jewish people of Europe from extinction at the hands of Nazi Germany."[3] The Treasury Department, engaged in a months-long battle with the State Department over sending humanitarian aid to Europe, uncovered the fact that Assistant Secretary of State Breckinridge Long had instructed U.S. diplomats in Switzerland to stop sending information about mass murder to the United States. On January 16, 1944, Treasury Department staff brought their findings to President Roosevelt. The confluence of public, congressional, and intra-administration pressure convinced the president to act.

One of the many suggestions repeated by multiple humanitarian relief groups after the War Refugee Board's creation was the need for the United States to create or encourage havens for refugees. On March 6, 1944, Josiah DuBois and Joseph Friedman, both on the WRB's staff, collaborated on a memo about the possibility of a refugee haven in the United States. They argued that the War Refugee Board could not ask other countries to take in refugees when the United States has not expressed a willingness to do so. "The enemy must not be given the pretense of justification that the Allies, while speaking in horrified terms of the Nazi treatment of the Jews, never once offered to receive these people.... The moral aspect of the problem is pre-eminent."[4] To make the idea palatable to Roosevelt in an election year, DuBois and Friedman proposed that the refugees be treated like the thousands of prisoners of war already in the United States. The refugees could enter outside of immigration quotas, as the United States would mandate their repatriation to Europe after the war. DuBois and Friedman reasoned there could be no complaints of mistreatment, since an American prisoner of war camp was much better than a Nazi concentration camp.

Roosevelt took some convincing. At a press conference on March 24, 1944, he told a journalist that the United States was not planning to open itself as a refugee haven since "there aren't enough [refugees] to come, which is one reason—a pretty good one."⁵ So the War Refugee Board staff mobilized to quietly drum up public support for the idea by utilizing sympathetic journalists. Newspaper columnist Samuel Grafton dedicated his April 5 column to the issue of "free ports" in the United States. Free ports, Grafton explained, were places where goods were stored tax-free, while importers waited to bring them into the country. The United States could provide similar space for refugees from Nazism, allowing them to enter outside of immigration laws and returning them to their homelands after the war.⁶ Radio commentator Norman Jay turned his "Very Truly Yours" broadcast into an open letter to WRB director John Pehle, expressing his hope that with the establishment of free ports, "America can heave a national sigh of relief as it forsakes the unnatural role it has played in barring refugees from its shores."⁷ A White House–sponsored Gallup poll revealed 70 percent of the public respondents supported the plan—provided the refugees did not work in the United States and would return to Europe after the war.

The public support seemed to sway Roosevelt. He was still hesitant to bring in large numbers of refugees without congressional approval but suggested Pehle find "an emergency situation" involving about a thousand refugees. Roosevelt would welcome them into the United States as his "guests" and be able to justify his action to Congress.⁸ Within days Leonard Ackermann, the WRB's representative in North Africa, contacted Pehle. Refugees from Yugoslavia were trying to land in Italy, but the American military had been directed to "discourage the evacuation of refugees" and "not to provide transportation to Yugoslav refugees when returning to Italy."⁹ Ackermann protested vehemently to the Allied authorities, especially since he had just received word from Yugoslavia that partisans there were willing to help Hungarian Jews escape to their territory. They would need someplace to go, and now the Allied military was trying to stop the rickety wooden boats carrying refugees from crossing the Mediterranean. Pehle wrote another report, reminding the president of his instruction to find an emergency. He helpfully enclosed drafts of a message to Congress, orders to the Allied military to transport refugees, and instructions to various departments to prepare a camp.¹⁰ Pehle sent his report to the White House and waited.

On May 30 Roosevelt was again asked about free ports at a press conference, but this time his answer was quite different than it had been two months earlier. The president emphasized that most refugee havens would be overseas but claimed the government was working on a potential free port in the United States.[11] In private Roosevelt told Pehle that the War Refugee Board could bring a thousand refugees to the United States if the staff could secure a camp. Roosevelt also expressed his preference for the term "Emergency Refugee Shelter" rather than "free port" since it "connoted the temporary character of the refugees' stay in the United States and also because the word 'shelter' is an honest word and that we won't be able to provide much more than shelter."[12] A little over twenty-four hours later, the War Department offered the War Refugee Board the use of Fort Ontario, a recently decommissioned military installation on Lake Ontario with a history dating back to the Seven Years' War.[13] Oswego, a small city of approximately twenty-two thousand residents, had not been warned prior to the announcement that Fort Ontario, located in the center of the city, would soon house World War II refugees. Yet less than a week after the War Department announced the selection of Fort Ontario, the Chamber of Commerce had already formed a special "Fort Ontario Committee" and wrote to thank Roosevelt for choosing them for this honor. "Fort Ontario," the Chamber of Commerce wrote, "will continue to measure up to its worthy tradition."[14]

The War Refugee Board did not have the staff or expertise to run a camp, so it turned to an agency that did: the War Relocation Authority (WRA). The WRA, under the Department of the Interior, already administered the camps containing approximately 120,000 Japanese and Japanese Americans imprisoned after Roosevelt's executive order 9066, which had declared the West Coast a military zone and authorized their removal. Joseph Smart, who had supervised the Heart Mountain, Minidoka, and Grenada camps, was appointed director of the Fort Ontario Emergency Refugee Shelter. The War Relocation Authority, working with the U.S. Army, began to build and retrofit the fort's barracks and buildings for the refugees' arrivals, while across the Atlantic aid workers began to interview and select the group.

At a meeting between the WRB and the WRA, representatives discussed selection criteria for the refugees. "Family units must be given first consideration," the list began. The refugee group should also include at least three doctors, as many nurses as available, journeymen to help with the upkeep of the buildings, people "possessing leadership qualifications," interpreters, one or more rabbis, and religious leaders for all the groups represented.[15] Roosevelt's message to the Allied authorities instructing them of the plan, though, had no such criteria. That instruction merely said to pick refugees "for whom other havens of refuge are not immediate available," to "include a reasonable proportion of various categories of persecuted people," and to screen for "any loathsome, dangerous, or contagious disease."[16] Roosevelt told them to hurry: "The procedure for the selection of the refugees and arrangements for bringing them here should be as simple and expeditious as possible, uncomplicated by any of the usual formalities involved in admitting people to the United States under the immigration laws."[17] Leonard Ackermann, tasked in Italy with overseeing the selection of the refugees, assembled a team of aid workers and other bureaucrats to fan out through Allied-occupied southern Italy, advertise the opportunity, interview, and choose. They decided to avoid men of military age, both for optics in the United States (so Americans would not see military-aged men being cared for in safety by the government while their own sons were fighting in Europe) and because partisan and Zionist groups wanted these men for their own. Unfortunately, Sir Clifford Heathcote-Smith, a British representative of the Intergovernmental Committee on Refugees assisting with the selection, ignored this instruction and seemingly neglected to tell the refugees he chose that they would be required to repatriate after the war.[18] Even those refugees who had been informed would be forgiven for not taking the United States seriously. In the draft notice Ackermann shared with the War Refugee Board, refugees were merely informed their postwar repatriation was "contemplated."[19]

In less than a month, the team had interviewed approximately three thousand interested refugees and selected one thousand (several dropped off the list prior to departure). "It has been one of the most difficult and heartrending jobs that I have ever undertaken," Ackermann wrote to Pehle. "It was necessary in a number of cases to be hard and say 'no' when it would have been merciful and proper to say 'yes.' . . . I only wish we could have taken more."[20]

After a two-week voyage, on August 4, 1944, the *Henry Gibbins* arrived in New York harbor carrying 982 refugees destined for Fort Ontario. The trip had been relatively uneventful, although some of the refugee groups, who self-divided by nationality and language, had begun to bicker among themselves and complain about their treatment. This continued after their arrival in Oswego, particularly after the refugees saw the practical yet meager accommodations, saw that the camp was surrounded by a fence topped with barbed wire, and realized that they would be confined in the camp, unable to work outside it, for the duration of the war. They were "guests of the president" with no legal status in the United States.

Ruth Gruber, a Department of the Interior staff member, had also joined the refugees on the *Henry Gibbins*—and quickly became beloved by many of them—to gather stories to provide the press upon the ship's arrival. Five days after the group's arrival at Fort Ontario, she wrote: "They are adjusting themselves to the life of eating and walking; they are once more voicing their discontents. They want freedom; they want education; they want more food; they want work. They have already begun to use the press as their weapon."[21] Although most of the press about the opening of the camp was positive, there were a few exceptions. One refugee even took a reporter to the fence and told him to put his face against it, so he could get a sense of the betrayal some of the refugees felt.[22] Gruber blamed Heathcote-Smith directly for the complaints. "It is from this group that our 5 to 10 percent of malcontents have come. . . . Sure, they knew they were going to a camp; but they figured, the Americans are easy. They'll let us out right away."[23] Others, of course, may have been disappointed but expressed gratitude to the United States. "This is more beautiful than anything in Europe," one refugee supposedly told *Life* magazine. "Now I have a villa on the Lake Ontario."[24]

Although most American officials remained publicly and privately committed to returning the refugees to Europe after the war, ties between the refugees and the United States began to challenge that commitment.

First, officials noticed something as the refugees arrived at the camp: "It appears that several of the women selected in Italy for admission to the Emergency Refugee Shelter at Fort Ontario in Oswego, New York are pregnant."[25] Would their children, therefore, be natural-born American citizens? Milton Sargoy, a War Refugee Board lawyer, was assigned to write a legal memorandum on the question. Sargoy pointed out the *United States v. Wong Kim Ark*, in which the Supreme Court in 1898 held that despite the Chinese Exclusion Act, children born to resident alien Chinese parents within the territorial boundaries of the United States would, in fact, be considered natural-born citizens. A potential exception could be made if Fort Ontario, as an Emergency Refugee Shelter, was not considered part of the United States for the duration of the shelter's existence or if the refugees had not officially "entered" the United States. This was a real consideration for Sargoy, as Attorney General Francis Biddle had assured Senator Robert Reynolds (who opposed the creation of the shelter) after Roosevelt's announcement that "the refugees will not be permitted to enter the United States under the immigration laws and thereby to obtain any rights to be at liberty in the United States or to remain here."[26] Therefore, unlike *Wong Kim Ark*, the refugee parents could not be considered resident or domiciled in the United States. "No court has yet considered the question of the citizenship of a child born in the United States to an alien woman who had been refused admission to the country," Sargoy wrote. But he also discovered a precedent. In 1919 the Labor Department had weighed the case of Teresa Mendicino, an immigrant excluded from entering the United States after her arrival who gave birth while awaiting deportation. The Solicitor of Labor ultimately concluded that "since the American view of citizenship is governed by the rule of *jus soli*, the place of birth, the resident or domicile of the parent has no bearing on the child's citizenship." Under the Fourteenth Amendment "the sole criteria are birth in the United States and subject to its jurisdiction," which would apply, Sargoy concluded, to any child born at Fort Ontario.[27] Miriam Mary Franco, the daughter of Jewish refugees Victor and Lidia, was born in late September 1944. She was the first of sixteen babies born to refugee parents at Fort Ontario, all birthright citizens of the United States.[28]

There was also the question of the many refugees' close links to Americans, particularly to American servicemen and -women. Within hours of the *Henry Gibbins* docking in Hoboken, New Jersey, military policeman Lt. Herbert Altman, himself a refugee from Germany, spotted two people he had not seen in six years: Eisig and Golde Diamant, his father and mother-in-law. The family was able to embrace on the dock and exchange a few words before the Diamants were shuffled away.[29] Within a week, newspapers reported that Sgt. Joseph Flick, who grew up in Berlin and escaped to the United States in 1938, learned from a Yiddish newspaper that his parents, Naftali and Rywa, had arrived at Fort Ontario. They were able to speak on the phone for twenty minutes, and Joseph's parents updated him on their internment experiences, the imprisonment of one of Joseph's brothers, the death of another, and a sister in Belgium who, with her family, had not been heard from.[30] Georg and Helga Sternberg, also originally from Berlin, were able to speak to their daughter-in-law, Lee, for the first time in eight years and learned that their son Frederick, now a captain in the U.S. Army, was stationed in England.[31] More than sixty newly arrived refugees had immediate family serving in the U.S. military, and at least 131 had extended family in the service. One young refugee was engaged to an American serviceman.

Additionally, nearly one hundred refugees had parents, spouses, or children in the United States whom, in many cases, they not seen in many years. Nearly 250 were members of families in which one of the adults had a sibling, or siblings, already settled in the country.[32] Elsa Graner, working as a domestic and a seamstress to support her two children, read in a newspaper that her husband, Dr. Hugo Graner, was in Oswego. They had been separated since March 1939 when Elsa, seven-year-old Otto, and five-year-old Hildegarde had obtained U.S. immigration papers under the German quota. Hugo had been subjected to the much smaller Hungarian quota and unable to immigrate with the family. Although visitors were not permitted to enter the Fort Ontario for a month-long quarantine period, these phone calls—and then the physical reunions—were featured in heartwarming newspaper articles. "I have no money to go to him," Elsa Graner told the *New York Herald*. "Not even to send him a telegram. But I will go to him when I can . . . some time, somehow."[33]

The town of Oswego largely welcomed the refugees, and this too was captured in photographs and articles. The *New York Post* printed interviews with Oswego residents who had visited the fence surrounding the camp to speak with the refugees. "I don't think any of us expected there would be so many outstanding people out at the fort," Edwin Waterbury, the head of the Chamber of Commerce noted. One woman, who had originally hoped to hire a refugee woman as a housekeeper, met refugee Margarette Frank at the fence and commented to the reporter, "Why she's so attractive. My, don't you want to do something to help people like that."[34] A large photo spread in *Life* magazine in late August and publicity surrounding First Lady Eleanor Roosevelt's visit to the fort in mid-September further humanized the refugees for the American people.

Although the War Refugee Board's impetus for opening the camp had been to demonstrate that the United States was willing to accept refugees—which the WRB staff hoped to convince other nations to do—the Fort Ontario refugees remained segregated, visibly identified as temporary refugees. Many could have likely qualified for U.S. immigration visas; during the war the quotas for immigrants from Europe remained unfilled. In fact, three hundred of the refugees had already applied for immigration to the United States prior to 1941, and at least fourteen had received visas but had been trapped in Europe by the war.[35] Yet Roosevelt's promise that the refugees would be returned to their homelands and the need for the symbolism of the fort meant that the State Department was not instructed to examine the refugees for possible admission, even for refugees with close family to support them. Nor were the refugees permitted to sleep anywhere outside the camp, save for approved hospital stays. Reunions only took place in Oswego. Babies were born, marriages celebrated, men and women died and were buried, and still the administration officials remained publicly committed to the refugees' return.

President Franklin Roosevelt died on April 12, 1945, less than a month before the end of the war in Europe. The Fort Ontario refugees held three memorial services for the president, although twelve-year-old Liesl Bader later claimed she was sad to hear of his death, but not sorry. "Maybe we would not have to go back where we come from as we agreed to with him."[36] Roosevelt's death did not immediately change the government's decision. Henry Morgenthau Jr., the Treasury secretary who was closely linked with the WRB, remained committed to fulfilling his late friend Roosevelt's wishes. But with war ending in Europe, President Harry Truman ordered the War Refugee Board to end its operations. On June 8, 1945, the Department of the Interior officially took over all administration and control of the camp.

The War Relocation Authority remained in charge, but without the camp's director, Joseph Smart. In early May Smart suddenly resigned from the federal government to devote himself to advocating for the refugees to be permitted to stay in the United States. He assembled supportive aid agencies and celebrities to his cause and sought to place newspaper articles pleading with the Truman administration to grant relief.

Congressman Samuel Dickstein, the head of the House Committee on Immigration and Naturalization, who also represented large Jewish and immigrant constituencies, announced hearings, titled "Investigation of Problems Presented by Refugees at Fort Ontario Refugee Shelter." He and members of a subcommittee traveled to Fort Ontario over two days in late June 1945, interviewing dozens of refugees and Oswego residents. Fourteen members of the fort's Boy Scout troop individually testified under oath that they would take up arms in defense of the United States, should they be permitted to stay. One after another, Oswego's supervisor of schools, the public high school principal, and elementary school educators testified to the quality of the refugee students and what valuable citizens they would make. The hearing was aptly named: the refugees had presented a clear problem. Their neighbors liked them. Many had American relatives. The refugees who had given birth had native-born American children. The congressmen left, and the refugees were left to wait. Some, tired of living in limbo, chose to voluntarily repatriate, mostly to Yugoslavia, or emigrated to join family abroad. In the camp newspaper, the *Ontario Chronicle*, refugee cartoonist Max Sipser commemorated the one-year anniversary of the group's arrival through artwork. The top of the cartoon depicted the refugees on August 5, 1944, excitedly waving at the Statue of Liberty. The cartoon below, for August 5, 1945, showed a refugee using a telescope to peer at the far-distant statue as other refugees crowd at the fence topped with barbed wire. The meaning was clear: freedom, once in their grasp, felt far away.

With the approach of a second cold winter in Oswego, some refugees planned a performance of a new opera, *The Golden Cage*, about their experiences as refugees and at Fort Ontario. The lyrics to one song expressed their desperation: "We are in a cage without reason, We are in a cage, golden cage; We're missing nothing but our freedom. . . . Behind the fence of Fort Ontario. We are sitting, awaiting the glorious day: When our unchained feet may finally go; Over the most wonderful country's way."[37]

They had to write a new segment prior to the play's debut. On December 22, 1945, not long before opening night, the president issued what became known as the Truman Directive. The quota system would remain, but displaced persons would be granted preference, and the Fort Ontario refugees who qualified would be permitted to officially "enter" the United States as new immigrants. Over six weeks in January and February 1946, the remaining refugees boarded buses to Canada, registered at the U.S. consulate in Niagara Falls, and officially entered the United States for the first time. The National Refugee Service assisted them in joining relatives or in finding new cities in which to establish new lives.

In the fifty-nine years between 1921 (when the House of Representatives voted down a refugee provision to the Emergency Quota Act) and 1980 (when Congress finally passed the Refugee Resettlement Act), more than four million refugees and displaced persons arrived in the United States outside of the immigration system.[38] Almost all came after World War II. They came from postwar Europe, from 1950s Hungary, from 1960s Cuba, and from southeast Asia in the 1970s. Congress passed individual bills to aid them, setting narrow definitions of who qualified, based on where they were displaced from, and when, and how. These refugees arrived by plane to military bases, by battleship to makeshift welcome centers, or by small wooden boats onto south Florida beaches. Sometimes, in lieu of congressional action, the president utilized humanitarian parole to allow these people to stay. They quickly spread throughout the country and blended in as much as their accents and experiences would allow. In contrast, the 982 refugees who arrived at Fort Ontario in Oswego, New York, in August 1944 were the only Holocaust-era refugees to enter the United States outside of the immigration system. Yet their experiences—and the experience of the U.S. government in trying to figure out how to deal with them—have reverberated over the subsequent decades. The bottom line, bureaucrats quickly discovered after the Fort Ontario refugees' arrival, is that once refugees arrive on American shores, forced repatriation or deportation becomes much more difficult. They have American ties, American children, and, perhaps most importantly, Americans who like them and fight for them to stay. Despite the intentions of the authors of the Johnson-Reed Act, the United States was and remains a multicultural society; Fort Ontario was and is, an unmistakably American story. The Fort Ontario refugees remain an early example of the promise that refugees provide and a symbol of the tortured debates the United States continues to have regarding refugee admissions.

Notes

1. "Immigration Bill Passed by Senate," *New York Times*, May 4, 1921, 1.
2. The American Jewish Yearbook (http://ajcarchives.org/, vols. 41 and 42, accessed November 28, 2021) reports that 43,450 Jews arrived in the United States in 1939 out of a total of 82,998 quota immigrants (52.53 percent). In 1940 it was 36,945 out of 70,756 total (52.21 percent).
3. H. Res. 350, War Refugee Board Papers (hereafter WRBP), Box 33, Folder 2, Franklin D. Roosevelt Presidential Library and Archives, Hyde Park, New York (hereafter FDRL).
4. Josiah DuBois and Joseph B. Friedman, March 6, 1944, Morgenthau Diaries (hereafter TMD), vol. 707, 235–44, FDRL.
5. Franklin Roosevelt, March 24, 1944, Presidential Press Conferences, Series 1, FDRL.
6. Samuel Grafton, "I'd Rather be Right," *New York Post*, April 5, 1944, TMD, vol. 717, 187, FDRL.
7. Norman Jay, "Very Truly Yours" radio transcript, April 25, 1944, TMD, vol. 724, 108–12, FDRL.
8. John Pehle, May 20, 1944, Holocaust Refugees and the FDR White House (hereafter HRFDR) (Microfilm Collection, Bethesda MD: UPA collection from LexisNexis, 2006), LM 0255, Reel 4, Folder 1, 24–25, USHMM.
9. Robert Murphy, Memo to Military Government Section, AFHQ, April 29, 1944, WRBP, Box 78, Folder 2, FDRL.
10. John Pehle, "To the President," May 18, 1944, TMD, vol. 733, 10–17, FDRL.
11. Transcript, phone conversation between John Pehle and Henry Morgenthau Jr., May 31, 1944, TMD, vol. 737, 85, FDRL.
12. John Pehle, June 1, 1944, TMD, vol. 738, 39–51, FDRL.
13. Pehle, June 1, 1944.
14. Harry Mizen, Letter to FDR, June 14, 1944, HRFDR (Microfilm Collection, Bethesda MD: UPA collection from LexisNexis, 2006), LM 0255, Reel 4, Folder 1, 56, USHMM.
15. Anne Laughlin, Memo of meeting, June 12, 1944, RG-48, Office of the Secretary of the Interior, Central Classified Files, 1937–1953, Box 2331.
16. Franklin Roosevelt, Cable 1823, June 8, 1944, TMD, vol. 741, 151, FDRL.
17. Roosevelt, Cable 1823.
18. Ralph Stauber, Memo for Myer and Smart, August 3, 1944, RG-210, Classified General Files, Box 1, Folder 4, National Archives, Washington DC (hereafter NADC).
19. Leonard Ackermann, Letter, June 22, 1944, WRBP, Box 1, Folder 1, 90–94, FDRL.
20. Leonard Ackermann, Letter, July 12, 1944, WRBP, Box 1, Folder 1, 74–81, FDRL.

21. Ruth Gruber collection, Folder Memos—Refugees, August 9, 1944. My thanks to the late Ruth Gruber for sharing these documents, which are currently housed at New York University.
22. Ruth Gruber collection, Folder Memos—Refugees.
23. Ruth Gruber collection, Folder Memos—Refugees.
24. "Refugees Arrive from Europe," *Life*, August 21, 1944, 27.
25. Milton Sargoy, Memorandum re: Citizenship, August 1944, RG-210, War Refugee Board Basic Documents, Box 2, Folder 3, NADC.
26. Francis Biddle, Letter, June 23, 1944, TMD, vol. 745, 59–60, FDRL.
27. Milton Sargoy, Memorandum re: Citizenship, August 1944, RG-210, War Refugee Board Basic Documents, Box 2, Folder 3, NADC; emphasis in original.
28. Sharon Lowenstein, *Token Refuge: The Story of the Jewish Refugee Shelter at Oswego, 1944–1946* (Bloomington: Indiana University Press, 1986), 198.
29. "Once a Refugee, Soldier on Guard at Pier Finds Kin Fleeing Nazis," unidentified newspaper, August 9, 1944, RG-210, Classified General Files, Box 7, Folder 8, NADC.
30. "Sergeant Surprised," *New York Sun*, August 10, 1944, RG-210, Classified General Files, Box 7, Folder 8, NADC.
31. "Oswego Refugees Talk to Kin Here," *Evening Sun* (New York), August 11, 1944, RG-210, Classified General Files, Box 7, Folder 8, NADC.
32. "Investigation of Problems Presented by Refugees at Fort Ontario Refugee Shelter," June 24–25, 1945 (Washington DC: Government Printing Office, 1945), 117–23.
33. "Family Broken Up by Gestapo to Meet Again at Fort Ontario," *New York Herald*, August 8, 1944.
34. "Oswego Opens Its Hearts to Refugees," *New York Post*, August 9, 1944.
35. "Investigation of Problems Presented by Refugees," 124.
36. Lowenstein, *Token Refuge*, 165.
37. Edward Marks, *Token Shipment* (Washington DC: Government Printing Office, 1946), 84.
38. Carl J. Bon Tempo, *Americans at the Gate: The United States and Refugees during the Cold War* (Princeton NJ: Princeton University Press, 2008), 1.

9

Limiting the Undesirables
Jewish Refugee Migration to Australia in 1938 and 1939

PAUL R. BARTROP

The first few years after Adolf Hitler's attainment of power in Germany in 1933 saw neighboring European countries willing to receive Jewish refugees from Nazism and accommodate them temporarily. Those admitted were, however, encouraged to find a permanent home in some other country as soon as practicable.

In Australia it was always assumed that because of its remoteness from Europe, and its lack of proximity to other immigrant-receiving countries, German Jews seeking to flee Hitler would arrive intending to settle permanently as immigrants—and at the beginning of the Nazi period the country's parlous economic situation caused by the Depression dictated that immigration was at its lowest ebb since Federation in 1901. Moreover, German Jews were not at first considered as refugees; indeed, in 1933 Australia did not even have a refugee policy. By June 1933, however, when it seemed likely that Germany's Jews might seek to escape antisemitic persecution, a rapidly improvised position was developed by the conservative United Australia Party government and the officials of the Department of the Interior administering immigration. This held that care would have to be taken to see to it that no "serious influx" of Jews came to Australia.[1] From then until the end of the struggle against Nazism twelve years later, the responsible authorities held fast to this principle. It seemed always to be in the back of the bureaucrats' minds, guiding their every step as tens of thousands of refugee Jews from Germany, Austria, Czechoslovakia, and other parts of Europe pleaded desperately for admission.

Further, it can be argued that the government and the popular will coalesced to produce an unsympathetic and anti-refugee Australia—in an environment where all refugees were considered to be Jews fleeing Nazism. The government, preferring exclusion over acceptance, consistently searched for ways to ensure that refugees could be kept out. The reasons for this require examination. After all, Australia was a liberal-democratic nation founded on immigration, proud of its high level of perceived tolerance, and with a strong image as a humanitarian and caring community. Four themes stand out.

First, Australia at the outset of the period carried prejudices toward foreigners that had been formed according to racial criteria. In the nineteenth and early twentieth centuries, Chinese, Pacific Islanders, and Indians had all been the subject of special legislation or anti-foreign agitation, and this antipathy was projected onto selected European nationalities, particularly southern Europeans (who, in addition to not being British, were viewed by many Australians as unfair workplace competitors, especially in depressed rural regions), after the Great War.[2] The second reason for rejection of Jewish refugees related to the economy.[3] During the Depression decade of the 1930s, there was opposition from both the labor movement and from middle-class Australia to the migration of immigrants from non-British backgrounds—the labor movement on the ground that refugees would allow themselves to be exploited, lowering living and industrial standards; middle-class opposition relating to a fear that wherever employment possibilities did exist, Australians would be crowded out of the workplace.

Interwoven with these fears was the third motif running through the Australian rejection of refugees: an intolerance of "alien" immigrants. It is probably in the nature of immigrant reception and integration that recent arrivals are those most likely to bear the brunt of local animosities and prejudices. Australians, with a relatively short history of foreign migration by the 1930s, saw every new foreign arrival as an object of suspicion. An anti-foreigner stance played a huge role in the rejection of foreign Jews before and, unquestionably, during the Second World War.

The question of antisemitism must be examined: it is an issue that should not be considered lightly. The ironic aspect of this, however, is that in the 1930s Australia did not have an antisemitic tradition in the same sense as did the countries of Europe or the Americas.[4] Australia had not been such a society up to this time.[5] That the Nazi period saw an anti-alien and anti-immigrant stance adopted, moreover, should not automatically imply that the Australian people had become antisemites overnight. Given that the main targets of prejudice during the 1930s and early 1940s were Jewish *and* foreign, however, saw them placed in an invidious position. (British-born Jews, on the other hand, did not suffer discrimination in Australian society.) The overwhelming conclusion to be drawn from the evidence is that the Australians rejected them in the first instance because they were foreign: their Jewishness, at least until 1938, was employed to reinforce the rejection, not to establish it. After then the issue became clouded by fears of Jewish migration on a much larger scale, and activities were directed toward denying Jews entry because of their Jewishness alone.

Further, while the government searched consistently for ways in which to keep out refugees,[6] most Australians, if they thought about the problem at all, and if judged from the volume of supportive letters received by the government and printed in the newspapers, probably came down on the side of an abstract sympathy for Germany's Jews—though not sufficiently to accept them into the country as immigrants. This was especially the case from late 1938, after which the refugee issue assumed hitherto unparalleled dimensions.[7]

Public opinion, however, could be difficult to measure. Opinion polls did not yet exist, and the only standards available for government analysts were newspaper editorials, letters to the editor, correspondence forwarded directly to politicians, and public statements from leading citizens. Where competing positions were put forward, it was usually up to officials in the Commonwealth Departments to interpret them and provide an approximation of which way the winds of opinion were blowing.[8]

In short, the whole refugee issue in the 1930s was a major inconvenience imposing upon the nation a jolting period of reassessment concerning its place in the world and its responsibilities toward other human beings in need of help, coupled with a large measure of indifference to the fate of the persecuted. Refugees were always looked upon as alien immigrants and judged on that basis rather than on the urgency of their situation. The government's position fluctuated throughout the 1930s and was certainly far from consistent when deciding who was desirable and who was not, but on the whole Australian officialdom exhibited an ongoing opposition to the entry of Jewish refugees. The conservative governments of Joseph Lyons and Robert Menzies had an ideological commitment to favoring the immigration of British settlers; the bureaucrats objected to an immigration policy being thrust onto them by circumstances over which they had no control; and large sections of the Australian public had concerns surrounding labor displacement and racial blending. Moreover, while there were many who felt that Nazi antisemitic persecution was abhorrent and evil, an oft-repeated opinion was that Australia was not accountable, and it should be the responsibility of other countries to find a solution.

Much has been written on the Australian response to the Evian Conference on refugees held in July 1938, but to a large degree the statement made there by its delegate Thomas White, that Australia had "no real racial problems" and was "not desirous of importing one," merely served to underscore what was already the majority position in government.[9] The immediate aftermath of the conference did not see a change in Australian policy. In a memorandum prepared by the Prime Minister's Department on July 27, 1938, the existing policy was outlined and reaffirmed: applications for admission of foreigners (in this context, Jews from Germany and Austria) could be granted to (1) dependent relatives of persons already settled in Australia; (2) aliens other than dependent relatives who possessed at least £50 landing money and were nominated and guaranteed by persons in Australia; and (3) aliens without guarantors in Australia who could introduce at least £200.[10]

Some other groups, however, were subject to special conditions beyond these general rules. The Dutch, for example, required only £50 for a single man or £100 for a married man where a guarantee was furnished by the Netherlands Migration Office. Where no guarantee existed, £100 landing money for a single man might still be considered sufficient.[11] These arrangements, however, did not apply to Dutch immigrants "of Jewish race." Admission of northern Europeans was always viewed as preferable, and the minister for the interior was granted discretionary power to reduce the amount of landing capital for individual cases involving non-Jewish applicants from such countries. Reductions of landing money were also granted in respect of Maltese immigrants due to their standing as British European subjects.[12]

The varying amounts of landing money demonstrated the government's discriminatory approach and were deemed sufficient to safeguard Australian living standards. Prospective immigrants might be able to meet health, character, and other criteria for acceptance, but without the required landing money as well, these were largely irrelevant. This was therefore a vital tool in immigration management: it was one thing to have set criteria for entrance, but entirely another to be faced with large numbers of applicants, all of whom seemed to meet them. Ways had to be found to reduce eligible numbers. The question was really whether the government's policy would discriminate against Jewish refugees *as Jews* or classify them along with other "unassimilable" aliens. This issue had to be addressed when considering whether British Jews would be entitled to receive assisted passages for emigration.

The provision of financial assistance for immigrants from Britain had been suspended indefinitely when the worst effects of the Depression hit Australia in 1932. On March 4, 1938, it was reestablished, though some states had strong reservations about how successful it might be given that significant aftereffects of the Depression remained. The federal government therefore agreed to apply the scheme only to those states agreeing to participate. When the question of assisted passages for British Jews was raised in August 1938, the government decided that they could not be debarred from receiving assisted passages, though in a memorandum for Cabinet the Department of the Interior implied that approvals for British Jews should be kept subject to federal oversight and at the discretion of the minister.[13]

The second half of 1938 saw extensive comment throughout Australia regarding the "undesirable" aspects of foreign (but not British) Jews.[14] Some opponents focused their concerns on the economic consequences of Jewish refugees; for others, the issue was one of race. Rarely, however, were antisemitic expressions directed toward Judaism as a religion. The appearance in significant numbers of protest letters sent to the press or government ministers in mid-1938 indicates the extent to which the refugee issue dominated the thinking of a vocal group of Australians. By the middle of 1938 several sectors of the community were directing the government's attention to the fact that feeling was growing very strongly against what seemed to be the wholesale arrival of what were deemed to be "undesirable aliens."

Against such negative statements, advocates of refugee immigration found themselves fighting a losing battle. The ingress into Australia up to mid-1938 was still relatively slight, but the potential menace of unspecified numbers of non-English-speaking foreigners pouring into Australia provoked an increasingly negative reaction. And until the government provided the public with a clear direction on how it was going to confront this issue, it seemed as though such disquiet would intensify. The task of enlightening the population fell to the Department of the Interior. The minister, John McEwen, handed the task to his assistant minister, Victor Thompson.

A member of the rural-based Country Party, which governed as the junior member in the conservative coalition government dominated by the United Australia Party, Victor Thompson was born in Sydney on September 10, 1885. From 1919 onward he was instrumental in the Northern New State secessionist movement in New South Wales, focusing on the New England region. In this endeavor he worked closely with Dr. Earle Page, founder of the Country Party, and was rewarded in December 1922 by election to Parliament as the member for New England. Serving on several parliamentary committees, he was Country Party whip and parliamentary secretary between 1934 and 1937. From 1937 to 1940 he was assistant minister to the treasurer and the minister for Repatriation, Commerce, and the Interior;

in this latter capacity he had much of the work relating to Jewish refugee migration delegated in his direction.[15]

When handed the brief to consolidate all information regarding the current state of the Jewish refugee situation, he decided it would first be best to clarify just where the alien immigration issue stood at that time. In a memorandum dated August 17, 1938, he outlined several matters for Cabinet's information: precisely where Australia's immigration intake was heading; who was coming into the country; how they were being admitted; and what the overall consequences of their presence might be.[16] This key document, purportedly dealing with alien migration generally, concentrated only on two groups: southern Europeans and Jews. Its intention was to allay any fears Cabinet members may have had about the number of "undesirables" coming to Australia.

Indicative of the limited extent to which Interior recognized the gravity of the situation is the fact that German Jews were even now not yet viewed as refugees with a legitimate and desperate need for protection but remained on the same level as other immigrants. The memorandum made no reference to their plight, other than to refer to "many of the Jewish applicants [who] are under the necessity of leaving Austria or Germany at an early date."[17] There was neither a sense of urgency nor a desire to alleviate distress. In the entire memorandum there was not a single reference to Jews as "refugees." They were simply "Jewish residents of Europe."[18]

Thompson recounted the various ways in which German Jews were being permitted to enter Australia: 500 annually who had been handed over to the government-approved Australian Jewish Welfare Society (AJWS), which would, after investigating their cases, provide guarantees on their behalf; approximately 1,000 annually guaranteed by individual relatives or friends already resident in Australia; and a scheme allowing entry to 300 without guarantees per month, provided they possessed at least £200 landing capital. This made for a potential yearly total (never realized) of 5,100 Jews from Germany.

Of these, Thompson noted, the last category—independent non-guaranteed migrants who fitted all the government's entrance criteria—created "a difficult position." The rate of applications was so great, he wrote, that it was "necessary to defer or reject many applications *which would have been considered satisfactory if the necessity had not arisen to limit the number of approvals.*" With vast numbers of people applying for entry, "under present conditions . . . only about *one in ten* applications can be approved."[19] In other words, 90 percent of eligible applications were being rejected.[20] The position had intensified since Austria's *Anschluss* (union) with Germany, which brought the full weight of Nazi antisemitism to bear against the Austrian Jewish community. This saw a rise in applications to over five hundred per week. Considering this—a situation in which nine out of every ten Jewish applicants who met government criteria for entry, and would normally have been acceptable, were now being rejected—Thompson was satisfied that the existing safeguards were holding firm. The present position would, of course, need to be watched "very carefully" in the future, though for the present the percentage of Jews in Australia was only about 0.35 percent.[21]

Still, the pressure being exerted upon the Department of the Interior by large numbers of applications from non-guaranteed Jews gave rise to a concern that the officials were losing the battle to deal with everybody fairly. Their task was not being made any easier, Thompson added, by the "numerous enquiries and representations from Members of Parliament, solicitors and others who have been urged to make such enquiries and representations on behalf of the applicants." New staffing proposals for the department had been drawn up and approved some time ago; but when they were being considered, "it was not contemplated that so many people in Australia would be taking up the cases of the Jews and making representations to the Department."[22] Reassessing the situation, the department's Immigration Branch was expanded after August 1938 to facilitate the handling of increased refugee applications.

The overall challenge before the policymakers was thus a steep one. After weighing the pros and cons, the government took a position allowing the entry of some Jewish refugees, while refusing the entry of most of those who applied to be admitted. In doing so, it was held, Australia would not be seen as renouncing its humanitarian obligations, and the nation's racial composition would remain essentially intact. Unquestionably the government adopted racial criteria when determining its policy. Its solution was to carry out a covert policy of discrimination against Jewish admissions, in which the bureaucracy played a major role in shaping and executing policy decisions.

Alert to the possibility of being forced to expand its intake owing to pressure from overseas (read, Britain), Jewish immigration intakes increased after December 1, 1938—but it is highly questionable whether the increase was matched in understanding or compassion.[23] On the surface, there was no reason it should have. The refugees were still foreign, still Jewish, and still applying to come in what were seen as alarming numbers. No government could hope to legislate tolerance or approval; that could only come through wholehearted commitment and an intensive education program, but no one in the Australian power elite possessed that level of foresight. Multiculturalism was yet to arrive as an ideal; indeed, it took another four decades before being introduced, and even after that it took generational change to be accepted.[24] The policy of the Australian government was ungenerous when it began in 1933 and remained so throughout the prewar period.

As mentioned, public opinion was vitally important in helping the government to chart its course over the refugee issue. Just how far positive forces may have come into their own had the government pursued a policy of openness and welcome can, of course, never be ascertained, but the potential for positive action was far from promising as war clouds loomed in the autumn of 1939.

Several events were to play out in the months following Victor Thompson's memorandum of August 1938, notably a bogus "liberalization" of refugee migration policy by the federal government on December 1, 1938, according to which fifteen thousand refugees would be admitted over the next three years. Not all were Jews, it must be pointed out, though it is often mistakenly believed that this was the case.[25]

Regardless of the applicant's origin or circumstances, however, all applications for foreign immigration to Australia had to be filled out on one of two official forms. Form 40 ("Application for Admission of Relative or Friend to Australia") was submitted by an Australian resident guaranteeing an immigrant's maintenance after arrival. Form 47 ("Application for Permit to Enter Australia") was to be completed by all non-guaranteed intending migrants. In a bolt from the blue in March or early April 1939, however, both forms were revised so that all intending immigrants, from anywhere other than the British Empire, had to state whether they were "of Jewish race." It is not altogether clear why the change was made. It is likely that the increase in applications for entry following the *Anschluss* led to officials in the Department of the Interior seeking a way to reduce the inflow by a clear means of identification, though there is no evidence of this having been articulated in government documents.

The timing of the amendment was crucial, with Europe's Jews more dependent than ever on impartiality. Some government officials responded negatively to the new form. Inspector Roland S. Browne of the Commonwealth Investigation Branch (Australia's federal security agency), for one, considered the Department of the Interior's position thoroughly unjustifiable and possibly even unconstitutional. He suggested that if the department wanted to elicit certain information from the applicants it should simply ask what race the person in question was. Browne was concerned that the amendment would "raise a controversy as to what is the Jewish race," as even "eminent scientists hold that the Jewish race is a myth."²⁶ Would Australia, he asked, "be about to accept Hitler's definition of a Jew?" This would be nonsensical: there are "thousands of mixed marriages among the refugees, and the Jews are as mixed a crowd as the English." Browne recorded that the amendment was

> an amazing and disquieting departure, for a Government form, and the question is impossible to answer in a great number of cases, that is answered with any degree of authority. . . . If such discrimination is to be shown, will the Department go a step further and logically define what is the Jewish race? I should think even the most ardent Nazi will praise the author of this form, who, modest in the fame which his work brings, may desire to add a new line such as "Roman Catholic or not," or "Salvation Army or not."²⁷

He concluded with the hope that "for the sake of Australia's good name" the form would be immediately withdrawn, as "it is monstrous, offensive, quite absurd and provocative."²⁸

The director of the Commonwealth Investigation Branch, Colonel Harold Jones, took up the issue with the Department of the Interior and had a reply within a week showing that the department had already reconsidered its position. He was informed that as exception had been taken by some members of the Jewish community to the use of the words "Jewish race," the words "of" and "race" were henceforth to be crossed out on the forms already distributed, so that the phrase read simply "is/is not Jewish."²⁹ This change in procedure was to commence forthwith.

Prior to this, the Australian Jewish Welfare Society (AJWS) had already drawn attention to the "numerous protests" it had received from members of the Jewish community in Victoria and New South Wales, "who have taken great exception to the words 'JEWISH RACE.' They are most emphatic in their protests and wish to point out that they are BRITISH SUBJECTS of JEWISH FAITH, and the word 'RACE' especially, is most obnoxious to them."³⁰ The department backed down immediately, informing the AJWS that "it will be arranged for the word 'RACE' to be deleted and the form amended to read simply 'is/is not Jewish.'"³¹ This was sufficient for the AJWS, which neither broached the subject again nor demonstrated any objection to the continued employment of the discriminatory categorization. Its only objection was that Jews were being classified as a "race"; there was no opposition to the general idea of a Jewish identifier appearing on immigration forms, as the AJWS saw benefits to the selection process if Jewish applications could be known in advance.

The motives of the officials in the Department of the Interior, however, must be viewed critically. It was they who drew up the forms and put them into operation. With the move to insert the "Jewish race" clause arising at a time when the main aim of the department was seeking ways of reducing (or at least slowing) refugee admission, we must question the amendment. Until the introduction of the new forms there was no fixed way of ascertaining whether an applicant was Jewish: the forms as altered now required any white person desiring to migrate to Australia—from Europe, the United States, European territories abroad, or anywhere else—to state whether he or she was (or was not) "racially" Jewish.

The question as to how far the Jewish race clause was discriminatory is open to debate. While it might have been introduced to facilitate the entry of Jews to Australia, it also had a terrible potential to be used negatively. In sum, a conclusion can be drawn that the Department of the Interior tried to camouflage its obviously discriminatory ploy by the subterfuge of trying to ease refugee admissions. The clause was, moreover, retained until November 1952, at a time of booming postwar immigration. Any discussion of this, however, should not overlook its overtly racist foundation back in 1939.

In August 1938 Victor Thompson established that only about 10 percent of applications from non-guaranteed refugees were being accepted, emphasizing that this was not because the applications were in any way deficient. Soon after this Minister John McEwen declared that refugees were being refused entry to Australia because they were "not able to comply with the standards we set for white aliens," even though the Department of the Interior had already agreed that many Jewish refugees met the prescribed standards.[32] McEwen knew this but misled Parliament into believing that only those refugees who did not meet the government's standards were being denied permission to enter—when in fact the Department of the Interior was seeing to it that over 90 percent of applicants who met the government's prescribed standards were being refused permits. The minister's statements were accepted without question and in good faith.

As the refugee immigration issue was not one in which politicians generally sought to become embroiled, the Department of the Interior was effectively left to administer policy unhampered, and it took a stronger and stronger grip on the Jewish issue until the point was reached where *any* refugee matter—from immigration to security to employment to external relations—was passed through it as a matter of course. The implications of this position, as the prewar period gave way to the most devastating conflict in history, remained to be seen, though the portents throughout 1938 and 1939 of Australia as a haven for the persecuted Jews of Germany looked very dark indeed. It was clear that those who managed to arrive did so despite the government's best efforts, not because of them.

Notes

1. "Admi. of German Jews—Cabinet Decision Re.," Interior memorandum for Cabinet, handwritten minutes from Sir George Pearce for Prime Minister, June 2, 1933, National Archives of Australia (hereafter NAA), A434, file 49/3/7034.
2. For a general survey, see Andrew Markus, *Australian Race Relations, 1788–1993* (Sydney: Allen and Unwin Australia, 1994).
3. A good early study of the Great Depression in Australia is C. B. Schedvin, *Australia and the Great Depression: A Study of Economic Development and Policy in the 1920's and 1930's* (Sydney: Sydney University Press, 1970).
4. As an example, the relationship between Jews and non-Jews in late colonial Victoria has been traced. See Frank Fletcher, "The Victorian Jewish Community, 1891–1901: Its Relationship with the Majority Gentile Society," *Australian Jewish Historical Society Journal and Proceedings* 8, no. 5 (July 1978): 221–71.
5. A detailed account of the early period can be found in Suzanne D. Rutland, *Edge of the Diaspora: Two Centuries of Jewish Settlement in Australia* (Sydney: Collins Australia, 1988), chaps. 1–6.
6. See Paul R. Bartrop, *The Holocaust and Australia: Refugees, Rejection, and Memory* (London: Bloomsbury, 2022); also Michael Blakeney, *Australia and the Jewish Refugees, 1933–1948* (Sydney: Croom Helm Australia, 1985).
7. For a discussion of one expression of this, see Paul R. Bartrop, "'Not a Problem for Australia': The *Kristallnacht* Viewed from the Commonwealth, November 1938," *Journal of the Australian Jewish Historical Society* 10, no. 6 (May 1989): 489–99. Also see Kim Richard Nossal, "'No Repercussions Down Under?' Australian Responses to *Kristallnacht*," in *Violence, Memory, and History: Western Perceptions of Kristallnacht*, ed. Colin McCullough and Nathan Wilson (New York: Routledge, 2015), 130–50.
8. See Paul R. Bartrop, "Foreign Immigration between the Wars: The Role of the Public Service," in *Towards National Administration: Studies in Australian Administrative History*, ed. J. J. Eddy and J. R. Nethercote (Sydney: Hale and Iremonger, 1994), 157–67.
9. For a general introduction, see Paul R. Bartrop, *The Evian Conference of 1938 and the Jewish Refugee Crisis* (London: Palgrave Macmillan, 2018), quote on 72. It has often been stated that at Evian, White committed Australia to accepting a quota of fifteen thousand Jewish refugees over a three-year period. This has been disproven conclusively in Bartrop, *Holocaust and Australia*, chap. 4.
10. "Immigration Encouragement: Landing Money," Prime Minister's Department memorandum (*White Alien Immigration*), July 27, 1938, NAA, A461, file G349/1/2.
11. "Immigration Encouragement."

12. "Immigration Encouragement."
13. "Jews (British Subjects) Resident in the U.K. Assisted Passages For," Interior memorandum for Cabinet (*Jews [British Subjects] Resident in the United Kingdom—Question as to whether they should be granted assisted passages*) prepared by V. C. Thompson, August 29, 1938, NAA, A1, file 38/30786.
14. See, for example, letters protesting Jewish immigration in "Protests re. Jewish Immigration," NAA, A455, file 235/5/6.
15. John Atchison, "Thompson, Charles Victor (1885–1968)," *Australian Dictionary of Biography*, accessed November 21, 2021, https://adb.anu.edu.au/biography/thompson-charles-victor-8782/text15397.
16. "Refugees (Jewish and Others)—General Policy File," Interior memorandum for Cabinet (*Immigration*) prepared by V. C. Thompson, August 17, 1938, NAA, A433, file 43/2/46.
17. "Refugees (Jewish and Others)."
18. "Refugees (Jewish and Others)."
19. "Refugees (Jewish and Others)"; emphasis added.
20. "Refugees (Jewish and Others)." By July 1939 approvals had risen to 20 percent: an improvement, certainly, but one that still excluded 80 percent of those eligible to land under existing government criteria for all immigrants (*The Argus*, July 25, 1939, 9).
21. "Refugees (Jewish and Others)."
22. "Refugees (Jewish and Others)."
23. A figure of perhaps 2,500 Jewish admissions can be calculated between 1933 and 1938. It is difficult to be more precise than this given that the government did not keep records identifying immigrants as Jews or non-Jews. From December 1, 1938, after which exact figures were kept, 5,080 Jews entered the country. See Paul R. Bartrop, *Australia and the Holocaust* (Melbourne: Australian Scholarly Publishing, 1994), 246, 277n114.
24. See, for example, Klaus Neumann, *Across the Seas: Australia's Response to Refugees: A History* (Melbourne: Black, 2015); also see Andrew Jakubowicz and Christina Ho, eds., *"For Those Who've Come across the Seas . . .": Australian Multicultural Theory, Policy and Practice* (Melbourne: Australian Scholarly Publishing, 2013).
25. This has been discussed in depth in Paul R. Bartrop, "The Australian Government's 'Liberalisation' of Refugee Immigration Policy in 1938: Fact or Myth?" *Menorah: Australian Journal of Jewish Studies* 2, no. 1 (June 1988): 66–82.
26. Inspector Roland S. Browne to Director, Commonwealth Investigation Branch, April 19, 1939, NAA, A367, file C3075, "Miscellaneous: Admission of Aliens, Forms, Instructions, etc."
27. Browne to Director.
28. Browne to Director.
29. Interior memorandum (*Applications by Persons Resident in Australia for the Admission of Alien Relatives or Friends—Form No. 40*) prepared by A. R. Peters for Director, Commonwealth Investigation Branch, April 26, 1939, NAA, A367, file C3075.

30. Frank Silverman to A. R. Peters, April 21, 1939, NAA, A445, file 235/5/9, "Alleged Discrimination against Admission of Jews [question of Jewish or not on Dep. I Forms]"; emphasis in text.
31. J. A. Carrodus to Frank Silverman, April 27, 1939, NAA, A445, file 235/5/9.
32. Commonwealth Parliamentary Debates, House of Representatives, vol. 158, November 22, 1938, 1851.

10

Reviewing the Past, Re-Viewing the Nation
Early Canadian Responses to Abella and Troper's *None Is Too Many*

RICHARD MENKIS

From the moment of its publication in September 1982, *None Is Too Many: Canada and the Jews of Europe, 1933–1948* (*NITM*) by Irving Abella and Harold Troper became *the* book that explored the intersection between the Holocaust and Canadian history. The first hardcover edition of the book sold out within three weeks of its printing and was reviewed widely. By October it began to appear on bestseller lists. One of CBC radio's most influential broadcasters, Peter Gzowski, featured Abella and Troper for an almost unheard of week of interviews on his program *Morningside*. The authors delivered lectures across the country, leading to more newspaper articles and interviews about the book. The publisher, Lester & Orpen Dennys, issued a second and third printing in the next year and sold over ten thousand copies in Canada.[1]

The volume's fame also reached into the United States. In early 1983 the *New York Times* featured an article on the runaway success of the book in Canada.[2] Later that month the international Jewish Telegraphic Agency reviewed the book, and the article was picked up by Jewish newspapers and magazines in the United States and elsewhere. In that same year Random House came out with an American edition of the book, and Lester & Orpen Dennys issued it in paperback format, both leading to more reviews. By late 1983 the book had also won two distinguished awards. The Canadian Historical Association awarded to *NITM* its prize for best book in Canadian history to appear in 1982, and the New York–based Jewish Book Council conferred on the volume a National Jewish Book Award in the category of books relating to the Holocaust.

This chapter uses the high profile of *NITM* to explore debates on the Canadian past and their implications for the Canada of the 1980s. Samuel Moyn's excellent study of the controversies over Jean-François Steiner's *Treblinka: The Revolt of an Extermination Camp* demonstrates the rich potential of studying the reception of a popular book.[3] *NITM* was more embraced than disputed, at least in the first years after its publication. Academics and nonacademics almost universally praised the work for the thoroughness of its research in support of its provocative thesis. Nevertheless, reviewers and other writers disagreed with Abella and Troper, and each other, on aspects of the actions and attitudes of Canadians regarding Jewish refugees and immigration between 1933 and 1948. In this chapter I draw on Canadian reviews of the book in the first few years after publication to explore how critics offered a variety of understandings of Canadian behavior during the Nazi era, and I invite readers to reexamine their assumptions about the past, and present, of Canada.[4]

Background: Canada and Its Jewish Community

As if focusing a camera, Abella and Troper's *None Is Too Many* brought two separate images together. One was of a Canada in the throes of a reinvention, including in its exploration of new approaches in the management of its linguistic, cultural, and ethnic diversity. The other was of a Canadian Jewish community that was moving the memory of the Holocaust from the periphery to the center of communal life and identity. In order to examine the immediate reactions to the book, and their impact on the self-definitions of Canada and its Jews in the early 1980s, we first need to appreciate the evolution of each of those images.

The economic and population transformations after the Second World War were a surprise to many Canadians. In the wake of the First World War, discontented workers and returning soldiers clashed with authorities, the most notable confrontation being the Winnipeg General Strike of 1919, which was about collective bargaining among other issues. In the interwar period, the Canadian government doubled down on the policy of preferring agricultural workers to other immigrants and viewing some potential immigrants—such as the Jews—as potential leftist political troublemakers. But several years after the Second World War, at the urging of industrialists, Canada looked to populate its cities and to do so with new kinds of workers.[5]

Canada also distanced itself from Great Britain, culturally and politically. Not everybody was keen on this change, with some of the most intense confrontations taking place during the Flag Debate in the 1960s. Much to the chagrin of many Canadians, the Liberal government dropped the Union Jack from the Canadian flag, to be replaced by a single red maple leaf bounded by red bars on either side.[6] Another major signpost of a new era, which was much more than symbolic, occurred in 1982, when Canada "patriated" its constitution, placing all legislative power in the hands of the federal and provincial governments and out of the authority of the British Parliament.

Of the many changes in postwar Canada, some of the most significant had to do with interethnic relations. In the 1950s a number of groups, including the Jews, used the courts and political lobbying to challenge unfair practices in employment and housing.[7] They also opposed the restrictions that supposedly did not exist at "exclusive" social and sport clubs.[8] Anglo-Canada was also forced to acknowledge that French Canada had legitimate discontents with Canada. In the early 1960s French Canada was in the midst of its "Quiet Revolution," which looked to create a new nationalism and minimize the role of the Catholic church and the right-wing politics that had dominated postwar Quebec. They pressed the federal government for greater protection of the French language and cultures. The Royal Commission on Bilingualism and Biculturalism, established in 1963, identified many areas that required greater legal recognition and support of French language in the federal government and beyond.[9]

The Royal Commission also responded to pressure from below for recognition of the ethnic minorities within Canada. The government thus called on the commission to take into account "the cultural contribution made by the other ethnic groups to the cultural enrichment of Canada and the measures that should be taken to safeguard that contribution."[10] In 1971 Prime Minister Pierre Elliot Trudeau introduced a policy to support multiculturalism within a bilingual framework. The policy encouraged the study of minority groups by the widening of the holdings of its national library and archives and by supporting the publication of works on and by these minorities. Beyond its rather practical impact, scholars Harold Troper and Morton Weinfeld insist that the symbolic recognition of ethnic groups was significant and became part of the national myth of Canadian multiculturalism, often contrasted to the American "melting pot."[11] They also point out that numerous groups were suspicious of the ability of the policy and myth to challenge racist policies and promote a just society. These problems were on the minds of both people and legislators, and in 1982 (the same year as the publication as *NITM*), the Canadian Charter of Rights and Freedoms was entrenched in the newly "patriated" Constitution of Canada. The charter includes a section (27) that did not directly confer rights but provided guidance for its interpretation, stipulating that the charter "shall be interpreted in a manner consistent with the preservation and enhancement of the multicultural heritage of Canadians."[12]

Canadian Jews faced this shifting Canada while negotiating, inter alia, the social and cultural impacts of the Holocaust. When Canada loosened its restrictions on immigration in the late 1940s, refugees from the Holocaust found a home in Canada. Many arrived on immigration schemes for Jewish orphans and occupational groups, such as tailors. In the early years others arrived in Canada to join already-established family members, and after 1950 the doors were opened without the same restrictions.[13] With an estimated thirty-five thousand coming to Canada in the decade after the end of the war, approximately 15 percent of the total Jewish population were survivors, a large number in comparison to most other communities. In the United States, for example, survivors comprised about 4 percent of the Jewish population.

Although the survivors were not a homogeneous group, they all shared a deep sense of loss and struggled with ways to cope with those losses. Many survivors looked for public support from other members of the Jewish community. Survivors came together with other survivors and with Jews from the same town in Eastern Europe in their *lansmanshaftn* (aid or benefit societies) for special programs and to create, with *landsmen* in other countries, memorial books or *yizkerbikher*. During the 1950s there were also public events, when survivors and non-survivors came together in acts of commemoration, as on the anniversaries of the Warsaw Ghetto Uprising.

But the memory of the Holocaust had only limited impact on the Jewish public sphere in the 1950s. After the war the so-called Parliament of Canadian Jewry—the Canadian Jewish Congress (CJC)—was actively involved in numerous political and cultural questions. According to historians Irving Abella and Franklin Bialystok, throughout the 1950s only two resolutions explicitly connected to the Holocaust were made at its general assembly (at the assembly of 1993, in contrast, ten of the fifty resolutions were related to the Holocaust).[14]

International and national events changed the dynamic within the Jewish community in the 1960s and affected the salience of the Holocaust within Canadian Jewish life. The capture of Adolf Eichmann and his trial in Israel in 1961 brought details of the Holocaust, and the stories of the victims, to a wider audience than ever before and affected survivors and non-survivors alike. Other events were often divisive. Survivors reacted with horror and anger at evidence of new Nazi vitality. During Christmas 1959 synagogues in Germany were defaced with swastikas, and the decade began ominously for Jews around the world, as in the first two weeks of January similar desecrations had occurred in twenty-five countries, including Canada.[15] Neo-Nazi activism seemed on the uptick, and later that year Canada's state-supported national broadcaster, the Canadian Broadcasting Corporation (CBC), chose to conduct a long television interview with

American neo-Nazi George Lincoln Rockwell. In Canada small groups of neo-Nazis became more vocal and distributed various types of antisemitic propaganda, and in 1965 a group in Toronto announced that it would hold a rally at a local park. Although CJC worked behind the scenes to infiltrate the neo-Nazis and played an important role in documenting antisemitism and encouraging legislation against hate propaganda, it also advised against public displays of protest.[16] Many in the survivor community viewed the reactions of the non-survivor community as inadequate and patronizing, and they created their own organizations to challenge CJC's judgment and leadership on these issues. The relatively large survivor community, in short, was asserting itself.[17]

Some of the tensions persisted into the early 1970s and beyond. A number of survivors continued to criticize the established community for being weak in its fight against antisemitism or for not exerting enough pressure on the Canadian government to search for Nazi war criminals within its borders. However, by the mid-1970s the CJC leadership began to include more survivors in its ranks. Moreover, the importance of the Holocaust in the community's agenda was acknowledged by the creation of a variety of committees, including the National Holocaust Remembrance Committee, established in 1973, which, according to historian Franklin Bialystok, quickly became "the locus of Holocaust education and commemoration."[18] Popular culture, however, far outstripped the reach of educational and commemorative programs. While critics and historians lambasted the 1978 TV miniseries *The Holocaust*, it was watched by millions around the world, including in Canada. Even its detractors had to admit that the show raised questions, including: Why wasn't the educational system doing a better job in the education of Canadian children, as evidenced by the inadequacy of the country's textbooks? Around the same time historians of the United States and Great Britain asked another relevant question: What was the rest of the world doing as the Holocaust was unfolding in Europe?

The Authors and the Book

Irving Abella and Harold Troper belonged to a new generation of Canadian historians, with new concerns. Abella studied labor history, and Troper worked on immigration history. The first installment of *NITM* appeared as an article in the *Canadian Historical Review* in 1979.[19] By bringing together immigration history and policy with the history and activities of a minority group, Abella and Troper's article satisfied the demand of the editors for historical pieces that went beyond an older political history.[20] The authors also benefited from new developments in archival collecting policies. As a result of a new federal policy of multiculturalism introduced in 1971, the Public Archives of Canada began to collect and preserve the records of previously marginalized ethnic minorities. At the same time, Jewish agencies supported community-based archives.[21] These new collections, in addition to the government records, allowed Abella and Troper to describe and analyze the interactions of the Jewish community with politicians and bureaucrats.

Using this wide array of records, *NITM* examines Canadian responses to the plight of Jewish refugees from the time that the Nazis came to power in 1933 until several years after the war. Canada's restrictive policy toward Jewish immigration had already been in place in the mid-1920s, when Canada joined the United States and other countries in reducing Jewish immigration to a trickle. Canada prioritized immigrants who farmed or worked in the forests or mines. There were also national and ethnic preferences. British and American emigrants were favored, followed by immigrants from Scandinavia. Below them were immigrants from eastern and southern Europe. The losers of these "racial sweepstakes" were immigrants from Asia as well as Jews. An individual in these "non-preferred" categories could arrive only under a special order-in-council. Getting one was a political process requiring cabinet approval.

NITM narrates how Canada kept these restrictions in place from the time Hitler came to power in early 1933 until several years after the war. Before the war Jews could legally emigrate from Nazi Germany, but they needed a place to go. Canada was not a choice. During the war there were several rescue schemes to help Jews who might be rescued from the Nazis, as well as to help Jewish refugees who had already escaped from Nazi-occupied territories, but again they needed a place to go. After the war the few surviving Jews—especially in displaced persons camps—hoped to rebuild their lives. Canada, however, did not ease restrictions until three years after the war, when industry clamored for workers, and the technocrats and politicians rejected the priorities of the previous generation.

Canada was not the only country to shut its doors. The Jews of Nazi-occupied Europe could find few countries willing to offer help. Abella and Troper, however, consider Canada's record to be one of the worst. They estimate that only five thousand Jews were allowed to immigrate to Canada between 1933 and 1945, and another eight thousand between 1945 and 1948. Regarding these figures, they conclude, "That record is arguably the worst of all possible refugee-receiving states."[22]

The book describes and analyzes the interactions of Canadian Jewry with civil servants and federal politicians. Once the book was reviewed, historiographic issues emerged in the discussions of each group. Did the Jewish community use all its resources to challenge government policy, and did it use those resources wisely? Were the civil servants simply the implementers of government policy, or did they have their own views and the "space" to promote their agenda? What was the role of antisemitism in the framing of government policy? Each of the debates on these issues will be discussed at length in a future publication. In this chapter I summarize the debates, especially over the last two questions, as they lead directly to the broader question that concludes this essay: How did these evaluations affect understandings of Canada, both past and present?

Reviewing the Actors

Abella and Troper give a full accounting of the strategies and strenuous actions of the Canadian Jewish community, especially the umbrella organization Canadian Jewish Congress. The authors also assert that the community's aspirations were very far from achieving changes in policy: "It is, therefore, a harsh but undeniable conclusion that the Jewish community—no matter what it did ... could never get more than the government ... was prepared to give, which was never much."[23] The authors find no fault in the community and warn against anachronistically calling on the marginalized Jews of the 1930s and 1940s to wield late twentieth-century tactics. Most of the reviewers agreed with that assessment. Some did so conscious of a debate south of the border about the tactics of the Jewish establishment toward the Roosevelt administration. They sided with historian Henry L. Feingold, who had argued in 1979 that "a close perusal would indicate that virtually every means of public pressure ... [were] used by American Jewry during the war years to bring their message to American political leaders."[24] There were, however, some on the formerly pro-Soviet communist left who found the intercessions of the established Jewish community to be ineffective, elitist, and obsequious.[25]

Civil servants figure prominently in *NITM*, with the most prominent and notorious being Frederick Charles Blair (1874–1959). As director of the Immigration Branch of the Department of Mines and Resources between 1936 and 1943, he ensured that the number of Jews admitted to Canada was kept to a bare minimum. Drawing from the correspondence of Blair with colleagues, Abella and Troper establish that Blair harbored antisemitic views that energized his resolve to keep Jews out of Canada.

Several reviews explore the relationship between Blair and the politicians, the "space" Blair had to act in, and how he used it. According to political scientist Gerald E. Dirks, "The ability of one senior public servant to manage a policy, a minister, and even at times the prime minister, has seldom been as well documented."[26] Sandford F. Borins, a scholar of public management, uses his understanding of government administration to detail how a civil servant could pursue his own course of action. Borins pulls out from *NITM* a number of initiatives and tactics used by Blair: he examined files himself; he duped his minister into tightening immigration rules when the minister thought he was loosening them; he put off the processing of files; he interpreted regulations narrowly; and he told his political masters that immigration during war would undercut the government's need to focus on a victory. Borins then flips the script and states what a different and more benevolent civil servant could have done.[27] For Borins, civil servants have choices and the tools to actualize their choices.

The portrayal of civil servants in the book and in subsequent reviews prompted a backlash. Jack Granatstein reports in a 1984 review that "Abella and Troper's charges against civil servants have stirred up some controversy."[28] Granatstein challenges Abella and Troper and de-emphasizes the agency of the bureaucrats (and unlike most other reviewers, he does not mention Blair by name). He indicates that the authors may have quoted and cited the bureaucrats accurately, but they did not acknowledge that civil servants were overworked, handling multiple files, and focused on doing the bidding of the politicians.[29] At least one other reviewer also softens the portrayal of the civil service by only naming one of the few civil servants who showed some benevolence toward Jews and then quoting him at length.[30] Other reviewers point to civil servants who behaved differently than Blair, but they also warn against the temptation to soften the image of the civil service with these exceptions.[31]

Of all the groups, the prime minister and his cabinet exercised the greatest control over immigration and refugee policies. They could change the restrictions by regulation, and within the existing framework they could issue orders-in-council. William Lyon Mackenzie King and his Liberal Party governed during the period covered in the book, with the exception of 1933–35, and King was the prime minister until November 1948. The members of the cabinet who figure most prominently in the book are Thomas Crerar and Ernest Lapointe. Crerar was minister of mines and resources, which was the ministry responsible for immigration. Abella and Troper portray him as weak, moved occasionally to suggest a more liberal policy, but easily brought back into line by the civil servants in his department (especially the aforementioned Blair) and by King. Lapointe was the minister of justice and served as King's "Quebec lieutenant." This followed the tradition of Anglophone prime ministers relying on a prominent francophone cabinet minister from Quebec to advise on the opinions of French Canada regarding government policies. Abella and Troper stress that Lapointe warned King that French Canada had no interest in opening up immigration, especially to Jews.

Abella and Troper argue that any evaluation of the politics of immigration by King and his cabinet must acknowledge domestic concerns, such as high unemployment during the Depression. Nevertheless, the authors emphasize that antisemitism, among the politicians and their electorate, played a crucial role. King himself was known to express concerns over racial mixing in Canada, and the system of immigration encoded racialization, including antisemitism. Abella and Troper list several elected officials who tried to offer an alternative view, especially those in the small socialist Co-operative Commonwealth Federation (CCF). But the authors also indicate that there were few counterweights to the attitudes toward Jews and Jewish migration. They called the churches "silent," a perspective that several historians later scrutinized carefully.[32]

Not all the reviewers agreed with Abella and Troper's discussions of the role of antisemitism. Dirks, who authored an earlier work on immigration, argues: "Self-interest caused Canadians to perceive the shattered Canadian economy as a more immediate priority than the oppressive laws of a far-off European government."[33] Another group of reviewers emphasize Canadian preparation for World War II as evidence of motivations other than antisemitism. While praising the thoroughness of the archival research of the book and acknowledging the tragic consequences of the Canadian policies, Jack Granatstein complains that Abella and Troper come up short when trying to explain why events unfolded as they did. He argues that the government was not prepared to compromise the war effort: "The simple fact is that the politicians and bureaucrats had decided that their aim had to be to bring a united Canada into the coming war against Hitler. If letting Jews in created tensions in Quebec and elsewhere in Canada, that was too high a price."[34] This response, however, is problematic. The book discusses Canadian hierarchical policies that preexisted the rise of Hitler. It also deals with the responses to the first years of the Nazi regime, before it was clear to anyone that there was a "coming war against Hitler," as well as the period after the war. Granatstein's critique is problematic and is discussed further in the final section of the chapter.

Specialists in the history of Quebec took special note of Abella and Troper's presentation of antisemitism in that province. An early (and ongoing) critic of NITM is anthropologist and historian Pierre Anctil.[35] In his review he praises the authors for their research and analysis and does not deny that there were some antisemites in Quebec. He argues, however, that Abella and Troper do not understand French Canada's reactions. The responses of Quebecers, he insists, have to be understood as those of a vulnerable minority (like the Jews) within Canada and with limited political power. He complains that the authors examined antisemitism with secondary sources and through the eyes of CJC documentation, at a time when CJC and French Canada had no real contacts and very limited mutual understanding.[36]

Other historians specializing in Quebec's history, however, were inclined to agree with Abella and Troper. Historians Marie Poirier and Frédéric Seager accept that antisemitism was a potent force in Quebec.[37] They allude to the hostility of the Quebec press toward Jewish refugees and immigration. The exception was the weekly *Le Jour*, established in 1937 by the fiercely independent Jean-Charles Harvey. Laval University historian Richard Jones, who is the author of a seminal work examining the ideology of the major Catholic daily newspaper *L'Action catholique*, offers the fullest exploration of the issue. While he suggests that Abella and Troper could have devoted more attention to the question of antisemitism in Quebec, he uses his extended review to provide evidence of antisemitism in Quebec in its anti-liberal Catholic Church and among its Catholic intellectuals. Their views may not have been as virulent as the Nazism of Adrien Arcand, but "all these people saw themselves as opinion-makers and moulders, and to them Jewish immigration was anathema."[38]

Re-Viewing the Nation

The reviewers largely addressed the implications of NITM without reference to specific contemporary events. There were, however, some exceptions. The book appeared several months after the beginning of the 1982 war between Lebanon and Israel. The massacre of Palestinians by Israel's allies in Sabra and Shatila occurred in the same month the book was published. Some members of the Jewish community, and some reviewers of NITM, thought the press coverage of events was antisemitic.[39] The book also appeared when the issue of Nazi war criminals in Canada was getting some press. Canada had finally arrested one of them, Helmut Rauca, in June 1982 and deported him to Germany five months later.[40] It seemed a sad truth that some Nazi war criminals had a clear path to Canada, while immigration restrictions were in place for Jews. It is possible that the salience of these immediate events influenced the sales of the book, and that some of the reviews were indirectly responding to them. However, the reviews mostly addressed the more general question: What should we think and feel about Canada in response to the findings of the book?

Reviewers in English Canada presented the book as a challenge to national complacency and to self-images of Canada as a land of tolerance. The headlines—often the creations of the newspaper or magazine staff, and not necessarily of the authors—framed the articles for the readers. Many incorporated the language of a trial, including "indictment," "authors charge," and "complicity." Many of the reviewers accepted the evidence and delivered a verdict of guilty. E. D. Ward-Harris, writing for the *Time Colonist* in Victoria, British Columbia, re-creates an internal dialogue where he evaluates the "case" made by the authors. First, he lists all the ethnic groups in the postwar "mosaic" of Canada, as well the postwar waves of immigrants and refugees. With that is evidence for Canada's tolerance: "'Come off it fellows' . . . I said to myself, 'Canada doesn't operate that way and never has and if you want to shatter my belief you had better be convincing.'" After the first few pages, he is willing to concede that the authors have a "tenable case," and after several chapters: "I was utterly convinced their case was unassailable."[41]

Many reviewers agreed with Ward-Harris. "Destroyed forever," writes Gerald Dirks, "is any feeling that Canada has had a long and honourable tradition of giving succour and providing sanctuary for the world's troubled peoples."[42] A reviewer of the paperback edition of *NITM* believes the less expensive version should sell even better than the hardcover, "if there is a market for stories of terrible injustice, for a book that should make every Canadian think twice about our eternally sweet sense of Canada as conscience of the world."[43]

A related set of responses warned that a contemporary commitment to multiculturalism could lull Canadians into a deceptive view of Canada and its past. Few, however, are as lucid and perceptive as historian David Stafford: "In April 1945, Georges Vanier, then Canadian ambassador to France, visited the recently liberated concentration camp at Buchenwald. Vanier later broadcast his impressions over the CBC and expressed shame that nothing had been done for the victims. . . . It would be comforting to think that most Canadians shared Vanier's shame at our severely restrictive immigration policy toward Jewish refugees from Nazi Europe. . . . This would not only flatter our self-image, *it would anchor the current rhetoric of multiculturalism in a bedrock of historic Canadian tradition.* Alas, the evidence of *None Is Too Many* . . . provides no such comfort."[44]

Many of the reviewers concurred that Canada was guilty, but that NITM was new evidence for a trial already in progress. William French of the *Globe and Mail* introduces his review by referring to recent books that dealt with the wartime relocation of the Japanese, and he explains that "while officially for security reasons, [the relocation] was covert racism, carried out for political advantage."[45] Reviewer Geoff Martin, in the *Dalhousie Gazette*, agrees: "I cannot say I am surprised at the gross callousness of the government of Canada. . . . Canada's now legendary treatment of the Japanese-Canadians during World War Two has shocked many."[46] For historian Robert Bothwell, the first "breach in the edifice of self-satisfaction was by reflections on the treatment received by Canada's Japanese."[47] It is both revealing and distressing that only a handful of reviewers even mention Canada's treatment of First Nations.

Several authors pursued a different comparison. Historian Gershon Hundert contrasted NITM to research on other bystanders to the Holocaust, especially Great Britain and the United States. Jewish journalist Gila Wertheimer also discussed work on the United States and Great Britain that demonstrated "similar heartlessness." For neither, however, does the poor record of other countries mitigate the harshness of the Canadian treatment. "Canada was not different;" writes Hundert, "Canada was worse."[48]

The authors of these headlines and articles did not just engage *intellectually* with the guilty verdict. Many of the articles imbued the verdict of guilty with the emotion of shame.[49] Sara Ahmed explores how "righteous shame" can affect nation building. In *The Cultural Politics of Emotion*, she describes how, at an individual level, shame can both identify and reject departures from the "scripts of normal experience." But expressions of shame also "reproduce" the nation in several ways. One way is especially pertinent: "the nation brings shame 'on itself' by its treatment of others; for example, it may be exposed as 'failing' a multicultural ideal in perpetuating forms of racism." As such, the multicultural ideal is reinforced for the present, even when the past behavior was "shameful." Moreover, the sense of shame can foster the creation of a new community of "well-meaning individuals."[50] In our case the critics who called out, and accepted, the guilt and shame were calling on well-meaning individuals (such as themselves) to reconstitute a generous Canada committed to pluralism.

Some remain outside this reconstituting community. The impact of NITM in Quebec was limited. Two leading French-language newspapers reviewed NITM, and both accepted the realities of antisemitism in Quebec, while arguing that the Quebec of the 1930s was not the same as the Quebec of 1982.[51] Outside francophone Quebec, however, some insisted that the connection between past and present was not so easily dismissed. One newspaper interviewed Abella about eight months after the appearance of the book and asked why NITM was having so little impact among francophone Quebecers. He answered that the issues of the 1930s had their parallels to the issues of Quebec separation in the 1980s and that the lack of reaction suggests that little has changed from the 1930s; he concluded: "One wonders what is going on in that province."[52]

The wondering never ceased. NITM has not been translated into French, perhaps because of critiques that the book was excessively critical of Quebec politicians and society. Or perhaps a book about Canadian national politics was not of great interest in that province. The discussions of the relationship of Quebec society and culture to its minorities, and specifically to its Jews, would erupt in the wake of publications by Mordecai Richler and Esther Delisle.[53] Richler considered the behavior of his contemporary Quebec nationalists shameful and rooted it in the past. Delisle focused on Quebec nationalism in the 1930s. The reactions to NITM anticipated the debates and sensitivities that would later arise in the Richler/Delisle affairs, but without the same prominence.[54]

Canadian Jews would have a special relationship to the reconstituting community. Almost all the reviewers—including those who identified as Jews—agreed with Abella and Troper that Canadian Jews had little power and thus deserved no verdict of guilty for what happened to Jewish refugees. However, Jews could still feel angered by their past frailty. In an academic journal Sandford Borins includes heartfelt personal remarks: "My reaction as a Jew was one of both incredulity and anger.... *None Is Too Many* came as a shock to me because it paints such a different picture of my people.... The Jews of the thirties were timid, deferential to (Gentile) authority, and fearful of public displays of overt race hatred."[55] The implicit message is that his Jewish contemporaries need to behave differently in their wish to reinforce ideals of pluralism and to protect themselves. Others stated this explicitly, as when Michelle Landsberg reflects on the political climate during the war in Lebanon:

> So why rock the boat now? Two reasons. One is that I've been reading the astounding book *None Is Too Many*.... Canadians need to know that genteel polite antisemitism ... can lead not only to human hardheartedness, social injustice and material harm, but even to death.

And why should I stick my neck out now, just when Israel has earned the condemnation by the world for the massacre ... in Beirut? Precisely now I'm sticking my neck out because the war has created a new, tolerant, climate for anti-Semitism.[56]

One group of reviewers resisted the verdict of guilty and did not accept blame and shame, or at least not to the same degree as most others. They used a variety of strategies to make their case. One reviewer minimizes the significance of the findings of the book: "Man's inhumanity to man is not new and restrictive immigration policies—not that they are forgivable—are small change in the face of the Holocaust and even smaller in the face of the Second World War."[57] (By contrast, another reviewer suggests that the book "could have been sub-titled 'Canada's contribution to the Final Solution.'")[58] Michael Bliss states that Canadians were not completely responsible for their actions: "Canadians were not an evil people. During the agony of European Jewry they *happened to be* prisoners of naive and vicious ideas and so contributed, *almost unwittingly*, to monstrous crimes."[59] How it "happened" is left unstated.

Some of the reviewers used a redemptive narrative to provide a different picture of Canadians and Canada. They alluded to Canada's participation in the war against the Nazis. As discussed above, Granatstein problematically explains that government policies were motivated by a desire to enter the war as a united nation. Political scientist Freda Hawkins writes of sacrifices on the battlefield to defy Nazism: "If there is one criticism to be made of *None Is Too Many* it is that, although written by historians, the historical context provided in this study is very limited. ... Apart from its beginning and ending and the disastrous events affecting the Jewish community in Europe, World War II is missing from these pages. One would never know from *None Is Too Many* that Canadians were fighting and dying in it and supporting the Allied cause in many other ways."[60] Michael Bliss also alludes to the sacrifices of Canadian soldiers and their families during the war: "The charge that Canada was not doing enough was a hard one to make to Canadian men and women who were sacrificing their sons. Do the men who fought at Dieppe or flew the Lancasters over Germany need to feel guilty about what Canada did in Hitler's war? Do they need to feel as guilty as the men who spent the war years riding around Montreal on their motorcycles?"[61]

Several reviewers challenged this line of argumentation by offering non-redemptive narratives. E. D. Ward-Harris writes with indignation at the national unity argument used by King (and Granatstein): "Mackenzie King claimed he did not want to disrupt national unity.... I find it difficult to accept but then I'm biased, having experienced the horrors of Belsen death camp on the day of its liberation."[62] Other reviewers pointed out that Canada's response to the refugees existed side by side with Canada's military response. Historian Robert Bothwell rejects the view that we must allow for a moral victory because of Canada's war record: "Fighting German nazism and Italian fascism and Japanese imperialism, Canadians seldom paused, at that time or later, to consider whether their own country was doing as much to uphold the values politicians proclaimed and its propagandists trumpeted."[63] The most concise response came in a review by David Snell several years after the book appeared: "Despite a magnificent military contribution to the Allied war effort, Canadians must recognize that we had an opportunity to save many lives and we chose not to."[64]

Conclusion

The reviewers of *NITM* largely agreed with Abella and Troper's historical assessments of the behavior of the Jewish community, the civil servants, and the politicians. In their reviews many used the behavior of the elected and nonelected officials to place Canada's past on trial. The verdict of guilty caused most of the reviewers to speak of their shame and put forward shame as the correct response for all Canadians. But this was no longer only about the past. The shame was to remind Canadians to work with other well-meaning individuals to get Canada to live up to ideals of pluralism and generosity so that multiculturalism has real social potency.

These responses represent an early moment in a long process. Under pressure from the Jewish community and others, in 2018 the Canadian government apologized for refusing admission to the passengers of the hapless *St. Louis* in 1938 and more generally for its refugee policy from 1933 to 1948.[65] The apology acknowledged that in Canada, "as far as Jews were concerned, none was too many" and that Canadians must now do better.[66]

Notes

1. Irving Abella and Harold Troper, *None Is Too Many: Canada and the Jews of Europe, 1933–1948* (Toronto: Lester & Orpen Dennys, 1982); Hamish Cameron, "Trade News," *Quill and Quire*, March 1983, 38; Lew Gloin, "A Book Canadians Should Read—with Anguish," review of paperback edition of *None Is Too Many: Canada and the Jews of Europe, 1933–1948*, by Irving Abella and Harold Troper, *Sunday Star* (Toronto), September 11, 1983.

2. Michael T. Kaufman, "Canada Admitted Few," *New York Times*, January 2, 1983.
3. Samuel Moyn, *A Holocaust Controversy: The Treblinka Affair in Postwar France* (Waltham MA: Brandeis University Press, an imprint of University Press of New England, 2005).
4. Although the book did attract attention by non-Canadians, in this chapter I focus on how the book was reviewed in the Canadian press and on the reviews by Canadians in non-Canadian newspapers and journals.
5. See Harold Troper, "New Horizons in a New Land: Jewish Immigration to Canada," in *From Immigration to Integration: The Canadian Jewish Experience*, ed. Ruth Kline and Frank Dimant (North York ON: Institute for International Affairs, B'nai Brith Canada, 2011), 3–18, 267–69, for the best summary of immigration policies vis-à-vis the Jews.
6. See José E. Iguartua, *The Other Quiet Revolution: National Identities in English Canada, 1945–71* (Vancouver: UBC Press, 2006), 175–92.
7. James W. St. G. Walker, "The 'Jewish Phase' in the Movement for Racial Equality in Canada," *Canadian Ethnic Studies* 34, no. 1 (Spring 2002): 1–29.
8. Harold Troper, *The Defining Decade: Identity, Politics and the Canadian Jewish Community in the 1960s* (Toronto: University of Toronto Press, 2010), 248–63.
9. For a recent review of the Royal Commission on Bilingualism and Biculturalism, with an emphasis on its limitations from Quebec's perspective, see Valérie Lapointe-Gagnon, *Panser le Canada: Une histoire intellectuelle de la Commission Laurendeau-Dunton* (Montréal: Boréal, 2018).
10. Lapointe-Gagnon, *Panser le Canada*.
11. Harold Troper and Morton Weinfeld, "Canadian Jews and Canadian Multiculturalism," in *Multiculturalism, Jews, and Identities in Canada*, ed. Howard Adelman and John H. Simpson (Jerusalem: Magnes Press, the Hebrew University, 1996), 21–24.
12. Government of Canada, The Canadian Charter of Rights and Freedoms, section 27, accessed March 24, 2025, https://www.justice.gc.ca/eng/csj-sjc/rfc-dlc/ccrf-ccdl/check/art27.html.
13. For the best overall survey, see Adara Goldberg, *Holocaust Survivors in Canada: Exclusion, Inclusion, Transformation, 1947–1955* (Winnipeg: University of Manitoba Press, 2015). On the orphans and tailors' project, see, respectively, Fraidie Martz, *Open Your Hearts: The Story of the Jewish War Orphans in Canada* (Montreal: Véhicule Press, 1996); Andrea Knight, Paula Draper, and Nicole Bryck, *The Tailor Project: How 2,5000 Holocaust Survivors Found a New Life in Canada* (Toronto: Second Story Press, 2020).
14. Irving Abella and Franklin Bialystok, "Canada," in *The World Reacts to the Holocaust*, ed. David S. Wyman (Baltimore: Johns Hopkins University Press, 1996), 765.
15. Franklin Bialystok, *Delayed Impact: The Holocaust and the Canadian Jewish Community* (Montreal: McGill-Queen's University Press, 2000), 98–99.
16. Kenneth Grad, "A Gesture of Criminal Law: Jews and the Criminalization of Hate Speech in Canada," *Osgoode Hall Law Journal* 59, no. 2 (Spring 2022): 375–427.
17. Troper, *Defining Decade*, 94–121.
18. Bialystok, *Delayed Impact*, 181.
19. Irving Abella and Harold Troper, "'The Line Must Be Drawn Somewhere': Canada and Jewish Refugees, 1933–9," *Canadian Historical Review* 60, no. 2 (1979): 178–209.

20. Marlene Shore, "'Remember the Future': The *Canadian Historical Review* and the Discipline of History, 1920–95," *Canadian Historical Review* 76, no. 1 (1995): 410–63.
21. Richard Menkis, "Identities, Communities, and the Infrastructures of History: Creating Canadian Jewish Archives in the 1930s and 1970s," in *History, Memory, and Jewish Identities*, ed. Ira Robinson, Naftali S. Cohn, and Lorenzo Ditommaso (Boston: Academic Studies Press, 2015), 233–56; Amir Lavie, "'The Past Is Not a Foreign Country': Archival Mentalities and the Development of the Canadian-Jewish Community's Archival Landscape during the Nineteen Seventies" (PhD diss., University of Toronto, 2019), ProQuest, accessed March 24, 2025, https://utoronto.scholaris.ca/items/1d32df95-7b06-415a-a4fd-bd2dbce4b13e.
22. Abella and Troper, *None Is Too Many*, vi.
23. Abella and Troper, *None Is Too Many*, 283.
24. Henry L. Feingold, "Who Shall Bear Guilt for the Holocaust? The Human Dilemma," *American Jewish History* 68, no. 3 (March 1979): 276.
25. Joshua Gershman, "Many Needed Saving but 'None' Was Too Many," review, *Canadian Jewish Outlook* 21, no. 3 (March 1983): 13–15.
26. Gerald E. Dirks, review of *None Is Too Many* by Abella and Troper, *Canadian Journal of Political Science* 163, no. 3 (Fall 1983): 609.
27. Sandford F. Borins, review of *None Is Too Many* by Abella and Troper, *Canadian Public Administration* 26, no. 4 (December 1983): 668.
28. J. L. Granatstein, review of *None Is Too Many* by Abella and Troper, *American Historical Review* 89 (1984): 886–87.
29. Granatstein, review, 886–87.
30. Michael Bliss, "The Shame of Bystanders," review of *None Is Too Many* by Abella and Troper, *Maclean's*, September 15, 1982, 58–59.
31. David Stafford, "A Daydream in Hell: To Jews Caught in the Nazi Europe, Canada's Immigration Policy Was Arguably the Most Restrictive in the World," review of *None Is Too Many* by Abella and Troper, *Saturday Night*, September 1982, 57–58; Adele Wiseman, "Complicity in Murder," review of *None Is Too Many* by Abella and Troper, *Whig Standard Magazine* (Kingston ON), October 16, 1982.
32. Abella and Troper, *None Is Too Many*, 284; Alan T. Davies and Marilyn F. Nefsky, *How Silent Were the Churches? Canadian Protestantism and the Jewish Plight during the Nazi Era* (Waterloo ON: Wilfrid Laurier University Press, 1998).
33. Dirks, review, 610.
34. Granatstein, review, 887.
35. For a recent restatement of his position, see Pierre Anctil, "Which Canada Are We Talking About? An English-Language Polemic about French in Canadian Jewish History," in *No Better Home? Jews, Canada, and the Sense of Belonging*, ed. David S. Koffman (Toronto: University of Toronto Press, 2021), 284–96.
36. Pierre Anctil, review of *None Is Too Many* by Abella and Troper, *Recherches Sociographiques* 25, no. 1 (1984): 138–41.
37. Frédéric Seager, review of *None Is Too Many* by Abella and Troper, *Revue d'Histoire de l'Amérique Française* 39, no. 2 (Autumn 1985): 271–72; Marie Poirier, "Un silence eloquent," review of *None Is Too Many* by Abella and Troper, *Jonathan* 11 (1983): 22, 24.

38. Richard A. Jones, "Canada and the Jewish Refugees of Nazi Europe," review of *None Is Too Many* by Abella and Troper, *Historical Reflections* 11, no. 1 (Spring 1984): 97–98.
39. Ronnie Miller, *From Lebanon to the Intifada: The Jewish Lobby and Canadian Middle East Policy* (Lanham MD: University Press of America, 1991), 74–77.
40. Sol Litman, *War Criminal on Trial: Rauca of Kaunas* (Toronto: Key Porter, 1998), 153–72.
41. E. D. Ward-Harris, "Shocking Saga of How Canada Kept Out Jews," review of *None Is Too Many* by Abella and Troper, *Times-Colonist* (Victoria BC), October 16, 1982.
42. Dirks, review, 610.
43. Anne Collins, review of paperback edition of *None Is Too Many* by Abella and Troper, *Books in Canada* 12, no. 9 (November 1983): 40.
44. Stafford, "A Daydream in Hell," 57; emphasis added.
45. William French, "Anti-Semitism a Shameful Chapter in Canada's History," review of *None Is Too Many* by Abella and Troper, *Globe and Mail* (Toronto), September. 9, 1982.
46. Geoff Martin, "Canadian Racism Is Exposed in 'None Is Too Many,'" review of *None Is Too Many* by Abella and Troper, *Dalhousie Gazette*, March 24, 1983.
47. Robert Bothwell, review of *None Is Too Many* by Abella and Troper, *Canadian Jewish Historical Society Journal* 7, no. 1 (Spring 1983): 55–56.
48. Gershon Hundert, review of *None Is Too Many* by Abella and Troper, *Canadian Historical Review* 64, no. 1 (1983): 56.
49. Although mental health professionals differentiate between the emotions of guilt and shame, I am only using the term "guilt" to register the "verdicts" rendered by the authors.
50. Sara Ahmed, *The Cultural Politics of Emotion*, 2nd ed. (Edinburgh: Edinburgh University Press, 2014), 107–9.
51. Arnold Ages, "Quand le Canada était antisemite," review of *None Is Too Many* by Abella and Troper, *Le Devoir* (Montréal), May 7, 1983; Arthur Hiess, "Le Canada et les Juifs d'Europe, 1933–1948," review of *None Is Too Many* by Abella and Troper, *La Presse* (Montréal), February 7, 1983.
52. Nancy Russel, "A Tale of Racism and Bigotry," *Star-Phoenix* (Saskatoon SK), April 16, 1983.
53. Mordecai Richler, *Oh Canada! Oh Quebec! Requiem for a Divided Country* (New York: Viking Penguin, 1992); Esther Delisle, *The Traitor and the Jew: Anti-Semitism and Extreme Right-Wing Nationalism in Québec from 1929 to 1939* (Montréal: R. Davies, 1993).
54. Nadia Khouri, *Qui a peur de Mordecai Richler?* (Montréal: Editions Balzac, 1995).
55. Borins, review, 666.
56. Michelle Landsberg, "I Now Feel Forced to Speak about Anti-Semitism," *Toronto Star*, November 9, 1982.
57. Jeff Holubitsky, "Chronicle of Canadian Shame Flounders in Minutiae," review of *None Is Too Many* by Abella and Troper, *Edmonton Journal*, November 1, 1982.
58. John H. Simpson, review of *None Is Too Many* by Abella and Troper, *Sciences Religieuses/Studies in Religion* 12, no. 3 (September 1983): 348.
59. Bliss, "Bystanders," 88–89; emphasis added.

60. Freda Hawkins, "Indictment," review of *None Is Too Many* by Abella and Troper, *Canadian Forum*, December/January 1982–83, 37.
61. Bliss, "Shame of Bystanders," 59.
62. Ward-Harris, "Shocking Saga."
63. Bothwell, review, 55.
64. David Snell, review of *None Is Too Many* by Abella and Troper, *History and Social Science Teacher*, Summer 1987, 236.
65. Adara Goldberg, "Making Present the Past: Canada's St. Louis Apology and Canadian Jewry's Pursuit of Refugee Justice," in *Agency and the Holocaust: Essays in Honor of Debórah Dwork*, ed. Thomas Kühne and Mary Jane Rein (London: Palgrave Macmillan, 2020), 215–35.
66. "PM Trudeau Delivers Apology Regarding the Fate of the Passengers of the MS St. Louis," Government of Canada transcript, November 7, 2018, https://pm.gc.ca/en/videos/2018/11/07/pm-trudeau-delivers-apology-regarding-fate-passengers-ms-st-louis.

11

Mexico and the Holocaust
The Contradictions of Postrevolutionary Immigration Policy

DANIELA GLEIZER

In 1947, when the United Nations was debating the partition of Palestine, the Mexican representative, Rafael de la Colina, took advantage of the situation to claim, referring to the Holocaust, "Mexico promptly raised its voice against such barbaric processes, and at the same time, opened its doors to thousands of refugees, thereby overcoming enormous difficulties of an economic and demographic order that were opposed and continue to oppose rising immigration."[1] Later, in 1975, in the context of the Mexican government's support for United Nations Resolution 3379—which condemned Zionism as a form of racism—the Mexican press accused the Mexican Jewish community of a lack of loyalty given the asylum that had been offered to Jews persecuted under Nazism.[2]

However, these assertions by Mexican authorities and the press do not reflect what really happened. On the contrary, in 1934 the Ministry of the Interior secretly prohibited Jewish immigration to Mexico, which led to the rejection of thousands of asylum requests and forced many ships that reached the port of Veracruz with Jewish refugees on board to be sent back to Europe. Despite exceptions, which allowed close to two thousand Jewish refugees to enter to the country between 1933 and 1945, Mexico's contribution to the Jewish refugee crisis was minimal, if we take into account that Latin America, as a whole, received close to ninety thousand Jewish refugees during that same period.[3] However, this process of reshaping the collective memory, which took several decades, was successful in reconfiguring what was actually a highly selective and restrictive policy into its diametrically opposite image—one of openness and receptivity—which has prevailed in many circles up to the present day.[4]

Part of the confusion is understandable because Mexico had an important tradition of political asylum in its historical record beginning in the 1920s—with the asylum granted to diverse figures in Latin American politics—that continued in the 1930s and 1940s, with the reception of close to twenty thousand refugees from the Spanish Civil War and a small group of German-speaking exiles fleeing Nazism (totaling one hundred to three hundred persons), including figures of the stature of Paul Merker, Anna Seghers, Ludwig Renn, Egon Erwin Kisch, and Leo Katz.

With respect to Jewish immigration, however, Mexican governmental authorities in the 1930s and 1940s were much clearer in their position than later reinterpretations might suggest. In fact, they explicitly differentiated between "racial refugees" and "political refugees," publicly justifying the closed-door policy for the former and the welcome given to the latter. In 1940, for example, the minister of the interior, Ignacio García Téllez, reported that the acceptance of racial refugees was "extremely limited," because due to their high numbers, Mexico was waiting for the democratic countries to make a "broad, generous and supportive effort" to resolve the problem together. He also stated that, except for Spanish refugees, the only ones who would be admitted in the country were "isolated and special cases of foreigners who were really and effectively persecuted, who could prove their situation and who did not enter the country to compete with the active local population."[5]

Part of the confusion also resides in the lack of differentiation between immigration and asylum policies. Although, as noted, Mexico had constructed an important tradition of political asylum, its immigration policy since the 1930s had been highly restrictive and entirely discretionary; and it was precisely this immigration policy that framed the Jewish exile.

The Prohibition of Jewish Immigration

Although during the nineteenth century and the first two decades of the twentieth the arrival of foreigners to the country was promoted both to increase the population and to exploit natural resources, believed to be inexhaustible, starting in the 1920s a process of constriction began that would change the character of immigration policies from liberal and open to selective and discretionary. To understand this shift, we must look back to the Mexican Revolution, which broke out in 1910 with a strong nationalistic and even xenophobic character, largely a reaction to the xenophilia of the preceding period (the administration of Porfirio Díaz, spanning the years from 1867 to 1911) and various experiences of foreign intervention and national sovereignty violations in the past.

It is not easy to characterize postrevolutionary nationalism, but perhaps the adjective that best describes it is "defensive."[6] In its economic dimensions it sought to protect national interests from real or potential foreign threats, which included defending Mexican workers from competition from foreign wage earners. In its social aspects it sought to protect the population from outside influences. Based on the scientific racism inherited from the nineteenth century,[7] and on the internal assessment of Mexico's problems, which included the "backwardness" of the population attributed to its Indigenous roots, the state assumed the task of safeguarding Mexican *mestizaje* (miscegenation). Although it was understood that the Mexican population was the result of a mixture, and racial purity was never overtly defended, it did indeed recognize the need to protect Mexican mestizaje from the influence of certain "races," some because they represented a potential of "racial degeneration," and others because they were regarded as "impossible to assimilate" into the Mexican population.[8] This, of course, was not a conviction of Mexican originality. Practically all countries' immigration policies at the time began to introduce mechanisms of defense against "presences deemed to be threats."[9]

Therefore, starting in the mid-1920s, diverse confidential circulars issued by the Ministry of the Interior began to prohibit the entry of specific ethnic groups into the country, based on a blend of racial criteria with political and economic considerations. The summary of those prohibitions can be found in two confidential circulars: no. 250, of October 1933, and no. 157, of April 1934. Together they prohibited, among others, the entry into Mexico of Asians (except for Japanese), those of African descent, Arab populations, "Gypsies" or Roma, USSR citizens, and Poles, as well as foreign workers—at different times, but especially after the 1929 crisis.[10]

Jews were added to the list in 1934, with the distinctive feature of being characterized as the most undesirable of all, based on their "psychological and moral characteristics," the sort of activities they were involved in, and the work in commercial businesses that—according to the document—they invariably undertook.[11] Even if foreigners belonged to an accepted "race" or nationality, if they were Jewish, their entry was prohibited. However, an exception was made for American Jews, after the complaints of those who wished to enter the country and were rejected in Mexican consulates threatened to spark a diplomatic rift between the two nations.[12]

As Pablo Yankelevich has demonstrated, anti-Jewish prejudice was added to a "space imbued with longstanding anti-Jewish imagery of Catholic origin and a modern antisemitism rooted in the racialization of hatred for Jews."[13] Although the presence of Jews in Mexico (and foreigners in general) was scant, during the 1920s the population of the Jewish community grew fivefold, going from 2,000 to 10,000 persons (in a country of close to 16 million inhabitants). This was largely the result of immigration policy restrictions introduced by the United States, particularly the 1924 Immigration Act, which caused part of the immigration flow to the United States to be channeled to Mexico, where the immigrants hoped to cross the border by land or wait out admission authorization. Thus, between 1924 and 1929—when Mexican immigration policy was still open—close to 7,500 Jewish individuals of diverse origins, both Ashkenazi and Sephardic, reached Mexico, and most of them ultimately stayed on.[14] The presence of Jews in Mexican society was perceived in some sectors as a threat, because together with the Lebanese, they competed with Mexicans in retail activities (especially retail installment sales). Later, their incursions into formal business and industry stirred discontent in economic sectors impacted by their competition.[15]

The Mexican Government Policy on Jewish Refugees

The prohibition of Jewish immigration in 1934 did not have immediate effects. Mexico, like the rest of Latin America, was not among the top emigration options during the early years of Nazism, when refugees thought that their situation was temporary and found countries, such as France, that offered them asylum and allowed them to stay in Europe, making it easy to return to Germany as soon as possible.[16] However, the Nazis' goal of removing all Jews from Germany and, starting in March 1938, also from Austria provoked a true refugee crisis in the first months of 1938; then the Kristallnacht, in November of that year, was a graphic, violent message of the urgent need to flee. The rupture of diplomatic ties between the United States and Germany in 1941 and the closure of U.S. consulates in the zones controlled by the Nazis turned Latin America into a favored place of refuge.[17]

The earliest Jewish requests for asylum in Mexico came from 1937, but it was in 1938 when they began to multiply. An analysis of the oral testimonies of the Jewish refugees who came to Mexico shows that they knew practically nothing about the country, which was rarely their first choice for refuge, but rather the last. The refugees applied for visas for many countries simultaneously—trying to reach the United States first—and when they saw that possibility fade, they tried other destinations. Mexico appeared as a refugee option during the months or years when the refugees were in countries that offered them temporary asylum, while they were looking for permanent places of residence. Given that Mexican legislation permitted the entry of relatives, the role played by family members who had arrived in Mexico in the 1920s was key for securing them visas, as described below, although the process was complicated and tortuous.

The Lázaro Cárdenas Administration (1934-40)

During the early years of Nazism, the Mexican government, headed by General Lázaro Cárdenas, characterized the problem of Jewish refugees as a European matter that was beyond the country's sphere of interest. The question was seen as a migration problem; in other words, the Jews who were fleeing the Nazi regime were not given the status of refugees or exiles, but of migrants, so they were subject to the rules derived from immigration rather than asylum policy. It is important to point out that the new General Population Law, issued in 1936, first introduced a quota system that annually defined the number of foreigners of each nationality who could enter the country, and that in 1937, Confidential Circular no. 157, which prohibited Jewish immigration, was replaced by other provisions that, in practice, continued the ban.[18]

Despite the Mexican government's more or less rigid stance, President Cárdenas seriously considered relaxing his position when Mexico participated in the Evian Conference, an international meeting convened in July 1938 in that French city to address the subject of refugees from Nazism. This was evident in the instructions given to Primo Villa Michel, Mexico's representative at the conference, who was told to loosen Mexico's position if the organizing powers (England, France, and the United States) applied sufficient pressure.[19] However, once the Evian Conference was over, the Mexican representative was satisfied to report that it had been unnecessary to use the instructions received, because no country was really willing to modify its immigration policy to receive Jewish refugees, which implied there were no international commitments Mexico needed to fulfill. This led the Mexican government to return to its more closed stance.

In 1939 the minister of the interior, Ignacio García Téllez, informed the minister of foreign affairs, Eduardo Hay, that the country had already received at least 150,000 asylum applications, but the selection of individual cases had followed such rigid guidelines that "only a number not even reaching the monthly quota determined by the Differential Tables has been approved."[20]

The toughening of Mexico's position on Jewish refugees can be seen in the lowering of immigration quotas, because permits for foreigners from Germany, Belgium, Czechoslovakia, Denmark, France, the Netherlands, England, Italy, Japan, Norway, Sweden, and Switzerland were reduced from five thousand per country in 1938 to one thousand in 1939, and to one hundred in 1941. Policy changes in 1939 also prohibited the entry of stateless individuals (which affected Jews who had been stripped of their citizenship by the Third Reich); specified that only asylum requests made from the actual country of persecution would be evaluated (which ruled out most applicants, who had to temporarily seek safety abroad before beginning the process of requesting visas for permanent destinations); and warned that no tourist would be accepted as a refugee. Finally, the quotas for 1939 required that applicants—quite paradoxically—had to categorically declare they would not harbor racial prejudices and were willing to "form a Mexican mestizo family."[21]

The Manuel Ávila Camacho Administration (1940-46)

The change in government took place in December 1940, when General Manuel Ávila Camacho took office. A moderate man, he sought "national unification" after the Cárdenas administration had generated strong social polarization. His presidency heralded a phase of open cooperation with the United States—due to World War II—in diplomatic, military, and economic fields.

In immigration matters, the Ávila Camacho administration respected the commitments made by his predecessor, especially in the field of political asylum, although bureaucratic red tape and internal and external obstacles made it increasingly difficult for refugees to reach Mexico. As mentioned earlier, a part of the quotas for 1941 was further reduced, but these quotas established that those foreigners who had fled from their places of origin for political or *religious* reasons would be given protection. This consideration was reiterated in the president's first state of the union address, in which he alluded to Mexico's hospitality to victims of *racial* and political persecution. However, because of World War II, the Mexican government reserved the power to deny entry to foreigners and even to cancel prior permits, which made the immigration policy even more discretionary.

Without discarding the possibility of greater opening to Jewish refugees on a governmental level, corruption cannot be overlooked in understanding the admission of refugees from 1941 to 1942. Although this was also an issue under the previous government, it seemed to increase during the six-year term of Manuel Ávila Camacho, due to both the changes that took place in the Ministry of the Interior (now in the hands of Miguel Alemán) and the refugees' urgent need, which led to an increase in the cost of visas and bribes at ports of entry. According to the United States Department of Justice: "The Mexican authorities seem to be so corrupt that visas can be obtained at any time for the right price."[22] Various documents allude to the sale of Mexican visas, which cost anywhere from $300 to $1,000 per person at any given moment in time, depending on who made the request. Near the end of 1941 the Comité Central Israelita de México (Israelite Central Committee of Mexico, CCIM) reported that legal immigration to Mexico was possible, but that it was necessary to have a competent attorney, whose fees were "very inflated." In mid-1942 a lawyer charged $600 per person, $750 for two people, and an additional $100 for each family member.[23]

In May 1942 Mexico joined the war on the side of the Allies, which prompted border closings to all non-American immigration, and the possibilities for Jewish immigration shrank even more. However, an agreement issued by the Ministry of the Interior alleged force majeure in authorizing foreigners to stay in Mexico if they were unable to return to their countries of origin, while also granting them work permits. In addition, the Ávila Camacho government permitted the legalization of many immigrants who had arrived in the country in earlier years under the umbrella of political asylum seekers.

In 1943 the CCIM recorded the entry of only 72 persons. For that year the committee had 612 refugees registered (although they were not all Jewish, because it also aided other types of refugees). The low number was because at the beginning there was no requirement to register before the CCIM to receive help.[24]

The Jewish Community Leadership

Most Jewish immigration, as mentioned, took place in the 1920s. However, it was not until 1938 that the Jewish refugee problem prompted the creation of the Pro-Refugee Committee to address all questions related to them, and the CCIM was established as the political representative of the Jewish community in the country. From then on, the Pro-Refugee Committee became a subcommittee within the CCIM.

Despite the CCIM's limited resources (in terms of human resources, budget, and political ties with the government), it did extremely important work. Always keeping a low profile, the Jewish group's leadership promoted the Mexican anti-fascist movement by financing many of its public acts, while it worked diligently to secure visas, help refugees disembark once they reached Mexico, pay their repatriation bonds, and support them in the early months after their arrival. Similarly, it had a legal department to formalize the immigration situation of those who arrived, secure work permits for them, and avoid their deportation.

To contribute to this work, the CCIM had certain resources sent by the Joint Distribution Committee (JDC) for specific purposes, while the Jewish emigration agency (HICEM) or the Hebrew Immigrant Aid Society (HIAS) provided a monthly subsidy of $200.[25] In 1939, for example, the JDC sent $1,700 for a special fund to legalize the refugees' status and secure work permits, and in 1941 it sent $8,000 for the disembarkation costs of the steamship *Serpa Pinto*. The CCIM also carried out fundraising campaigns for which it created the Emergency Rescue Committee for Victims of War. The campaigns brought to the fore the ideological differences within the Jewish committee: the communists believed the money should be sent to the USSR to support the efforts of the Red Army; the Zionists thought the creation of a Jewish state in Palestine should be strengthened, whereas the Bundists insisted on sending the money directly to Europe to try to alleviate the suffering of Jewish communities there. In the end the Jewish community in Mexico supported the JDC's campaign to aid Polish Jews; some money was earmarked for the Allies—the British Army, in particular—and other funds were raised to sponsor the emigration of Jewish refugees to Palestine.

One of the Central Committee's main accomplishments was to ensure that German and Austrian Jews would not be considered "enemy citizens" once Mexico entered the war on the side of the Allies. In this way the committee prevented them from being sent to internment camps and from having restrictions imposed on their mobility or economic activities, as in the case of most of the nationals from those countries.

Those Who Arrived

As mentioned earlier, there were no collective immigration projects for Jewish refugees. Whoever arrived did so with their own means, sometimes relying on the aid of Jewish or non-Jewish relief organizations, which included diverse political networks and humanitarian organizations. These included the World Jewish Congress, the Joint Distribution Committee, the Hebrew Immigration Aid Society, HICEM, the Jewish Labor Committee, and other, non-Jewish agencies, such as the American Friends Service Committee, the Unitarian Service Committee, and the Emergency Rescue Committee.

Therefore, the refugees who arrived in Mexico came from a sweeping variety of highly different experiences. Most came from Germany, Austria, Belgium, France, Czechoslovakia, Poland, and Hungary, although some also arrived from Greece and Bulgaria. Most reached the Veracruz coasts by ship, but some went halfway around the world to set sail from Japan and reach Mexican ports on the Pacific. Others entered by train, crossing the northern border of the country (because New York was often an obligatory stop on their journey), and a few arrived over the southern border or by airplane.

As for their immigration status, some arrived legally, thanks to the law permitting the arrival of relatives.[26] For the family members already in Mexico, it was not only a matter of obtaining authorization for the visas; they also had to keep careful track of the administrative processes until the document reached the hands of its recipients. Multiple bureaucratic walls cropped up along the way. In addition, the visas were only valid for six months, and on many occasions, they had to be renewed. That was primarily due to the shortage of ships to transport civilians in times of war, as well as the number of papers the refugees had to secure to be able to leave. Those who had contacts in the upper echelons of the Mexican government or who paid out money were more likely to secure visas, but not all of them were successful.

A second group of refugees reached Mexico without papers, and they were able to disembark thanks to the corruption in ports of entry, as mentioned above. A third group arrived under the category of political asylum refugees, with the prior authorization of the Ministry of the Interior. Although in this case the generosity of the Lázaro Cárdenas administration (which extended the authorizations in 1940) has been alluded to, there were also other arrangements that permitted the entry of political refugees. A detailed study of the collaboration between the Jewish Labor Committee of New York and its Mexican subsidiary, the Society for Culture and Aid, shows that to secure authorizations for their coreligionists, they had to pay $500 per person to someone inside the Ministry of the Interior, through a Jewish intermediary who helped to obtain the visas.[27]

Once the war was over, Mexico's immigration policy continued to close doors to Jewish refugees. According to Hans Wollny, while between 1947 and 1951 the International Relief Organization was able to relocate more than 32,000 refugees in Argentina, 28,000 in Brazil, and 17,000 in Venezuela, Mexico received no more than 1,000.[28]

Concluding Remarks

Against a backdrop of displays of sympathy over the fate of the individuals persecuted by totalitarian regimes and government declarations of openness to political refugees, explaining how Mexican doors were shut to Jewish refugees is no simple matter.

As seen through this discussion, there were changes in the personal positions of some key officials, the most important being the president, Lázaro

Cárdenas, who shifted between opening and closing doors, seriously considering the possibility of receiving a specific group of Jewish refugees in the country, only to ultimately backpedal, leaving the decision in the hands of the Ministry of the Interior, which was opposed to Jewish immigration. With this move the case of Jewish refugees became an immigration problem, more than a matter of asylum. In clear contrast, he would personally see to providing asylum to Spanish refugees.

The Mexican experience shows how one specific administration could simultaneously adopt contrary positions on different groups of refugees seeking asylum. In this case the consideration of the Spaniards as one of the original branches of Mexican mestizaje, their potential to "whiten" the population, and the political identification between the Cárdenas regime and the Spanish Republic led to the offer of asylum in Mexico; moreover, once they were in the country, they were even exempted from the legal requirements to acquire Mexican nationality. On the contrary the consideration of Jews as "undesirable foreigners," the cultural distance, specific prejudices against Jews, the fear of massive immigration, and the voices within Mexican society against Jewish immigration led to the closed-door policy. What comes through clearly is that the government's xenophobia did not only operate on theoretical levels but also translated into exclusionary public policies that, in practice, prevented refuge from being offered to people who needed it desperately.

Collective memory has reconfigured this episode of closed doors into its exact opposite: an image of openness and protection extended to Jewish refugees. It is up to history to recover the experiences of those who were not able to enter the country, in order to offer a more complex and balanced vision.

Notes

1. Rafael de la Colina, "Declaración de abstención en torno al problema de Palestina," in *Rafael de la Colina, Sesenta años de labor diplomática*, ed. Archivo Histórico Diplomático Mexicano (Mexico: Secretaría de Relaciones Exteriores, 1981), 192. See also Judit Bokser, "Alteridad en la historia y en la memoria: México y los refugiados judíos," in *Encuentro y alteridad: Vida y cultura judía en América Latina*, ed. Judit Bokser and Alice Gojman de Backal (Mexico: UNAM/FCE/Universidad Hebrea de Jerusalén/Amigos de la Universidad de Tel Aviv, 1999), 355. Mexico ultimately abstained in the voting.
2. Judit Bokser, "Fuentes de legitimación de la presencia judía en México: El voto positivo de México a la ecuación sionismo-racismo," in *Judaica Latinoamericana*, vol. 3 (Jerusalem: Magnes, 1997), 339.

3. Patrick von zur Mühlen, "The 1930s: The End of the Latin American Open-Door Policy," in *Refugees from Nazi Germany and the Liberal European States*, ed. Frank Caestecker and Bob Moore (New York: Berghahn, 2010), 103–8.
4. Bokser, "Alteridad en la historia"; Bokser, "Fuentes de legitimación." See also Daniela Gleizer, "Recordar lo que no pasó: Memoria y usos del olvido en torno a la recepción de los refugiados judíos del nazismo en México," *Revista de Indias* 72, no. 255 (2012): 465–94.
5. Ignacio García Téllez, "Puntos de vista de la Secretaría de Gobernación en relación con el otorgamiento de asilo a los refugiados políticos," *Migración y Población* 1, no. 1 (1940): 4.
6. Pablo Yankelevich, "Nación y extranjería en el México revolucionario," *Cuicuilco* 11, no. 31 (2004): 8.
7. This is the moment when the concept of "race," consolidated around the body, nature, and biology, became "the intellectual key to thinking about human difference." Peter Wade, "Raza, ciencia, sociedad," *Interdisciplina* 2, no. 4 (2014): 36, 41.
8. On the ideology of mestizaje, see, among others, Guillermo Zermeño, "Del mestizo al mestizaje: Arqueología de un concepto," *Memoria y sociedad* 12, no. 24 (2008): 79–95; Olivia Gall, "Mestizaje y racismo en México," *Nueva Sociedad*, no. 292 (2021): 53–64.
9. See Tomás Pérez Vejo, "Exclusión étnica en los dispositivos de conformación nacional en América Latina," *Interdisciplina* 2, no. 4 (2014): 179–205; Pablo Yankelevich, "Extranjería y antisemitismo en el México posrevolucionario," *Interdisciplina* 2, no. 4 (2014): 143–59.
10. Confidential Circular no. 250, October 17, 1933, and no. 157, April 27, 1934, Archivo Histórico del Instituto Nacional de Migración (hereafter AHINM), file 4-250-2-1933-54.
11. Confidential Circular no. 157.
12. Confidential Circular no. 157.
13. Yankelevich, "Extranjería y antisemitismo," 145.
14. Yankelevich, "Extranjería y antisemitismo," 145; Daniela Gleizer, "De la apertura al cierre de puertas: La inmigración judía en México durante las primeras décadas del siglo XX," *Historia mexicana* 60, no. 2 (238) (2010): 1204–7.
15. Yankelevich, "Extranjería y antisemitismo," 145.
16. Haim Avni, "La guerra y las posibilidades de rescate," in *Entre la aceptación y el rechazo: América Latina y los refugiados judíos del nazismo*, ed. Avraham Milgram (Jerusalem: International Institute for Holocaust Research Yad Vashem, 2003), 20.
17. Yehuda Bauer, *American Jewry and the Holocaust: The American Jewish Joint Distribution Committee, 1939–1945* (Detroit: Wayne State University Press, 1981), 64.
18. In May 1937 Confidential Circular no. 157 was replaced by Circular no. 930, which left to the discretion of consuls the documentation of those who met the criteria of the General Population Law for tourists and transmigrants. Circular no. 930, however, was revoked less than a year later, on March 12, 1938, through Circular no. 84, which established that European tourists whose immigration was deemed as "undesirable" had to request authorization from the Ministry of the Interior to visit the country. AHINM, file 4-350-2-1933-54 and file 4-350-2-1938-69, respectively.
19. Primo Villa Michel had been the legal consultant of the Ministry of the Interior and was the Mexican ambassador to the United Kingdom at that time. Before the con-

ference he had expressed the opinion that the admission of undesirable foreigners should be prohibited. Pablo Yankelevich and Paola Chenillo, "La arquitectura," in *Nación y Extranjería*, ed. Pablo Yankelevich (Mexico: UNAM, 2009), 198–99.

20. Téllez to Hay, Mexico City, August 3, 1939, AHINM, file 4-350-1940-883.
21. "Tablas diferenciales a que se sujetará la admisión de inmigrantes durante el año de 1939," *Diario Oficial*, October 31, 1938.
22. Letter from the Department of Justice, July 23, 1942, National Archives and Records Administration (hereafter NARA), Record Group (hereafter RG) 59, file 812.111 10551/2.
23. NARA, RG 59, Reel 23, Parts I and II.
24. Financial report sent by CCIM to JDC, Mexico City, February 21, 1944, Archive of the Joint Distribution Committee, Collection 33/44, file 744.
25. Centro de Documentación e Investigación Judío de México (CDIJUM), Archivo de la Kehilá Ashkenazi, CCIM, Actas, vol. 1, act no. 6, November 29, 1938. Dollars here refers to U.S. dollars.
26. Article 82 of the 1936 General Population Law established that immigrants had the right to bring their spouse, single children, parents, and blood relatives up to the third degree into the country. *Diario Oficial*, August 29, 1936. This right was restricted in 1941 to the direct relatives of Mexicans or foreign immigrants (the category of "immigrant" entailed permission to reside in the country indefinitely). *Diario Oficial*, October 15, 1940.
27. See Daniela Gleizer, "Gilberto Bosques y el consulado de México en Marsella (1940–1942): La burocracia en tiempos de guerra," *Estudios de Historia Moderna y Contemporánea de México* 49 (2015): 54–76.
28. Report of the International Refugee Organization, in *Yearbook of the United Nations* 1952, 492, quoted in Hans Wollny, "Asylum Policy in Mexico: A Survey," *Journal of Refugee Studies* 4, no. 3 (1991): 225.

Part 3

Representation

12

Holocaust Education in South Asia
The Much-Needed Response to Holocaust Denial, Trivialization, and Inversion

NAVRAS J. AAFREEDI

This is a study of the absence of Holocaust education in South Asia, why it is needed there, and how it can be introduced in the region.[1] Most South Asians know little about Jews, let alone the Holocaust, subjects rarely taught in schools. However, Adolf Hitler enjoys immense popularity among them. Paradoxically, what drives this popularity is both ignorance and distorted awareness of the Holocaust. The awareness of the Holocaust makes him popular among the antisemites in certain sections of Muslim community and those Islamophobes among the Hindu nationalists who would like Muslims to be persecuted and even massacred the way the Nazis murdered the Jews on a massive scale. Both Islamist antisemites and Hindu nationalist Islamophobes admire him for the genocide he perpetrated on the Jews. The Hindu nationalist Islamophobes' admiration for Hitler is mediated by their attitude toward Muslims in India and does not originate in any hatred for Jews. In fact, the Hindu nationalist Islamophobic admirers of Hitler are philosemites who hold the Jewish State of Israel in high esteem for what they perceive as its having put Arab Muslim foes (including both the hostile Arab neighbors and the Arab Muslim minority within Israel) in their place. They see the Holocaust as a model to emulate, as illustrated by recent open, explicit calls for genocide against Muslims in India.[2] The Islamist antisemites' admiration for Hitler emanates out of their desire for a genocide against Jews, for which they seek validation in the vision of the impending apocalypse or the end of times in the highly controversial hadith *Sahih Bukhari*.

Hitler's popularity among those South Asians who are neither antisemites nor Islamophobes largely emanates out of the ignorance of the Holocaust and a fascination with strong leadership.[3] South Asians learned about the Holocaust largely from the Jews who found refuge there because the press in pre-1947 undivided India was focused on reporting the struggle for national independence from the British and gave little space to news of the then ongoing Holocaust.[4] Even the Jews among Indians (India is the only country in South Asia today to have a Jewish population),[5] like most of their fellow countrymen, know fairly little about the Holocaust, let alone comprehend the scale and magnitude of the colossal tragedy, as indicated by the Indian Jewish novelist Esther David. In an anecdote that she narrates in her novel *Shalom India Housing Society*, a Jewish character mistakes Yom HaShoah for a joyous Jewish festival meant to be celebrated and organizes a party to do so.[6] Holocaust commemoration events in Mumbai (Bombay), which has the highest concentration of Jews in India, register the participation of Jews in very small numbers. The English language national daily newspaper *Hindustan Times* reported in 2011 that only twenty people turned up for a Holocaust commemoration event, jointly organized by the Israeli and German consuls in Mumbai.[7] This testifies to the widespread ignorance of the Holocaust among South Asians and their lack of interest in learning about it.

The presence of casual or unwitting antisemitism cannot be denied in many cases. This casual antisemitism emerges as a result of the fact that most South Asians never come into any direct contact with Jews because of their miniscule numbers. They know them only through secondary sources, often unreliable. There are only five thousand Jews in India, in a population that nearly reaches 1.5 billion. The sources of information about Jews that shape the South Asian perceptions of them range from fiction (the problematic depiction of a Jew as Shylock in Shakespeare's *Merchant of Venice* and Fagin in Charles Dicken's *Oliver Twist*) to prejudiced, inaccurate, and exaggerated news reporting and op-eds by Islamists and leftists. In the case of Muslims, in addition to the two mentioned above, there is also the literal interpretation or misinterpretation of scriptural polemics, something not applicable in the case of Hindus because there is no reference to Jews in the Indic scriptures.[8] Those afflicted with casual antisemitism are often not even conscious of their antisemitism, and they may or may not be aware of the history of the Holocaust. Aatish Taseer describes in his memoir cum travelogue, *Stranger to History* (2009), how his father, Salmaan Taseer, governor of Punjab (2008–11), the most populous state in Pakistan, indulged in Holocaust minimization by calling the figure of six million deaths "wildly exaggerated." In support of his argument Salmaan points out his visit to Belsen, which he found to be too small to fit "in more than three hundred people a day."[9] He clearly does not realize that Belsen was a concentration camp, not an extermination camp. Aatish calls South Asia a "safe area for casual hatred" where people can voice ugly opinions of the weak and the marginalized, numerically or politically, without challenge, comforted by homogeneity. And a popular target, particularly in certain sections of Muslims in South Asia, are the Jewish people. Of the different forms of antisemitism, the one that is genocidal in nature is without doubt the most dangerous, but even the unwitting antisemitism, such as expression of a prejudiced opinion of Jews, which is more common, can be dangerous in the long run. In a society where there are hardly any Jews, as in Pakistan, there are no repercussions for speaking ill of them. The Pakistani Muslim propensity to blame the Jews for everything is pointed out by Mehnaz Afridi in her book *Shoah through Muslim Eyes* and by the Pakistani comedian Aqdas Waseem in an episode titled "Yahudi Saazish" (Jewish Conspiracy) in the Urdu satirical comedy series *Pichkaari* on the YouTube channel LoomBerry Studio.[10]

Holocaust denial and minimization are the most common expressions of antisemitism in South Asia. Holocaust denial is not illegal in the region, unlike in several countries in Europe. Far from condemning Holocaust denial, Pakistan's prime minister, Imran Khan, equates any criticism of the prophet Muhammad (blasphemous to the believers) with it. In the wake of anti-France Muslim protests after the beheading of a schoolteacher by a Muslim enraged by the teacher showing his students cartoons of Muhammad in a discussion on free speech, Khan tweeted, "I also call on Western govts who have outlawed any negative comment on the holocaust to use the same standards to penalise those deliberately spreading their message of hate against Muslims by abusing our Prophet PBUH."[11] The fact that the tone of his tweet betrayed an attempt to minimize the Holocaust did not go unnoticed. Seth J. Franzmann wrote in the *Jerusalem Post*: "The tone of his tweet, like comments by other far-right Islamist leaders, is to try to minimize the Holocaust—as he says, 'negative comments about the Holocaust'—to get back at European governments. European countries and their collaborators carried out the Holocaust; the same countries today are the ones where there are sometimes cartoons offensive to Muslims."[12] Franzmann adds: "None of the leaders, including Khan, Mahathir, Erdogan and Ahmadinejad, argued that Holocaust denial should be banned in their countries as well as blasphemy. Instead, their argument is that blasphemy should be banned in Europe and that they should have a right to free speech denying the Holocaust. In general, the cycle of these groups is to encourage Holocaust denial the more they see offensive comments against Islam in Europe."[13]

It appears that the Muslim Holocaust deniers believe, according to Meir Litvak, "that the memory of the Holocaust" provided "the foundation of

Western support for the establishment of the State of Israel." Therefore, it is felt that negating the Holocaust "would severely undermine Israel's legitimacy in the West and help in its eradication."[14] For them, "it never happened or else was hugely exaggerated," as Robert S. Wistrich points out.[15] The fact is that the State of Israel owes its foundation to the Yishuv (the Zionist Jewish entity residing in the pre–State of Israel), rather than the Holocaust. The 360,000 survivors would not have found a shelter there had there not been a thriving self-governing community or 600,000-strong Yishuv built over years since the first settlement in 1860. "And the UN November 1947 partition resolution, voting for the establishment of a Jewish State," as Dina Porat states, "came indeed after the Holocaust but not as its direct result. Political considerations, such as the Soviet interest in replacing Britain in the Middle East and in preventing American future influence in the area, were much more instrumental than belated empathy."[16]

Most of the literature on the Holocaust in Urdu, the lingua franca of linguistically diverse South Asian Muslims, aims at either denying or minimizing it. The few exceptions include Rahman Abbas's novel *Zindeeq*, which has references to the Holocaust, and the Urdu section of the website of the United States Holocaust Memorial Museum.[17] Another exception is the Urdu portion of a trilingual brochure published to commemorate the Holocaust films retrospective I held in 2009 at the two biggest universities in Lucknow, a major center of Muslim scholarship.[18] The brochure also contained an Urdu poem written by Anwar Nadeem (1937–2017) of Lucknow, the only Urdu poem on the Holocaust.[19] The event was a befitting response to the Holocaust denial conference held in Iran just three years before, in 2006. While the retrospective was in progress, the two most widely read Urdu daily newspapers in Lucknow, *Aag* and *Rashtriya Sahara*, tried to sabotage the event by publishing front-page stories denying the Holocaust.[20] The articles were based primarily on the arguments made by well-known Holocaust deniers. But even awareness of the Holocaust is no deterrent to antisemitism, as pointed out by Porat, who writes: "Holocaust education has also not yet proved itself to be barrier against antisemitism, for youngsters, whose ignorance is coupled by naivete, often raise questions such as these: Why the Jews? Why all the Jews? What's wrong with them? Was their murder really initiated without any logical reason, or other good motive? Six million—how indeed did so many Jews, who do not seem to be helpless today, allow this to be done to them."[21] Only Jewish history can answer such questions. Hence, it is so badly needed across the world. Global Jewish history cannot be divorced from the history of antisemitism.

The two are intertwined. Therefore, merely teaching about the Holocaust is not enough. It has to be accompanied by the long history of antisemitism, or in other words, put simply, global Jewish history.

As for the Indian admirers of Hitler, they, in general, are ignorant of Hitler's views on India. As a racist, Hitler considered Indians as outright rejects. Vaibhav Purandare observes that in forcefully outlining his prejudices against them, Hitler combined "hatred with contempt."[22] Harsh references to Indians in his autobiography *Mein Kampf*, a bestseller in India, go unnoticed or deliberately overlooked. Free of copyright in India, *Mein Kampf* is printed by half a dozen publishers. Hundreds of thousands of its copies have been sold in the last two decades. It has registered a steady rise in demand for it. Perhaps the genesis of Hitler's popularity in South Asia can be traced to the Nazi propaganda there. From 1933 to 1939, when the Nazi propagandists were active in India, newspapers such as *Spirit of the Times, Sālār-é-Hind, Princely India, Karnataka Bandhu, Lokhandi Morchā,* and *Trikāl* served their purpose to some degree by winning Indian moral support for Germany, even if only from certain sections of Hindus and Muslims. They targeted both Hindus and Muslims. They used the issue of Palestine to win Muslim support. To lure the Hindus, the Nazi propagandists highlighted the Nazi symbol of the swastika and the Aryan race theory, aware as they were that the swastika is an ancient Hindu symbol and that the North Indians consider themselves Aryan. They also tried to give the impression that India belonged to them alone and not to the Muslims and other communities just as Germany belonged only to Germans and not to the Jews, who were outsiders. The Nazis operated in India through various cultural and business organizations, both Indian and European.[23]

The Nazi propagandists found a particularly receptive audience in the Hindu nationalists. In a speech Vinayak Damodar Savarkar, president of the Rashtriya Swayamsevak Sangh (RSS; National Volunteer Union or National Union Corps, a far-right, Hindu ethno-religious nationalist volunteer paramilitary organization), made on October 14, 1938, he presented the Nazi treatment of Jews in Germany as a model to emulate to solve the Muslim problem in India: "A nation is formed by a majority living therein. What did the Jews do in Germany? They being in minority were driven out from Germany."[24] This provides a context to calls for genocide against Muslims in India.

The fact that Subhas Chandra Bose met Hitler and tried to win his support in raising an army against the British in India often deludes the Indians into believing that their struggle for freedom from the British rule received a significant contribution from Hitler. Bose was convinced that "the next phase in world history will produce a synthesis between Communism and fascism," and that "it will be India's task to work out this synthesis." *Sāmyavāda'* or "the doctrine or synthesis of equality" is how he described it.[25] His grandniece Sarmila Bose published an open letter to Jewish organizations on March 13, 2023, in which she apologized "to Jewish people, other victims of the Holocaust, and their loved ones" "for the failure" of her "grand-uncle" "to acknowledge and condemn the persecution and extermination of Jews, other minority groups, disabled people and political opponents, by Nazi Germany."[26]

Satya Sivaraman points out that far from being a new development, "From the time Hitler rose to power in Germany in the 1930s there have been strong currents in the Indian mainstream that admired the Fuhrer for all he stood for and indeed even sought transplantation of his perverted philosophy to Indian soil."[27] According to historian Benjamin Zachariah, "The Nazi model of all organisations under the control of one party and one leader is an appealing one" to the Hindu nationalists, and "the depiction of Hitler as a German patriot serves that purpose."[28] The Hindu Right Wing has always admired the Nazis. Their "discussion of Nazi policies towards the Jews was mediated by their general stand on the religious minorities of India, particularly on the Muslim community."[29] They see the Nazi treatment of Jews as a model to emulate in the case of the Muslim minority in India. This explains the growing popularity of Hitler among the Hindu youth.

The Hindu nationalists resort to Holocaust distortion. They appropriate the term "Holocaust" for the atrocities committed on Hindus and their alleged mass murder over a period of several centuries that these nationalists allege to have happened without any substantial historical evidence to support these claims. They do so not to equate the Holocaust with this alleged genocide of Hindus, but in order to dwarf the Holocaust in magnitude and scale through their largely baseless and exaggerated claims. It is competitive victimhood at its worst. For the Hindu nationalists it emanates out of majority victimhood, based on myths and distortion of history, rather than facts. Their claim of being heirs to "ancestral martyrs" illustrates their embrace of vicarious victimhood. They become what Zygmunt Bauman describes as "martyrs by appointment, martyrs who never suffered."[30] This is not to imply that the Muslim rulers never oppressed their Hindu subjects, but nothing can be further from truth than calling it a centuries-long genocide, many times bigger in scale and magnitude than the Holocaust (Shoah).

Basam Tibi is of the view that among the Islamists "the argument that the Jews are 'evil' leads to genocidal antisemitism. This ideology was imported from Europe and has been indigenized in process of Islamization."[31] A number of Islamist clerics have an apocalyptic vision of the annihilation of Jews.[32] This apocalyptic genocidal antisemitic vision draws primarily upon a highly disputed hadith, *Sahih Bukhari*, according to which the day of resurrection comes with a fight against the Jews who will hide behind trees and rocks to save themselves, but even they will cry out, "Oh Muslim, oh server of Allah, a Jew is hidden behind me, come and kill him." This alleged hadith states that only "the *gharqad* tree fails to betray the hiding Jew, because it is Jewish." Tibi finds reference to this hadith as telling, for "it prescribes the 'killing of the Jew' as 'religious obligation' and thus demonstrates the most perilous implication of the religionization of antisemitism."[33] It is important to note here that the Qur'an does not anywhere call to "kill the Jews."[34] Tibi rightly observes that when Hamas in article 7 of its charter quotes the above-mentioned hadith and applies it to Israel, the hadith turns into a call for the eradication of the Jewish state, which makes the possibility of another Holocaust even more substantial. Blaming the Jews for creating a schism among Muslims leading to their breakup into Shias and Sunnis, for creating a rift among Christians leading to the emergence of Protestantism, for triggering a number of wars in Europe including the two world wars, and for controlling the European economies for their own vested interests, prominent Islamic theologian in Pakistan, Israr Ahmed (1932–2010) both validated and justified the perpetration of the Holocaust on Jews, when he said: "Hitler realised that their real enemy was the Jew sitting over their heads and sucking their blood. Why this genocide, this Holocaust? He had identified them, because he was not a WASP (White Anglo-Saxon Protestant) who were enamoured and completely influenced by Jews."[35] He was honored with Pakistan's third highest civilian award, Sitārā-i-Imtiāz (Star of Excellence) in 1981. The impact of this validation and justification of the Holocaust is evident when popular Pakistani film actor Veena Malik tweeted a quote in endorsement, wrongly attributing it to Adolf Hitler, "I would have killed all the Jews of the world . . . but I kept some to show the world why I killed them."[36] She deleted it later when severely criticized for it.

A further problem around the Holocaust in South Asia is that of its inversion or reversal in the press. "Holocaust inversion" or "Holocaust reversal" is what we call the point of view that "the Israelis not only have forgotten the lesson of the Nazis but also have even become the new Nazis, doing to others what was done to them."[37] The section of the English-language press in India influenced by the left has often been found indulging in Holocaust inversion. Its significance lies in the following statistics. India, the region's largest and most populous country, home to one-sixth of the global population, has 82,237 newspapers and newsmagazines, out of which 12,000 are daily newspapers, with 1,406 out of these in the English language, and 462 million internet users.[38] India is the third largest internet user after the United States and China.[39] Thirty-nine percent of 1.2 billion Indians read newspapers.[40] Newspapers sell 125 million copies every day in India.[41] According to the World Association of Newspapers, one in every five daily newspapers in the world is published in India.[42] In 2015 the newspaper industry in India grew by 8 percent.[43] In India, print publications attract 43 percent of all corporate advertising, whereas in the United States the figure is less than 15 percent.[44] Between 2010 and 2014 advertising revenues from newspapers in India grew by 40 percent.[45] India is the world's second largest English-speaking country. It is estimated that around 10 percent of its population or 125 million people speak English, which is second only to the United States. The number is expected to quadruple in the next decade.[46]

In an article titled "The Nazis Are in Gaza" that appeared in the newspaper *Hill Post* in 2014, retired Indian bureaucrat Avay Shukla wrote: "It is a cruel irony of history that the Jewish government in Israel is doing to the Muslim residents of Gaza exactly what the Nazis did to them 70 years ago.... It is now the face of a reinvented Nazism."[47]

One major commonality in two more examples of the vilification of the State of Israel below is that the author in both cases is aware of his Jewish lineage and feels that his admission of it makes his argument(s) more compelling. It is not rare for anti-Zionist Jews to mobilize their Jewish identities in their rhetoric with the objective of creating an air of legitimacy to hostility to Israel. David Hirsh has identified this phenomenon as influential in the rise of anti-Zionism and antisemitism.[48] One of India's best known novelists, playwrights, film and drama critics, and screenwriters, Kiran Nagarkar (1942–2019), conscious of the prominent position he enjoyed in the Indian civil society, opened his essay "Alone-ness of Being Palestine," in the newspaper the *Indian Express*, with a disclaimer: "Perhaps at the outset, I should make it clear that I am a quarter Jewish."[49] As his essay progressed, he mentioned how the Israeli prime minister Benjamin Netanyahu reminded him of Adolf Hitler: "He is blood brother, perhaps the unrecognised identical twin, of Hitler. At least in one respect they shared the same objective: Come what may, get rid of an entire people."[50] He went on to write: "The only difference between the two unlikely twins is that while the Führer planned the Holocaust on the quiet at the Wannsee Conference and executed it in various concentration camps with such finesse over several years that few Germans and outsiders knew about it; the Israeli PM does it in the full glare of the media machine, claiming that he and his people are the victims of non-stop, violent Palestinian attacks."[51] The *Indian Express*, which published Nagarkar's essay, is a centrist newspaper.[52] Like Nagarkar, Kamal Mitra Chenoy also feels the need to divulge his personal Jewish connection as he questions the rationale behind the Indian prime minister Narendra Modi's visit to Israel is his essay titled "Modi in Israel: I Am Aghast as an Indian, Ashamed as a Secular Jew," published in the newsmagazine *Daily O*.[53] He ends his essay with the words, "As a secular Jew, I am deeply ashamed." "The force of the 'as a Jew' preface is to bear witness against the other Jews," as David Hirsh puts it.[54] Its basis is the presumption that being Jewish provides a sort of privileged insight into what is antisemitic and what is not—as Hirsh states, "The claim to authority through identity substitutes for civil, rational debate."[55] Hirsh observes that "antizionist Jews do not simply make their arguments and adduce evidence; they mobilize their Jewishness to give themselves influence. They pose as courageous dissidents who stand up against the fearsome threat of mainstream Zionist power."[56] Chenoy's essay was republished by the Communist Party of India, Marxist-Leninist (ML) on its official website.[57] According to them, the legitimacy of the State of Israel is questionable.

There are similar examples of Holocaust inversion from the Pakistani press as well, such as columnist Arshiya Zahid's article titled "A Holocaust to Create Israel, and Another to Achieve Greater Israel" in the *Daily Times*.[58] Another prominent example of anti-Zionism and antisemitism in the Pakistani press is given by Bernard-Henri Lévy in his book *Who Killed Daniel Pearl?* (2003), in which he describes his first glimpse of the English version of the Jihadist newspaper *Zarb-e-Momin*. It accused Israel of a genocide and carried "an editorial declaring the murder of Jews, all Jews, throughout the world, a 'sacred duty' that 'pleases Allah.'"[59] These are just a few examples of the anti-Zionist and antisemitic propaganda that Pakistan's 945 newspapers, with the exception of perhaps a few, indulge in.[60]

Finally, as far as education and textbooks are concerned, the Holocaust is rarely ever mentioned by name. The Nazi genocide against Jews is generally nothing more than a passing reference. Certain steps if taken could go a long way in creating awareness of the Holocaust in South Asia, so badly needed, such as the introduction of Holocaust studies at the secondary level of teaching and the training of teachers to teach it, publication of Holocaust pedagogical literature and the dubbing of Holocaust cinema in South Asian languages, establishment of faculty positions in Holocaust studies at institutions of higher education and the opening of Holocaust museums and commemoration of the United Nations Holocaust Memorial Day (January 27).

Notes

1. South Asia in this study refers to the region occupied by the member countries of the South Asian Association for Regional Cooperation, popularly known by its acronym, SAARC. Its member countries are Afghanistan, Bangladesh, Bhutan, India, Nepal, Maldives, Pakistan, and Sri Lanka.
2. A call for genocide against Muslims in India was made during a three-day conference called Dharma Sansad (literally, "religious parliament"), held in Haridwar in Uttrakhand, India, December 17–19, 2021.
3. The percentage of Indians who supported democracy dropped from 70 percent to 63 percent between 2005 and 2017, according to a study done by the Centre for the Study of Developing Societies (CSDS). That study found that the proportion of people "satisfied with democracy" plunged from 79 percent to 55 percent. Less than half (47 percent) of "graduates and above" were found to be satisfied with democracy. More than half of all respondents expressed their willingness to support "a governing system in which a strong leader can make decisions without interference from parliament or the courts." In 1999–2004, some 43 percent of Indians supported rule by a strong leader. This figure rose to 56 percent by 2010–14. Recent Pew surveys have found Indians to be the most ardent supporters of "autocratic rule." Together with South Africa, Vietnam, and Indonesia, India is one of only four countries in the world where a majority of citizens (53 percent) are willing to support military rule. See John Gramlich, "How Countries around the World View Democracy, Military Rule and Other Political Systems," Pew Research Center, October 30, 2017, https://www.pewresearch.org/fact-tank/2017/10/30/global-views-political-systems/.
4. Shalva Weil, "From Persecution to Freedom: Central European Jewish Refugees and Their Host Communities in India," in *Jewish Exile in India: 1933–1945*, ed. Anil Bhatti and Johannes H. Voigt (New Delhi: Manohar, in association with Max Mueller Bhavan, 2005), 64–84.
5. There were 1,235 Jews in Pakistan when it came into existence in 1947. However, over the years most of them left Pakistan for Israel and the West. Today the only openly Jewish person in Pakistan is Fishel Benkhald (b. 1987), whose maternal grandmother was an Iranian Jew. The only two Jews who remained in Bangladesh converted to Christianity, marking the end of Jewish life there. The last remaining Jew in Afghanistan recently left the country. No Jewish community is known to exist in the rest of SAARC countries.
6. Esther David, *Shalom India Housing Society* (New York: Feminist Press at City University of New York, 2009).

7. "Jews Pay Homage to Holocaust Martyrs," *Hindustan Times* (Mumbai), May 3, 2011, Appendix 1, 2.
8. Buddhist, Hindu, and Jain.
9. Aatish Taseer, *Stranger to History: A Son's Journey through Islamic Lands* (Melbourne: Text Pub., 2009) (e-book).
10. Mehnaz Afridi, *Shoah through Muslim Eyes* (Boston: Academic Studies Press, 2017), 182; *Yahudi Saazish | PICHKAARI | Pakistan Elections 2018*, YouTube video, 1:10, posted by "LoomBerry Studio," July 18, 2018, https://www.youtube.com/watch?v=vbt89IyZFp4.
11. Imran Khan, quoted in Seth J. Frantzmann, "Pakistan Targets Holocaust to Appease Far-Right Anti-French Islamists," *Jerusalem Post*, April 18, 2021, https://www.jpost.com/middle-east/pakistan-targets-holocaust-to-appease-far-right-anti-french-islamists-665496.
12. Frantzmann, "Pakistan Targets Holocaust."
13. Frantzmann, "Pakistan Targets Holocaust."
14. Meir Litvak, "The Islamic Republic of Iran and the Holocaust: Anti-Semitism and Anti-Zionism," in *Anti-Semitism and Anti-Zionism in Historical Perspective: Convergence and Divergence*, ed. Jeffrey Herf (New York: Routledge, 2006), 251.
15. Robert S. Wistrich, "Anti-Zionist Connections: Communism, Radical Islam, and the Left," in *Resurgent Antisemitism: Global Perspectives*, ed. Alvin H. Rosenfeld (Bloomington: Indiana University Press, 2013), 407.
16. Dina Porat, "Holocaust Denial and the Image of the Jew, or 'They Boycott Auschwitz as an Israeli Product,'" in Rosenfeld, *Resurgent Antisemitism*, 477.
17. Rahman Abbas, *Zindeeq* (Delhi: Arshia, 2023); "Urdu Resources," United States Holocaust Memorial Museum, accessed July 8, 2023, https://www.ushmm.org/ur.
18. Navras Jaat Aafreedi, *The First Ever Holocaust Films Retrospective in South Asia: Lucknow, September 2009* (Pune, India: Centre for Communication and Development Studies, 2009), Academia, https://www.academia.edu/102053921/Trilingual_English_Hindi_and_Urdu_Brochure_of_the_First_Ever_Holocaust_Films_Retrospective_in_South_Asia; Navras Jaat Aafreedi, "The First Ever Holocaust Films Retrospective in South Asia," *Journal of Indo-Judaic Studies* 11 (2010): 149–53, online April 17, 2019, Middle East Institute, New Delhi, http://www.mei.org.in/jijs/aafreedi11.
19. The poem's English translation by Saira Mujtaba was published in *Anwar Nadeem*, a blog dedicated to the memory of the deceased poet, on August 11, 2009, http://anwarnadeem.blogspot.com/2019/08/the-series-of-this-pain-should-not.html.
20. Anonymous, "Sadī kā Sabsé Badā Jhūt? Holocaust," *Aag* (Lucknow), October 18, 2009 [Urdu]; Qutubullah, "Holocaust: Bīsvīñ Sadī Kā Sabsé Badā Jhūtā Afsānā," *Roznāmā Rāshtriya Sahārā* (Lucknow), September 16, 2009 [Urdu].
21. Porat, "Holocaust Denial," 472.
22. Vaibhav Purandare, *Hitler and India: The Untold Story of His Hatred for the Country and Its People* (Chennai, India: Westland, 2021), 24.
23. These organizations include International Railway Information Bureau of Madras, Bombay Press Service, Indo-German News Exchange of New Delhi, Aligarh University German Society, Bhatachar Movement in Bengal (Bhattachari), German

Institute of Bombay and certain branches of Hindu Mahasabha in Maharashtra (Casolari).
24. MSA, Home Special Department, 60 D(g) Pt III, 1938, cited in Marzia Casolari, "Hindutva's Foreign Tie-Up in the 1930s: Archival Evidence," *Economic and Political Weekly* 35, no. 4 (January 22–28, 2000): 218–28.
25. Purandare, *Hitler and India*, 128.
26. Sarmila Bose, "An Apology to the Victims of the Holocaust for the Silence of My Great-Uncle Subhas Chandra Bose," *Scroll*, March 13, 2023, https://scroll.in/article/1045098/an-apology-to-the-victims-of-the-holocaust-for-the-silence-of-my-great-uncle-subhas-chandra-bose.
27. Satya Sivaraman, "Musings on the Popularity of Mein Kampf," *Infochange India*, 2009, 51.
28. Benjamin Zachariah, quoted in Manimugdha S. Sharma, "Why Hitler Is Not a Dirty Word in India," *Times of India*, April 29, 2018, online August 11, 2020, https://timesofindia.indiatimes.com/india/why-hitler-is-not-a-dirty-word-in-india/articleshow/63955029.cms.
29. Yulia Egorova, *Jews and India: Perceptions and Image* (London: Routledge, 2006), 67.
30. Zygmunt Bauman, "The Holocaust's Life as a Ghost," *Tikkun* 13 (July–August 1998): 34, cited in Anne Rothe, *Popular Trauma Culture: Selling the Pain of Others in the Mass Media* (New Brunswick NJ: Rutgers University Press, 2011), 21.
31. Bassam Tibi, "From Sayyid Qutb to Hamas: The Middle East Conflict and the Islamization of Antisemitism," in *Global Antisemitism: A Crisis of Modernity*, vol. 4, *Islamism and the Arab World*, ed. Charles A. Small (New York: Institute for the Study of Global Antisemitism and Policy, 2013), 26.
32. Clerics with this vision include Mufti Abdu Lubaba, Mufti Salman Azhari, engineer Muhammad Ali Mirza, Mohammed Bin Ishaq, and Pirzada Muhammad Raza Saqib Mustafai.
33. Tibi, "From Sayyid Qutb to Hamas," 40.
34. R. Firestone, "Is the Qur'an 'Antisemitic?'" in *Confronting Antisemitism from the Perspectives of Christianity, Islam, and Judaism*, ed. A. Lange, K. Mayerhofer, D. Porat, and L. Schiffman (Berlin: De Gruyter, 2020), 106, https://doi.org/10.1515/9783110671773-007.
35. Dr. Israr Ahmad, "Lectures in English," YouTube, https://www.youtube.com/c/DrIsrarAhmadEnglish.
36. "Pakistani Actress Veena Malik Quotes Adolf Hitler amid Unrest between Israel and Palestine; Account Withheld," ABP Live, May 14, 2021, https://news.abplive.com/entertainment/bigg-boss-4-contestant-pakistani-actress-veena-malik-quotes-adolf-hitler-amid-unrest-between-israel-and-palestine-1458328.
37. James Wald, "The New Replacement Theory: Anti-Zionism, Antisemitism, and the Denial of History," in *Anti-Zionism and Antisemitism: The Dynamics of Delegitimization*, ed. Alvin H. Rosenfeld (Bloomington: Indiana University Press, 2019), 8.
38. Smruti S. Pattanaik and Ashok K. Behuria, "Media-Scape in South Asia and the Issue of Regional Cooperation," in *The Role of Media in Promoting Regional Understanding in South Asia*, ed. Priyanka Singh (New Delhi: Pentagon Press, 2016), 28–30.

39. "India Is Now World's Third Largest Internet User after U.S., China," *The Hindu* (New Delhi), August 24, 2013, updated November 16, 2021, http://www.thehindu.com/sci-tech/technology/internet/india-is-now-worlds-third-largest-internet-user-after-us-china/article5053115.ece.
40. Dibyajyoti Sarma, "39% of Indians Read Newspapers: IRS 2017 Report," *PrintWeek India*, January 19, 2018, http://www.printweek.in/News/-indians-read-newspapers-irs-2017-report-27836.
41. Atul Kumar Mishra, "Newspapers in India and Their Political Ideologies," *TFIPOST*, July 13, 2015, https://tfipost.com/2015/07/newspapers-in-india-and-their-political-ideologies/.
42. Rajini Vaidyanathan, "Newspapers: Why India's Newspaper Industry Is Booming," BBC News, August 1, 2011, https://www.bbc.com/news/business-14362723.
43. A.A.K., "Why India's Newspaper Business Is Booming," *The Economist*, February 22, 2016, https://www.economist.com/the-economist-explains/2016/02/22/why-indias-newspaper-business-is-booming.
44. A.A.K., "Why India's Newspaper Business Is Booming."
45. A.A.K., "Why India's Newspaper Business Is Booming."
46. Zareer Masani, "English or Hinglish—Which Will India Choose?" BBC News, November 27, 2012, https://www.bbc.com/news/magazine-20500312.
47. Avay Shukla, "The Nazis Are in Gaza," *Hill Post*, August 7, 2014, http://hillpost.in/2014/08/the-nazis-are-in-gaza/100392/.
48. David Hirsh, *Contemporary Left Antisemitism* (London: Routledge, 2018), 9.
49. Kiran Nagarkar, "Alone-ness of Being Palestine," *Indian Express*, April 12, 2018, https://indianexpress.com/article/opinion/columns/alone-ness-of-being-palestine-jounalist-yasser-murtaza-death-5133603/.
50. Kiran Nagarkar, "Alone-ness of Being Palestine."
51. Kiran Nagarkar, "Alone-ness of Being Palestine."
52. Mishra, "Newspapers in India."
53. Kamal Mitra Chenoy, "Modi in Israel: I Am Aghast as an Indian, Ashamed as a Secular Jew," *Daily O*, July 4, 2017, https://www.dailyo.in/voices/modi-in-israel-palestine-netanyahu-jews-nakba-shimon-peres-kashmir/story/1/18175.html.
54. David Hirsh, *Contemporary Left Antisemitism* (London: Routledge, 2018), 228.
55. Hirsh, *Contemporary Left Antisemitism*, 228.
56. Hirsh, *Contemporary Left Antisemitism*, 228.
57. Chenoy, "Modi in Israel."
58. Arshiya Zahid, "A Holocaust to Create Israel, and Another to Achieve Greater Israel," *Daily Times* (Lahore, Pakistan), June 4, 2018, https://dailytimes.com.pk/248495/a-holocaust-to-create-israel-and-another-to-achieve-greater-israel/.
59. Bernard-Henri Lévy, *Who Killed Daniel Pearl?*, trans. James X. Mitchell (Hoboken NJ: Melville House, 2003), 362.
60. Pattanaik and Behuria, "Media-Scape in South Asia," 28–30.

13

Approaches to Holocaust Education in the Arab World
Obstacles and Solutions

MOHAMMED S. DAJANI DAOUDI AND ZEINA M. BARAKAT

This chapter provides an overview of the need to promote Holocaust education in Palestine and in the Arab and Muslim worlds. It addresses the following questions: What are the barriers to Holocaust education in Palestine, as well as the Arab and Muslim worlds? Does learning about the Holocaust promote empathy for Jews? Would teaching about the Holocaust translate into building peaceful relations between Jews and non-Jews? How important is it to the Arab-Israeli peace process to integrate Holocaust studies into the educational curriculum of the Arab world?

This chapter examines the roots of antisemitism in the Arab world. It sheds light on Holocaust denial, the efforts to cast doubts on the existence of gas chambers, and the attempt to diminish the crimes committed in Nazi extermination camps. It concludes with outlining a strategy for Holocaust education, recommending that Arab governments revise their school curriculum to ensure that this tragic episode in history is part of their ongoing educational strategy.[1]

Impediments and Barriers

There is no one "Palestinian" or "Arab" narrative dealing with the Holocaust. Most narratives are marred by shades of Holocaust denial and characterized by intolerance, prejudice, racism, bigotry, bias, and sheer ignorance. Some adopt the discriminatory approach that there was no Holocaust. The refusal to acknowledge the Holocaust not only means denying that it ever occurred; it also includes other ways of diminishing the genocide of European Jews. For example, there is the attempt to minimize the number of victims, accusing others of inflating the numbers killed, making claims that Jews are exploiting their tragedy while denying the pain of others, denying the existence of gas chambers, blaming the Jews for being responsible for the Holocaust, and even accusing Jews of exploiting the genocide to gain international support and sympathy for the creation and existence of Israel.[2] The refusal to recognize the Holocaust is connected to the loss of

Palestinian self-determination and what Arabs refer to as the Naqba, the displacement of Palestinians from their homeland.

It is necessary to distinguish between two types of modern antisemitism. The first type manifests itself in hatred of and prejudice against Jews. The second type of antisemitism includes criticisms of Israel and enmity toward Jews in terms of their faith and ethnicity. Arabs accept the first and refuse to view the second as antisemitic. Therefore, there are serious barriers to combatting antisemitism and promoting Holocaust education in Palestine and the Arab world.

Throughout the four hundred years of Ottoman rule in the Arab world between 1517 and 1917, Jews often lived a more stable life than those living in many parts of Europe, practicing their religion freely and without discrimination. During the nineteenth century, European clerics and missionaries introduced traditional Christian antisemitism into parts of the Muslim world, stemming from the claim that Jews caused the death of Jesus.[3] Nazi propaganda in the 1930s and the 1940s incited antisemitism among the Arab population who viewed Zionism as a dangerous threat to Arab national aspirations of self-determination, liberty, and independence. The Mufti of Jerusalem Hajj Amin al-Husseini (1921–37) helped spread antisemitism among the illiterate masses by quoting the infamous book *The Protocols of the Elders of Zion* and misinterpreting Quran scripture as anti-Jewish.[4] In the aftermath of the 1948 Naqba and the declaration of the Jewish State of Israel on what was considered by Arabs as the homeland of the Palestinians, antisemitic, anti-Zionism, anti-Jewish, anti-Israel, anti–United States, anti-imperialist, and anti-Western rhetoric was frequently conflated by government officials, political leaders, parties, and individuals.

Arab ignorance of the Holocaust led to the perception that they were being blamed for the Holocaust. Therefore it was seen as the direct cause of the 1948 Naqba, which left more than 750,000 Palestinian refugees.[5] The ongoing Israeli occupation of Palestinian lands and settlement expansion causes daily pain and suffering. The Arab-Israeli conflict influenced the refusal of ordinary citizens to learn about the Holocaust. Learning about the Holocaust or Jewish history became connected to the political and social taboos about Jews and Jewish society.

The continuous identification of Arab societies with the Palestinian cause has infused antisemitism in Arab politics and the public political discourse. The humiliating Arab defeats in their wars with Israel in 1947–48, 1956, 1967, 1973, and 1982, the Israeli occupation of the West Bank and East Jerusalem, and the siege and bombardment of the civilians in Gaza have profoundly influenced how Palestinians and Arabs write about, look at, and perceive Holocaust education.

Most of the Arab masses still ignore the genocide of the Jewish people in political and national solidarity with the Palestinian cause. They frequently connect what happened in Nazi-occupied Europe with the contemporary situation in Palestine. For example, there is a propensity to compare life under the Israeli military occupation to the lives of Jews in the ghettos and Nazi concentration camps. In *Al-Masry Al-Yawm*, November 18, 2023, a cartoon appeared with a flag with a swastika on top of a heap of skulls, "Israel Raises Its Flag on Shifa Hospital."

Palestinians compare their suffering with the Israeli army checkpoints, curfews, imprisonment, and closures to those imposed on the Jews by the Nazis. The conditions of Palestinian prisoners in Israeli jails are portrayed equally to the Nazi atrocities in the concentration camps. They raise the question: how are the Jews, who had suffered so much, capable of causing similar pain to others? For some, the Holocaust happened and ended, whereas the Naqba continues into the present. They maintain that Christian Europeans perpetrated Holocaust atrocities, and Palestinians were held responsible for this evil endeavor. Many Palestinians feel that Jews were compensated for their suffering at the Palestinian expense. They believe that they lost their homeland to allow Jews to establish their state.

"There are no people that has not suffered, to some extent, from the Nazi threat to the future of mankind," observes Emile Habibi, a prominent Palestinian writer, in an article titled "Your Holocaust, Our Catastrophe," first published in the *Tel Aviv Review*.[6] "In the eyes of the Arabs," he continues, "the Holocaust is seen as the original sin which enabled the Zionist movement to convince millions of Jews of the rightness of its course. If not for your—and all of humanity's—Holocaust in World War II, the catastrophe that is still the lot of my people would not have been possible."[7] Habibi concludes that the Europeans cleansed their conscience by recognizing Israel at the expense of the Palestinians.

Holocaust education can be a painful journey and a controversial educational practice for Palestinians. Israeli occupation policies have impacted Palestinian memory of the past, and thus Holocaust education fell through the cracks. The Holocaust is not taught in Palestinian schools and universities in the occupied territories; nor is it presented and narrated in history and social studies curricula. Islamic religious education in Arab schools advocates hostility toward Jews, accusing them of poisoning the Prophet. For example, the textbook *Al-Qadia al-Filistiniya* (The Palestinian Cause) states, "Their usury and love of money was the reason that people hated them, and this caused them to hate the societies they lived in."[8] The Arab educational system not only lacks Holocaust education but also omits education on Judaism, Jewish history, culture, philosophy, and civilization.

The Islamic roots of antisemitism stem from the religious misinterpretation of the Quran and the prevalent anti-Jewish hadith attributed to the Prophet. Muslim extremists describe the Holocaust as God's "punishment" inflicted on Jews for disobeying him. Islamists accuse Jews of plotting to control Arab trade and economies, monopolize essential commodities, manipulate prices of products to impoverish the Arab states, and have political and military hegemony over the Arab world. Islamists accuse Jews of plotting to control Arab trade and economies, monopolize essential commodities, manipulate prices of products to impoverish the Arab states, and have political and military hegemony over the Arab world. Islamists portray Israel as a dagger in the heart of the Arab lands, a usurper that could only be conquered by armed Jihad (Islamic struggle). Consequently, they contest all forms of peaceful coexistence with Israel and deny the religious connection of the Jewish people to the city of Jerusalem and its holiest sites and Palestine. Anti-Jewish sentiments are encouraged by the Islamic parties of al-Ikhwan al-Muslimun (Muslim Brotherhood), al-Jama'a al-Islamiya (Islamic Group), al-Jihad (Holy Struggle), al-Najoun Minal-Nar (Survivors from Hell), Takfir wa'el-Hijra (Denunciation and Holy Flight) in Egypt; Hamas (Islamic Resistance Movement), al-Jihad al-Islami (Islamic Struggle), and Hizb al-Tahrir al-Islami (Islamic Liberation Party) in Palestine; al-Jama'ah al-Islamya al-Musalhah (Armed Islamic Group), Jaysh al-Khalas al-Islami (Islamic Salvation Army) in Algeria, and the militant Islamic party, Hizb Jabhat al-Amal al-Islami (Islamic Hope Front) in Jordan.[9]

Religious sermons delivered in mosques and published in books contain antisemitic themes. In April 1995 the mufti of Egypt, Muhammad Sayyid Tantawi, declared: "As to the reference in the Quran that they [the Jews] were given preference over all other people, the context relates to a specific time and place when the Jews were committed to divine laws. Later, no people were as strongly vilified in the Quran as the Jews."[10] The interpretation does not explain that those who are vilified in the Quran broke their covenant with God and does not relate only to Jews but other believers. For example, official religious programs often broadcast on public television and radio, invoking religious rhetoric to promote antisemitism and discredit Judaism and Christianity, claiming that God has cursed Jews and Christians for falsifying the holy books that God sent them. Jews are accused of having forged their sacred scriptures and being killers of prophets, destroying the revelation of God and spreading corruption on earth, incurring God's wrath and anger. "Islam is the truth and the only truth" is the proclamation of Islamists.

There are several ways in which the Holocaust has become a taboo topic, with many Arabs preferring not to discuss it in its factual context. Those who want to learn about the Holocaust raise suspicions, doubts, and concerns about their affiliation, nationalism, and identity. Arabs exist in an environment where the Holocaust is generally viewed as a narrative marketed to them by the "other." Literature about the Holocaust in Arab writings does not accurately depict the horrors of the extermination of the Jews during World War II. Arab readers are fed misleading sources that misrepresent critical Holocaust facts, provide readers with negative perceptions about Jews and Jewish culture, and do not try to show the Jewish perspective.

Culturally, antisemitic literature impacts Arab minds. *The Protocols of the Elders of Zion* is a widely disseminated book in the Arab world, circulating among the masses as a factual treatise. It is a forgery claiming Jewish conspiracy for global domination by controlling its press and economies.[11] The book stresses the antisemitic notion that Jews believe non-Jews "are mentally inferior to Jews and can't run their nations properly. We need to abolish their governments and replace them with a single government for their sake and ours. This will take a long time and involve much bloodshed, but it is for a good cause."[12] Copies of *The Protocols of the Elders of Zion*, with new translations, continue to circulate in the Arab world and inspire other antisemitic publications. In 1968 the famous Lebanese poet Said Akl wrote in his review of Nuwayhed's book that "Israel, before you published this book, could have been considered a military threat only, but after your publication, it became a civilization and metaphysical danger."[13] Another popular antisemitic publication in the Arab library is the Arabic translation of Henry Ford's *The International Jew: The World's Foremost Problem*. It blames the Jews for the world's problems and plays a significant role in inspiring antisemitism and spreading anti-Jewish hatred.

Adolf Hitler's *Mein Kampf* (*My Struggle* in English; *Kifahi* in Arabic) has a broad audience among Arab youth and has been reprinted more times than almost any other international work.[14] In one version of the book, translator Lewis al-Hajj describes Hitler as "one of the few greats who nearly stopped the process of history, changing its direction, and altering the shape of the world; he, therefore, belongs to history."[15] He adds: "Hitler, the man of ideology, has left a huge intellectual heritage that includes politics, sociology, education, art, and war as an art and science."¹⁶ Lewis al-Hajj asserts that his translation of Hitler's book has not been published honestly before in Arabic. He claims his version is adapted from the original copy and has not been corrupted or altered by censors.[17]

Books that factually document the Holocaust are banned or censored in the Arab world. Books translated into Arabic claim the Holocaust is a hoax. They reflect negative, stereotyped images of Jews, such as *The Hypocrisy of Jews* by Martin Luther, translated from German into Arabic in 1974 by Hajaj Nuwayhed with an introduction by PLO leader in Lebanon Shafik al-Hut.[18] Luther's earlier views and expressions of antisemitism and anti-Jewish sentiment leave a strong impression among Arab Christians and the Muslim community.

Prominent Arab personalities often express hateful Jewish stereotyping. In his book *Al-Ha't wal Dumu'* (The wall and the tears), published in 1979, the well-known Egyptian writer and journalist Anis Mansur demonizes and ridicules Jews. He states Jews are allowed by their faith to ravish women from other religions and that they, as obstetricians, specialize in abortion to reduce the number of non-Jews, suggesting that the Talmud instructs Jews to kill all non-Jews.[19] In his book *Al-Shakhsiah al-Yahudiah* (The Jewish personality), Egyptian professor Muhammad Jala Idris of Tanta University describes Jews as "not humans, but something in the form of humans."[20] He concludes by stating that "the Jewish personality, as presented in the course of analysis and based on findings by psychologists, is abnormal and irregular, marked by considerable deviation and derangement."[21]

In his book *The Bible Came from Arabia*, published in 1985, the Lebanese historian Kamal Salibi suggests that God gave Abraham his Israelite descendants. Solomon and David's kingdoms were in Arabia south of Mecca, not Palestine.[22] In *Sayf al-Samiah: Qesati ma' Ukthubat al-Holocaust* (The sword of Semitism: My story with the lie of the Holocaust), published in 2005, Rifaat Sayed Ahmed discusses the political controversy in Egypt when he was accused of antisemitism for writing about the "myth of burning Jews in Nazi gas chambers."[23] He argues that the real Holocaust is taking place in Palestine, Iraq, and the rest of the Arab and Muslim world.

One of the few books published in Palestine in Arabic about the Holocaust is Mohammed Abu Samra's *Mahraqat al-Naziat bayn Raich Berlin wa Yahud Falastin* (The Nazi Holocaust between the Berlin Reich and the Jews of Palestine), published in 2008. It questions whether "the Holocaust is a reality, and if it did occur, was it by acts of Nazis or Jewish conspiracies aiming to support the idea of a national Jewish homeland and to return from the Diaspora to Palestine?"²⁴ He describes the Holocaust as a hoax and a myth improvised by Nazi and Jewish conspiracies, aiming to encourage the creation of a national Jewish homeland in Palestine and pressure Jews to immigrate from the Diaspora to Palestine.

In 2011 Egyptian writer Ayman Sharaf published *Al-Holocaust al-Muaakess: Kayf qatal al-Yahud 80 alf almani waazabu 3 malayeen akhareen* (The reversed Holocaust: How Jews killed 80 thousand Germans and tortured 3 million more).²⁵ He claims in his book that Jews took revenge on Germans in a manner that exceeds in its cruelty and brutality in comparison to what happened to the Jews during the Holocaust.²⁶ The book adapts John Sack's *An Eye for an Eye: The Story of Jews Who Sought Revenge for the Holocaust*, a work that suggests a group of Jews at the end of World War II sought revenge for the Holocaust by setting up concentration camps to torture and murder German civilians.²⁷ Sack aimed to show that Germans were also victims of Polish and Jewish revenge when the opportunity arose.

As mentioned earlier, French Lebanese author Gilbert Achcar in his well-documented book, *The Arabs and the Holocaust: The Arab-Israeli War of Narratives*, brings a new perspective on how the Arab world perceives the Holocaust in political and historical contexts. The author explores clashing narratives about the Holocaust: "As is the case concerning the events of 1948, there is a deep gap between the narratives of the two peoples about almost everything—and the Holocaust as a major trauma in modern Jewish history is no exception. It is natural for Arabs to interpret this tragic event from their point of view and according to their understanding of its implications for their history."²⁸ What is needed, then, is an agreement on the verifiable facts of the past.

Prominent figures accused of antisemitism in the West are highly praised in the Arab world. One such figure is the well-known British historian Arnold J. Toynbee, who observes in his major work, *A Study of History*, that the Israeli treatment of Arabs during the 1948 war was morally comparable to the Nazi treatment of the Jews.²⁹ Another is the French philosopher Roger Garaudy, who wrote in his book *The Founding Myths of Modern Israel* that the death of six million Jews is a "myth/hoax."³⁰

Conspicuously, there are no books in Arabic that thoroughly refute the claims and arguments of Holocaust deniers. Nor are there any present-day, in-depth accounts of what happened during the Holocaust, either written by an Arab author or as a translation into Arabic of a book dealing with the subject of denial, such as Richard J. Evans's *Lying about Hitler*, Michael Shermer and Alex Grobman's *Denying History: Who Says the Holocaust*

Never Happened and Why Do They Say It, and Deborah Lipstadt's *History on Trial: My Day in Court with a Holocaust Denier*.

Various songs, paintings, poems, comics, and different cultural activities in the Arab world incite antisemitism and Holocaust denial in one way or another, often without people realizing they are being antisemitic. Antisemitic slogans, images, and cartoons are still prevalent in the media, cultural activities, and public demonstrations. The Moroccan cartoonist Naji Benaji was awarded a special prize for drawing two bottles, one featuring the "Holocaust" containing a few skulls, and another, "Palestinian," which is full of skulls. He was lauded in the Arab world for his cartoons.[31]

Films depicting the terrors of the Holocaust, including Steven Spielberg's *Schindler's List* and Tim Nelson's *The Grey Zone*, are banned in many Arab countries such as Egypt, Lebanon, and Jordan, claiming they are "pornographic" and under the pretext that scenes of torture, nudity, and violence would offend public sensibilities. The Palestinian people find it difficult to express sympathy for the "colonizer" and "occupier" by expressing any empathy for the suffering of the Jews during the Holocaust. Thus the heated controversy that took place in April 2014 regarding the trip of Palestinian students to the Nazi death concentration camp in Auschwitz, Poland. They are deeply wounded emotionally and psychologically by the continuation of the Israeli occupation, and these wounds impact the rest of Arab society. On the individual level many Israelis fail to understand the impact of the Naqba on Palestinians. Similarly, Palestinians also fail to appreciate the impact of the Holocaust on the Jewish psyche.

Palestinians hold profound feelings of victimization as an essential part of their identity. They cannot relinquish their feelings of being the absolute victim in this conflict. Their attitude toward the Holocaust is comparative rather than sharing and empathizing with the other. The Holocaust was a crime of extraordinary dimensions. Dissidents, Roma and Sinti, and other European minority groups were also victims of the horrors of the Nazi regime. Many were sent to the concentration camps, and some were killed in the gas chambers. However, the Palestinians and Arabs fail to realize that it was the Jews who were the central target of discrimination and ultimately extermination, and they were the only ones who faced the fate of destruction as a religion.

Embarking on Holocaust Education in the Arab World

Holocaust education in the Arab world can only thrive under conditions of conflict resolution, the establishment of peace, and Israeli recognition of an independent Palestinian state. Education can help students view themselves and others as human beings first, with a moral code dedicated to cherishing the welfare and happiness of one another. Holocaust education introduces students to an inherently painful subject matter. It facilitates their understanding of why genocides happen and how they might recur. For genocides not to happen again in the future, people need to look at the truth respectfully, not ignore or deny it.

Peace education in post-conflict societies is gaining popularity as the recognition grows that unresolved disagreements about historical narratives often lead to renewed conflict and increased violence.[32] It is an effective tool to foster mutual recognition and reconciliation. Knowledge of the past fosters a more profound understanding, opens new horizons, and enables individuals to distinguish between shades of truth and falsehood.

Holocaust education can provide students with a moral foundation by offering them the opportunity to study a painful history and affording them the chance to show respect for the victims of tragedy. It helps shed light on what happened in the Nazi camps during World War II. It gives hope that people will learn from the lessons of the past.

Holocaust education allows students to alter their misperceptions about the Holocaust. Teaching about the genocide of European Jews in the educational curriculum, especially in the Arab world, reflects moral courage since it demonstrates respect for human life and esteem for human dignity.[33] Understandably, teaching the Holocaust in Arab schools can be challenging due to the prolonged Arab-Israeli conflict. One way to surmount this impediment is to teach about the Holocaust, the Naqba, and other human sufferings in modern history. They should not be integrated into one narrative nor necessarily compared. However, by engaging in these complicated and painful histories, both sides would acknowledge the narrative of the other and show respect for it.

Holocaust education can help open the eyes of students to realize that the Holocaust was not an anomaly but rather a culmination of unchallenged antisemitic sentiments and atrocities committed against Jews, forcing them to live in secluded neighborhoods and overcrowded ghettos. Holocaust education also brings awareness about the importance of ethical standards and conduct, showing the wide gap between right and wrong. It sheds light on episodes of darkness and offers hope in the face of despair. It stresses that nothing is more important than our commitment to acquiring knowledge and defending the truth. It helps students understand how ordinary people could become vicious perpetrators and how medical doctors, who swore the Hippocratic Oath, could save lives but also take lives without any remorse.

Holocaust education could become a prism through which Arab societies find the courage to address what for them is a taboo topic of the past. To that end not only students but educators in these countries should become familiar with the culture and history of the Jewish people and Nazi crimes. In this instance educators would play an essential role in correcting the distorted perceptions of a complex historical fact. They would create space for students to contribute their own past experiences. The supportive role of educators is crucial in achieving this objective.[34] Specialized organizations would train the educators and then have them return to their classrooms to design and implement the training within the school. An ethical dilemma confronting Holocaust education lies in avoiding the dangers of teaching the Holocaust in ways that might somehow promote antisemitism.[35]

Strategies for Holocaust Education Teaching

The Holocaust should be a mandatory part of the Arab education curriculum. Arabs should confront the past in their educational system to move toward a peaceful future. In *The Jews of Islam*, Bernard Lewis points out that in the Middle Ages, when polemics against Jews were typical in the Christian world, they were rare in the Islamic world. In the early centuries of Islamic rule, he writes, there existed "a kind of symbiosis between Jews and their neighbors that has no parallel in the Western world between the Hellenistic and modern ages. Jews and Muslims had extensive and intimate contacts that involved social and intellectual association—cooperation, commingling, even personal friendship."[36] Studying the historically positive and constructive relations between Muslims and Jews is a good starting point for combatting antisemitism and promoting Holocaust education. It is important to stress how the Holocaust is intertwined with Arab history and culture by not ignoring Arab efforts to save and give refuge to Jews during the Holocaust.[37]

Many Arab students have never heard of the Auschwitz extermination camp system. They should be allowed and encouraged to visit Nazi camps with their teachers as part of their studies. Students should read, watch, and discuss documentary films about the Holocaust in their classes. Nazi camps such as Auschwitz-Birkenau and Holocaust museums in the United States and Israel have played a unique role in educating people about the horrors of the Holocaust. They witness how the vicious crimes were carried out within their cement walls and barbed wires. While millions of people visited Auschwitz-Birkenau and Sachsenhausen, the number of Arabs visiting such sites is meager. However, there is hope that this might change, and more Arab visitors will join the rest of the world in paying homage to the memory of the victims of the Holocaust.

The Battle for Tolerance, Empathy, and Moderation

Arab and Muslim countries should do much more in dealing with the Holocaust to prevent the spread of antisemitism and to fight the spread of Islamophobia in the West.

Palestinian history since 1948 has been painful. Despite this fact, Palestinians should choose between right and wrong, good and evil, and black and white with no in-between gray zone when it comes to recognizing the Holocaust. It is imperative to make this choice. There is a universal consensus that the Nazi efforts to exterminate the Jewish race were wrong. Palestinians suffered and are still suffering through the Israeli occupation. However, that does not mean that the Holocaust should be ignored or denied. This is not the legacy they should leave for future generations.

There are several reasons why Holocaust education is expected to have a positive impact on the Arab world. First, Holocaust denial is historically incorrect and factually wrong. It constitutes a significant threat to morality and human dignity. Second, recognizing the Holocaust is a sign of respecting historical truth. When the reality of the past is denied or ignored, it destroys values. Third, learning the tragic lessons of the past is necessary to avoid their recurrence in the present and future. Fourth, showing empathy and compassion for the suffering of others, even if no relations, friendship, or love bonds exist with them, would make this world a better place to live in. Fifth, the Quran and the Prophet encourage the pursuit of knowledge and learning. The Quran says: "And say, 'My Lord, advance me in knowledge'" (Taha Surah, verse 20). The Prophet hadith: "Seek knowledge from the cradle to the grave." This compels us to seek knowledge and the truth: "I do not know, but I want to know." Sixth, without knowing about evil, we cannot understand the meaning of good. Lastly, being criticized for doing the right thing is still a worthwhile responsibility for seeking historical truth. It is imperative to have books dealing with the Holocaust objectively, such as Robert Satloff's *Among the Righteous: Lost Stories from the Holocaust's Long Reach into Arab Lands* and Mehnaz Afridi's *Shoah through Muslim Eyes*, translated into Arabic to enhance Holocaust education.

Conclusion

Antisemitism in Europe has deep roots and a lengthy history of pogroms extending back to the Crusades, the expulsion from Spain, and the horrors of the Holocaust.[38] In the Arab world Jews became the target of slander, defamation, stereotyping, and conspiracy theories recently after the establishment of the Jewish state of Israel in 1948. Palestinians, and Arabs in general, need to realize that understanding the complexity of the Holocaust is central to diminishing the enmity and hatred that fuel antisemitism and Islamophobia. Palestinians should learn about the Holocaust as a unique event without it casting a shadow on their 1948 Naqba. They should recognize that they have nothing to fear from opening their eyes to the truth concerning these dark chapters of modern human history.

Showing respect for the memory of the Holocaust and expressing empathy with its victims rightly acknowledges the past and offers a way to support the struggle against racism, bigotry, intolerance, antisemitism, and Islamophobia globally. The lack of Holocaust education in Palestine and many Arab/Muslim countries has created a vacuum in historical and educational curricula. More importantly, the depiction of Jews in the media and social networks has created a perspective that can be called antisemitic. We can achieve a better educational system by disseminating articles, journals, media, and books in Arabic about the Holocaust and other genocides.

Notes

1. Other scholars have surveyed some of the above issues. For example, Gilbert Achar, *The Arabs and the Holocaust: The Arab-Israeli War of Narratives*, trans. G. M. Goshgarian (New York: Metropolitan Books, 2010); Sarah Ozacky-Lazar, "Holocaust Memory among Palestinian Arab Citizens in Israel: Personal Sympathy and National Antagonism," in *Holocaust Memory in a Globalizing World*, ed. Jacob S. Eder, Philipp Gassert, and Alan E. Steinweiss (Göttingen: Wallstein Verlag, 2017); Samira Alayan, "The Holocaust in Palestinian Textbooks: Differences and Similarities in Israel and Palestine," *Comparative Education Review* 60 (February 2016): 80–104.
2. Edy Cohen, "Arabs and the Holocaust," BESA *Center Perspectives Paper*, no. 1,438, February 5, 2020. On January 26, 2007, the 192-member UN General Assembly approved a resolution by consensus, introduced by the United States, condemning "without any reservation any denial of the Holocaust."
3. Institute of Jewish Affairs and American Jewish Committee, *Antisemitism: World Report 1995* (London: Institute of Jewish Affairs; New York: American Jewish Committee, 1995), 250.
4. Abdel Karim Al-Omar, ed., *Muthakarat Hajj Amin al-Husseini* [Memoirs of Hajj Amin al-Husseini] (Damascus, Syria: Al-Ahali, 1999). These memoirs were origi-

nally published as articles in the Egyptian magazine *Akher Sa'ah* and the monthly *Palestine Journal* and were later collected into a book. Another source is his interviews with the weekly magazine *Roz al-Yusuf*, collected as a book.

5. See Ilan Pappe, *The Ethnic Cleansing of Palestine* (London: Oneworld, 2007); Rashid Khalidi, *The Hundred Years' War on Palestine: A History of Settler Colonialism and Resistance, 1917–2017* (New York: Metropolitan Books, 2020).
6. Emile Habib, quoted in Leon Wieseltier, "Palestinian Perversion of the Holocaust," *New York Times*, June 12, 1988, sec. 4, 27.
7. Wieseltier, "Palestinian Perversion of the Holocaust," 27.
8. *Al-Qadia al-Filistiniya*, quoted in *Wasatia Education: Exploring the Palestinian Curriculum* (Jerusalem: Wasatia Academic Institute and IMPACT-se, 2019). See "Education in Times of Conflict," *Palestine-Israel Journal* 8, no. 2 (2001).
9. See Bernard Lewis, "Muslim Anti-Semitism," *Middle East Quarterly*, June 1998, 43–50.
10. Institute of Jewish Affairs and American Jewish Committee, *Antisemitism*, 253.
11. For example, see Ajaj Nuwayhed, *Protuqulat Hukama' Sahyoun* [The protocols of the Elders of Zion: Its text, symbols, and Talmudic origins], 4th ed. (Beirut: Al-Istiklal and Arab Institute for Research and Publishing, 1996); Ajaj Nuwayhed, *The Protocols of the Elders of Zion and the Talmudic Teaching*, trans. Shawki Abdel Nasser (Beirut: al-Taqween, 2003); see also N. Cohn, *Warrant for Genocide: The Myth of the Jewish World–Conspiracy and the Protocols of the Elders of Zion* (New York: Harper & Row, 1966); S. Bronner, *A Rumor about the Jews: Reflections on Antisemitism and the Protocols of the Learned Elders of Zion* (Oxford: Oxford University Press, 2003).
12. See Richard Landes and Steven Katz, eds., *Paranoid Apocalypse: A Hundred-Year Retrospctive on "The Protocols of the Elders of Zion"* (New York: New York University Press, 2012); E. Webman, ed., *The Global Impact of "The Protocols of the Elders of Zion": A Century-Old Myth* (London: Routledge, 2011).
13. Said Akl, *al-Muharer* newspaper, August 10, 1968, quoted in the introduction to Nuwayhed, *Protocols of the Elders of Zion*.
14. Adolf Hitler, *Kifahi* [*Mein Kampf*], trans. Lewis al-Hajj (Ramallah, Palestine: Palestinian Institute for Publishing and Distribution, 1995).
15. Hitler, *Kifahi*, 5.
16. Hitler, *Kifahi*, 5.
17. Hitler, *Kifahi*, 6.
18. Martin Luther, *Al-Yahud wa Akazibahum* [*The Jews and Their Lies*], translated from German to Arabic by Hajaj Nuwayhed, with an introduction by Shafik al-Hut (Beirut: Dar al-Fikr, 1974); Martin Luther, *On the Jews and Their Lies*, trans. Martin H. Bertram, in *Luther's Works* (Philadelphia: Fortress Press, 1971).
19. See Raphael Israeli, "Arab and Islamic Anti-Semitism," ACPR Policy Paper, no. 104, 2000.
20. Institute of Jewish Affairs and American Jewish Committee, *Antisemitism*, 253.
21. Israeli, "Arab and Islamic Anti-Semitism," 253.
22. Kamal Salibi, *The Bible Came from Arabia* (London: Jonathan Cape, 1985).
23. Rifaat Sayed Ahmed, *Sayf al-Samiah: Qesati ma' Ukthubat al-Holocaust* [The sword of Semitism: My story with the lie of the Holocaust] (Cairo: Madbuli Library, 2005).

24. Mohammad Abu Samra, *Mahraqat al-Naziat bayn Raich Berlin wa Yahud Falastin* [The Nazi Holocaust between the Berlin Reich and the Jews of Palestine] (Amman, Jordan: Dar Usamah, 2008).
25. Ayman Sharaf, *Al-Holocaust al-Muaakess: Kayf qatal al-Yahud 80 alf almani waaz-abu 3 malayeen akhareen* [The reversed Holocaust: How Jews killed 80 thousand Germans and tortured 3 million more] (Cairo: Jazeerat al-Ward Library, 2011).
26. Sharaf, *Al-Holocaust al-Muaakess*, 5.
27. John Sack, *An Eye for an Eye: The Story of Jews Who Sought Revenge for the Holocaust*, 4th rev. ed. (New York: Basic Books, 2000).
28. Gilbert Achcar, *The Arabs and the Holocaust: The Arab-Israeli War of Narratives* (New York: Metropolitan Books, 2010; Paris: Picador Paper, 2011).
29. Arnold J. Toynbee, *A Study of History*, 12 vols. (Oxford: Oxford University Press, 1934–61); Francis Neilson, "Arnold Toynbee's 'Study of History,'" *American Journal of Economics and Sociology* 14, supplement (April 1955): 1–77.
30. Roger Garaudy, *The Founding Myths of Modern Israel* (Paris: Aaargh, 1996); Roger Garaudy, *The Mythical Foundations of Israeli Policy* (London: Studies Forum International, 1997).
31. See Manfred Geerstenfeld, "Holocaust Inversion: The Portraying of Israel and Jews as Nazis," no. 55, April 1, 2007, Jerusalem Center for Security and Foreign Affairs, https://jcpa.org/article/holocaust-inversion-the-portraying-of-israel-and-jews-as-nazis/.
32. Simone Lassig, "Post-Conflict Reconciliation and Joint History Textbooks Projects," in *History Education and Post-Conflict Reconciliation: Reconsidering Joint Textbook Projects*, ed. Karina V. Korostelina and Simone Lassig (London: Routledge, 2013), 1.
33. Zeina M. Barakat, *From Heart of Stone to Heart of Flesh: Evolutionary Journey from Extremism to Moderation* (Munich: Herbert Utz Verlag GmbH, 2017), 177.
34. Elke Gryglewski, "Teaching about the Holocaust in Multicultural Societies: Appreciating the Learner," *Intercultural Education* 21, supplement 1 (2010): S41–S49.
35. Geoffrey Short, "Teaching about the Holocaust: A Consideration of Some Ethical and Pedagogic Issues," *Educational Studies* 20, no. 1 (1994): 53–67.
36. Bernard Lewis, *The Jews of Islam* (Princeton NJ: Princeton University Press, 2014); quoted by Fareed Zakaria, "Anti-Semitism Is like Cancer in the Islamic World," *Durango (CO) Herald*, February 21, 2019.
37. Robert Satloff, *Among the Righteous: Lost Stories from the Holocaust's Long Reach into Arab Lands* (New York: Public Affairs, 2007).
38. See William I. Brustein, *Roots of Hate: Anti-Semitism in Europe before the Holocaust* (Cambridge: Cambridge University Press, 2003).

14

"When This Happens, Whoever Can Write"
The Testimonial Representation of the Holocaust in Colombia

LORENA CARDONA GONZÁLEZ

The rewriting of different types of accounts about the Holocaust appears as a drive, an irreverence, a desire for justice, and even as an irrepressible vitality for some survivors, who, like Primo Levi, make their own experience an impulse to tell and a need to listen, because writing and talking about Auschwitz is not only allowed but even necessary.[1]

Understanding the insufficiency of language with which any account could describe what happened in the concentration camps or during the war in general and challenging the violent impositions of the Holocaust were, among other things, the answers to those who tried to make this "An event without witnesses" and to those who were convinced that if the truth were revealed, the world would not believe it, considering them as facts too monstrous to be believed.[2]

In this sense the witnesses of the Shoah make their testimony a possibility of representation despite how overwhelming their experience was, and yet they carry in their respective accounts the stories of hundreds of absent people who did not survive to tell. We know of them only because their experiences have taken shape through the words of those witnesses.

It could be said that after Auschwitz the stories of survivors began to appear in the public sphere as both literature, memoirs, *and* testimony. Auschwitz and its consequences transformed the narrative spectrum and have brought together in their orbit not only survivors but also other types of writers who have made it a leitmotif to talk about the continuities of barbarism and the dissolution of human beings. This type of testimonial literature affirms Esther Cohen's argument that such literature "revolves around the barracks, gas chambers, crematoria, hunger, the self-destruction of man at the hands of man."[3] Its particularity allows one to sense a new genre of testimonial literature that Cohen calls Nazi concentration camp literature.

A concern about this genre lies in its transient nature because of the irremediable death of its authors. The end of witnessing will lead to an array of literature and its disappearance. Alternatively, recognizing the permanent nature of the works has generated additional texts and productions in the words of other writers who would speak of harsh life in camps using other narrative devices and resources. This makes this genre of testimonial literature a form of memory preservation and reflection on the atrocities of the Holocaust. Consequently, an analytical and contextual approach to this literature about the Holocaust is fundamental because it allows for registering these stories within the places where they happened and concerning the authors who constructed them.

In Colombia the Holocaust typically appears as a distant event that took place in Europe, and it is not commonly linked to local history. Although the Holocaust is seen as a European crime, this essay expands the Holocaust to local history in Colombia. There are testimonial accounts of a few survivors who, at some point, lived in Colombia, and there they captured their memories and impressions of this event.[4] Three such accounts are briefly referenced in this chapter: *No olvidarás* (*Thou Shalt Not Forget*) by Israel Lapciuc; *Otoño dorado: Inicio del Holocausto* (Golden fall: The inception of the Holocaust) by Polish survivor Edith Korman; and *Anyu* by Anamaria Goldstein.[5]

Published in different decades, these works of testimonial literature speak to the phenomenon of survival and its link with Colombia. These survivors came from places such as Romania, Poland, and Hungary, and they give an account of the uniqueness of the extermination in each of their countries, of the struggles to overcome barbarism, of family members lost in the war, and of how they were saved. However, beyond the uniqueness of these texts, what stands out is their reaffirmation of leaving an imprint and commitment to life and of expressing a way of understanding the violence to which they were subjugated and the aggressions they suffered during the civil war in Colombia—creating an intersection between suffering at different times and remembering their past trauma during the Holocaust.

No olvidarás

At the end of the 1970s, some North American newspapers reported that "Colombian Jews are victims of a racial stereotype" because several community members had been kidnapped at the hands of common criminals and subversive organizations because of the collective antisemitic trope that is associated with Jews and wealth.

During this wave of harassment against the Jewish community in Colombia, *No olvidarás* by Israel Lapciuc was published in 1976. That same year, the author's father, Samuel Lapciuc, who had been kidnapped a few months prior, was released in the city of Medellín through the payment of a large sum of ransom money.[6]

Given the limited security that the country offered, the Lapciuc family decided to emigrate to Miami, leaving as a legacy this story in which their experiences of the war during the Nazi occupation in Romania are narrated. It is significant that the first document of the Holocaust in Colombia, written in Spanish, emerged at a time when there was hostility toward the Jewish community. The complexity of these stories records not only the war but also the circumstances to which some survivors were subjected while trying to rebuild their lives.

No olvidarás is a narrative about the author's wartime memories that exemplifies a personal imperative that seeks to share and talk on behalf of those who could not do so. It is a story about an eleven-year-old boy who survives the Holocaust, and who decides thirty years later to narrate it from memory as if it was written in the present without the context of the present time. He attempts to show how he faced the war from a childhood perspective in which he details the events under the terrible conditions during the Holocaust.

The text is extremely rich in details and insights. Step by step the book places the reader within the Nazi concentration camp system: the defeat of the Romanian army by the German outpost, the occupation of the cities and subsequent antisemitic measures, the establishment of the ghetto (in this case, in the city of Czernowitz), the deportations, the tedious and cruel train voyages, his passage through two concentration camps (Ladischin and Cariera de Piatra),[7] his confinement in an orphanage within the Bershat Ghetto, and finally his liberation by the Soviet army.

It is striking that this story does not belong to the dominant group of Holocaust narratives that revolve primarily around Nazi camps. It stands out for describing a process of extermination that is marked by hunger, exhaustion, forced labor, and especially shootings by the operation groups (Einsatzgruppen) in collaboration with the local Ukrainian police.[8] Furthermore, he also demonstrates the importance of the 1943 Jewish resistance in Romania and its connections to the Soviet army at the time of the Russian counteroffensive.

The book gradually delves into the loss of Lapciuc's childhood, which involves estrangement and misunderstanding. It then goes through survival strategies and finally through a process of violent radicalization forced by the conditions of the war. The author recalls his childhood and the mature role that he had to assume to avoid death, highlighting the implications, internal dilemmas, and the weight of the decisions he makes to survive. The narrative demonstrates the power of memory and narrative for a survivor.

The plot begins with the German occupation and the surrender of Romania in June 1941. From the moment that Lapciuc is led to the Czernowitz ghetto with his family, he creates friendships with other boys that enable them to take advantage of their skills and agility to escape and get food.[9]

In November 1941 deportations from the ghetto began to the area of Transnistria, a Soviet region occupied by German and Romanian forces, whose natural borders were the Dniester River and the southern bank of the Bug River.[10] The long train journeys and the deplorable overcrowded conditions are described as strategies to undermine the will of the victims and in turn to starve people to death. Notions of madness and delirium become visible as the narrative describes increasingly extreme and cruel situations.

The story presents associations that compare Germans with beasts, such as when the author writes: "From then on, I began calling them beasts. Yes, they were uniformed beasts who instead of growling talked in German. The beasts were waiting for us all in the ghetto. You could see them around the clock at the end of the streets."[11] The responses of the victims are explained through a madness that ensues, and one of these associations appears in the description of the transfer and the loss of reason of the victims inside the train cars:

> My neighbor beats with both hands and challenges death while crying. It scares me to see the expression his face has taken on. It is discomposed and his eyes roll around inside the holes. There is a fixation that turns him into something he was not a moment ago. . . . His hands, somewhat chubby, are cracked and a smear of blood covers his knuckles. He is crazy, his actions are those of a man possessed. As he punches, jumps, and bursts into laughter, he stops crying to laugh. He has no reason to laugh unless madness has entered his head. When he stops banging, I grasp my mother's apron. I'm afraid that the madman will turn his banging against me.[12]

These two associations are particularly interesting, a delirium that creates a condition for survival. First, this helps in reducing barbarism to the brutality of the perpetrator, or the insanity of the victim is a strategy for which it is impossible to be responsible. Finally, animals and humans do not share the same sense of reason, and the insane are not subjected to the same measures as ordinary people in ordinary situations.

Beyond surviving, one of the missions of every survivor is to tell the story of their experience, to create a work of justice in which the witness not only appears as the one who was there but also as the one who, by narrating, gives back the word to the *drowned*, who could not escape from barbarism.[13]

Among the many events described in the book, there are also the extermination camps and children's orphanages.[14] The book also describes the organized groups of Jewish resistance. Their work emerged not only through action and uprisings but also through writing as denunciation and relief and to ensure the significance of the events; the experiences would be documented so that others would not forget.

The book also delves into reflections on the loss of childhood and innocence, the imperative need to survive during war, and the thirst for revenge. Furthermore, it also gives an account of later events such as the return to the devastated cities, the questions about what the survivors would become in the future, the search for relatives, and Lapciuc's arrival in Bucharest, a stopover before he arrived in Colombia. According to Lapciuc's narrative, violence, hatred, and revenge are natural reactions to the atrocities of the Nazis and their collaborators. This reading of violence applies to adults and strongly politicized people; however, adulthood or political concerns do not correspond to Lapciuc's case; here the violence is vital and therefore completely justified. It is impossible to deduce the reasons for this type of narrative, but what is clear is that "the memory of violence and the memory of what was done to commit it is difficult to manage in times of peace," not in times of war.[15] This is rare and shows that the Colombian context enables the condition of being able to create this kind of story and continue talking about past violence through the prism of present violence without further reflection.

In summary, it is important to note that *No olvidarás* is a book that offers the reader another perspective on the Holocaust. The crudeness of the crimes of Nazism can be read from other situations, in other geographies, and with a childlike perception of the facts. Its density is marked by violence, and the bloody scenes of the testimony are emptied of hope or promising endings. This book is only a possibility in the present violence in Colombia and reasserts the marks of trauma.

An edition of *No olvidarás* published by Editorial Bedout of Medellín has a single reference in the book of Colombian testimonial chronicles by the author Simón Guberek, "Yo vi crecer un país," where the crudeness of the testimony of Israel Lapciuc is described.[16] Perhaps his early departure from the country, due to the kidnapping of his father, has left this text, ironically, in "oblivion." However, its value can be seen as the first registry of the Shoah in Colombia, which can be approached from multiple perspectives.

Otoño dorado: Inicio del Holocausto

Otoño dorado by Edith Korman appeared in 1996, and as Rudolf Hommes notes in the book's prologue, it is the result of Steven Spielberg's film *Schindler's List*. As is the case in the United States and elsewhere, the film has become a symbolic reference for many survivors. After the film's premiere, many survivors decided to start telling their stories, as is the case of Edith Korman.

Otoño dorado is described by Korman as a debt that she felt she owed to her family for years of silence. The book is an attempt to explain the numerous questions that were asked of her and for which she had not found the right words until writing *Otoño dorado*.

The text narrates the war years that Korman and her family endured in Poland. Korman was born in Kozienice, a small shtetl about twenty kilometers from Warsaw, and begins by offering an account of her life in the village, a quiet place that revolved around the industry of the shoe trade. The people of the village were traditional and had a deep attachment to Judaism. Their coexistence with Polish Catholics did not appear to be one of conflict, except for some manifestations of antisemitism. At first the book shows Korman's connection with Colombia due to the early migration of her father, Abraham Kestemberg, to the country in 1928. He had hoped to open a new path in the Americas, improve his economic situation, and reunite his family on a different continent.

Once in Colombia, the family moved to Mompox, a riverside town in the Department of Bolivar, where her father set up a small shop to import merchandise and to sell and distribute it. The village was like a tropical tranquility where strangers were welcomed to new customs, traditions, and language. Korman makes the following observation: "The tropics were a novelty that as children we enjoyed, no more harsh winters, no more boots, and uncomfortable coats. We ate exquisite and unknown fruits; these, which for Eastern Europe were a scarce delicacy and supremely expensive, were picked without trouble from the trees in the courtyards. The walks were to the vast and majestic Magdalena River, where the momposinos sailed in canoes and sifted the sand in flat bowls, to separate the tiny grains of gold that were deposited at the bottom."[17] In Korman's words, Colombia was late to industrialize as it was more traditional with a positive atmosphere. After this short stay in Colombia, the family had to return to Poland in 1932 due to the health problems experienced by her mother because of the weather and changes in her diet. Once they returned to Poland they began to hear frequent comments about the situation in Germany and the advent of Hitler.

By 1937 the changes in Kozienice were evident. There was no talk of anything other than the risks and dangers of Nazism. Polish Jews returning from Germany came with stories of increasingly heartbreaking news about their experiences of mockery, segregation, and restrictive decrees.

Faced with this scenario, Korman's father again tried to return to Colombia. On behalf of his family, he managed to obtain only one visa, so he had to leave without any other family members. On June 15, 1939, Korman's father left Poland with the hope of being able to process the consular documents for his wife and children in Colombia. Unfortunately, the beginning of the war impeded the process, and the rest of the Korman family had to face the difficult years of the Nazi occupation separately.

At this point in the story, we are transported to interesting nuances and contradictions. The book reveals a testimony of survival as well as a denunciation of Colombian immigration measures and a political reaffirmation based on Zionism.[18] The text confirms the importance that Judaism played for the author and documents the struggle of the Jews in the context of the Warsaw ghetto uprising.

On September 25, 1939, the transfer order for those imprisoned in the ghetto was issued. Despite the extreme conditions of starvation and misery, Korman emphasizes that the ghetto was also a place of mutual aid. She joined a voluntary unit as a nurse, taught children in the underground, and provided food for the neediest.

The conditions of the war caused Korman to reaffirm her religious beliefs. Her Judaism was not a reason for humiliation or shame. In this sense celebrating the holidays and respecting the Shabbat remained a ritual obligation each Friday.

In 1941, despite the imminence of the transfers and deportations, Korman, with the help of some friends of her parents, managed to hide in the town of Ostrowiec. For this to happen, her relatives in the ghetto were required to arrange a false identity for her as a Catholic, and she was required to memorize important dates in Catholicism and acquire knowledge of the main celebrations and prayers.

While in hiding, Korman gained a broader view of the war, the political circumstances, the blackmail of Schmáltzovniks, and the diverse resistance movements that operated in Warsaw.[19] After the war she eventually found her family in Poland, and before the Soviet government prevented her from leaving the country, she escaped to Austria, in the Allied zone. After additional trips through Europe, she reunited with her brother Gilek in Paris. There they received the documents and the funds necessary to go to Colombia. Finally, in July 1946, at the age of twenty-three, she found her father again in the city of Cali.

An essential part of the text is the author's description of uprisings, resistance actions, and Jewish sabotage within the ghetto against the Germans. For example, she highlights how the tenets of religion and the fundamentals of life appeared to be in opposition to the will of legitimate defense, resistance, and the general actions of war. The struggle and the defense required a strong character, which contrasts with the stereotype of the cowardly and incapable Jew, docile in the face of adversity. The uprising of the Jews in the ghetto undermined the belief that Jews fled without resistance, indicating the courage and heroic measures taken by the Jews.

The written testimony is urgent and important because, as Korman emphasizes, it contributes to the search for answers, to the intention of leaving a legacy, and it allows the experiences of many survivors in time to have remained and be "heard" even after death. There are several reasons why *Otoño dorado* is a critical text: it is a reflective work in which the past and the present are in constant dialogue, generating in the reader an expanded and meaningful look at the experiences through its author of persecution at the hands of the Nazis. Likewise, it offers an account of a range of topics that reveal other perspectives and other facts about the Holocaust, such as a woman's perspective on combating her situation. The text is full of contradictions, as in all testimony, but allows one to ask new questions, and it leaves a more profound impact on the war in Colombia.

Anyu

The final work, *Anyu*, appears as a familiar and self-contained testimonial project, in which Anamaria Goldstein recounts her life story, especially her experiences during the war.[20] It is a well-structured text and is not only a testimonial but is also informative and precise historical documentation. It is presented like a photo album with commentary in which familial aspects are intertwined with the history of Hungary during the war. It shows how this history is intertwined with the fate of the Jews.

Born in 1942, Goldstein, when barely three years old, survived the war hidden in the house of a baroness who agreed to hide her with her parents by obtaining false Christian documentation and a significant sum of money. That is why Goldstein defines herself as a survivor of the war, a reflection of the trauma suffered by the generation that remained, one of the 7,712 Jewish children left alive in Hungary, many of whom were orphans.

This is a story that emerges from other stories; it shows how Goldstein came to the story of her loved ones from the narration of her parents, her aunt Ila, her friends, and her teachers. It also draws on documents of another nature, such as historical research, geographic references, statistical data, family trees, press archives, questionnaires, job lists, bibliographies, and references. This does not mean that the text is tedious or unempathetic; on the contrary there are deep reflections in it and questions, especially those that arise after the catastrophe and those that have to do with the reconstruction of life in a communist context in postwar Hungary.

The book historically frames the situation of the Jews within Hungary and their relations before the war. It shows that the relations between Magyars and Jews were relatively pleasant, even friendly. The anti-Habsburg rebellion of 1848 granted minorities economic and legal equality. Jews enjoyed citizenship, as well as extensive rights such as voting and the possibility to pursue areas such as commerce, agriculture, and education.

However, in 1920 this atmosphere of trust gradually changed with the rise to power of Miklós Horthy, who promoted an ambiguous policy concerning the Jews. Although it was in this country where one of the first antisemitic measures was established in Europe—before the arrival of Nazism—such as the Numerus Clauses, which limited school admissions, at the same time it was one of the countries in which the degree of collaboration with the German government was not as radical as in France or the Netherlands.

Goldstein's father, Sándor Vajda, was a lawyer and throughout the war was involved in obtaining residence permits for Jews fleeing southern Poland and Russia and traveling to Hungary in the hope of safety.

In 1941 the government of Marshal Horthy issued a law prohibiting Jewish lawyers from practicing their profession. As a result Goldstein's father had to close his office, although he continued with the task of obtaining residences and visas clandestinely. The government also determined that Jewish males between the ages of eighteen and forty-eight (later on the range would be extended to between sixteen and sixty) had to perform forced labor. Goldstein's father thus had to dedicate himself to building dams, working in quarries, and loading trains with packages of flour weighing 70 kilos (over 150 pounds).[21]

His aunt Ila was one of the first people deported from Hungary to Auschwitz, traveling with seventy others in a cattle car for five days. She was sent to Lager B III, Block 7.[22] From Auschwitz, she was transferred to Germany, specifically to Allendorf, and once there she worked as a slave in the Dynamite Nobel factory owned by IG Farben.

With her father in prison and her family's whereabouts unknown, Goldstein and her mother, Erzsebet, were hidden during the last days of the evacuation, looking for an alternative to escape death. Between basements, temporary residences, and houses on the outskirts of Budapest, Goldstein and her mother managed to save themselves; her father was released from jail at the end of October 1944 and was able to meet them.

The accounts of the reunion and the conditions after the war are devastating. They indicate the number of relatives killed in Auschwitz and elsewhere, adding to this the state of material and economic ruin of Budapest, which in 1945 was under Soviet occupation. This period meant a lot of changes and new prohibitions for the survivors in the countries with communist influence: there were no cultural or religious distinctions, and beliefs were suppressed. This made it impossible to speak from each different ethnicity and to describe the conditions of each extermination.

Faced with this panorama and with renewed fears, Goldstein and her family managed to emigrate to Colombia in 1957, after the Hungarian Revolution. In Colombia, many years later, she was able to begin the reconstruction of the events, so that in later decades she could write her story.

As Alessandro Portelli affirms, family stories are not constructed in an orderly and chronological manner. The family stories of the Holocaust did not suggest that idyllic way in which the father or grandfather under the warmth of a fireplace set out to tell a story—in this case a miserable and complex one.[23] The narratives of the Shoah have reached the new generations randomly and haphazardly, more from silence and prudence than from freedom of speech.

The Holocaust is a subject that is represented in language through fear, in the repetition of suffering, or in the numerous accounts of those who suffered it. They are often stories that are elaborated with fragments and explanations, which is why each author must make sense of them and find their logic. This is a clear exercise in the way *Anyu* is constructed, and that is what Goldstein appeals to in her book. It seems that the reader is taken through the labyrinth of experiences to piece together the testimony and experiences of the survivor.

Conclusion

It is important to point out that these three books offer an immense variety and richness, approaching the Holocaust from multiple instances, not only geographically but also critically. In historical matters, depending on each case, they treat Nazi policies, state collaboration, the phenomenon of ghettoization, deportations, the world of mass killing—both in extermination camps and in the operations of the shooting squads—the phenomenon of liberation, migration, and communist dictatorships. Likewise, they are gestures constructed with ample narrative resources, passing through Lapciuc's pure and passionate narration, Korman's reflexivity and poetics, and Goldstein's arrangement and documentation. Their views on survival are also different: for Lapciuc, it is the lost childhood and the management of barbarism through violence and revenge; for Korman, it is the strength of a legacy, the exaltation of courage, and the value of her religion; and for Goldstein it is the search for answers and the challenge of speaking out after surviving a war and suffering a dictatorship. However, in each literary testimonial lies the idea of hope translated to their children and grandchildren, in transmitting not only their faith but also a history that will become a memory in each of their steps.

Along the same lines, these documents are instructive about the specificity of other forms of violence that, although they may seem distant, constantly speak to us and knock on the doors of the violence in Colombia. Many of these survivors have lived with the war in Colombia and are also constantly reliving past horrors—the connections between conflicts, the parallel readings of the war in Europe and the war in Colombia, the intersections with violence and, above all, with kidnappings. The testimonial accounts mention these connections, and thanks to these books it is possible to trace these instances not as an isolated phenomenon. With these books and the information, one can ascertain that many surviving Jews desired to leave the country in the years after their arrival. In one way or another, the Holocaust, which for Colombians is something that happened to others in the heart of Europe, can be a prism through which we can read our excesses and extract from it other lessons.

Notes

1. Primo Levi, *Entrevistas y Conversaciones* (Barcelona: Península, 1998), 130.
2. Giorgio Agamben, *Lo que queda de Auschwitz: El archivo y el testigo; Homo sacer III* (Barcelona: Pre-Textos, 2000), 18; Primo Levi, *The Drowned and the Saved* (New York: Simon & Schuster, 2017), 1.
3. Esther Cohen, *Los narradores de Auschwitz* (Monterrey, Mexico: Editorial Fineo, 2006), 26.
4. There are very few testimonial productions of survivors registered in Colombia, and they are not widely disseminated.

5. Israel Lapciuc, *No olvidarás* (Medellí, Colombia: Editorial Bedout, 1976); *Thou Shalt Not Forget: A Child's Memoir of the Holocaust* (Hoboken NJ: KTAV, 2004); Edith Korman, *Otoño dorado: Inicio del Holocausto* (Bogotá, Colombia: Ediciones Tercer Mundo, 1996); Anamaria Goldstein, *Anyu* (Bogotá, Colombia: Escala LTDA, 2007).

6. In 1978, according to Israeli diplomatic authorities, the belief that such kidnappings were motivated by antisemitic intentions was false. However, this stereotype was significant since all the victims were nationally recognized industrialists and businessmen. Ana Posner, a victim of such a crime, even reported that her captors had repeatedly beaten her and insulted her with antisemitic insults. The situation of violence and insecurity in Colombia was such that many of the members of the community began to emigrate to other countries in the hope of finding quieter places to continue their lives. An article by Azriel Bibliowicz (2001) reviews the way in which Colombia has encouraged a double migration of the Jewish community in the country: "60% of the members who left emigrated to Miami; 25% to Israel; 10% to Costa Rica and 5% to other countries." Azriel Bibliowicz, "Intermitencia, ambivalencia y discrepancia: Historia de la presencia judía en Colombiam," *Amérique Latine Histoire et Mémoire* 3 (2001): 20.

7. These concentration camps are currently in Ukrainian territory. See "Transnistria," Shoah Resource Center, http://www.yadvashem.org/odot_pdf/Microsoft%20Word%20-%205883.pdf.

8. After the occupation of Ukraine, some anti-Stalinist groups joined the German forces, creating the Russian National Liberation Army (RONA), also called "hiwis"—auxiliary volunteers—who were used as collaborators of the SS in the concentration camps and in the shooting operations in Bessarabia, Bukovina, Romania, and Ukraine. See "Hilfswillige," Shoah Resource Center, https://www.yadvashem.org/odot_pdf/Microsoft%20Word%20-%206372.pdf.

9. The Czernowitz ghetto was created by the Romanian dictator Ion Antonescu on October 10, 1941. About fifty thousand jews were interned there. See "Traian Popovici and the Jews of Czernowitz," Jewish Virtual Library, https://www.jewishvirtuallibrary.org/jsource/biography/Popovici.html.

10. The Government of Transnistria was a territory granted by the Nazis to the Romanians, as compensation for the northern Transylvanian territories given to Hungary in the second Vienna arbitration in 1940. Some 150,000 Jews from the regions of Bessarabia, Bucovina, and northern Moldavia were deported to this area, of which only 60,000 survived. See "Transnistria," Shoah Resource Center.

11. Lapciuc, *Thou Shalt Not Forget*, 48.

12. Lapciuc, *Thou Shalt Not Forget*, 106.

13. Levi, *Drowned and the Saved*, 1.

14. For more details, see Lorena Cardona González, "Sobre ciertas cosas que no se pueden nombrar: La Representación del Holocausto en Colombia (1976–2015)" (master's thesis, Universidad Nacional de la Plata, 2015), 68–77, https://www.memoria.fahce.unlp.edu.ar/tesis/te.1163/te.1163.pdf.

15. Alessandro Portelli, *Absalom, Absalom! Storia orale e letteratura* (Rome: Donzelli Editore, 2007), 9.

16. Simón Guberek, *Yo vi crecer un país: Crónicas testimoniales colombianas* (Bogotá, Colombia: Fundación Cultural Simón y Lola Guberek, 1982).
17. Korman, *Otoño dorado*, 23.
18. Immigration to Colombia was difficult despite the determination and disposition that the Hebrew Federation in Colombia and the newspaper *Nuestra Tribuna* (journal of the Ashkenazi Jewish community in Colombia) made to facilitate the way for immigration. The Colombian legislation added new elements to restrain the arrival of immigrants; for instance, Decree 1194 of 1936 expressed in detail the requirements and documents for "certain nationalities." These documents included a certificate of behavior for the last ten years, where the migrant's moral qualities were certified. A health certificate was required stating the absence of infectious diseases, disability, dementia, or addictions. Likewise, this decree for the first time banned the entrance of a specific foreign group. According to Article 11, gypsies, regardless of their nationality, could enter the country. Finally, requirements were added for a landing bond to be paid at the port of entry, which fluctuated between 100 and 500 pesos, depending on the kinship and the number of entrants. All these measures were in response to the different pressures—particularly from labor unions—that considered the migratory flows as unfair competition that would complicate the already difficult labor situation in the cities.
19. The Schmáltzovniks were a Polish group that reported to authorities about converted Jews or Jews with false documentation.
20. The word "Anyu" means "mother" in Hungarian.
21. Goldstein, *Anyu*, 22.
22. Goldstein, *Anyu*, 27.
23. Alessandro Portelli, *Historias orales: Narración, imaginación y diálogo* (Buenos Aires, Argentina: Prohistoria Ediciones, 2016), 107.

15

Holocaust Education in Australia
History, Importance, and Challenges

SUZANNE D. RUTLAND

The twentieth century is recognized as a century of genocide. Since the Armenian genocide in 1915, millions of people have been murdered in the name of racial, religious, national, or tribal purity. Over time Holocaust education has come to be seen as one way of countering hate ideologies and genocidal campaigns. The aim of this chapter is to discuss whether Holocaust and genocide education can play a role in countering these campaigns, using developments in Australia as a case study. It argues that a general approach to antiracist education, covering the different events in recent history and introducing study of the Holocaust as a paradigmatic example of genocide, is an effective way to counter prejudice and racism. A nuanced approach is needed to confront the challenges and problems of using Holocaust education to counter prejudice and racism.

While mass violence has been an ongoing phenomenon throughout human history, the concept of genocide is comparatively new. In 1944 Polish Jewish jurist Raphael Lemkin coined the term "genocide," endorsed by the United Nations Genocide Convention in 1949.[1] Initially Jewish Holocaust survivors and historians opposed any comparisons between the Holocaust (known in Hebrew as the Shoah) and other genocides. However, in the 1990s, as the Bosnian and Rwandan genocides occurred, some key Jewish thinkers changed their mind. In his introduction to his groundbreaking work *Rethinking the Holocaust*, preeminent Holocaust historian Yehuda Bauer argues: "The Holocaust has, therefore, become the symbol for genocide, for racism, for hatred to foreigners, and of course for anti-Semitism, yet the existence of rescuers on the margins provides a hope that these evils are not inevitable, that they can be fought. The result is the beginning of international cooperation to educate as many people as possible—to warn them."[2] Bauer's message is that despite the Holocaust's unprecedented nature, with its use of industrialized murder and international impact, if it has happened once in human history, it can happen again. He reminds us that people must be able to differentiate "between mass murder, genocide and . . . the amok killing of children in a Scottish village by a disturbed individual."³ He argues: "Just as we cannot fight cholera, typhoid and cancer with the same medicines, mass murder for political reasons has to be fought differently than genocides and Holocaust(s)."⁴

The Australian Jewish Community and Holocaust Education

Between 1946 and 1961 Australia received around twenty-seven thousand Holocaust survivors, supplementing the approximately nine thousand prewar Jewish refugees and Jewish internees sent by the British in the early 1940s. Of that number, approximately 60 percent of survivors, mainly Polish, settled in Melbourne, with 40 percent, mainly Hungarian and Central European, in Sydney. Melbourne had the highest percentage of Holocaust survivors on a pro rata population basis outside of Israel. However, the early postwar years were marked by the code of silence. Most survivors did not talk of their traumatic experiences.⁵ Many believed that the best way to secure continuity of Jewish life was by building a new life in Australia and having children to replace those who had died, with these children often bearing the names of lost loved ones. They wished to shelter their children from the horrors they had experienced during the Holocaust.⁶ A child of survivors, Ruth Wajnryb, describes her experience of growing up in Campbelltown, a Sydney suburb distant from the Jewish center, stressing: "It was as if we'd arrived from another planet, with no records or recollections, no memory. We lived in the present and for the future. . . . But there was no past. The past was cordoned off, sealed out. There was a complete severance with what went before."⁷

When they began to share their stories starting in the late 1970s, most Australian Jewish survivors wanted to focus on the specificity of Jewish suffering, resisting any comparisons, including with the genocide against the Indigenous Australians. For them the Holocaust was unique. Due to the suffering they experienced in Poland, they also strongly opposed the community participating in the March for the Living, an international program involving visits to Auschwitz and other Holocaust memorial sites introduced in 1987. This only changed in 2001 with the second generation, some of whom started to return to Poland and write about their personal experiences. Over time the pain of the survivors receded, and there were significant changes on the international scene, particularly following the disintegration of the Soviet Union in 1991.⁸

The initial endeavors in Holocaust education were all based on efforts within the Jewish community, beginning in the 1970s.⁹ A specific program was initially introduced into the Sydney Jewish day school, Moriah College, in 1976.[10] In the 1980s there were major developments largely because of survivors wanting to counter Holocaust denial. This included the opening of Holocaust museums in Melbourne, Sydney, and later in Perth, initially by survivors. As Helen Light comments: "It is here that they have felt safe to break their silence, to record their sufferings, and to share their trauma. Their message: beware of racism, of fascism, of discrimination. Be sure, 'Never Again.'"[11] School education programs were introduced with increasing numbers of students from across the spectrum of government and private schools visiting as part of their studies in history, religion, or English.

Over the two last decades, the Jewish community has developed several additional programs that seek to reach into the schools to combat antisemitism and racism. These include Courage to Care, a student-centered program dealing with the Holocaust and non-Jewish rescuers of Jews, introduced in 1998. Its traveling exhibition and pedagogic materials center on the non-Jewish rescuers, those who had the "courage to care," risking their lives to save Jews. Its aim is to convey messages of tolerance and living in harmony, emphasizing the importance of standing up against persecution, especially against minority groups.[12] It also emphasizes the ability of the individual to make a difference. Other programs have been introduced with an interfaith element, with various programs run by the New South Wales Jewish Board of Deputies, which use an intercultural approach, including a visit to the Sydney Jewish Museum with the aim to teach genocides, incorporating the Holocaust, with each speaker dealing with a different genocide.

Clearly professional development is vital in terms of Holocaust education. Over the years the community has introduced programs to sponsor teachers, mainly non-Jewish, who wish to study at Jerusalem's Yad Vashem, Israel's Holocaust Memorial and Education Centre. One motivating factor for participating teachers is concern about anti-Jewish sentiments expressed in their schools. Acting on their own initiative, they have applied for these scholarships to study at Yad Vashem. In 2009 the Melbourne Jewish philanthropist John Gandel introduced the Gandel Holocaust Studies Program for Australian Educators, aimed specifically at high school teachers, with the inaugural course held in January 2010. This program offers generous grants for successful applicants to attend the course and attracts between twenty and forty Australian teachers each year.

Over time the community has also moved to a more universalistic approach to Holocaust education, meeting current student needs, both Jewish and non-Jewish. In 2018 the Sydney Jewish Museum underwent a major renovation and added a broader section on human rights. Thus, as is happening globally, Holocaust education is linked with human rights education in Sydney.[13]

Holocaust Study and Its Universal Messages

The United States Holocaust Memorial Museum outlines the value of Holocaust education on its website: "The Holocaust provides one of the most effective subjects for examining basic moral issues. A structured inquiry into this history yields critical lessons for an investigation into human behavior. It also addresses one of the central mandates of education, which is to examine what it means to be a responsible citizen."[14] Holocaust education also gives us a template toward understanding the importance of genocide education and the need to include it in school curricula, as is now proposed, at least in principle, at the federal level in Australia.

Education about the Holocaust and genocide has come to be seen as an important element in preventing the incitement to hate. Bruce Carrington and Geoffrey Short have argued that the universal approach allows educators to address the Holocaust in broad pedagogic terms, using it as a case study in education against racism and "helping students to understand that ethnic and cultural prejudice and discrimination can take diverse forms."[15] They posit that the topic of the Holocaust can assist students gain a deeper understanding of the abuse of human rights violations based on different parameters relating to ethnicity, nationalism, and religion, as well as a better understanding of the dangers of scapegoating and stereotyping. This can ensure that students become more effective citizens for democracy. Similarly, Margot Brown and Ian Davies have stressed the vital importance of Holocaust education. They point out that a study of the Holocaust "raises questions about general intercultural relationships" since other groups such as the Roma and homosexuals were also persecuted.[16]

At the same time, there are dangers in the universal approach because the Holocaust can be used and misused for various political purposes.[17] As well, the media can also trivialize the Holocaust. Renowned Holocaust historian Michael Marrus has warned: "Reduced sometimes to slogans, the lessons can become familiar through packaging, but more often than not, I suspect, are discarded as easily as are advertisements."[18] Thus, Marrus stresses that historians need to take care with the concept of universal lessons from the Holocaust.

The challenges of using the Holocaust to teach ethics and morality have also been raised by Australian historian and Holocaust educator Avril Alba.

She asks how can one bring the complexities of the past to bear on the minds of the present? To illustrate this difficulty, she quotes from the Australian author Jackie French's celebrated children's novel, *Hitler's Daughter*, when the central protagonist, the young boy Mark, confounds his teacher with the following question:

> "Mr. MacDonald..."
> "Yes, Mark?"
> "The things Hitler did, or Pol Pot... all that genocide stuff. I mean could they have ever thought they were right?"
> Mr. MacDonald looked uncomfortable. "I don't know," he said at last. "Sometimes people think they are doing the right thing even when it is bad. But with Hitler and Pol Pot... I just don't know. Maybe they did think what they were doing was good."
> "But how can we know we're doing the right thing?" cried Mark.[19]

Alba points out that Mark's response indicates the complexity to understanding what is right and wrong. As with Marrus, Alba also argues, "Holocaust curricula cannot abdicate either historical rigor or ethical complexity. Educators must be equipped to work with the difficulty of the history while laying bare and contending with the implicit ethical messages and 'lessons' embedded in the educative process itself." She stresses that even though there is a debate as to whether the study of the Holocaust and other mass atrocities can lead to more ethical approaches in the present, the "demand that we consider them anew" is surely undeniable.[20] Therefore, she advocates that teachers need to challenge students and encourage them to "recognise the contingency of their own 'presents,' encouraging complexity rather than complacency in the negotiation between present and past."[21]

Government Policy and Holocaust Education

Historically, Australian school education has been a state responsibility, with each state having its own department, resulting in different approaches and matriculation examinations. The Holocaust has been included within history courses, particularly in year ten and in the senior school history syllabi, which include World War II for matriculation. However, the federal government in Australia has not mandated the commemoration of Holocaust Memorial Day of January 27, and there has been no Australian-coordinated Holocaust education program, although this could change with the new National Curriculum, the draft of which has more focus on the Holocaust but is not yet implemented.

Until recently, the Jewish community's focus has been on what is called in Hebrew Yom HaShoah (Holocaust Remembrance Day), held annually on the Hebrew date of 27 Nisan (April/May) to commemorate the Warsaw Ghetto Uprising, the three-week Jewish insurgency in 1943. Recently the Australian Jewish community has also begun to commemorate the International Holocaust Remembrance Day on January 27, with ceremonies being held at the Jewish museums with members of the general community and dignitaries invited to participate. In 2021 this was changed to an Australia-wide virtual commemoration involving key political figures.

Australian governments, at the federal, state, and local levels, have been particularly active in promoting the story of the Swedish diplomat Raoul Wallenberg. His activities in Budapest, Hungary, helped save the lives of tens of thousands of Jews through his distributing protective Swedish passports and creating safe houses in diplomatic buildings. In 1985 Anna Cohn's sculpture honoring Wallenberg was dedicated in a park in the Sydney suburb of Woollahra. In the same year a monument was erected in the Melbourne suburb of Kew, designed by the Austrian-born sculptor Karl Duldig. According to the artist, "The stones symbolize the destruction of the Holocaust, whilst the portrait of Wallenberg at the top symbolizes how one man was able to make a difference and save so many lives."[22] Subsequently, another memorial was established at Melbourne's Jewish Holocaust Museum and Research Centre, and a tree and memorial seat have been located outside the St. Kilda Town Hall.[23]

In order to highlight Wallenberg's courageous efforts and tragic end, the Australian Labor government, led at the time by Julia Gillard, granted him honorary Australian citizenship in 2013. In addition, on April 23, 2013, Gillard signed The London Declaration, which was drafted and signed in 2009 by members of parliaments from across the democratic world—a group known as the Inter-Parliamentary Coalition for Combating Antisemitism. This was strongly supported by the Liberal Party, then in Opposition, with 105 parliamentarians from the Opposition signing the declaration. In February 2016 the Department of Foreign Affairs and Trade further paid homage to Wallenberg's courageous stance by hosting a traveling exhibition on his life's story titled "To Me There's No Other Choice," sponsored by the Swedish Embassy. All these activities help educate the government officials and the general public about the Holocaust, through the personal story of one individual who had the "courage to care."

The various efforts by the government discussed above were piecemeal, and while in principle the Australian government supported the concepts of Holocaust memory and education, few specific, concrete steps were taken until very recently. The initial Holocaust museums and memorials were funded largely by the Jewish community, and there was no broader government involvement, as occurred with the United States Holocaust Memorial Museum in Washington DC or the Imperial War Museum in London, where the Holocaust exhibit was incorporated into the broader museum. However, in 2021 the Liberal federal government committed to fund a new Holocaust museum in Canberra, the nation's capital. It also provided additional funding to the Holocaust museums in the state capitals of Adelaide, Brisbane, Melbourne, Perth, and Sydney.[24]

While the Australian government was represented at the Stockholm meeting in 2000, Australia did not immediately apply to become a member nation of the International Holocaust Remembrance Alliance (IHRA). This changed in 2015 when, because of efforts within and without the Jewish community, the government applied for observer status. In June 2019 Australia gained full membership status, and in 2021 Scott Morrison, the Australian prime minister, announced that Australia had adopted the IHRA Working Definition of Antisemitism that was adopted by the organization in Bucharest in 2016.

Challenges Facing Holocaust Educators

Several different challenges face Holocaust educators. One major issue is whether the Holocaust should be taught under the umbrella of the discipline of history, English, religious, or citizenship education.[25] Many countries include the topic of the Holocaust within the history curriculum, but its objective nature limits discussion of broader moral, ethical, and philosophical issues that do not fall within its rubric.[26] There are also pedagogic issues relating to the amount of time allocated to teaching the Holocaust; it is often included as part of World War II, so the issues are only dealt with superficially; and there may be a lack of teacher knowledge.[27] All these issues are directly relevant to Holocaust education in Australian schools.

Another issue is whether Holocaust education can counter antisemitism, which primarily comes from three sources: the far right, the far left, and radical Islam. Recent studies have highlighted that antisemitism in Australian schools can come from different school populations and possibly reflect these different triggering sources.

I studied attitudes of Muslim school children living in the largest concentration of Australia's Muslim population in Sydney's southwestern suburbs. Many attend local government schools, and Arabic-speaking students can constitute up to 80 percent of a school's population. This study was based on original data derived from interviews with teachers in these schools, as well as with Jewish educators who were involved with the programs discussed above, such as Courage to Care. Despite their very diverse religious and ethnic heritages from Asia and the Middle East, many children of Muslim background expressed strong anti-Jewish attitudes, reflecting some of the myths circulating in the Arabic media, such as the belief that Israel was responsible for 9/11 and that Jews control the media. Muslim students also often expressed an admiration for Nazism and Hitler; some drew swastikas on the desks and had posters of Hitler. They also made statements in class such as, "Hitler did the right thing" and "Hitler didn't go far enough."[28] Jewish teachers have experienced harassment from their Muslim students, as have Jewish students in these schools, to the extent that their parents have had to move them to another school.

The belief that Israel was created as compensation for the Holocaust exists in the Muslim world, as demonstrated by an action-based Israeli study that found that the interviewees saw a direct analogy between the Jewish Holocaust in Europe and the flight and expulsion of the Palestinian refugees in the 1948 war, the Naqba, or what they called "the Palestinian Holocaust."[29] From the data that emerged from my research, the belief that the Palestinians are the real victims of the Holocaust is also strong in Sydney, based on similar concepts elsewhere in the Muslim world.[30]

However, antisemitism can also be an extreme problem for students at monocultural schools, often located in geographical locations where the Muslim population is very small. There have been several recent examples of playground antisemitism, which a recent study also highlighted.[31] In the last three years, particularly troubling incidences occurred in Melbourne, the state of Victoria's capital, at both the primary and secondary levels. A recent survey of seventy teachers regarding their experiences teaching the Holocaust in New South Wales revealed this geographical and socioeconomic diversity and found that antisemitism can be more prevalent in Protestant than Catholic nongovernment schools. This indicates that there can be different factors contributing to antisemitism and Holocaust denial.

Several studies have also found that there is a gender factor. Philip Mendes's 2008 study of antisemitism among Muslim youth found Muslim antisemitism was confined to boys' schools, reporting on the boys downloading "beheadings and attacks against 'infidels' onto their mobile phones and then swapping them with their friends."[32] He argued that these sentiments come almost exclusively from boys, and that it "appears to be a form of male violence which is not mirrored by girls in the same cohort."[33] My study supported this finding, as has the more recent study of seventy teachers involved in Holocaust education, where all the comments in regard to antisemitism came from either boys or coed schools.[34] Thus, there are different factors contributing to the problem of antisemitism in schools, which need to be considered.

Conclusions and Recommendations

These findings indicate that the different ethnic, religious, and political factors contributing to antisemitism may require different teaching strategies. The Victorian government's response to the recent problems of antisemitism in government schools has been to make Holocaust education mandatory for years nine and ten and to develop new teaching and learning resources, which also include local references. In addition, the government has established a dedicated "Reporting Racism Phone Line," provided additional funding to address the problem of playground antisemitism, and established a Jewish Student Advisory Group to keep the government informed.

There is a debate in educational circles as to the best way to approach anti-Jewish attitudes. Together for Humanity (T4H), an organization dedicated to promoting interfaith harmony and accepting the "Other," does not use the Holocaust at all because of its belief that including the Holocaust could be counterproductive to the program's aims, especially for Muslim children.[35] In comparison, other teachers in the Sydney schools believe that the best approach is to teach the Holocaust within the genocide framework, beginning with the Bosnian genocide of 1995, which some of the Muslim students' parents experienced. The students need to understand that hate can lead to genocide before addressing the Nazi genocide. After that, a visit to a Holocaust museum is more meaningful.

In terms of non-Muslim antisemitism in schools, particularly in Protestant schools, more research is needed to establish the basis of this prejudice. The prevalence of antisemitism and Holocaust denial in social media, particularly on right-wing sites, is certainly a major trigger for students across the diverse population spectrum. The recently released IHRA "Recommendations for Teaching and Learning about the Holocaust" includes a section on how to counter antisemitism spread on the web, and this is an aspect where better strategies are needed.[36]

Museums aim to counter racism, but when preparing their education programs, they need to consider the religious and ethnic background of their student school groups. Philipp Schorch argues in regard to the

Melbourne Immigration Museum: "At the same time, the research findings suggest that the life worlds of students, their personal backgrounds and schools, are intertwined with their interpretive engagements with the exhibition and need to be considered for museum practices and further research."[37] This also applies not only to Jewish Holocaust museums but also to Holocaust education. As discussed, while there are key messages to be conveyed through Holocaust education to counter prejudice and racism, Holocaust education is no simple panacea. Educators need to ensure that they are thorough in their preparation for teaching the subject, and that they convey the key ethical and moral issues within all the complexity of the period.

Notes

1. "Coining a Word and Championing a Cause: The Story of Raphael Lemkin," United States Holocaust Memorial Museum, Holocaust Encyclopedia, accessed September 6, 2016, https://encyclopedia.ushmm.org/content/en/article/coining-a-word-and-championing-a-cause-the-story-of-raphael-lemkin.
2. Yehuda Bauer, *Rethinking the Holocaust* (New Haven CT: Yale University Press, 2001), xi.
3. Bauer, *Rethinking the Holocaust*, 67.
4. Bauer, *Rethinking the Holocaust*, 67.
5. Ruth Wajnryb, *The Silence: How Tragedy Shapes Talk* (Sydney: Allen & Unwin, 2001), 6.
6. Suzanne D. Rutland and Sophie Caplan, *With One Voice: The History of the New South Wales Jewish Board of Deputies* (Sydney: Australian Jewish Historical Society, 1998), 318.
7. Wajnryb, *The Silence*, 6.
8. Suzanne D. Rutland, "'Returning to a Graveyard': Australian Debates about March of the Living to Poland," in *Aftermath: Genocide, Memory and History*, ed. Karen Auerbach (Melbourne: Monash University Pub., 2015), 141–65.
9. Judith E. Berman, *Holocaust Remembrance in Australian Jewish Communities, 1945–2000* (Perth: University of Western Australia Press, 2001), 82–84.
10. Suzanne D. Rutland, "In the Shadow of the Holocaust: The Development of Moriah College, Sydney," special issue, "The Memory of the Holocaust in Australia," *Holocaust Studies: A Journal of Culture and History* 13, no. 2-3 (2007): 35–58.
11. Helen Light, "Jewish Museums: The Space to Explore," in *New under the Sun: Jewish Australians on Religion, Politics and Culture*, ed. Michael Fagenblat, Melanie Landau, and Nathan Wolski (Melbourne: Black Inc, 2006), 290.
12. Sharon Kangisser Cohen, "'Courage to Care': A First Encounter between the Holocaust and Australian School Students," *Australian Journal of Jewish Studies* 19 (2005): 121.
13. Suzanne D. Rutland and Suzanne Hampel, "Holocaust Studies in Australia: Moving from Family and Community Remembrance to Human Rights and Prevention of Mass Violence," in *Conceptualizing Mass Violence: Representations, Recollections,*

and Reinterpretations, ed. Navras Aafreedi and Priya Singh (London: Routledge, 2021), 107–9.

14. "Rational and Learning Objectives," United States Holocaust Memorial Museum, accessed December 1, 2021, http://www.ushmm.org/educators/teaching-about-the-holocaust/why-teach-about-the-holocaust.

15. Bruce Carrington and Geoffrey Short, "Holocaust Education, Anti-Racism and Citizenship," *Educational Review* 49, no. 3 (1997): 271.

16. Margot Brown and Ian Davies, "The Holocaust and Education for Citizenship: The Teaching of History, Religion and Human Rights in England," *Educational Review* 50, no. 1 (1998): 81.

17. Michael R. Marrus, *Lessons from the Holocaust* (Toronto: University of Toronto Press, 2015).

18. Marrus, *Lessons from the Holocaust*, 152.

19. Avril Alba, "Lessons from History? The Future of Holocaust Education," in *A Companion to the Holocaust*, ed. Simone Gigliotti and Hilary Earl (Hoboken NJ: Wiley Blackwell, 2020), 599.

20. Alba, "Lessons from History?," 614.

21. Alba, "Lessons from History?," 614.

22. Alan Gil, "New Hope for Wallenberg as Park, Sculpture Dedicated," *Sydney Morning Herald*, May 13, 1985, 3.

23. "Raul Wallenberg Memorial/Kew," Only Melbourne, accessed December 1, 2021, http://www.onlymelbourne.com.au/raoul-wallenberg-memorial#.V8944rU1Q7A.

24. Rob Harris, "'A Brighter, More Tolerant Future': $750,000 Funding for Holocaust Museum in Canberra," *Sydney Morning Herald*, January 27, 2021, https://www.smh.com.au/politics/federal/a-brighter-more-tolerant-future-750-000-funding-for-holocaust-museum-in-canberra-20210126-p56wx6.html.

25. Neil Burtonwood, "Holocaust Memorial Day in Schools—Context, Process and Content: A Review of Research into Holocaust Education," *Educational Research* 44, no. 1 (2002): 69–82.

26. See, for example, Susan Hector, "Teaching the Holocaust in England," in *Teaching the Holocaust*, ed. Ian Davies (London: Continuum, 2000), 105–15; Carrie Supple, *From Prejudice to Genocide: Learning about the Holocaust*, rev. ed. (Stoke-on-Trent, UK: Trentham Books, 1998).

27. Geoffrey Short, "The Role of the Holocaust in Antiracist Education: A View from the United Kingdom," *New Community* 23, no. 1 (1997): 75–88; Brown and Davies, "Holocaust and Education for Citizenship"; Greg Keith, "The Holocaust in Australian Secondary Schools: An Analysis of a Quantitative Survey of History Teachers in the Greater Sydney Area," unpublished manuscript, 2021.

28. Suzanne D. Rutland, "Genocide or Holocaust Education: Exploring Different Australian Approaches for Muslim School Children," in *As the Witnesses Fall Silent: 21st Century Holocaust Education in Curriculum, Policy and Practice*, ed. Zehavit Gross and E. Doyle Stevick (Geneva: Springer, 2015), 225–43.

29. Edna Shoham, Neomi Shiloah, and Raya Kalisman, "Arab Teachers and Holocaust Education: Arab Teachers Study Holocaust Education in Israel," *Teaching and Teacher Education* 19 (2003): 617.

30. Mehnaz M. Afridi, *Shoah through Muslim Eyes* (Boston: Academic Studies Press, 2017), 28.
31. Zehavit Gross and Suzanne D. Rutland, "Combatting Antisemitism in the School Playground: An Australian Case Study," *Patterns of Prejudice* 48, no. 3 (2014): 309–30.
32. Philip Mendes, "Antisemitism among Muslim Youth: A Sydney Teacher's Perspective," *ADC Special Report*, no. 37 (Melbourne: B'nai B'rith Anti-Defamation Commission, 2008), 2.
33. Mendes, "Antisemitism among Muslim Youth," 2.
34. Rutland, "Genocide or Holocaust Education," 234; Keith, "Holocaust in Australian Secondary Schools."
35. Interview with Rabbi Zalman Kastel, "Rotary Youth Talks: Bringing Humanity Together with Youth Engagement," December 15, 2021, YouTube, https://www.youtube.com/watch?v=RKI8d8y7yik.
36. "Recommendations for Teaching and Learning about the Holocaust," International Holocaust Remembrance Alliance, https://holocaustremembrance.com/resources/recommendations-teaching-learning-holocaust.
37. Philipp Schorch, "Experiencing Differences and Negotiating Prejudices at the Immigration Museum Melbourne," *International Journal of Heritage Studies* 21, no. 1 (2015): 47.

16

Aotearoa New Zealand

ANN BEAGLEHOLE

Though the Holocaust took place in distant countries, it has continued to reverberate in New Zealand in the years since—at least symbolically—and through policies and laws relating to refugees. In addition to New Zealand's actions and inactions regarding refugees, this essay considers Holocaust commemorations and education in the twenty-first century, human rights, and reverberations of the Holocaust for the Indigenous Māori people.

Refugee Policy, 1930s and 1940s

New Zealand severely restricted non-British immigration in the 1930s and 1940s. Yet around 1,100 refugees (mainly Jewish), fleeing Nazi Europe, were able to enter before the outbreak of World War II. Thousands of others who applied to enter were declined for reasons discussed below. After the war New Zealand continued to place restrictions on the entry of Holocaust survivors and other refugees.[1]

While New Zealand rescued some Jewish refugees trying to flee the Holocaust, the country's main action to help victims of Nazism was to fight in World War II to defeat Nazi Germany. New Zealand soldiers, twelve thousand from a population of under two million, contributed their lives to ending the war.[2]

In the 1930s and 1940s, Pākehā (New Zealanders primarily of European descent) took for granted that the only desirable immigrants to New Zealand would be British. Jews, Chinese, and other "race aliens," as they were then termed, were not wanted. Desperate Jewish refugees were subject to the tight controls of the 1931 Immigration Restriction Amendment Act, which meant that most were declined entry.

Walter Nash, minister of customs in New Zealand's first Labour Government, was responsible for immigration policy. He thought Jewish refugees would be difficult to "absorb" without raising "antipathy" to them.[3] Many of the refugees were professional or business people. Professional and business associations were wary of possible rivals. Nash's justification for restricting the entry of refugee business people was that "anti-Semitism, never far from the surface, was very apt to emerge in the case of the talented race whose members can often beat us at our own game, especially the game of money making."[4] Nash also argued that the refugees should be refused entry because they would add to the number of the unemployed looking for work or did not have the skills that were needed in New Zealand.

The government was under some pressure from Britain to accept refugees to ease their flow to Britain and Palestine. There was significant Jewish immigration to Palestine until Britain, which had been granted the mandate by the League of Nations in 1922, started severely restricting immigration in 1939 in response to concerns of the Arab population.

Pressure came too from the Intergovernmental Committee on Political Refugees, set up by the Evian Conference on refugees, initiated by the United States in 1938. At Evian, New Zealand indicated that the number of refugees the country accepted would be limited by economic conditions.

To gain the sought-after entry permit to New Zealand, European Jews would need a mix of contacts, money, and chance. The heroic efforts of some individuals helped a lucky few. Japanese diplomat and vice consul Sugihara Chiune, based in Poland in 1940, acting without his government's consent, issued around 2,500 transit visas to Japan, saving up to 6,000 Jewish lives, known today as "Sugihara Survivors." Some of those Sugihara rescued eventually reached New Zealand, including Peter Baruch and his family. They came to New Zealand via Russia, Japan, and Indonesia.[5]

New Zealand's restrictions on the number of refugees seemed to be justified by public concerns that the refugees might be Nazi sympathizers. Refugees from Germany, classified as enemy aliens during the war, were subject to tight controls, and at least eight Jewish refugees were interned.[6]

When the war ended, Holocaust survivors encountered serious obstacles to reuniting with their families in New Zealand, including shipping problems the priority given to the more than nine thousand servicemen and other New Zealanders in Britain, and New Zealand's restrictive policy.[7] As before the war, chance, contacts, and money seemed to be the crucial factors.

New Zealand's policy after the war needs to be seen in the context of how much New Zealanders were aware of the atrocities committed against Jews. By 1942–43 the government had fairly accurate information. A telegram in December 1942 from the secretary of state for dominion affairs to the New Zealand prime minister referred to "the existence of a detailed German plan for extermination of Jews."[8] The general population had the opportunity to read about Jewish persecution, including concentration camps, from around 1942, and eyewitness accounts from 1945.

As well as restricting Holocaust survivors, New Zealand was initially reluctant to settle displaced people (or DPs, as they were known) between 1948 and 1950.[9] While New Zealand wanted new settlers, as before the war, it preferred British immigrants. There are various estimates of how many of the DPs were Jewish. A New Zealand official's estimate in 1946 was that there were 1,375,000 DPs in Europe of whom "a large number are Jews."[10] An International Refugee Organization (IRO) estimate in 1948 was that 15 percent of the total remaining refugees under care of the IRO were Jewish. Of these, 70 percent said they wanted to go to Palestine. The IRO had plans for resettling 50,000 in Palestine in 1948 "if condition there permitted."[11]

The IRO asked New Zealand and various other countries to settle some of the refugees. New Zealand was also under pressure from Britain to accept DPs, and northern Europeans were considered acceptable.[12] When New Zealand subsequently agreed to accept some of the DPs, the selection process was biased in favor of northern Europeans and against Jews and "Slavs."[13] This was despite an IRO requirement that DP selection be carried out without discrimination against specific groups.[14]

New Zealand eventually admitted over four thousand (mainly non-Jewish) displaced people. After 1948 New Zealand's restrictions on Jewish DPs could conveniently be justified on the grounds that the refugees of Jewish origin had a national home to go to: Israel. New Zealand, as did other Western countries, saw the creation of a Jewish homeland in Palestine as a ready solution to the refugee problem, though some officials warned of the creation of a new refugee problem (Palestinians). New Zealand supported proposals to enable Jewish refugees to go to Palestine and the creation of independent Jewish and Arab states.[15]

While excluding Jews and others due to their ethnicity, New Zealand inadvertently settled up to fifty alleged Nazi war criminals after the war, as later identified by Dr Efraim Zuroff of the Simon Wiesenthal Centre. The government investigated the allegation in the early 1990s, but none of the suspects were brought to trial and no legal action was taken.[16] This is despite legislation that would have allowed for the domestic prosecution of those charged with crimes against humanity, such as Nazi war criminals. The lack of legal action showed a failure to meet New Zealand's international obligations, according to a 1991 article in the *Auckland Law Review*.[17] In 2021 the *Times of Israel* reported that the government had declined a request to declassify the relevant files about the alleged migration of Nazi war criminals.[18]

Refugee Policy since the Holocaust

While the humanitarian impulse has not been absent in New Zealand's response to refugees since the Holocaust, other considerations (economic, social, and political) have predominated. The country's refugee policy evolved as a result of global circumstances and the changing needs of refugees. New Zealand was signatory to the postwar international agreements that established the rights of refugees to seek safety and the obligations of countries to protect them. The United Nations Convention relating to the Status of Refugees was adopted in 1951 and applied only to people who had become refugees as a result of events taking place in Europe before 1951. The 1967 protocol made the 1951 provisions applicable to refugee situations worldwide. New Zealand also signed the Agenda for Protection in 2002, which covered a range of measures relating to the status of refuges not addressed in 1951 and 1967.[19]

Governments have adopted generous and innovative policies in relation to small numbers of refugees with disabilities, welcoming them together with their families in the early 1960s, when other countries would only accept them separately from their families. New Zealand has had compassionate policies for refugees with illness (for example, HIV/AIDS) from the 1990s and for refugee women at risk.[20]

As before the Holocaust, New Zealand has welcomed some refugees more than others. The careful selection of settlers to ensure they would "fit in" continued to be an important aspect of refugee policy, particularly until the late 1980s. Changes since that time have included the ethnic diversification (away from Europe) of refugee intakes, marking a break, at least in theory, with earlier policies of discriminating on grounds of national origin and ethnicity. New Zealand's annual refugee quota was set up in 1987.[21]

New Zealand has settled over 40,000 refugees since the Holocaust. The number of refugees arriving annually after the late 1980s remained between 750 and 800 until in 2020, when the refugee quota increased to 1,500. This number was not reached until 2023 due to COVID-19.[22] In addition to quota arrivals, a small number of asylum seekers and convention refugees, who sought refugee status after their arrival, have also been settled.[23] Average claims per year have numbered 384, with 184 the average number accepted, mainly from China, Afghanistan, Iran, and Sri Lanka.[24]

In May 2022 the government announced that asylum seekers would no longer be detained at a corrections facility.[25] In March 2023 the government proposed changes to how New Zealand treats arrivals by boat of more than thirty asylum seekers. The proposal includes electronic tagging of asylum seekers and an increased period of detention. Yet, the country has never had a refugee boat reach New Zealand.[26]

Several refugee intakes have taken place through the creation of emergency visas—for Afghan nationals after the Taliban's return to power in 2021, for example, and for refugees from Ukraine in 2022 after the Russian invasion.[27] While the number of refugees New Zealand accepts has remained small, the settlement of refugees became an ongoing and important humanitarian priority in immigration policy, not just an occasional gesture of compassion.[28]

At the same time, policy has sometimes discriminated against Muslim refugees and refugees from the Middle East and Africa, in part on security grounds after the terror attacks of 9/11 in the United States. In 2009 the government refocused the refugee quota in favor of refugees from the Asia Pacific region. A "family links" policy, also implemented, excluded most refugees from the Middle East and Africa until scrapped in 2019.[29] Refugee settlers, particularly Muslim, have sometimes encountered prejudice and racism. The victims of the attacks on Christchurch mosques of March 15, 2019, included several recent refugees.

According to some reports, the attacker of the mosques had links with resurgent right-wing extremists overseas, holding neo-Nazi ideology. In his writings he had attacked Nazi targets: Roma people, as well as Muslims and Jews.[30] Since the attacks, the New Zealand media have reported on the growth of neo-Nazi groups in New Zealand, with links to white supremacist groups overseas.[31] A national research center to prevent and counter violent extremism, a key recommendation of the Royal Commission of Inquiry into the Christchurch mosque attacks, was opened by the government in June 2022.[32] In March 2023 the government delayed the recommendation of the Royal Commission to establish a standardized way to react to threats and set national security priorities, with the option of establishing a new security agency. Muslim and Jewish communities were reported to be concerned by the delay.[33]

In response to the mosque attacks, the New Zealand government launched the Christchurch Call in 2020. The initiative seeks to ensure that an open and free internet is not used by extremists to organize and share their messages and to encourage governments to make sure that existing legislation around extremist content is followed and enforced.[34] In April 2023 former prime minister Jacinda Ardern was appointed special envoy for the Christchurch Call.[35]

Māori

Māori have not had direct input into New Zealand's refugee immigration policy. This is despite immigration being a crucial aspect of the Treaty of Waitangi, signed in 1840 between Māori tribes and the British "Crown," which facilitated British colonization and settlement of the country. Immigration was "the blueprint setting out the relationship between Māori and these new peoples . . . all New Zealanders of non-Māori origin, both Pākehā and other tauiwi [foreigners] in return for the right of the British Crown to govern its own peoples."[36]

Some Māori have consistently shown dissatisfaction with immigration policy over the years, particularly with resources—such as jobs, health care, and housing—being diverted from Māori in deprived circumstances to immigrants, including refugees. Several Māori academics and other commentators have expressed concern about the lack of consultation with Māori over immigration policy.[37]

At the same time, some Māori have been exceptionally welcoming to refugee settlers. Refugees have benefited from Māori protocols of welcome (manaakitanga) developed to govern internal migration within Māori society. Some Māori have identified with the plight of refugees who had lost their land, as many Māori themselves did. There is anecdotal evidence of Māori support for Jewish refugees. An elder of the Ngāpuhi (largest iwi or tribe, located on the North Island) told of his forebears traveling to Wellington to offer the government land for Jewish refugees who had escaped the Nazis and reached New Zealand. The offer was refused.[38] Some Jewish refugees have recalled the ways that Māori befriended them, at a time when they had not felt welcomed by Pākehā society.[39]

In recent years Kaupapa Māori approach to immigration has received increased attention. In May 2022 two Kaupapa Māori refugee settlement providers were contracted to develop new refugee settlement practices with the aim of applying Te Tiriti (the Treaty of Waitangi) principles to immigration policy "in ways that recognize and provide for indigenous rights and recognition, while sharing our land in the spirit of manaakitanga."[40]

The notion of historical trauma (initially drawn from Holocaust research) has sometimes been used in North America to describe the impact of colonization on Indigenous people. The Holocaust has functioned in New Zealand too as a way to articulate aspects of Māori victimization.[41] Some New Zealand researchers have applied this wider meaning of historical trauma to the experience of Māori to highlight the negative impact of colonization: wars, land confiscations (raupatu), population decline, loss of mana, the onslaught of European diseases, cultural suppression, and much else.

Since 1985, efforts have been made through the Waitangi Tribunal (a permanent Commission of Inquiry) to address past injustices to Māori. Typically, the tribunal publishes reports with recommendations on claims brought by Māori relating to Crown actions that breach the promises of the 1840 Treaty of Waitangi. The tribunal's Taranaki Report of 1996 provoked controversy, including among some Jewish groups, when it described what had happened to Taranaki Māori in the 1860s as being akin to the Holocaust: "The graphic muru (plunder) of most of Taranaki and the raupatu (confiscation) without ending describe the holocaust of Taranaki history and the denigration of the founding peoples in a continuum from 1840 to the present."[42] Some commentators objected to the comparison between the Holocaust and colonization on grounds of "emotional wording," though use of the strong language "possibly arises from effort to convey the deep feeling of loss Taranaki Māori have."[43] Others have thought the comparison apt. "New Zealanders who react with 'horror' to the use of the word holocaust 'are being a bit precious or indulging in collective amnesia.'"[44]

Then Associate Minister of Māori Affairs Tariana Turia's support of the use of the term "Holocaust" led to her reprimand by then Prime Minister Helen Clarke, who was quoted in the *New Zealand Herald* as saying: "I know the [Waitangi] Tribunal used it [Holocaust] with respect to Taranaki. I do not agree with that and I do not want to see ministers using the term and causing offence again." She reiterated the message: "I don't accept that the word holocaust can be validly used about the New Zealand experience."[45] A 2010 Ngāi Tahu Research Centre report acknowledged the issues around the use of the word "Holocaust" and concluded that the term was useful in the exploration of the impact of historical trauma, including colonization, on Māori. (Ngāi Tahu is the principal Māori iwi/tribe of the South Island.) The report noted that the phrase "historical trauma" was coined to provide a framework for understanding the traumatic experiences of Holocaust survivors and the impact on following generations, and it concluded that historical and intergenerational trauma theory, alongside Kaupapa Māori theory, was relevant for Māori research, for example, into health disparities experienced by Māori.[46] (Kaupapa Māori theory is based on Māori philosophy and principles.)

Human Rights since the Holocaust

The devastation of World War II, including the flagrant violation of rights by Nazi and fascist countries during the Holocaust, provided an impetus for the Universal Declaration of Human Rights in 1948. Aiming to prevent the scourge of another war, the declaration reaffirmed faith in fundamental human rights and in the dignity and worth of people. New Zealand prime minister Peter Fraser played a significant part in the drafting of the Universal Declaration.

To provide better protection of human rights, the New Zealand Human Rights Commission (HRC) was set up in 1977. New Zealanders who have survived the Holocaust have supported the work of the HRC. An example is their contribution to the HRC's antiracism campaign "Give Nothing to Racism" in 2017. Then Race Relations Commissioner Susan Devoy acknowledged that the campaign "was in part inspired by our very own Kiwi survivors of the Shoah who went on to spend their lives talking about the horrors they had witnessed. Survivors as children remember that the hatred started small in newspapers, classrooms, workplaces and neighbourhoods. We need Kiwis to recognize the seeds of hate and to call them out. Don't stand by, stand up."[47] The campaign was launched by 2017 New Zealander of the Year Taika Waititi, who urged New Zealanders to recognize that racism starts small with acts of casual racism. Waititi, whose background is Māori and Jewish, directed the 2019 film *Jojo Rabbit* about a boy in Nazi Germany who discovers that his mother is hiding a Jewish girl in their attic.

Recently the HRC has been involved in responding to increasing racism in New Zealand, particularly online, targeting Māori, Muslim, and Jewish people.[48] Racism has come both from the right and the left and has included longstanding antisemitic tropes, using the racist language of the Third Reich. In 2021 the HRC included action to counter antisemitism in the government's National Action Plan against Racism.[49]

Also in 2021, the government proposed changes involving the HRC to make hate speech a criminal offence, with the intent of maintaining balance between protecting free speech and protecting people from hate speech.[50] Proposed legislation would remove existing free speech/hate speech provisions from the Human Rights Act to the Crimes Act, with the Human Rights Act 1993 revised to include protection for religious groups and for disabled and rainbow communities.[51] In February 2023 Prime Minister Chris Hipkins delayed the proposed legislation to allow further consideration of a highly contested area.[52]

The insertion of rainbow communities into the Holocaust narrative was a part of gay liberation in New Zealand in the 1970s and 1980s. The first "serious" New Zealand gay periodical, *Pink Triangle*, the publication of the National Gay Rights Coalition, stated: "We chose the name because of its historical connections with the gay movement in that the pink triangle was first used as a symbol of degradation against gay women and men in concentration camps of Nazi Germany. From a symbol of degradation, it has been adopted by the international gay community as a symbol of pride."[53]

Echoes of the Holocaust may be found in New Zealanders' response to a wide range of international human rights violations, including the 1994 Rwandan genocide (when a New Zealander was president of the United Nations Security Council), Uyghur repression, and Naqba in 1948 (when many Palestinians were displaced by the creation of the State of Israel).

Holocaust Commemoration and Education

As the number of Holocaust survivors and people who can give eyewitness accounts grows smaller, and as the tragedy of the Holocaust is misappropriated and, worse, attacked and undermined by deniers and others, there is additional urgency to finding new and meaningful ways of "remembering." Indeed, Holocaust remembrance, in New Zealand as elsewhere, tends to take place in highly political environments and can be infiltrated by non-Holocaust agendas.

There are many examples of recent uses and abuses of Holocaust memory. A prominent leader of the Mongrel Mob (an organized street gang with predominantly Māori and Pasifika members) was featured in a video speaking to a group of members about voting, several times using the Nazi phrase "Sieg Heil."[54] The eighty-third anniversary of Kristallnacht took place as protesters, likening COVID-19 virus restrictions and vaccination requirements to Nazi behavior during the Holocaust, used Nazi images and the Star of David emblem to associate themselves with Holocaust victims, invoking that tragedy for political point-scoring.[55] The Holocaust is used by these groups to promote hate.

Holocaust memorialization became institutionalized and globalized in 2005, when in Resolution 60/7 the United Nations General Assembly recognized the universal significance of the Holocaust by establishing an International Holocaust Remembrance Day (UNIHRD) on January 27. UNIHRD has been marked in New Zealand since its inception. The 2022 UNIHRD commemoration included a parliamentary reception in Wellington (the capital city) with candle lighting to honor the six million Jews killed during the Holocaust. An event highlight was the singing of the Partisans' Song in Yiddish and in Te Reo Māori (the Māori language). In 2023 UNIHRD marked the eightieth anniversary of the Warsaw Ghetto Uprising.[56]

Commemorations are led by the Jewish community, bringing together the various organizations that coexist in the small New Zealand Jewish community (of approximately eight thousand people in 2019).[57] Despite some government participation and some involvement by diverse organizations such as the Human Rights Commission and the Wellington Islamic Centre, the Holocaust occupies a minor space in New Zealand cultural memory. While the meaning of the memorialization—"never again"—is not contested, the Holocaust does not usually receive much national attention and is largely ignored by wider society. Historian Giacomo Lichtner has noted evidence of a "backlash" against the way the Holocaust has been memorialized and elevated to a universal symbol of evil. This, combined with inadequate knowledge of the Holocaust, may be why some people are asking: "Why is the Holocaust relevant to New Zealand?"[58] In 2005, for example, then Labour Government member of Parliament John Tamahere was reported to say that he was sick and tired of hearing how many Jews were gassed and of being made to feel guilty.[59]

New Zealand's leading organization in Holocaust education and remembrance is the Holocaust Centre of New Zealand (HCNZ), founded by a small group of Holocaust survivors.[60] The mission of HCNZ is to witness, remember, educate, and act; to ensure that the lessons of the Holocaust are relevant to fight intolerance and racism, to promote human rights; and to celebrate diversity.[61]

HCNZ aims to align its education program for secondary school students with the mainstream curriculum. HCNZ's recent initiatives have included developing a memorial for the children killed in the Holocaust and organizing Holocaust education programs for New Zealand teachers at Yad Vashem in Israel. Anne Frank's diary has been translated into Te Reo Māori to make it accessible to more students. New Zealand's first Anne Frank Memorial opened in June 2021. Speakers at the opening made connections between the Holocaust and present-day issues such as bullying and exclusion.[62]

Two former HCNZ board members have been active in Holocaust education and scholarship at the tertiary level. Former chairperson of the board Simone Gigliotti (coeditor of *The Young Victims of the Nazi Regime*) taught several Holocaust related topics between 2004 and 2016 at Victoria University of Wellington.[63] Also at Victoria University, Giacomo Lichtner (author of *Fascism in Italian Cinema*) has taught representation of the Holocaust since 2003. A recent course topic is the Holocaust and Genocide.[64]

The Holocaust and Antisemitism Foundation Aotearoa New Zealand (HAFANZ) shares HCNZ's objectives of remembering, educating, and bearing witness to the Holocaust.[65] Sheree Trotter (Te Arawa) of HAFANZ has highlighted ignorance about the Holocaust in the wider community and has long been critical of the New Zealand government for not joining the International Holocaust Remembrance Alliance, which promotes education, commemoration, and research.[66] In June 2022 the government decided to join as an observer.[67]

Reverberations of the Holocaust

The Holocaust has been significant in New Zealand's past and has cast a metaphorical shadow ever since. New Zealanders have taken pride in being exceptionally humanitarian to refugees. Yet New Zealand did not do as much as it could to rescue the Jewish refugee victims. The country's record in helping other groups of refugees since the Holocaust is mixed.

The tragedy that befell Jewish people and others has been politicized and co-opted for other uses. Anti-vax protesters, wearing the Star of David with "unvaccinated" lettered in the center, waved banners at protests in Wellington in 2022. At the same time, as noted earlier, the Holocaust has been usefully referenced in contemporary debates about the plight of victimized groups (such as the Uyghurs) and in relation to human rights and antiracism campaigns (such as hate speech legislation).

For Māori, insights from historical trauma research, some of it originating in Holocaust research, have been pertinent in their search for justice and redress for losses arising from colonization and exploitation. The Holocaust Education Centre of New Zealand and other groups and scholars have focused on memorializing the Holocaust and providing education relevant to future generations, using the legacy and lessons of that tragedy to combat intolerance and racism.

Notes

1. This section of the essay is a summary of Ann Beaglehole, *A Small Price to Pay: Refugees from Hitler in New Zealand, 1936–1946* (Wellington, New Zealand: Allen & Unwin, 1988) and Ann Beaglehole, *Refuge New Zealand: A Nation's Response to Refugees and Asylum Seekers* (Dunedin, New Zealand: Otago University Press, 2013), 30–51.
2. "Fact Sheet 1: New Zealand and the Second World War," New Zealand History, accessed May 4, 2021, https://www.nzhistory.govt.nz/files/documents/28mb/fact-sheetl.pdf.
3. F. A. de la Mare, "The Refugee Problem," 1, ANZ Nash 1311/0592/3, quoted in Beaglehole, *Small Price to Pay*, 16. On the long history of right-wing activism, including antisemitic conspiracy theories in New Zealand in the 1930s, see Matthew Cunningham, Marinus La Rooij, and Paul Spoonley, eds., *Histories of Hate: The Radical Right in Aotearoa New Zealand* (Dunedin, New Zealand: Otago University Press, 2023).

4. De la Mare, "Refugee Problem," 1, quoted in Beaglehole, *Small Price to Pay*, 16.
5. Val Graham, "Chiune Sugihara: Righteous Gentile among Nations," Jewish Lives, accessed September 20, 2021, https://www.jewishlives.nz/our-people/chiune-sugihara?rq=chiune%20sugihara. Estimates of the number of visas Sugihara issued vary.
6. Ann Beaglehole, "Locked Up and Guarded 'Lest [They] Escaped to Help Their Mortal Enemies': Jewish Internees in New Zealand during the Second World War," in *National Socialism in Oceania: Germanica Pacifica*, ed. Emily Turner-Graham and Christine Winter (Frankfurt, Germany: Peter Lang, 2010), 147–67.
7. Beaglehole, *Refuge New Zealand*, 196n35, citing figures in an undated report to the Interchurch Council of New Zealand by O. S. Heymann, cited by L. M. Goldman, *The History of the Jews in New Zealand* (Wellington, New Zealand: A. H. & A. W. Reed, 1958), 234.
8. Telegram from Secretary of State for Dominion Affairs to Prime Minister of New Zealand, December 8, 1942, ANZ, ABHS, W4627, 950, Box 2491, 108/3/1, part 1, International Affairs, Social Affairs—Jewish question, general, 1942–1947, quoted in Ann Beaglehole, "Kiwi in a Kaffiyeh or a Tui in a Tallis?" *New Zealand International Review* 43, no. 1 (January/February 2018): 3.
9. This section of the essay is a summary of Beaglehole, "Kiwi in a Kaffiyeh?," 2–6.
10. Foss Shanahan, Acting Permanent Head, PM's Department to Prime Minister, September 20, 1946, ANZ, EA2, 206, 108/4/1, part 2, 1947/9A, Social Affairs, Refugees, General, 1946–1947, quoted in Beaglehole, "Kiwi in a Kaffiyeh?," 3.
11. Notes of a meeting held on September 20, 1948, at which were present: Wing Commander R. Innes, Director of Resettlement, International Refugee Organization, H. L. Bockett, Secretary of Labour and Director of Employment, and Messrs F. Shanahan and A. R. Perry, ANZ, EA2, 262, 108/4/1, part 3, 1948/14B, Social Affairs, Refugees, General, 1947–48, quoted in Beaglehole, "Kiwi in a Kaffiyeh?," 3.
12. W. G. Stevens to T. P. Davin, October 24, 1947, ANZ, L1 22/1/27, part 1, cited in Beaglehole, "Kiwi in a Kaffiyeh?," 3.
13. Director of Employment to Minister of Employment, "Resettlement of International Refugees," December 23, 1947, ANZ, EA2, 262, 108/4/1, part 3, Social Affairs, Refugees, General, 1947–1948, quoted in Beaglehole, "Kiwi in a Kaffiyeh?," 4.
14. Director of Employment to Minister of Employment, "Resettlement of International Refugees," quoted in Beaglehole, "Kiwi in a Kaffiyeh?," 4.
15. Foss Shanahan, Acting Permanent Head, Prime Minister's Department, to Prime Minister, September 20, 1946, ANZ, EA2, 206, 108/4/1, part 2, 1947/9A, Social Affairs, Refugees, General, 1946–1947, quoted in Beaglehole, "Kiwi in a Kaffiyeh?," 4.
16. Beaglehole, *Refuge New Zealand*, 48–49; Anthony Hubbard, "A Nazi Mass Murderer in Our Midst?" *Listener*, August 14, 2021, 30–35.
17. Tristan Gilbertson, "Legal Implications of the Presence of Nazi War Criminals in New Zealand," *Auckland Law Review* 6, no. 4 (August 1991): 552–74, https://www.nzlii.org/nz/journals/AukULRev/1991/5.pdf.
18. Lance Morcan, "New Zealand Still Not Opening Files on 'Resettled' Alleged Former Nazi Emigres," *Times of Israel*, June 5, 2021, https://www.timesofisrael.com/new-zealand-still-not-opening-files-on-resettled-alleged-former-nazi-emigres.
19. Beaglehole, *Refuge New Zealand*, 10.

20. Beaglehole, *Refuge New Zealand*, 113–16, 186–87.
21. Beaglehole, *Refuge New Zealand*, 14, 164.
22. "New Zealand Refugee Quota Programme," New Zealand Immigration, accessed September 22, 2021, https://www.immigration.govt.nz/about-us/what-we-do/our-strategies-and-projects/supporting-refugees-and-asylum-seekers/refugee-and-protection-unit/new-zealand-refugee-quota-programme.
23. Beaglehole, *Refuge New Zealand*, 129–62.
24. New Zealand Red Cross, *Humanitarian Migration Report: Current and Emerging Issues in Aotearoa New Zealand*, November 2022, 24, https://www.redcross.org.nz/assets/Uploads/Files/About-Us/News/Reports-and-publications/RC-Migration-Scoping-Report-2022-v10_final.pdf.
25. "NZ to Stop Imprisoning People Seeking Asylum," Amnesty International, press release, May 3, 2022, https://amnesty.org.nz/nz-to-stop-imprisoning-people-seeking-asylum/.
26. "Government Announces Plan to Electronically Tag Asylum Seekers Who May Pose Risk," Radio New Zealand, March 28, 2023, https://www.rnz.co.nz/news/political/486890/government-announces-plans-to-electronically-tag-asylum-seekers-who-may-pose-risk.
27. New Zealand Red Cross, *Humanitarian Migration Report*, 22, 42.
28. Beaglehole, *Refuge New Zealand*, 165.
29. Murdoch Stephens, "Unfair and Discriminatory: Which Regions Does New Zealand Take Refugees from and Why," *Policy Quarterly* 4, no. 2 (2018): 74–79, https://doi.org/10.26686/pq.v14i2.5097.
30. Joe Heim and James McAuley, "New Zealand Attacks Offer Latest Evidence of a Web of Supremacist Extremism," *Washington Post*, March 15, 2019, https://www.washingtonpost.com/world/europe/new-zealand-suspect-inspired-by-far-right-french-intellectual-who-feared-nonwhite-immigration/2019/03/15/8c39fba4-6201-4a8d-99c6-aa42db53d6d3_story.html; Cliff Harvey, "Parajmos: Roma Genocide" (Power Point/Zoom presentation, Holocaust Centre of New Zealand, Wellington, September 19, 2021).
31. Elliot Weir, "Investigation Sheds Lights on Aotearoa's Largest Neo-Nazi Group," *Critic*, August 9, 2021, https://www.critic.co.nz/news/article/9609/investigation-sheds-light-on-aotearoas-largest-neo-nazi-group.
32. "Centre for Preventing and Countering Violent Extremism Officially Open," New Zealand Government, news release, June 3, 2022, https://www.beehive.govt.nz/release/centre-preventing-and-countering-violent-extremism-officially-open.
33. Phil Pennington, "Muslim and Jewish Community Leaders Concerned by Delay of New National Security Agency," RNZ, March 30, 2023, https://www.rnz.co.nz/news/national/487034/Muslim-and-Jewish-community-leaders-concerned-by-delay-of-new-national-security-agency.
34. New Zealand Red Cross, *Humanitarian Migration Report*, November 2022, 117.
35. Christchurch Call, "New Zealand Special Envoy for the Christchurch Call Announced," April 4, 2023, https://www.christchurchcall.org/new-zealand-special-envoy-for-the-christchurch-call-announced/.

36. Khylee Quince, "Immigration Reset Allows Us to Honour the Bargain Struck at Te Tiriti," *Stuff*, June 26, 2021, https://www.stuff.co.nz/pou-tiaki/125559229/immigration-reset-allows-us-honour-the-bargain-struck-in-te-tiriti.
37. Beaglehole, *Refuge New Zealand*, 175–76.
38. Sheree Trotter, "NZ Must Step Up against Antisemitism," Newsroom New Zealand, February 3, 2020, https://www.newsroom.co.nz/ideasroom/nz-must-step-up-against-antisemitism.
39. Beaglehole, *Small Price to Pay*, 50–51.
40. Quince, "Immigration Reset."
41. David B. Macdonald, *Identity Politics in the Age of Genocide: The Holocaust and Historical Representation* (London: Routledge, 2008), 104–5.
42. Waitangi Tribunal, *The Taranaki Report: Kaupapa Tuatahi, Muru Me Te Raupata: The Muru and Raupata of the Taranaki Land and People*, WAI 143, report 1 (Wellington, New Zealand: Government Printer, 1996), 312.
43. "The Taranaki Report: Muru me te Raupatu," June 1996 Contents, *Māori Law Review*, accessed September 24, 2021, https://www.maorilawreview.co.nz/1996/06june-1996-contents/.
44. "Extracts from Simon Upton's Valedictory Speech: 12 December 2000," December–January 2001 Contents, *Māori Law Review*, accessed September 24, 2021, https://www.Maorilawreview.co.nz/2001/01/december-january-2001-contents/.
45. A. Young, "Holocaust Apology Puts Minister in Hot Water," *New Zealand Herald*, September 6, 2000, para 13, quoted in Leoni Pihama, Paul Reynolds, Cherryl Smith, John Reid, Linda Tuhiwai Smith, and Rihi Te Nana, "Positioning Historical Trauma Theory within Aotearoa New Zealand" (Ngāi Tahu Research Centre report), *AlterNative: An International Journal of Indigenous Peoples*, no. 3 (September 2014): 248–62, https://researchcommons.waikato.ac.nz/handle/10289/12397.
46. Pihama et al., "Positioning Historical Trauma Theory," 248–62.
47. "New Zealand Holocaust Survivors Inspire Award Winning Anti-Racism Campaign," Human Rights Commission, January 25, 2018, https://www.hrc.co.nz/news/new-zealand-holocaust-survivors-inspire-award-winning-anti-racism-campaign.
48. Meng Foon, "Anonymous New Zealand Group Set Up to Combat Racism Praised by Amnesty International," TVNZ, July 14, 2021, https://www.TVNZ.co.nz/one-news/new-zealand/anonymous-nz-group-set-up-combat-racism-praised-amnesty-international.
49. Paul Hunt and Meng Foon, "The Growing Issue of Anti-Semitism in New Zealand," *Stuff*, January 26, 2021, https://www.stuff.co.nz/national/300215269/the-growing-issue-of-antisemitism-in-new-zealand.
50. "Silence over Hate Speech Laws Has Allowed Misinformation in, Minorities Say," Radio New Zealand, July 23, 2021, https://www.rnz.co.nz/news/political/447500/silence-over-hate-speech-laws-has-allowed-misinformation-in-minorities-say.
51. Warren Brookbanks, "Submission to the Ministry of Justice on the Proposals against Incitement of Hatred and Discrimination," Maxim Institute, August 6, 2021, https://www.maxim.org.nz/content/uploads/2021/08/SUB-Hate-Speech-Consultation-2021.pdf.

52. "Post-Cabinet Media Conference," Radio New Zealand, February 8, 2023, https://www.rnz.co.nz/news/political/483875/hate-speech-laws-delayed.
53. *Pink Triangle*, editorial, no. 1 (May 14, 1979): 2, Auckland Museum, Collections online, https://www.aucklandmuseum.com/collection/object/874720.
54. Ireland Hendry-Tennent, "NZ Jewish Council Slams Video of Mongrel Mob's Harry Tam Saying 'Sieg Heil,'" *Stuff*, July 23, 2021, https://www.stuff.co.nz/politics/350518233/nz-jewish-council-slams-video-of-mongrel-mob-s-harry-tam-saying-sieg-heil.
55. Dan Satherly, "Coronavirus: Jewish Community Slams 'Ignorant' Anti-Vaccination Protesters Using Nazi, Jewish Imagery on Holocaust Anniversary," *Stuff*, November 9, 2021, https://www.stuff.co.nz/nz-news/350525005/coronavirus-jewish-community-slams-ignorant-anti-vaccination-protesters-using-nazi-jewish-imagery-on-holocaust-anniversary.
56. "When the Violin Falls Silent: Music in Hiding," Holocaust Centre of New Zealand, annual Kristallnacht concert, May 2024, https://www.holocaustcentre.org.nz/commemorations.html.
57. Leonard Bell and Miriam Natalya Bell, "Jewish Women in New Zealand," Shalvi/Hyman Encyclopedia of Jewish Women, Jewish Women's Archive, 1995, accessed September 20, 2021, https://www.jwa.org/encyclopedia/article/new-zealand. According to Statistics New Zealand 2018 Census figures, around 5,274 people identified as Jewish.
58. Giacomo Lichtner, "Is Poor Awareness of the Holocaust Just a Tip of the Iceberg?" *Stuff*, August 5, 2020, https://www.stuff.co.nz/national/education/115107459/is-poor-awareness-of-the-holocaust-just-the-tip-of-the-iceberg.
59. Macdonald, *Identity Politics in the Age of Genocide*, 112.
60. Inge Woolf, *Resilience: A Story of Persecution, Escape, Survival and Triumph* (Wellington: Holocaust Centre of New Zealand, 2023), 149–58.
61. "Mission Statement & Strategy," Holocaust Centre of New Zealand, 2007, accessed September 20, 2021, https://www.holocaustcentre.org.nz/mission--strategy.html.
62. Sophie Cornish, "New Zealand's First Anne Frank Memorial Unveiled in Wellington," *Stuff*, June 14, 2021, https://www.stuff.co.nz/national/125427759/new-zealands-first-anne-frank-memorial-unveiled-in-wellington.
63. Simone Gigliotti, LinkedIn, https://www.UK.linkedin.com/in/simone-gigliotti-3812ba65; Simone Gigliotti and Monica Tempian, eds., *The Young Victims of the Nazi Regime: Migration, the Holocaust and Postwar Displacement* (London: Bloomsbury Academic, 2016).
64. Giacomo Lichtner, https://people.wgtn.ac.nz/Giacomo.Lichtner; Giacomo Lichter, *Fascism in Italian Cinema since 1945: The Politics and Aesthetics of Memory* (New York: Palgrave Macmillan, 2013).
65. Holocaust and Antisemitism Foundation Aotearoa New Zealand, 2019, https://www.holocaustfoundation.com/home.
66. Trotter, "New Zealand Must Step Up."
67. RNZ, "Government's Decision to Join International Holocaust Remembrance Alliance Welcomed," June 25, 2022, https://www.newshub.co.nz/home/new-zealand/2022/06/government-s-decision-to-join-international-holocaust-remembrance-alliance-welcomed.html.

17

Representing the Holocaust in a Museum Setting in Post-Apartheid South Africa and Africa

TALI NATES

"Never again." These two words were declared for the first time in response to the Holocaust and are expressed again and again in speeches during Holocaust commemoration days as well as events marking genocides and mass atrocities around the world. They were also used by South Africa's first democratically elected president, Nelson Mandela, in his inauguration speech, saying, "Never, never and never again shall it be that this beautiful land will again experience the oppression of one by another and suffer the indignity of being the skunk of the world."[1]

Auschwitz survivor and writer Primo Levi cautioned us, saying: "It happened therefore it can happen again. This is the core of what we have to say. It can happen and it can happen anywhere."[2] It is therefore critical to deeply reflect and learn from this warning, as well as use it as a catalyst for memory activism.[3] This is the core of what we do at the Johannesburg Holocaust & Genocide Centre, where Levi's quote is prominently displayed.

However, genocide happened again on the African continent in April 1994. While millions of South Africans celebrated the country's first democratic elections and the end of apartheid, only a three-and-a-half-hour flight away from Johannesburg, hundreds of thousands of Tutsi had already been murdered in Rwanda. These events teach us that we not only need to learn from history; we also need to make connections between the past and the present. The histories of the Holocaust and genocide can teach us about human behavior, dilemmas, and choices, as well as their consequence.

History is a powerful tool that can be transformed into lessons for humanity that are relevant to our societies today. The question is, how is the Holocaust remembered in countries that were on the margins of the historical events of the Second World War? Can remembering and learning about it in these countries allow connections to local traumatic histories? Can learning about genocides in Africa uncover crucial lessons for the continent's individuals, communities, and governments?

Indeed, memory and education about the Holocaust and genocide in the twentieth century is a growing phenomenon on the African continent. Through special education programs and exhibitions, some African countries are utilizing the study of the Holocaust and genocide as a way of teaching about extremism and the prevention of human rights atrocities in their own countries.

This chapter thus reflects on Holocaust memory and education in Africa, with a focus on South Africa after the country's transition to democracy in 1994. As the founder and first executive director of the newest museum in the country, the Johannesburg Holocaust & Genocide Centre (JHGC), I use it as a case study to explore the connections between Holocaust and genocide history with contemporary human rights violations in South Africa. As the study of "Nazi Germany and the Holocaust" is mandated by the national curriculum of South Africa, this chapter further explores how students are able to better reflect on human rights and democracy in the past and present after participating in the JHGC's programs. Holocaust remembrance in Africa is only in its infancy. This chapter further explores the growing interest in Africa to learn about and memorialize local histories of the Holocaust and how the JHGC contributes to this growth. Finally, this chapter looks briefly at the period of the COVID-19 pandemic and some of the opportunities it brought for global partnerships on which the JHGC capitalized to significantly enhance Holocaust and genocide remembrance and education in Africa.

The Second World War and the Holocaust on the African Continent

The Second World War was a global war that included the African continent. The Nazis occupied Tunisia, Algeria, Morocco, western Egypt, and eastern Libya in their North African campaign (September 1940–May 1943). They targeted more than four hundred thousand Jews living there, implementing anti-Jewish policies and setting up internment and slave labor camps. The Nazis' ultimate plan was to murder the Jews using the Einsatzgruppen (mobile killing units) attached to Rommel's Afrika Korps. However, this plan was not implemented as the Allies began to liberate North Africa in November 1942.

Internment and forced labor camps were established in North and West Africa under Nazi Germany, Vichy France's government, and Mussolini's Italy. Among the prisoners were foreign refugees, prisoners of war, local Jews, Spanish Republicans, and dissidents. Libya was passed back and forth between Italian and British forces, and in 1942, for example, 2,600 Jews were deported to the camp of Giado, a former military post located 150 miles south of Tripoli.[4]

Dakar, the capital of Senegal, became the center of Vichy France in West Africa after May 1940. Several internment and forced labor camps in West Africa were established for Jews and other perceived local dissidents in Senegal, Mali, and Guinea. In June 1940 and November 1941, the Second World War was also fought in East Africa between the Allied Forces (including African troops under the then British Empire) and the Axis Forces (primarily from Italy).[5]

Africa also became a place of detention for Jewish refugees who were deported by the British. In December 1940, 1,581 Jewish refugees who had tried to escape Nazi-occupied Europe to safety in British Mandated Palestine were deported to the British colony of Mauritius. Between December 1940 and August 1945, the British authorities detained them in the Beau Bassin prison camp, where men and women were housed in different sections. These restrictions were gradually eased, and limited visitation times were permitted for married couples. By 1945, 60 babies were born on the island. However, 126 Jewish refugees died there, mainly from typhoid and malaria. They were buried in the St. Martin Jewish Cemetery near Port Louis.[6]

The South African Jewish community supported the refugees in Mauritius and also joined the South African army. South Africa joined the Allies on September 4, 1939, and its soldiers fought in North Africa, Ethiopia, Madagascar, and Italy, suffering 11,023 fatalities.[7] The South African Air Force's 60 Squadron, one of the leading aerial photographic units operating in Europe during the war, flew seventeen sorties to photograph the rubber refinery situated next to Auschwitz-Birkenau. However, only on examining the photographs in 1978 did it become clear that they included lines of Jewish deportees walking toward the crematoria and their death.[8]

In South Africa and many other African countries, despite fighting in the Second World War on the side of the Allies or being occupied by the Nazis and their allies and becoming a place of persecution and internment, after the end of the war Holocaust memory and education was barely evident until the 1990s.

Holocaust and Genocide Memory and Education in Post-1994 South Africa and Africa

In South Africa until 1994, Holocaust memory was mainly kept alive by the small Jewish community as well as the anti-apartheid movement, especially the political prisoners on Robben Island such as Nelson Mandela and Ahmed Kathrada.[9]

The Jewish community in South Africa, the largest in Africa, numbered at its height in the 1980s about 118,000.[10] From the 1930s, with the passing of the Quota Act (1930) and Aliens Act (1937), which restricted Jewish immigration from Eastern Europe and the Reich, there was limited Jewish immigration to the country.[11]

After the war approximately three hundred Holocaust survivors settled in South Africa and established an organization, Sh'erit ha-Pletah ("the surviving remnants"), that assisted in organizing Holocaust commemoration ceremonies around the country.[12]

The first Holocaust memorials were established in Jewish cemeteries around South Africa. Celebrated local sculptor Herman Wald's 1959 Johannesburg memorial is famous for its six symbolic ram's horns (Shofar). Wald explained: "Through the ram's horns the dead are blasting out the Sixth Commandment: 'Though shalt not kill.'"[13] Holocaust commemorations were held next to these Jewish cemetery memorials on Yom Ha'Shoah (Holocaust Remembrance Day, held on the Hebrew date of 27 Nisan) annually.[14]

From the 1990s there was growing interest and development in Holocaust research, memorialization, and education among the general population of South Africa as well as the continent. Traveling exhibitions played an important role. One of the most impactful was the exhibition "Anne Frank in Our World," which traveled around South Africa and Namibia in 1993–94 and was opened in Johannesburg by Nelson Mandela.[15] The exhibition, organized by Myra Osrin, a Cape Town Jewish community leader (in partnership with the Anne Frank House, Amsterdam), highlighted for the first time in South Africa's history the country's own apartheid past alongside the story of Anne Frank and the Holocaust. The exhibition was visited by thousands and raised issues of prejudice, abuse of power, racism, and historical memory. It inspired Osrin to create the first Holocaust center in Cape Town, the first such museum in Africa, which opened in 1999.[16]

The Cape Town Holocaust Centre serves as a memorial to the six million Jews who were killed in the Holocaust and all victims of Nazi Germany. It opened as an educational center with a permanent exhibition that includes an introduction to issues of race, racism, and apartheid in South Africa, alongside the history of the Holocaust. The exhibition includes a space dedicated to the Holocaust in Lithuania and Latvia (the source of the majority of Jewish immigration to South Africa), as well as the Jews of the island of Rhodes, as many survivors from the island settled in Cape Town after the war. The exhibition at the Centre went through a revamp in 2016 and now includes a brief introduction to the history of genocide in the twentieth century. It also changed its name to the Cape Town Holocaust & Genocide Centre.[17]

In 2007 the study of "Nazi Germany and the Holocaust" became a compulsory topic in the new national social sciences and history curriculum for grades 9 (13–14 years old) and 11 (16–17 years old) in South Africa, the first such curriculum in Africa.[18] The curriculum emphasizes human rights and aims to assist learners in understanding that during the 1930s and early 1940s, human rights, racism, and discrimination were not given much political or legal attention. Only after the Second World War and the Holocaust and with the establishment of the United Nations was there an acknowledgment of the importance of human rights. In December 1948, the United Nations passed both the Universal Declaration of Human Rights (UDHR) and the Convention on the Prevention and Punishment of the Crime of Genocide. However, in 1948 apartheid was legalized in South Africa, and it would take another fifty years for the country to sign the UDHR on December 10, 1998.

The curriculum emphasizes human rights, peace, and democracy, teaching first about the Holocaust and then about apartheid, with the hope that students will be better equipped to make connections to current issues, including human rights abuses in South Africa and throughout the African continent. Education Minister Angie Motshekga highlighted: "History encourages civic responsibility and critical thinking—these are key values needed in a democratic society. The study of History creates a platform for constructive and informed debates about peace, human rights, and democratic values."[19]

With the inclusion of the Holocaust and genocide in the national curriculum, it became crucial to train teachers on these histories, as well as to create reliable resources to support this teaching through textbooks and specialized museums. The development of museums in Cape Town, Durban, and Johannesburg, affiliated to an association, the South African Holocaust & Genocide Foundation, became an important source of support for education and memory in the country, assisting schools in fulfilling their mandate to teach about human rights and genocide.[20]

In 2004 the second museum in Africa dedicated to genocide, the Kigali Genocide Memorial (KGM) was opened. The KGM is also the final resting place for more than 250,000 victims of the 1994 genocide against the Tutsi. It is a place of remembrance and serves to educate visitors about the root causes, implementation, and consequences of the genocide in Rwanda as well as other genocides in history. The memorial also teaches about what can be done to prevent future genocides. The top floor of the memorial includes exhibitions about genocides in the twentieth century with a large gallery dedicated to the Holocaust.[21]

In 2009 a second Holocaust center was opened in South Africa. The Durban Holocaust Centre went through several extensions and changes, and its core exhibition tells the history of the Holocaust including the story of Anne Frank through a re-created "Secret Annex." Since 2017, this exhibition also has a space dedicated to understanding genocide in the twentieth century with a focus on the 1994 genocide against the Tutsi in Rwanda. Founded by Mary Kluk, it also changed its name in 2017 to the Durban Holocaust & Genocide Centre.[22]

The next memorial to open in Africa was the Beau Bassin Jewish Detainees Memorial & Information Centre, launched in November 2014 in Mauritius. Adjacent to the St. Martin Jewish cemetery, it was established to commemorate the 1,581 Jewish detainees in Mauritius. The memorial also commemorates the 126 Jewish detainees who died at Beau Bassin prison between 1940 and 1945 and are buried at the St. Martin cemetery.[23]

The newest museum in South Africa, the Johannesburg Holocaust & Genocide Centre, moved to its groundbreaking symbolic building in 2016 and held its official opening in March 2019.[24] The Centre is a public-private partnership with the city of Johannesburg. The next section expands on this newest and largest Holocaust and genocide museum on the African continent.

Creating the Largest Holocaust and Genocide Museum in Africa

When the Johannesburg Holocaust & Genocide Centre (JHGC) was founded, the administrators decided to tell the history of the Holocaust and genocide through a multidirectional, nonlinear and thematic lens. The exhibition and education programs focus on the history of genocide in the twentieth century, including the Herero and Nama Genocide in today's Namibia (1904–7), the Armenian Genocide under the Ottoman Empire (1915–23), the Holocaust (1933–45), and the Genocide against the Tutsi in Rwanda (1994). The exhibition also looks at Raphael Lemkin, the development of the word "genocide," and the passing of the Convention for the Prevention and Punishment of the Crime of Genocide and its aftermath. It makes connections to South Africa's history of crimes against humanity and also to human rights issues that the country still faces today. The exhibition ends in a reflection garden and a section dedicated to the current challenges in South Africa, highlighting xenophobic and Afrophobic violence that has plagued the country since 2008.[25]

The mission of the JHGC is to serve as a place of memory, education, dialogue, and lessons for humanity. It adopts a human rights approach that promotes social justice, cultural diversity, and inclusivity, as well as facilitating opportunities for audiences to develop citizenship skills. Throughout the exhibition and various educational programs, the Centre makes implicit and explicit connections to South Africa's own past and present human rights abuses, as the country continues to struggle with a legacy of apartheid and colonialism.

For many educators and learners, the history of apartheid is still difficult to deal with, thus learning about the history of the Holocaust and the 1994 genocide against the Tutsi in Rwanda, both removed in place and time from the South African experience, could allow for a more open discussion about national issues. Those histories can serve as an "entry point" for reflection in a non-prescriptive way about the country's own painful histories of colonialism, apartheid, racism, and "othering." Due to their own historical experience, South Africans tend to see human rights violations through the prism of "white versus black." The JHGC, through the case studies of the Holocaust and the 1994 genocide against the Tutsi in Rwanda, reminds people that racism operates beyond the color line and may occur as "black versus black" or "white versus white."[26]

Throughout the JHGC's exhibition, history is presented through the voices, dilemmas, and choices of witnesses: victims, resisters, rescuers, bystanders, and perpetrators. Visitors are encouraged to engage with photographs, artefacts, drawings, and testimonies at their own pace. The JHGC attempts to promote active citizenship by utilizing the arts to concentrate on the life the victims led before their murder and not only on their suffering and their moment of death. The exhibition includes art, poetry, and music in all its spaces, allowing visitors to use multiple senses. It requires visitors to activate their bodies throughout, looking up and down, pulling out drawers or panels, listening to testimonies or to specially composed pieces of music of Holocaust and Rwandan survivors singing and sharing their testimonies with each other in the garden of reflection.[27]

The JHGC building's architecture is full of symbolism that inspires visitors to reflect on past and current human rights atrocities. The railway lines embedded in concrete and rock around the building, a clear symbol of the Holocaust, allow the visitor to make the connection to the impact of colonial expansion, control, and exploitation on the African continent. They symbolize modernity and progress but also suffering and oppression. Other journeys may also be recalled, such as the journeys of those fleeing human rights atrocities today. While many museums present genocidal histories in

Holocaust in a Museum Setting

dark spaces, the exhibition area deliberately includes wide, high windows, reminding the visitor that genocide happens in broad daylight, in full view of neighbors. This architectural choice asks visitors to reflect on what they witness in their own communities and thus encourages social activism.

School and other groups join an interactive program fostering critical thinking and activism that focuses on various themes including identity formation, the concept of "us" and "them," and the range of human behavior presented in historical case studies. In one instance high school learners from Johannesburg translated memory into activism after hearing the testimony of Xavier Ngabo, a survivor of the 1994 genocide against the Tutsi in Rwanda, who volunteered at the Centre. Together they collected funds on his behalf to allow him to return to Rwanda in 2010 to attend the Gacaca process through which he found the remains of his parents and gave them a proper burial. In an interview with alumni of that school in 2020, it became evident that this experience made a lasting impact on their lives.[28]

In addition to a permanent exhibition, the JHGC is a multifunctional center that includes seminar rooms, temporary exhibition spaces, a resource and learning center, an archive, offices, and Issy's café, named after local Holocaust survivor Issy Gurwicz. These spaces allow for a rich public program on human rights education such as the rights of people with disabilities, fighting homophobia, racism, antisemitism, and gender violence. The various activities are presented by JHGC education facilitators, hosting national and international guest speakers, temporary exhibitions, film screenings, commemorations, workshops, theater productions, and conferences. All these activities attract large and diverse audiences that come again and again to engage in dialogue and challenge the status quo in a safe space.

With the temporary closure of the JHGC building during the COVID-19 lockdown in 2020 and 2021, the JHGC found new ways to interact with the community. By forging national and international partnerships, the Centre was able to offer weekly public webinars with diverse speakers, artists and activists, online lessons to schools and universities, podcasts, survivors' testimonies, commemorations, virtual tours, and more. As many of the schools in South Africa do not have access to data, the internet, or computers, the Centre created WhatsApp voice notes with survivors' testimonies and historical narratives that were sent to more than two hundred schools.

The JHGC developed a large collection of free digital resources for the public that were used by audiences worldwide. This included video and audio collections on YouTube, SoundCloud, and Spotify; educational short papers; two volumes of the book *Portraits of Survival*, featuring the stories of Holocaust and Rwandan survivors who settled in South Africa; online exhibitions; and themed virtual tours that are available on the JHGC's website.[29] When the Centre reopened to the public between lockdowns, it also continued to implement a hybrid model reaching a growing number of "online" and "in-Centre" visitors. In the first eighteen months of the pandemic, the JHGC engaged with approximately one hundred thousand people from over forty-five countries.

Holocaust and Genocide Memory and Education in Africa: New Developments

In 2017 the Johannesburg Holocaust & Genocide Centre and Aegis Trust (Rwanda), developed a new youth leadership program called the Change Makers Programme (CMP).

Initiating the project in December 2016 at the Salzburg Global Seminar, the partners worked on an idea of a collaborative, cross-regional program that would empower institutions and individuals to promote pluralism and democracy and to counter extremism. The educational project encourages learning from history's difficult past through the case studies of the Holocaust, the 1994 genocide against the Tutsi in Rwanda, and apartheid in South Africa and is aimed at the African continent to assist leaders in finding African solutions to local problems.

The CMP is a youth leadership and a "train the trainer" workshop for student leaders, facilitators, teachers, and thought leaders. It strives to build resilience and resistance to violence, helps develop the necessary skills to challenge the idea of extremism, and encourages participants to become upstanders and changemakers in their society. Using the three historical case studies, the program motivates participants from other countries in Africa to develop their own programs.[30] So far the project has been launched in thirteen countries in Africa.[31] Numerous resources, films, interactive activities, and a traveling exhibition about the Holocaust and genocide were developed. This exhibition is now permanently displayed in Mozambique, Nigeria, the Gambia, Rwanda, and Zambia.

The programs' pilot was facilitated with high school students and teachers in Johannesburg and Rwanda in October and November 2017.[32] In 2018 a successful evaluation of the pilot program was completed by the University of Pretoria, and in February 2019 another positive evaluation of the "train the trainer" program was concluded by the same university.[33] The report's conclusion stated: "Overall, the evaluation obtained adequate evidence which indicates that the Change Makers Programme is a feasible project that holds enough potential to empower young people to use history as a tool to promote pluralism and counter extremism." As remarkably recommended by all the participants, the program should be scaled up because "it changes the way people think and see things."[34]

Following the evaluation, the CMP "train the trainer" program was rolled out in South Africa and other African countries, including in July 2018 in Maputo, Mozambique (in partnership with the Ministry of Youth and Culture), in September 2018 in Yola, Nigeria (in partnership with the American University of Nigeria and the Rosa Luxemburg Foundation), in February 2019 in the Gambia (in partnership with UNESCO and the Ministry of Education), in February 2020 in Kigali, Rwanda (in partnership with the University of Leeds, the Global Challenges Research Fund [GCRF], and the Arts and Humanities Research Council [AHRC]), and in November 2021 in Lusaka, Zambia (in partnership with the Christian Churches Monitoring Group [CCMG] and KAS Media Africa), among others. At the end of their training, trainees facilitate youth workshops in their communities and countries and use the traveling exhibition to educate about the Holocaust, genocide, and crimes against humanity.

Interest in the Holocaust and genocide is growing on the African continent, including the study about the Holocaust in Africa and its multidirectional memory in universities, schools, and museums. New books, conferences, memorials, traveling exhibitions, websites, online webinars, podcasts, and commemorations allow this memory to spread even further.[35]

Conclusion

Learning about the Holocaust and genocide and how they relate to contemporary human rights issues can help us understand how prejudice, discrimination, and "othering" may lead to mass atrocities and genocide. By emphasizing the importance of empathy, critical thinking, and personal responsibility, the hope is that visitors at museums and memorials and participants in educational programs can become an active voice against hate speech and human rights violations and can work toward preventing future atrocities.

As interest in researching and educating about the Second World War and the Holocaust and its connection to South Africa and Africa grows, so does its memorialization. In South Africa, study of the Holocaust and genocide is increasingly becoming an entry point to speak about other related human rights issues. In 2018 the United States Holocaust Memorial Museum's traveling exhibition "Deadly Medicine: Creating the Master Race" was displayed in the three Holocaust and genocide centers in South Africa alongside "The Mark of the Life Esidimeni Decanting," a local photographic exhibition documenting the mistreatment and neglect of hundreds of mentally and physically ill state patients in the Johannesburg area, including the death of 144 patients.[36] In 2019 the JHGC highlighted the plight of refugees, asylum seekers, and stateless people through a digital storytelling exhibition, "My Congo, My Story," in partnership with Royal Holloway, University of London.[37] Educational resources and online exhibitions were being developed in 2023 in partnership with the refugee community in Johannesburg.

All learners visiting the Johannesburg Centre leave a message on what they have learned from their educational program and the actions that they would like to take moving forward. One of the thousands of such messages said: "I pledge to understand, respect and admire the differences one has compared to another. I acknowledge that no human is more human than others and I want to live by that."[38]

The JHGC's exhibition includes photos of two survivors side by side, both of whom volunteer at the Centre: Irene Klass, Holocaust survivor of the Warsaw Ghetto, and Sylvestre Sendacyeye, Rwandan survivor of a massacre at a church in Gitarama. Klass reflects: "I thought that when the world learned what had happened to us, it could never happen again. But it did"; and Sendacyeye responds: "And a genocide happened yet again to us here in Rwanda in full view of the world." They suggest that the world did not learn from history, that "never again" was not their reality. The question is, with the help of memorialization and education, can it become ours?

Notes

1. Nelson Mandela's inaugural address as president of South Africa, May 10, 1994, quoted in "Mandela: In His Own Words," *The Guardian*, modified February 11, 2001, https://www.theguardian.com/world/2001/feb/11/nelsonmandela.southafrica.
2. Primo Levi, *The Reawakening* (New York: Simon & Schuster, 1995), 215.
3. "Memory activism" is a term coined by Yifat Gutman. See Gutman, *Memory Activism: Reimagining the Past for the Future in Israel-Palestine* (Nashville: Vanderbilt University Press, 2017).
4. Sarah Abrevaya Stein and Aomar Boum have researched and published extensively about the Holocaust in North Africa. See their latest book: Aomar Boum and Sarah Abrevaya Stein, eds., *The Holocaust and North Africa* (Stanford CA: Stanford University Press, 2018).
5. Alioune Deme worked with the JHGC on the exhibition "The Holocaust in Senegal," Johannesburg Holocaust & Genocide Centre, accessed December 20, 2021, https://www.jhbholocaust.co.za/remembrance/online-resources/.
6. Geneviéve Pitot, *The Mauritian Shekel: The Story of the Jewish Detainees in Mauritius, 1940–1945* (Lanham MD: Rowman & Littlefield, 2000). Roni Mikel-Arieli is research-

ing this history and working with the Beau Bassin Jewish Memorial & Information Centre and the Johannesburg Holocaust & Genocide Centre. Information about the deportation to Mauritius is available on the Memorial's website written in collaboration with the JHGC: Beau Bassin Jewish Detainees Memorial & Information Centre, accessed December 20, 2021, https://jewishdetaineesmauritius.com.

7. South African Jewish Board of Deputies (SAJBD), *South African Jews in World War II* (Johannesburg: SAJBD, 1950).

8. South African Military History, last modified December 28, 2015, *The Observation Post* (blog), https://samilhistory.com/2015/12/28/the-south-african-air-force-discovered-auschwitz-extermination-camp. See also Yad Vashem, Aerial Photographs of Auschwitz, accessed March 20, 2025, https://www.yadvashem.org/from-our-collections/auschwitz-aerial-photos.html; Dino A. Brugioni and Robert G. Proirier, "The Holocaust Revisited: A Retrospective Analysis of the Auschwitz-Birkenau Extermination Complex," CIA (1975–79), accessed March 20, 2025, https://www.cia.gov/resources/csi/static/holocaust-revisited-auschwitz-birkenau.pdf.

9. R. Mikel-Arieli, "Reading the Diary of Anne Frank on Robben Island: On the Role of Holocaust Memory in Ahmed Kathrada's Struggle against Apartheid," *Journal of Jewish Identities* 12, no. 2 (2019): 175–95, https://muse.jhu.edu/article/730299.

10. At its height in 1980, the Jewish community numbered 117,963 Jews; G. Shimoni and G. Shimoni, *Community and Conscience: The Jews in Apartheid South Africa* (Hanover NH: Brandeis University Press, published by University Press of New England, 2003), 215.

11. *The Immigration of Jews into the Union, 1926–1936: An Analysis of Official Statistics* (Johannesburg: SAJBD, 1937), 6.

12. Xavier Piat-ka, "She'erith Hapletah," in *In Sacred Memory: Recollections of the Holocaust by Survivors Living in Cape Town*, ed. Gwynne Schrire (Cape Town: Holocaust Memorial Council, 1995), 194–98.

13. Herman Wald's website, accessed December 20, 2021, http://www.hermanwald.com/pages/FormViewAdd.aspx?id=187.

14. Shirli Gilbert, "Jews and the Racial State: Legacies of the Holocaust in Apartheid South Africa, 1945–60," *Jewish Social Studies* 16, no. 3 (Spring/Summer 2010): 32–64.

15. Shirli Gilbert, "Anne Frank in South Africa: Remembering the Holocaust during and after the Apartheid," *Holocaust and Genocide Studies* 26, no. 3 (2012): 366–93.

16. Tracey Petersen, "Teaching Humanity: Placing the Cape Town Holocaust Centre in a Post-Apartheid State" (PhD diss., University of the Western Cape, 2015).

17. The Cape Town Holocaust & Genocide Centre website, accessed December 20, 2021, https://ctholocaust.co.za.

18. Department of Education in South Africa, "Curriculum and Assessment Policy Statement: Grades 10–12," accessed December 20, 2021, http://www.education.gov.za/Portals/0/CD/National%20Curriculum%20Statements%20and%20Vocational/CAPS%20FET%20%20HISTORY%20GR%2010-12%20%20WeB.pdf?ver=2015-01-27-154219-397.

19. "Minister Angie Motshekga: 1st History RoundTable Discussion," Keynote Address, Pretoria, December 3, 2015, South African Government, https://www.gov.za/speeches/minister-angie-motshekga-1st-history-roundtable-discussion-3-dec-2015-0000.

20. The South African Holocaust & Genocide Foundation website, accessed December 20, 2021, http://holocaust.org.za.
21. The Kigali Genocide Memorial website, accessed December 20, 2021, https://kgm.rw.
22. The Durban Holocaust & Genocide Centre website, accessed December 20, 2021, https://dbnholocaust.co.za.
23. The Jewish Detainees Memorial & Information Centre website, accessed December 20, 2021, https://jewishdetaineesmauritius.com/home/visit-us/.
24. The Johannesburg Holocaust & Genocide Centre (JHGC) website, "Exhibitions," accessed December 20, 2021, https://www.jhbholocaust.co.za/visit-us/exhibitions/.
25. In 2021 the JHGC partnered with Jacana Media and the Rosa Luxemburg Foundation to publish the book [BR]OTHER, about xenophobic violence in South Africa, by photojournalists Alon Skuy and James Oatway. See [BR]OTHER: Exploring Xenophobia and Fear of the "Other," accessed December 20, 2021, https://br-other.webflow.io/.
26. Facing its complicated and painful history, all of it, including its abuse of power and atrocities committed in its name—for example, in South-West Africa (today's Namibia), which South Africa controlled from 1916 to 1990—proves to be challenging.
27. The Johannesburg Holocaust & Genocide Centre, "The Permanent Exhibition: Holocaust & Genocide," accessed December 24, 2021, https://www.jhbholocaust.co.za/visit-us/exhibitions/permanent-exhibition/. Listen to the specially composed music by Philip Miller on JHGC's SoundCloud, "Remember: Ibuka," accessed December 24, 2021, https://soundcloud.com/user-858426360/remember-ibuka.
28. An interview with three of the alumni for an education film for the Johannesburg Holocaust & Genocide Centre, Virtual Tour of the exhibition "Empathy and Humanity," "The Story of Xavier Ngabo and Learners from St Stithians," YouTube, April 30, 2020, https://youtu.be/TGvAxwrULKM.
29. See the Johannesburg Holocaust & Genocide Centre's website: *Portraits of Survival*, Online Publications, accessed December 24, 2021, https://www.jhbholocaust.co.za/remembrance/online-publications/; "Confronting Our Past through a Distant Mirror: Reflections on the Holocaust as a Tool for Teaching about memory and Justice in South Africa," Online Exhibitions, accessed December 21, 2021, https://www.jhbholocaust.co.za/remembrance/online-exhibitions/; "Educator Resources," accessed December 21, 2021, https://www.jhbholocaust.co.za/education/educator-resources/.
30. Edward Kissi, "Obligation to Prevent (O2P): Proposal for Enhanced Community Approach to Genocide Prevention in Africa," *African Security Review* 25, no. 3 (2016): 242–57.
31. "Change Makers Leadership Program Launches in Nigeria," Salzburg Global Seminar, January 29, 2019, https://www.salzburgglobal.org/news/latest-news/article/change-makers-leadership-program-launches-in-nigeria.
32. "First Class of Change-Makers Graduate from Salzburg Global–Inspired Program to Tackle Extremism," Salzburg Global Seminar, October 30, 2017, https://www.salzburgglobal.org/news/topics/article/first-class-of-change-makers-graduate-from-salzburg-global-inspired-program-to-tackle-extremism.

33. The evaluation of the Change Makers Programme appeared on UNESCO's website: "Phase One Critical Review: The Change-Makers (South Africa)," August 17, 2022, https://www.changingthestory.leeds.ac.uk/archive/sa-critical-review/.
34. Chaya Herman and Charity Meki-Kombe from the University of Pretoria (South Africa), working with the University of Leeds (UK), conducted two independent and objective assessments of the CMP and produced two comprehensive reports: "An Evaluation of the Change Makers Programme Piloted in South Africa and Rwanda," March 2018; "Change Makers Programme Roll Out through 'Train the Trainer' Workshop Mozambique and Nigeria," December 2018.
35. To see further examples, go to the JHGC's website, YouTube channel, and SoundCloud, accessed December 20, 2021, https://www.jhbholocaust.co.za/.
36. The exhibition and conference "Deadly Medicine: The Mark of the Life Esidimeni Decanting" was held at the Johannesburg Holocaust & Genocide Centre in November 2018, http://www.southafricanpsychiatry.co.za/temp/November_2018/South%20African%20Psychiatry%20-%20November%202018%20-%20Deadly%20Medicine%20-%20pg%2030.pdf.
37. This short film, *My Congo, My Story*, was produced for the exhibition in July 2019 by Ayesha Siddiqui, Royal Holloway, University of London, https://www.youtube.com/watch?v=p-AnHivXShg.
38. Johannesburg Holocaust & Genocide Centre, "Butterfly Project," accessed December 21, 2021, https://www.jhbholocaust.co.za/remembrance/butterfly-project/.

Conclusion

MARK CELINSCAK AND MEHNAZ AFRIDI

The chapters that comprise this volume call attention to the expanding scope of Holocaust studies. Each contributor adopts an approach, not exclusively European, to the study of the memory, history, and representation of the genocide. *Global Approaches to the Holocaust* thus offers a range of viewpoints to enrich and deepen our understanding of a transformational event of the twentieth century. Tzvetan Todorov has argued that history must be confronted if we are to prevent the past from controlling the present.[1] The brutal reality of the mass extermination of European Jewry and the persecution of other marginalized groups is something that must be fully engaged. The linkages to that destruction, both direct and indirect, need to be more closely studied if we are to better grasp the entirety of the Holocaust. The genocide of the Jews is not only a matter for Europe but has repercussions globally.

The evolution of our understanding of the Holocaust has gone through distinct phases. The earliest witnesses to the genocide, including the documentation provided by Filip Müller, Rokhl Auerbakh, and Emanuel Ringelblum, and the work of pioneering scholars such as David Boder and Eva Reichmann helped establish the foundations for Holocaust studies. Hans Günther Adler, Raul Hilberg, Frank Littell, and Hannah Arendt further elevated the field and allowed the subject to reach broader audiences. In the twenty-first century, scholars such as Aomar Boum, Michael Rothberg, Dirk Moses, and Tina Campt have endeavored to enrich the field of Holocaust studies by engaging with postcolonial thought, comparative genocide, world history, human rights, and other studies with a focus on racism and mass violence.

Nevertheless, Gerhard L. Weinberg has highlighted the persistent "false perception of the Holocaust as a purely European project."[2] He explains, "A critical difference between the Holocaust and all other genocides is that it was intended to be worldwide and not limited to a specific portion of the globe."[3] Similarly, this volume argues that the history of the Holocaust extends beyond continental Europe. As noted in the introduction, Maghrebi Jews were deported from North Africa to Nazi extermination camps in Europe.[4] Moreover, from June 1940 to May 1945, Alderney, an island in the English Channel, was occupied by Nazi Germany. The island was the furthest west Nazi Germany ever established a concentration camp. Recently the Alderney Expert Review Panel estimated the range of deaths as being between 641 and 1,027 people on the island out of a total inmate population of just under 8,000.[5] Nearly 600 Jewish prisoners were sent to the island, and as the report concludes, "The Holocaust therefore is part of Alderney's history."[6] Research on the "ratlines," the escape routes for Nazi fugitives through South America, which also included Canada, the United States, Australia, and elsewhere, reveal the important connections between the Holocaust and world history.[7]

In the twenty-first century, study of the Holocaust continues to expand in terms of its geographic, chronological, and thematic scope. This promising new research still requires scholars to engage with Europe but also demands consultation and engagement with archives and literature from around the world. For example, the British colony of Hong Kong, one of the last ports for Jewish refugees before their arrival at the Shanghai Ghetto, requires a shift in focus from "mass murder to mass migration."[8] Likewise, Mikhal Dekel's *Tehran Children: A Holocaust Refugee Odyssey* tells the story of the author's father and the nearly 250,000 Polish Jews who survived the Holocaust in Uzbekistan, Kazakhstan, Turkmenistan, Iran, India, and British-controlled Palestine.[9] Joanna Newman's research explores how European Jewish refugees ended up in Barbados, Trinidad, and Jamaica.[10]

Indeed, scholars in this volume highlight the different terrains of Holocaust memory, history, and representation in places such as Mexico and South Africa, two countries that are not commonly associated with the Holocaust. And yet, significant new research makes connections to the Holocaust in these countries and simultaneously links the subject to their respective Jewish communities. Indeed, the exploration of the Holocaust in the context of racism and discrimination, and its broader global impact, has been a pivotal area of study. *Global Approaches to the Holocaust* attempts to enrich academic dialogue by illustrating how the Holocaust has influenced diverse communities worldwide and explored how they have responded to their own challenges to immigration, refugees, denial, distortion, and antisemitism. This volume also evaluates the effectiveness of Holocaust education in combating antisemitism in diverse communities, offering insights into its global reach and providing valuable resources for educators and scholars worldwide. It underscores the enduring relevance of the Holocaust across different geographical regions, engaging with audiences unfamiliar with its history.

Many of the scholars in this volume adopted an interdisciplinary approach, drawing from history, literature, religious studies, anthropology, immigration studies, and more to offer a comprehensive exploration of the Holocaust's global impact. One crucial aspect of Holocaust education is the exploration of collective memory, which has generated extensive scholarship, including on memorialization. This volume highlights the need to incorporate the voices of non-Jews who played significant roles in rescue efforts, providing places of exile and combating Holocaust distortion. It also sheds light on the involvement of various countries in Holocaust history, including those that facilitated passage for Jews in places such as the Philippines, China, Mauritius, Morocco, and Chile. These histories, when integrated into educational curricula, can offer valuable insights for a broader audience concerning immigration and memory-related issues.

Global Approaches to the Holocaust emphasizes the worldwide reach of the Holocaust, one extending far beyond continental Europe, a fact often overlooked in educational contexts. It also analyzes the presence of numerous museums, memorials, and research centers worldwide. Educators and scholars are encouraged to continue with this type of engagement by showcasing the comprehensive global landscape of the Holocaust. As highlighted by a recent study commissioned by the Conference on Jewish Material Claims Against Germany, there is a serious lack of knowledge and awareness about the Holocaust in the United States and elsewhere.[11] Therefore, there is a pressing need to shift focus toward the global dimensions of the Holocaust to engage a more diverse and concerned audience.

In conclusion, the chapters that comprise this volume illustrate the challenges posed by emerging research and acknowledges that the memory of the Holocaust is influenced by shifting political and social dynamics. Our introduction notes Peter Novick's concept that the memory of the Holocaust can be understood as a "series of concentric circles."[12] We hope this volume allows readers to better appreciate the Holocaust as part of both European and global history.

Notes

1. Tzvetan Todorov, *Facing the Extreme: Moral Life in the Concentration Camps* (New York: Metropolitan Books, 1996).
2. Gerhard L. Weinberg, "A Worldwide Holocaust Project," in *Global Perspectives on the Holocaust: History, Identity, Legacy*, ed. Nancy E. Rupprecht and Wendy Koenig

(Newcastle, UK: Cambridge Scholars, 2015), 63. He also reveals, "It is only in recent years that there has been some—but very little—serious scholarship on issues relating to the extension of the Holocaust outside Europe" (61).

3. Weinberg, "Worldwide Holocaust Project," 63.
4. Aomar Boum and Sarah Abrevaya Stein, introduction to *The Holocaust and North Africa*, ed. Aomar Boum and Sarah Abrevaya Stein (Stanford CA: Stanford University Press, 2019), 7. Also see Edward Kissi, *Africans and the Holocaust: Perceptions and Responses of Colonized and Sovereign Peoples* (London: Routledge, 2020).
5. "The Lord Pickles Alderney Expert Review," UK Government (May 2024), 34, https://assets.publishing.service.gov.uk/media/6656f459dc15efdddf1a84bb/Lord_Pickles-Alderney_expert_review.pdf.
6. "Lord Pickles Alderney Expert Review," 15.
7. For example, see Gerald Steinacher, *Nazis on the Run: How Hitler's Henchmen Fled Justice* (Oxford: Oxford University Press, 2011); Philippe Sands, *The Ratline: The Exalted Life and Mysterious Death of a Nazi Fugitive* (New York: Alfred A. Knopf, 2021).
8. Cheuk Him Ryan Sun, "The Holocaust and Hong Kong: An Overlooked History," *Holocaust Studies: A Journal of Culture and History* 29, no. 3 (2023): 393–413.
9. Mikhal Dekel, *Tehran Children: A Holocaust Refugee Odyssey* (New York: W. W. Norton, 2019).
10. Joanna Newman, *Nearly the New World: The British West Indies and the Flight from Nazism, 1933–1945* (New York: Berghahn, 2019).
11. "New Survey by Claims Conference Finds Significant Lack of Holocaust Knowledge in the United States," Conference on Jewish Material Claims Against Germany, March 2018, https://www.claimscon.org/study/.
12. Peter Novick, "The Holocaust Is Not—and Is Not Likely to Become—a Global Memory," in *Marking Evil: Holocaust Memory in the Global Age*, ed. Amos Goldberg and Haim Hazan (Oxford: Berghahn Books, 2015), 48.

Epilogue

MARK CELINSCAK, MEHNAZ AFRIDI, AND ILAN STAVANS

The myriad essays in this volume highlight important themes in Holocaust studies and do so through a global lens. Accordingly, in the following epilogue we offer two narratives to exemplify the mosaic of Jewish survivor experiences through the perspective of identity, immigration, loss, and agency. The chapters in *Global Approaches to the Holocaust* focus on aspects that we think are essential to Holocaust studies, such as trauma, identity, loss, and memory. These essays illustrate the complicated and painful experience of persecution. We hope that the point of how the Holocaust can be viewed as a global event is deeply ingrained in this volume. Indeed, each essay focuses on a part of the world outside Europe. The volume asks the reader to think about the complex scope of the Holocaust in terms of race, religion, identity, nationalism, and historical rootedness. In this epilogue we want to further engage the reader with two expository essays that will describe individual life stories through multiple geographic landscapes, intellectual inventions, and meditations on displacement.

The first essay explores the arduous journey of Karl Kasiel Blitz (later known as Charles K. Bliss), whose life story illustrates the difficult challenges and choices faced by Jews during the Holocaust in a global context. The story takes the reader from modern-day Ukraine to Germany and then to England, Canada, Japan, China, and finally, with Blitz as a refugee, to Australia. His persecution, internment, and displacement alongside the various roles, languages, and dilemmas faced by a refugee, were common experiences during the Holocaust, as well as themes discussed throughout this volume.

The second essay tells the imagined story of Guita Blumenthal, also from modern-day Ukraine. To escape her persecution as a Jew, she embarked on the ill-fated MS *St. Louis*, which departed in May 1939 from Hamburg, Germany. Ilan Stavans creates both a historical and intellectual map of the influences on Blumenthal, including Moses Maimonides, Ludwig Wittgenstein, Mordechai Buber, and Franz Rosenzweig. The story of Blumenthal, a woman whose mother offered her the education and opportunity to study renowned intellectual giants, becomes a stream of consciousness that illuminates her intellectual curiosity and lucidity during her anxious voyage. The idea of time in this essay points to Wittgenstein's notion of "Information of Time" and "Memory of Time," which also refers to the volume's subtitle, "Memory, History, and Representation."

Global Approaches to the Holocaust was delayed by multiple factors beginning with the global pandemic. We completed this volume during a time fraught with rising antisemitism and Islamophobia, alongside a rethinking of the history of displacement, diaspora, and identity. We hope this volume, and the following two essays, are timely and significant in the current climate.

Charles Bliss and the Global Dimensions of the Holocaust

Mark Celinscak

Chernivtsi is situated on the upper Prut River in the Carpathian foothills in what is today southwestern Ukraine. It has been ruled by several different countries, and at one time Romanian, Polish, German, Yiddish, Hungarian, Ukrainian, and Russian were all spoken in the city.[1] In the nineteenth and twentieth centuries Chernivtsi was a focal point for both Ukrainian and Romanian nationalist movements. In 1908 the city held the first Yiddish-language conference. It was there that Yiddish was defined as a national language of the Jewish people.[2] By 1930 Jews made up more than a third of the residents of Chernivtsi.

Karl Kasiel Blitz became a prominent member of the Jewish community in Chernivtsi. Born in 1897 when the city was still part of the Austro-Hungarian Empire, Blitz and his family were plagued by poverty, hunger, and antisemitism. His parents, Michel Anchel and Jeanette (née Seidmann), struggled to make ends meet. His father, an optician, also worked as a mechanic, electrician, and woodturner to help support the family. His parents spoke Yiddish with one another and German with their children.

At the outbreak of the First World War, Karl Blitz joined a Red Cross field ambulance. Tasked with removing the dead and injured from the battlefield, he witnessed firsthand the violence of war. Upon graduating high school in 1915, Blitz enlisted in the army. He was demobilized two years later; in 1918 his father passed away.

After the war, Blitz enrolled at the University of Czernowitz, studying chemistry and physics.[3] When Chernivtsi became part of the Kingdom of Romania, Blitz transferred to the Technical University of Vienna to study chemical engineering, earning his degree in 1922. He was hired by a local firm as a chemist. In 1925 Blitz married Rosika Kottler, a union that ended in divorce two years later. He then began a lifelong relationship with Claire Adler, a German Roman Catholic.

In 1933 Blitz purchased an optometry business in Chernivtsi. His life changed forever in March 1938 when the Federal State of Austria was annexed into the German Reich. As a Jew, Blitz was arrested by the local authorities and ultimately sent to the Dachau concentration camp, northwest of Munich. In September 1938 he was transferred to the Buchenwald concentration camp near Weimar.[4] As a German Catholic, Claire worked tirelessly to secure his release. Finally, in April 1939, Blitz was released from Buchenwald, and within a matter of weeks he made his way to England, where he attempted to secure a visa for Claire.[5]

In September 1939 the Second World War began in Europe when Nazi Germany invaded Poland. Due to the German bombing campaign against the United Kingdom, which was known as the *blitzkrieg*, Blitz changed his surname.[6] He became known as Charles K. Bliss and worked as a factory manager in London. He arranged for Claire to leave Germany and stay with his family in Chernivtsi. In 1940, with the assistance of a friend, Bliss helped Claire travel to Greece. Her time in Greece, however, was short-lived as Italy invaded the country that same year. With extended family in China, Bliss devised a plan to reunite with Claire in the Shanghai International Settlement. Consequently, Claire made the arduous trip from Greece to Istanbul, Odessa, Moscow, across Siberia to Manchuria, and from Port Arthur across the Yellow Sea to Shanghai.[7]

Meanwhile, in June 1940, Bliss left London for Liverpool, where he boarded the *Empress of Canada*. By the time he arrived in Halifax, Nova Scotia, the Soviet Union had occupied Chernivtsi, and the family businesses were confiscated. While in Canada, Bliss attempted to secure his residency in the country. He traveled from Halifax to Montreal and Ottawa. Unable to secure a permit to stay in the country, Bliss journeyed across Western Canada.[8] In August 1940 he set sail for Shanghai to be reunited with Claire.[9]

Bliss arrived in Yokohama, Japan, aboard the *Empress of Asia*. He continued to Nagasaki before finally arriving in Shanghai. In December 1940, after years apart, Charles and Claire reunited. The former quickly established a business called Bliss Film Service. In January 1941 Charles and Claire officially married.

In December 1941 Japan attacked the United States and Britain, as well as occupying the remainder of Shanghai. Japanese rule thus disbanded the

International Settlement. For the Bliss family, life during the Japanese occupation proved challenging. The business struggled, and Bliss resorted to selling cameras to make ends meet. In January 1943 the Japanese announced that all Jews would be forced into a ghetto, formally known as the Restricted Sector for Stateless Refugees.[10] While in Shanghai, Bliss studied the Chinese language and worked to develop a new writing system.[11] He gave lectures while in the Shanghai Ghetto and continued to sell cameras.

The Japanese surrendered to the Allies on September 2, 1945, thus ending the Second World War. The following day, the Shanghai Ghetto was officially liberated. In July 1946 Charles and Claire immigrated to Australia, settling in Sydney.[12] His mother passed away in March 1947 before he could arrange for her to join them. By November of that year, members of his family managed to immigrate to Australia. In August 1961 Claire died after a long illness.[13] On July 13, 1985, at the age of ninety-seven, Charles passed away.

What might the story of Charles K. Bliss tell us about the global dimensions of the Holocaust? He was born in what is modern-day Ukraine. Nazi persecution forced him, first, into Germany and then on to England, Canada, Japan, China, and finally, as a refugee, Australia. Six countries, four continents, and countless cities. Bliss was imprisoned by Nazi Germany in multiple concentration camps. He was then detained, nearly ten thousand kilometers away, in a ghetto established by Imperial Japan, under pressure from Nazi Germany. His experiences during the war demonstrate the global scale of the Holocaust. They also illustrate how the international community, both directly and indirectly, both knowingly and unwittingly, became implicated in the Holocaust. His story characterizes both the expansiveness and magnitude of the Holocaust, which devastated the lives of individuals, families, communities, and countries.

The life of Charles Bliss is significant in other ways.[14] Semantography is an ideographic writing system comprising basic symbols that can be brought together to create new images and concepts. Invented by Bliss while he was in China, it came to be known as Blissymbols.[15] Its inventor explained that, growing up in the Austro-Hungarian Empire, he was surrounded by "twenty different nationalities [that] hated each other, mainly because they spoke and thought in different languages."[16] Human beings, he argued, could be induced by language to commit appalling crimes against one another.[17] Indeed, as a victim of Nazi Germany, Bliss revealed that he witnessed firsthand how words could "turn men into killers."[18] He argued that language helped convince people that harming defenseless human beings could somehow be justified.[19] Semantography thus strives to allow different linguistic groups to better communicate. It was intended to "open up a new world of thought and understanding across all barriers."[20] For his efforts, Charles Bliss was nominated for a Nobel Prize, and in 1969 he received the Order of Australia.[21]

Much like semantography, *Global Approaches to the Holocaust* aims to bring together scholars from diverse backgrounds, specializing in parts of the world not typically associated with the genocide of European Jews. It strives to remove barriers between scholars examining the Holocaust from a variety of perspectives and fields of study, as well as to open communication among different geographic regions.

Guita Blumenthal Waves to Abel Eisenberg from Aboard the MS *St. Louis*, Havana, Cuba, April 27, 1939, 11:21 a.m.

Ilan Stavans

And Abraham drew near and said: "Will You, in anger, for the sake of justice, destroy the righteous with the wicked?"
—Genesis 18:23

In chapter 7, titled "Three Simple Stories," of Julian Barnes's *A History of the World in 10½ Chapters* (1989), there is a passing reference to Guita Blumenthal, who "jumped ship"—the expression is prescient—from the diesel-powered German liner *St. Louis* in Havana, Cuba. Likewise, on page 136 of *Refuge Denied* (2006), by Sarah A. Ogilvie and Scott Miller, a comment by Sol Messinger, "a child of the *St. Louis*," refers to Guita, with equal brevity, as "a 27-year-old wisecrack" originally from Khlivyshche, which is near Stavchany, in Ukraine's Chemivtsi province, as well as "a friend, among others, of Buber and Wittgenstein" and "a stellar scholar of Maimonides," versed in the *Guide for the Perplexed*, "with more dexterity to decipher Rabbi Moshe ben Maimon's epigrammatic mind than any of her contemporaries." But again no further information is provided on Guita. Nor do Gordon Thomas and Max Morgan-Witts list her, in their *Voyage of the Damned* (1974), as "among the victims swallowed by oblivion."

This note, therefore, is a corrective:

Like the rest of the 937 Jewish refugees in the motor ship, built in the Bremen shipyards, Guita Blumental boarded it in Hamburg, on Saturday, May 13, 1939. And, again, just like everyone else, she knew that, while the ultimate destination of all Nazi refugees was America, the first stop would be Havana. On the pier relatives waved flags. A band played festive music on a wooden platform. The day was clouding over. Attentive to detail, Guita noticed that upon the platform a bee cast a nervous shadow. For some unexplained reason, people near her spoke in low tones, which—bizarrely—made her imagine them dead. The eight-decked vessel, with twin triple-blade propellers, capable of sailing at 16 knots, that is, 30 kilometers per hour, had a capacity for 973 passengers: 270 cabins, 287 tourist class, and 416 third deck. The price for the cabins was 800 Reichsmarks. There were also 500 tourist-class rooms at 600 Reichsmarks. Guita's ticket cost 475 Reichsmarks, was purchased twelve days before departure with money her "boyfriend" Abel Eisenberg had sent her from Mexico, and confirmed her as one of the last passengers on third deck. Should an unplanned return be required, the price included a "contingency fee" protecting the Hamburg-America Line.

The overall excitement made Guita feel self-conscious. She thought of her belongings—an old leather suitcase, which included several changes of clothes, two pairs of shoes, gloves, and a prayer book, along with the red dress and black winter coat she was wearing—as stage artifacts of an actress as if the journey on which she was about to embark belonged not to her but to the character in a mediocre novel. In a separate bag, Guita carried her precious copy of Maimonides's guide, along with a volume by Nahmanides, another by Hasdai Crescas, a journal, and a couple of introductory letters, one by Martin Buber, the other by Shaul Adler, a distinguished parasitologist on the faculty in Jerusalem's Hebrew University, who, long after the tragedy of the *St. Louis*, would translate Darwin's *On the Origin of Species* into Hebrew. And in her purse, she had a few extra Reichsmarks, a photograph of her parents on their wedding day, and the address of a "Jewish hotel" in Havana where, should chaos reign on her arrival, she would meet Abel as soon as she set her feet on "Prospero's lost island," as Wittgenstein, a couple of months prior, had mocked in the correspondence he sent from Cambridge.

Guita knew nothing about Cuba, except that it was a magnet for gamblers, mobsters, and empresarios. She didn't know much about Mexico. A decade ago, she had read a novella by an American playwright, *The Bridge of Saint Luis Ray*, from a friar's viewpoint, about the collapse of a rope bridge over a gorge, a canyon, or a river (she remembered the word *pongo*) and the people who perished while crossing it. Did it take place among the Aztecs in Mexico? Guita was phobic about bridges. She also disliked public transportation. Whenever she was on a tram, she felt trapped and susceptible. A little girl passed near her. Something had upset her. Guita looked for strength in the girl's facial gestures. Sailing would likely turn her stomach upside down. She was relieved that the vessel sailed on time. She attributed the fact to German punctiliousness, even though the British (Wittgenstein was persistently on her mind) modeled themselves too as "on the dot." She loosely recalled of a line from Oscar Wilde's *The Portrait of Dorian Gray*: "I am always late on principle, my principle being that punctuality is the thief of time." The *St. Louis* inauspiciously navigated the Elbe River toward the North Atlantic. The waters were calm. Guita looked at the hypothetical night sky. Discerning patterns in it, she thought of Maimonides's *Iggeret Teman*, known as the "Epistle to Yemen."

In the epistle, written around 1173, the Rambam, from his base in Egypt, advised Rabbi Ya'akov ben Nathanael ibn al-Fayyumi, son of the illustrious Rabbi Netan'el al-Fayyumi, against adopting astrology as a prognosticator of future human affairs. "I note that you are inclined to believe in the influence of the past and future conjunctions of the planets upon human affairs." Maimonides added: "At the time when Moses rose to leadership the astrologers had unanimously predicted that our nation would never be freed from bondage, nor gain their independence, but fortune smiled upon Israel, for the most exquisite of human beings appeared and redeemed them at the very time which was supposedly most inauspicious for them.... To the failure of their vaticination, Isaiah alludes when he says 'Where are they then thy wise men?'" Guita articulated the question in silence. Would the *St. Louis* travel without impediment? Was there some way, however minute, to glimpse what fate had in store for her? She felt a pinch in her back: every so often, especially when she was fretful, a nerve, entwined in her vertebrae, emitted a jolt that reached as far as her toes. There was nothing to do. In the future, should time allow it, she could visit a doctor in New York. But such privileges were beyond her now. Escape was her only task. She needed to be strong. She was aware that prayer services took place on board at sunrise and sunset. Another form of superstition, she thought, and she was intent on avoiding them. Fanaticism, she concluded, was the ailment of the present—even when practiced by non-fanatics.

Once in her cabin, Guita dropped her suitcase, quickly washed her face, and proceeded toward the dining room. As anticipated, the wealthy were on one end of the room, and tourists in another. She approached a table and sat next to a couple that spoke German with a Viennese accent, but she didn't say a single word. She looked at the menu. It featured items rationed in Germany that she couldn't afford. She asked instead for cabbage soup and a piece of bread. Once she finished, Guita made her way to the front of the ship. She felt mildly dizzy. Could she be pregnant? She had slept with a young physicist in Odessa a few weeks ago. On the way she noticed many children on board. She also knew there was childcare available. Was her biological clock in disarray? Or was the vertigo connected with the harmonious movement of the waters below her? If she was carrying a baby, she could still persuade Abel it was his, as long as their first night at the Hotel Raquel was the first or second night of their reencounter. What bothered her, though, was a vague feeling of foreboding. As she undressed, Guita remembered that in the *Guide for the Perplexed*, Maimonides comments a few times on a Hebrew word, *keri*, which appears seven times in chapter 26 of Leviticus. In it, the Almighty talks about "willful ignorance." Some translate *keri* as hostility, but she knew Maimonides opted for randomness. In his view the world is commanded by the Divine Providence, yet there is room for chance.

As she lay on the bed seeking the angels of sleep, Guita thought that chance ("the occurrence of events in the absence of any obvious design") was the prime organizer of things. A daughter of an orthodox butcher, she was destined for marriage, not to magnificent explorations of the mind. Her mother set her free by encouraging her passion about reading. She moved with a maternal uncle to Lvov, where she learned Russian and, to a lesser degree, German, and where she briefly met her teacher Mordechai Buber, who was a translator, with his friend Franz Rosenzweig, of the Bible into German, a Zionist, and a descendant of Rabbi Meir Katzenellenbogen of Padua, known in Hebrew as the Maharam. Her eyes closed, she met the rhythmic movement of the vessel enwrapping her. Her imagination made her visualize Buber's enveloped letter in her suitcase. He had encouraged her to emigrate to Palestine, "the only place where the Jewish mind is assured a vigorous future." He gave her the addresses in Jerusalem of a number of German émigrés. But Guita didn't write to them. She simply wasn't interested. Why relocate to a land where Jews would build a ghetto the size of an entire country?

Around that time, Guita met Abel, a twenty-three-year-old music student infatuated with Tchaikovsky and Brahms. Their first encounter was in Odessa, then in Vienna. He was a promising violinist with an interest in conducting orchestras. In Odessa the couple walked the grand Primorsky Boulevard and climbed the Potemkin Stairs, which lead to the waterfront, where the Vorontsov Lighthouse stood erect. His mother died when he was born and his father was an alcoholic. He was declared an orphan and, by Jewish law, "became the son" of his aunt. When she opted to take the family to Mexico, he stayed behind to pursue his studies at the Wiener

Volkskonservatorium, created by Emmerich Maday. They fell in love. Abel returned to Ukraine before following his mother and siblings to Mexico, from where he sent frequent letters. When Adolf Hitler became chancellor, she had a dream in which a lion roared near her bed. As a woman, she didn't want to marry for the sake of convenience. Her erudition in medieval philosophy was widely known. She was a tutor in Vienna, a block away from Kärntner Straße. Yet she felt time was running out. Around that time, through an acquaintance interested in the philosophy of language, she read Wittgenstein's *Tractatus Logico-Philosophicus* and was enthralled with the idea that thoughts are pictures, and that pictures are made up of elements that represent an object, and the combination of elements in the picture represents the combination of objects in a state of affairs. In other words, "the picture is a model of reality." Right now, in Guita's mind, a sequence of pictures allowed her to follow her narrative up to the very present. Time, she told herself, is cinematic. Was this conception too rooted in the pervasiveness of films in daily affairs? What obsessed her, though, was tomorrow as a sequence of non-pictures. She had written to Wittgenstein to inquire about his understanding of the future. His response resulted in her visiting him in Cambridge twice.

Guita's English was stilted, yet she made herself understood. Wittgenstein talked to her about the tyranny of clocks and about "moving outside of time." He distinguished—or she alleged he distinguished—between "information-time" and "memory-time." For some reason, she had forgotten the separation between the two. During her second visit Wittgenstein had promised to help her secure a position in England. After Kristallnacht, on November 9 and 10, 1938 (in Vienna at the time, she was in a state of disquiet for days), she had written him to remind him of it. But the offer never came. Instead, on March 22 Abel sent her a ticket to the MS *St. Louis*, assuring her it was "the last chance to escape purgatory." Truth is, Mexico for Guita was what Americans called "the boondocks." By joining Abel, she was likely rescuing her heart; she was also sacrificing her intellect. As an option, she preferred to think of New York. Still, whatever decision needed to be made couldn't wait long. Every day she waited for the postman's arrival. An envelope from Wittgenstein would push her in a certain direction. The mailbox only brought news from Abel: an itinerary and a reservation at Hotel Raquel, on Calle Amargura #103.

She couldn't remember anymore the exact day she contacted the Joint Distribution Committee for the special type of visa she needed. She secured the required items, among them a photograph, a relative or friend's foreign address, and proof of refugee status. She arrived in Hamburg on May 11. She experimented with increasing anxiety during the rest of the voyage. In total, she interacted with only a handful of fellow passengers. (One of them, from Lviv, Guita mistakenly thought she knew.) She couldn't hold the food she ate. To herself, she wondered if the intensity of her physical malady was similar to pregnancy. With her propensity to nervousness apparent since an early age, her father had once described her as a hysteric; her studious behavior over the years had proven him wrong. Now she wasn't sure. Twice she thought she should have waited longer in Vienna. Perhaps the anti-Jewish laws in Germany were just a fad. Evil is cyclical. It is impossible to say for sure when it is ready to stay for long. Yet Kristallnacht was palpably in her mind. Hitler's Foreign Office and the Propaganda Ministry were exploiting the unwillingness of other countries to admit large numbers of Jewish refugees. In the loneliness of her cabin, as she fell into deep slumber, she told herself she was lucky to have a path forward.

When she woke up, she was in a stupor. That state of insensibility, which overwhelmed for the rest of the trip, precludes me to tell her forthcoming days in any detail. Suffice to say that Guita barely left her cabin. Two passengers, aware of her situation, brought her hot soup. She made a total of seven visits to the restaurant. During one of them, she looked down at the undulating waves for as long as an hour. On May 25 she felt better, but her mood was somber. She might have lost several pounds. On the third deck she conversed with a number of people, one of them by the name of Max Loewe, who limped and, as he told Guita, was a First World War veteran (the limp came about after he was beaten by Nazi guards in Buchenwald), about a recent movie Guita hadn't seen, *Jezebel*, with Bette Davis and Henry Fonda. She saw Captain Gustav Schröder, the liner's chief in command, in a heated discussion with a member of the crew. Captain Schröder had been told of a cable just received in the vessel's home office: "MAJORITY OF YOUR PASSENGERS IN CONTRAVERSION OF NEW CUBAN LAW 937 AND MAY NOT BE GIVEN PERMISSION TO DISEMBARK." A day later, on Friday, more seagulls—these were no doubt real—flew over Guita. She felt the need to talk to them. A woman who one day becomes the mother of Harvard professor Doris Sommer recommended drinking tea with cognac. Guita laughed. Minutes later, on her way to the bar where she planned to spend her last Reichsmarks, she saw on a staircase a weed leaf growing from a wooden crevice.

She immediately fantasized the *St. Louis* at the bottom of the ocean, covered with algae, schools of fish navigating through marshes overtaking broken windows, and phytoplankton emerging from the German liner's oxidized chimineas. "The universe talks to us through the wilderness," she thought. Unbeknown to her, earlier that month an antisemitic rally in Havana, organized by the government and a few trade unions, amassed forty thousand people. All Jews were portrayed as communists. Meanwhile the Cuban Nazi Party requested a public investigation into Franklin Delano Roosevelt's past, arguing the American president, through his "Bad Neighbor Policy," was looking to create a Jewish state in the Caribbean archipelago. On Sunday, May 28, Lawrence Berenson of the Joint Distribution Committee sought to broker a deal with Cuban president Federico Laredo Brú and one of his ministers, Fulgencio Batista. In the end Brú offered to take every one of the passengers as long as the Joint Distribution Committee posted a bond for $500 per person—for a total of $453,500. Berenson made a counteroffer; it was summarily rejected.

Despite repeated efforts, Guita couldn't see Abel. He was part of a crowd on the Havana pier. He saw the anchor drop on May 27, at 4:17 p.m., waiting serenely for passengers to disembark. In turn, she put her clothes back into the suitcase, cleansed herself a bit, and moved into where the crowd of passengers were lining up to make their way out. Nothing happened. After an hour of no movement, Abel inquired with an officer at the entry port. He was told that the passengers' official documents were being checked. He thought it might be a lie yet proceeded calmly. Guita, in contrast, was frantic: she stepped on the railing to try locating Abel again. The motor ship was meters away from the pier. Guita raised her hands as if praying to God. Above her, the sky was clear. She took her coat off. "I'm in hell," she whispered. Also, "this is a jungle," although she had never been in one. A few minutes later, Captain Schröder, from the command center, announced people would soon be allowed to leave. It was another lie, even though twenty-eight passengers did disembark indeed: four Spaniards, two Cubans, and twenty-two Jews with valid United States visas. Four were Spaniards and two were Cuban.

The ordeal became unbearable. Abel tried an assortment of maneuvers to have a tête-à-tête with Guita. Unbeknownst to them, on May 5, four months before the Second World War officially began, the Cuban government had suddenly abandoned what was seen as a pragmatic immigration policy. Through a decree it "restricted entry of all foreigners except U.S. citizens, unless authorized by Cuban secretaries of state." This meant that the visas the *St. Louis* passengers held had been invalidated retroactively. Much of the information Abel got came from hearsay. Bystanders on the pier allowed themselves the pleasure of concocting rumors. He got updates about current events from radio stations and in *Diario de la Marina*, the pages of which, he opined, were rubbish. Exhausted, without knowing what to do with himself, every night he returned to the Hotel Raquel. His bed felt empty. Days earlier he had seen family members renting small boats and approaching the *St. Louis* to make contact. When he inquired about one, he found out several other relatives of passengers were attempting a full-blown rescue operation. While not known for his athleticism, Abel tried to find out details. But his quest was stonewalled when he was notified that the Cuban government no longer allowed citizens to come within a twelve-meter perimeter of the liner. Abel was undeterred. Along with two partners, he procured a simple row boat, which he intended to use the afternoon of May 30. It was too late. That morning, Guita heard from a Russian passenger that Captain Schröder, with 907 refugees on board, was ready to sail to Florida.

Inevitably, she heard about the tragedy, which Ogilvie and Miller refer to on page 22 of their book: shortly before, Max Loewe, after slitting his wrists, threw himself overboard. She saw him being rescued by the Cuban police. A policeman screamed the words "Hospital Calixto García." It was then that Guita made her most important decision: to jump as well. Through her studies of Søren Kierkegaard, she decided that the most auspicious—the most daring—of human acts is suicide. In *Either/Or*, he reflected on suicide using the metaphor of theater: we see ourselves on stage, yet when it is clear the play is over, what option is there but to depart? "I am sitting in the audience rather than observing the play from the outside." He adds: "Since I don't like to stand on the quotidian, unfriendly street, and since I enjoy sitting in the warm, comfortable auditorium, I must make a decision." As Guita pushed herself toward a fence on the upper deck, she appeared to see Abel from afar and waved her right hand. It was likely an apparition since at that precise time he was still in a workshop negotiating the rental deal. It was April 27, 1939, 11:21 a.m. local time.

She heard a siren. A seven-year-old boy, Sol Messinger, witnessed the act. He would describe it as a suicide, although, in truth, it was just an act of ultimate desperation. As Guita threw herself from aboard into the warm waters, her left foot was caught in a rope, which made her head hit the vessel's unforgiving iron hull walls. It was just the same since she didn't know how to swim. Her body sank with little resistance. At that moment Guita felt lonelier than she ever had in her entire existence. "Something unbelievable has happened to me," she reflected. "I thought life was about taking control. It was all a fabrication." She grasped for air without success. "I cannot think anymore. I am dead matter." Her belongings were left behind. Without a hint of interest, they were stored by members of the crew in a storage room, where they were forgotten. Not long after, the *St. Louis* sailed in search of the Miami lights. From there, it continued to Halifax, Nova Scotia, and then to Antwerp, Belgium. Of the 620 passengers it brought back to Europe, many died in Auschwitz and Sobibór. Others perished in internment camps or hiding from the Nazis. A total of 365 survived. The *St. Louis* returned to Hamburg without passengers.

From the vantage point of this last paragraph, it is possible to speculate what Guita's *other* fate might have been. Had she deboarded in Havana, she would have stayed with Abel at the Hotel Raquel for two nights. She would have arrived in Mexico City on April 31. She would have felt exhilaration, followed by depression. The experience in Havana would not leave her. Who died and who survived? Was it their fate to have ended one or the other, or were they part of a lottery? Guita would have tallied on a few philosophical disquisitions, but she would have distracted herself with other matters. After again attempting to reach Wittgenstein and Buber (neither ever received her last letters), she would have been plagued by a sense that Mexico was a habitat utterly alien to her. Fatefully, an automobile accident on Boulevard Paseo de Reforma, on Sunday, November 14, 1943, would have eliminated the possibility of Guita becoming my grand aunt. Upon his return to Mexico from Cuba, after a period of depression, in the dimension of reality, Wittgenstein called "information-time," Abel married Lilly Glantz, an unstable woman with whom he had four children; one of them, Henry—known as Saint Hershele—became an operative of the notorious Sonora drug cartel.

Notes

1. Marianne Hirsch and Leo Spitzer, *Ghosts of Home: The Afterlife of Czernowitz in Jewish Memory* (Berkeley: University of California Press, 2010), 90.
2. Tomasz Kamusella, *Words in Space and Time: A Historical Atlas of Language Politics in Modern Central Europe* (Budapest: Central European University Press, 2021), 12.
3. "Chernivtsi" in German is "Czernowitz."
4. C. K. Bliss, *Semantography (Blissymbolics)*, 2nd enlarged ed. (Sydney: Semantography Blissymbolics Publications, 1965), 11.
5. Bliss, *Semantography (Blissymbolics)*, 54.
6. Richard Ure, "The End of a Great Innings," *Semantography Blissymbolics Newsletter*, published by Semantography Trust Fund (Australia), n.d., 7.
7. Bliss, *Semantography (Blissymbolics)*, 814–15.

8. For further discussion about Canada's restrictive immigration policy toward Jewish refugees during the war, see Irving Abella and Harold Troper, *None Is Too Many: Canada and the Jews of Europe, 1933–1948*, 40th anniversary ed. (Toronto: Toronto University Press, 2023).
9. Bliss, *Semantography (Blissymbolics)*, 216.
10. Bliss, *Semantography (Blissymbolics)*, 817.
11. Bliss, *Semantography (Blissymbolics)*, 217.
12. Bliss, *Semantography (Blissymbolics)*, 219.
13. Bliss, *Semantography (Blissymbolics)*, 813.
14. Bliss was the subject of a documentary film. See *Mr. Symbol Man*, directed by Bob Kingsbury and Bruce Moir (Film Australia and the National Film Board of Canada, 1974), 47 minutes.
15. In 1942 Bliss called these symbols "World Writing." In 1947 he selected the term "Semantography," from the Greek *semanticos*, which refers to "significant meaning," and *graphien*, meaning "to write." See Bliss, *Semantography (Blissymbolics)*, 8.
16. Bliss, *Semantography (Blissymbolics)*, 10.
17. Bliss, *Semantography (Blissymbolics)*, 11.
18. Charles K. Bliss, "Semantography: One Writing for One World," *Australian Lithographer* 6, no. 31 (September–October 1971): n.p.
19. Bliss, *Semantography (Blissymbolics)*, 13.
20. Bliss, "Semantography," n.p.
21. See papers relating to a nomination by Douglas Everingham to award the 1969 Nobel Peace Prize to Bliss, 1968–71, MS 3884, National Library of Australia, Papers of Charles Bliss (File)-Box 52-53.

Contributors

Navras J. Aafreedi is an assistant professor of history at Presidency University, Kolkata, India; a research fellow at the Institute for the Study of Global Antisemitism and Policy, New York; a fellow of Salzburg Global Seminar under its Holocaust Education & Genocide Prevention Program and its Asia Peace Innovators Forum; and a member of OSCE (Organization for Security and Co-operation in Europe), ODIHR (OSCE Office for Democratic Institutions and Human Rights), UNESCO Advisory Group on Addressing Antisemitism through Education, and ISGAP-Woolf Institute Research Collective. His numerous publications include a monograph, *Jews, Judaizing Movements and the Traditions of Israelite Descent in South Asia* (2016), and a coedited volume, *Conceptualizing Mass Violence: Representations, Recollections, and Reinterpretations* (2021).

Mehnaz Afridi is a professor of religious studies and director of the Holocaust, Genocide, and Interfaith Education Center at Manhattan University. She teaches courses on Islam, the Holocaust, genocide, comparative religion, and feminism. Her last book, *Shoah through Muslim Eyes* (2017), was nominated for the Yad Vashem International Book Prize for Holocaust Research and the Jacob Schnitzer Book Award. She is currently working on her forthcoming book, *The Wounded Muslim*.

In 2019 she was awarded the Costello Award for teaching excellence in the School of Liberal Arts and the Lasallian Educator (2020) at Manhattan University. She is a U.S. State Department member on the delegation for the International Holocaust Remembrance Alliance. She also serves as a member of the Committee of Ethics, Religion, and the Holocaust at the United States Holocaust Memorial Museum, Washington DC.

Zeina M. Barakat, a Jerusalem-born Palestinian scholar, holds a PhD from Friedrich-Schiller University in Jena, Germany. She is a postdoctoral fellow and executive director of the European Wasatia Graduate School for Peace and Conflict Resolution at Europa-Universität, Flensburg, Germany. Additionally, she is a research associate at the Von Hügel Institute, University of Cambridge. She has authored numerous academic books and articles, including "From Heart of Stone to Heart of Flesh: Evolutionary Journey from Extremism to Moderation" (2017) and "Envisioning Reconciliation: Signs of Hope for the Middle East" (2022).

Paul R. Bartrop is a multi-award-winning scholar of the Holocaust and genocide. Until December 2020 he was a professor of history and director of the Center for Holocaust and Genocide Research at Florida Gulf Coast University, Fort Myers, where he is now professor emeritus of history. He is also a principal fellow in history at the University of Melbourne and an elected fellow of the Royal Historical Society in the United Kingdom. He is the author, coauthor, and editor of some thirty-five books, including *The Holocaust: Country by Country* (2024) and *The Holocaust and Australia: Refugees, Rejection, and Memory* (2023).

Ann Beaglehole (born Aniko Szegö in Hungary) is a historian and former public servant. She arrived in New Zealand in 1957 with her parents, who were Holocaust survivors, after the Hungarian uprising against the Soviet Union. She is the author of *Refuge New Zealand: A Nation's Response to Refugees and Asylum Seekers* (2013) and *A Small Price to Pay: Refugees from Hitler in New Zealand, 1936–1946* (1988), among other works. Her recent journal publication, titled "Beyond Polarisation?" is an essay, in the form of a conversation, on the Israel-Hamas conflict.

Aomar Boum is a historical anthropologist and member of the Academy of the Kingdom of Morocco. He is a professor and Maurice Amado Chair in Sephardic Studies in the Departments of Anthropology, History, and Near Eastern Languages and Cultures at the University of California, Los Angeles. He is also a faculty fellow at Université Internationale de Rabat, Morocco. He is interested in the place of religious and ethnic minorities such as Jews, Bahais, Shia, Amazigh, and Christians in post-independence Middle Eastern and North African nation-states.

Mark Celinscak is the Louis and Frances Blumkin Professor of Holocaust and Genocide Studies in the Department of History and the executive director of the Sam and Frances Fried Holocaust and Genocide Academy at the University of Nebraska at Omaha (UNO). He is the author of *Distance from the Belsen Heap: Allied Forces and the Liberation of a Nazi Concentration Camp* (2015), winner of a Vine Award for Non-Fiction, and *Kingdom of Night: Witnesses to the Holocaust* (2022), winner of a Canadian Jewish Literary Award for Holocaust literature. He is also the coeditor of *Artistic Representations of Suffering: Rights, Resistance, and Remembrance* (2021).

He currently serves as cochair of the Consortium of Higher Education Centers for Holocaust, Genocide, and Human Rights Studies. He was the principal investigator who established the Samuel Bak Museum: The Learning Center on the UNO campus. He is an elected fellow of the Royal Historical Society and editor of the *Journal of History*.

Mohammed S. Dajani Daoudi is a Jerusalemite scholar and peace activist. He holds a doctorate from the University of South Carolina, Columbia (1981) and another from the University of Texas at Austin (1984). He is the author of numerous books and academic articles. In 2007 he established the Wasatia Moderation Movement and the Wasatia Academic Institute. In 2014 Tufts University bestowed upon him the Dr. Jean Mayer Global Citizenship Award for his ongoing work to build peace, encourage dialogue, and find alternatives to extremism. In 2015–17 he joined the Washington Institute for Near East Policy as a Weston Fellow. In March 2023 the Austrian Parliament awarded him the Simon Wiesenthal Prize for his commitment to combating antisemitism. In September 2023 he received the Excellence in Leadership Award from Queens College, New York City University.

Rebecca L. Erbelding has been an archivist, educator, and historian at the United States Holocaust Memorial Museum since 2003. She was the lead historian on the museum's special exhibition "Americans and the Holocaust." She is the author of *Rescue Board: The Untold Story of America's Efforts to Save the Jews of Europe* (2018), which won the National Jewish Book Award. She served as the main historical adviser and an on-camera expert in Florentine Films' *The U.S. and the Holocaust*, directed by Ken Burns, Lynn Novick, and Sarah Botstein, which debuted on PBS in 2022.

Shirli Gilbert is a professor of modern Jewish history at University College London. She obtained her D.Phil. at the University of Oxford and was a postdoctoral fellow in the Society of Fellows at the University of Michigan. She is a historian of modern Jewish life, with particular interest in the Holocaust and its legacies; Jewish refugees in Africa; Jews, racism, and colonialism; and Jews in South Africa. Her publications include *Music in the Holocaust* (2005), *From Things Lost: Forgotten Letters and the Legacy of the Holocaust* (2017), and, with Avril Alba, *Holocaust Memory and Racism in the Postwar World* (2019). She is coeditor of the journal *Jewish Historical Studies*.

Daniela Gleizer is a researcher at the Institute for Historical Research at UNAM (Universidad Nacional Autónoma de México), specializing in the history of migration and exile in Mexico. She holds a PhD in history from El Colegio de México and authored *Unwelcome Exiles: Mexico and the Jewish Refugees from Nazism, 1933–1945* (2014). At UNAM she teaches graduate and postgraduate history courses. She is a member of the National System of Researchers and the Latin American Jewish Studies Association. Additionally, she is an affiliate researcher at the Center for Advanced Genocide Research at the University of Southern California.

Lorena Cardona González is a professor in the faculty of social and legal sciences at the Universidad de Caldas (Colombia). She earned a PhD in history and an MA in history and memory from the Universidad de la Plata (Argentina). Her research focuses on the representations of the Holocaust in Colombia and the history of Jewish and German migration during World War II. Her master's thesis, "Sobre ciertas cosas que no se pueden nombrar: La Representación del Holocausto en Colombia (1976–2015)," emerged from these two interests, as did her doctoral dissertation, "Una colectividad honorablemente sospechosa: Los alemanes, Colombia y la Segunda Guerra Mundial."

Bonnie M. Harris completed her PhD at University of California, Santa Barbara, her dissertation being the first academic study of the Philippine rescue of European refugee Jews from the Holocaust. Her book *Philippine Sanctuary: A Holocaust Odyssey* traces the story of Joseph Cysner, who was deported by the Nazis, detained at Zbaszyn, Poland, released to immigrate to Manila, and then interned by the Japanese in Manila during World War II. She taught history at San Diego State University and local community colleges in the San Diego area for over fifteen years. She has always regarded her family as her greatest accomplishment.

Emmanuel Kahan, PhD in history from the National University of La Plata, is a researcher at the National Council for Scientific and Technological Research of Argentina. He is a professor in the Department of History at the National University of La Plata and also is coordinator of the Center for Jewish Studies based at the Institute for Economic and Social Development. He has published various books and articles on Jewish life in Argentina, the reception of the Arab-Israeli conflict in Argentina, and the memory of the Holocaust. In 2013 he received the Best Dissertation Award given at the University of Texas at Austin by the Latin American Jewish Studies Association (LAJSA) and in 2015 the Scientific Work Award from the National University of La Plata.

Rotem Kowner is a professor of history and Japanese studies at the University of Haifa. He has led numerous projects examining broad themes in Asia and Japan from a global perspective. One such project explores the settlement of Jews in Asia, culminating in the edited volume *Jewish Communities in Modern Asia* (2023). Another recent project, focusing on the Japanese attitude toward Jews during the Holocaust, has resulted in several articles and a forthcoming book. A third project, examining Israel's relations with Asia, produced the edited volume *Israel-Asia Relations in the Twenty-First Century* (with Yoram Evron, 2023).

Nancy Nicholls Lopeandía is a historian at the Institute of History of the Pontifical Catholic University of Chile, with a PhD in sociology from the University of Essex, UK. Her areas of research and teaching are the recent history of Chile, memory, human rights, and the Holocaust. She is the author (with Yael Siman and Lorena Avila) of "Migration Narratives of Holocaust Survivors in Chile, Colombia, and Mexico" in *Lessons and Legacies XIV* (2020) and (with Yael Siman) of "New Homes and Transitional Spaces for Holocaust Survivors in Chile and Mexico" in *Beyond Camps and Forced Labour* (2020).

Richard Menkis is an associate professor of modern Jewish history at the University of British Columbia. His books include (with Pierre Anctil) *In a "Land of Hope": Documents on the Canadian Jewish Experience, 1627–1923* (2023) and (with Harold Troper) *More than Just Games: Canada and the 1936 Olympics* (2015). He is the author of numerous articles on Canadian Jewish historiography and Canadian responses to the Holocaust. In 2018 he won the Association for Canadian Jewish Studies' Louis Rosenberg Distinguished Service Award and in 2023 the Dean of Arts Award "for his outstanding contributions to the Faculty of Arts."

Roni Mikel-Arieli is a cultural historian interested in the intersections between Holocaust memory, Jewish history, and African studies. She is a postdoctoral and a teaching fellow at the Department of Sociology and Anthropology at the Ben Gurion University of the Negev. For the past two years she served as the academic director of the oral history division at the Institute of Contemporary Jewry of the Hebrew University of Jerusalem. Her first authored book, titled *Remembering the Holocaust in a Racial State: Holocaust Memory in South Africa from Apartheid to Democracy (1948–1994)*, was published in 2022.

Tali Nates is the founder and director of the Johannesburg Holocaust & Genocide Centre (JHGC) and a historian who lectures internationally on Holocaust and genocide education, memory, reconciliation, and human rights. She was born to a family of Holocaust survivors; her father and uncle were saved by Oskar Schindler. She has been involved in the creation and production of dozens of documentary films, curated exhibitions, published articles, and chapters in books. She won many awards in South Africa and globally, the latest of which was the Goethe Medal (2022, Germany) and the Secretary of State International Religious Freedom Award (2023, USA).

Suzanne D. Rutland (Medal of the Order of Australia, PhD), professor emerita, Department of Hebrew, Biblical, and Jewish Studies, University of Sydney, is a past president of the Australian Association for Jewish Studies, patron of the Australian Jewish Historical Society, and member of the Australian IHRA Delegation. She is a widely published author on Australian Jewry focusing on the Holocaust, immigration, Jewish and Holocaust education, Russian Jewry, antisemitism, and Jewish leadership. Her latest books are *Lone Voice: The Wars of Isi Leibler* (2021) and (with Zehavit Gross) *Special Religious Education in Australia and Value to Contemporary Society* (2021).

Yael Siman has an MA and a PhD in political science from the University of Chicago. She is an associate professor in the Department of Social and Political Sciences at Iberoamericana University, Mexico City. She teaches courses on the Holocaust and mass atrocities at the college and graduate levels. She is part of the UNESCO network on Holocaust education and is an associate researcher at the University of Southern California Dornsife Center for Advanced Genocide Research. Her recent publications include an article on thirty Jewish refugee families who immigrated to Mexico during the Holocaust (2024) and an edited volume on the Holocaust and Latin America (forthcoming).

Ilan Stavans is the Lewis-Sebring Professor of Humanities, Latin American and Latino Culture at Amherst College, the publisher of Restless Books, and a consultant to the *Oxford English Dictionary*. His work, translated into two dozen languages, has been adapted into film, TV, theater, and radio. His books include *The Oxford Book of Jewish Stories* (1998), *On Borrowed Words: A Memoir of Language* (2001), *The Schocken Book of Modern Sephardic Literature* (2005), *The Norton Anthology of Latino Literature* (2011), *El Iluminado* (2012), *How Yiddish Changed America and How America Changed Yiddish* (2020), *Selected Translations: Poems, 2000–2020* (2021),

The People's Tongue: Americans and the English Language (2023), *Otrarse: Ladino Poems of Juan Gelman* (2024), and *Sabor Judio: The Jewish Mexican Cookbook* (2024).

Ran Zwigenberg is an associate professor at Pennsylvania State University. His research focuses on modern Japanese and European history, with a specialization in memory and cultural history. He has published on issues of war memory, atomic energy, psychiatry, and survivor politics. His first book, *Hiroshima: The Origins of Global Memory Culture* (2014), won the 2016 Association for Asian Studies' John Whitney Hall Book Prize. His latest book, *Nuclear Minds: Cold War Psychological Science and the Bombings of Hiroshima and Nagasaki* (2023), deals with the psychological aftermath of the nuclear attacks on Japan.

Index

Aag (newspaper), 182
Abbas, Rahman, 182
Abella, Irving, 145–59
Abe Shinzō, 46
A-bomb trauma, 49–51
Achcar, Gilbert, 199
Ackermann, Leonard, 120–22
Aegis Trust (Rwanda), 257–58
Africa, 237, 249–59
Afridi, Mehnaz, 181
Afrikaner nationalism, 17–19
Agenda for Protection, 236
Ahmad, Tariq (Lord Ahmad of Wimbledon), 34
Ahmed, Israr, 185
Ahmed, Rifaat Sayed, 198
Ahmed, Sara, 156
Akl, Said, 197
Alba, Avril, 224–25
Algeria, 90–91, 92–93
al-Hajj, Lewis, 197–98
Al-Ha't wal Dumu' (Mansur), 198
Al-Holocaust al-Muaakess (Sharaf), 199
Aliens Act of 1937, 18–19, 252
Allende, Salvador, 73, 78, 79–80, 82
Al-Masry Al-Yawm (newspaper), 195
"Alone-ness of Being Palestine" (Nagarkar), 186–87
Al-Qadia al-Filistiniya (textbook), 195–96
Al-Shakhsiah al-Yahudiah (Idris), 198
Altman, Herbert, 124
American servicemen and -women, 124
AMIA. *See* Asociación Mutual Israelita de la República Argentina (AMIA)
Amicale Maurice Centre, 34
Anctil, Pierre, 154
"Anne Frank in Our World" exhibition, 23–24, 252

anti-Jewish legislation, 92–93
antiracism campaigns, 240
antiracist activists in South Africa, 19–22
antisemitism: and Afrikaner nationalism, 18–19; and apartheid, 20–22; in the Arab world, 194–204; in Australia, 132–33, 137; and Ben Shimon's text, 99–100; in Canada, 149, 153–54, 156–57; and Holocaust denial, 22, 51–52; and Holocaust education, 227–29; in Mauritius, 34; in Mexico, 167; in New Zealand, 240; in South Asia, 179–88
anti-Zionism, 185–86
Anyu (Goldstein), 214–16
apartheid, 17–25, 249–58
Appanah, Nathacha, 36–37
Arab-Israeli conflict, 194, 201
Arab-Israeli War of 1967, 61, 63
Arab revolt of 1936–39, 35
The Arabs and the Holocaust (Achcar), 199
Arab world, 193–204
Ardern, Jacinda, 237
Argentina, 59–67
arrival, experience of, 75–76
Asmal, Kader, 23
Asociación Mutual Israelita de la República Argentina (AMIA), 65
asylum and asylum seekers, 118, 165–66, 168–71, 236–37, 259
Atlantic (ship), 31
Atlit detention camp, 31
Auckland Law Review, 235
Auerbach, Franz, 20
Auschwitz, 48–49, 50–51, 77–78, 80, 207
Auschwitz Museum, 47
Australia, 131–41, 221–30
Australian Jewish Welfare Society (AJWS), 136, 139–40
Avigdor, Yaacov, 63

289

Ávila Camacho, Manuel, 170–71

Bader, Liesl, 126
Baruch, Peter, 234
Battle of the Three Kings, 94
Bauer, Yehuda, 221–22
Bauman, Zygmunt, 184
Beau-Bassin Jewish Detainees Memorial & Information Centre (BBJDMIC), 34–36, 254
Beau-Bassin prison, 29, 31–36, 251
Benadón, Ida, 63
Benaji, Naji, 200
ben Shimon, Nessim, 99–100
Ben Simhon, Mattatiya (Matityah), 97–98
Bensimon, David, 93
Bettelheim, Bruno, 49–50
Bialystok, Franklin, 148–49
The Bible Came from Arabia (Salibi), 198
Biddle, Francis, 123
Birger, Isia, 33
Blair, Frederick Charles, 151–53
Bliss, Charles K., 268–71
Bliss, Michael, 158
Blum, Léon, 93
Blumenthal, Guita, 271–79
Bocobo, Jorge, 113
Borins, Sandford F., 152, 157
Bose, Sarmila, 184
Bose, Subhas Chandra, 183–84
Bothwell, Robert, 156, 159
Boum, Faraji, 89–91
British Jews, 134–35
British Mandate of Palestine, 29, 31–32, 34–35, 234
Brown, Margot, 224
Browne, Roland S., 138–39
Buenos Aires, Argentina, 60–61, 63
Bungei Shunjū (magazine), 52

Calou, Vanessa, 35
Canada, 145–59
Canadian Broadcasting Corporation (CBC), 148–49
Canadian Charter of Rights and Freedoms, 147
Canadian Historical Review, 149
Canadian Jewish Congress (CJC), 148–49, 151, 154

Cape Town Holocaust & Genocide Centre (CTHGC), 24, 252–53
Cárdenas, Lázaro, 169–70
Carrington, Bruce, 224
Catholic Church, 154
CCIM. *See* Comité Central Israelita de México (CCIM)
Change Makers Programme (CMP), 257–58
Chenoy, Kamal Mitra, 187
Chernivtsi, 268–69
Chettiar, Anjini, 33
Chile, 73–83
Chinese Exclusion Act, 123
Christchurch Call, 237
Christchurch mosque attacks, 237
citizenship, 123–24
civil servants, 151–53
Clarke, Helen, 239
Clifford, Bede, 32
Cohen, Esther, 207
Cohen, Isaac, 117
Cohen, Prosper, 91, 95–96
Cohn, Anna, 226
Colina, Rafael de la, 165
Colombia, 207–17
colonial violence, 30–39
Comarmond, Pierre de, 32–33
Comité Central Israelita de México (CCIM), 171–72
Committee for Jewish Overseas Transports, 31
community-based archives, 150
Confidential Circular no. 157, 169
confidential circulars, 167
Congress, 105, 119–20, 126–27
Convention on the Prevention and Punishment of the Crime of Genocide, 253
Co-operative Commonwealth Federation (CCF), 153
Courage to Care, 223
Crémieux Decree, 92
Crerar, Thomas, 152
Cuba, 271–79
The Cultural Politics of Emotion (Ahmed), 156

Daily Times (newspaper), 187
Dakar, Senegal, 251
David, Esther, 180
Davies, Ian, 224

"Deadly Medicine: Creating the Master Race" exhibition, 258–59
Delisle, Esther, 157
Depression, 131–35
Desmarais, Jacques, 33
Devoy, Susan, 240
Diamant, Eisig, 124
Diamant, Golde, 124
The Diary of Anne Frank (play), 21
Diary of a Young Girl (Frank), 45–46
Dickstein, Samuel, 126
Did Six Million Really Die? (Harwood), 22
Diner, Hasia R., 60
Dirks, Gerald E., 152, 153, 155
displaced people (DPs), 127, 235
Dos Poylishe Ydntum, 61
DuBois, Josiah, 119
Dujovne, Alejandro, 60
Duldig, Karl, 226
Durban Holocaust & Genocide Centre, 24, 254

Echeverría, Luis, 63
Eichmann, Adolf, 22, 46–47, 61–62, 148
Emergency Quota Act, 118, 127
Emergency Rescue Committee for Victims of War, 172
emergency visas, 237
Eriksen, Thomas Hylland, 30
Evian Conference, 59, 105–6, 110, 133–34, 169, 234
An Eye for an Eye (Sack), 199

Feingold, Henry L., 151
Flick, Joseph, 124
Ford, Henry, 197
Fort Ontario Emergency Refugee Shelter, 117–28
The Founding Myths of Modern Israel (Garaudy), 199
Fourteenth Amendment, 124
France, 92–93
Franco, Miriam Mary, 124
Frank, Anne, 45–46, 53, 254
Frank, Margarette, 125
Frank, Otto, 47
Frankel, Neftali, 64
Frankl, Viktor, 46, 49

Franzmann, Seth J., 181
Fraser, Peter, 240
free ports, 120–21
Frei, Eduardo, 79
French, Jackie, 225
French, William, 156
Frieder, Alex, 112
Frieder, Morris, 111
Frieder, Philip, 111
Friedman, Joseph, 119
Friends of Israel in Mauritius (L'Amicale Maurice-Israel), 33
Furlong, Patrick, 18

Gandel, John, 223
Gandel Holocaust Studies Program for Australian Educators, 223
Garaudy, Roger, 199
García Téllez, Ignacio, 166, 169
gay liberation in New Zealand, 240–41
General Assembly United Nations Resolution 3379, 63
General Population Law, 169
genocide(s), 221–22, 249–59; and Holocaust denial, 193; and Holocaust education, 201, 223, 224–25, 229; and Holocaust memory, 64–66; and Islamist antisemites, 179; and the Johannesburg Holocaust & Genocide Centre, 254–57; and memory and education in Africa, 251–58; Rwandan, 24, 221, 241, 254–59; and the South African Holocaust and Genocide Foundation, 24, 35
Genocide Awareness Month, 35
German Forces Network, 92
German Jews, 107–10, 118, 131–33, 136
Gesuiwerde National Party, 18–19
Ghetto Fighters House Archives, 35–36
Gigliotti, Simone, 242
Gilbert, Shirli, 92
Gillard, Julia, 226
Gneisenau (ship), 107
Goebbels, Joseph, 91
The Golden Cage (opera), 127
Goldstein, Anamaria, 214–16
Goldstein, Eric L., 22
Gordon-Gentil, Alain, 37–38
Goumiers, 90
Gradmann, Louis, 32

Grafton, Samuel, 120
Granatstein, Jack, 152, 153, 158–59
Graner, Elsa, 124–25
Graner, Hugo, 124–25
Great Britain, 146, 156
Greyshirt Movement, 18
Griffiths, Owen, 34
Gruber, Ruth, 122–23
Guberek, Simón, 211–12
Guedj, David, 97
Gurwicz, Issy, 256
Gzowski, Peter, 145

Habibi, Emile, 195
Hajj Amin al-Husseini, 194
Halévi, Avraham, 98
Hall, Jeffrey, 54
Harvey, Jean-Charles, 154
Harwood, Richard, 22
Hassine, Asher-Prosper (Asher Hassin), 96–97
hate speech, 240
Hawkins, Freda, 158
Hay, Eduardo, 169
Heathcote-Smith, Clifford, 122–23
Hebrew Immigrant Aid Society (HIAS), 172
Henry Gibbins (ship), 117, 122–24
Herdan, Kurt, 76, 79
hibakusha (Japanese A-bomb survivors), 49–51
Higuchi Kiichirō, 53
Hilfsverein der Juden in Deutschland (Relief Association for Jews in Germany), 108–9
Hill Post (newspaper), 186
Himmel, Alice, 76–77, 80–81
Hindus, 183–84
Hindustan Times (newspaper), 180
Hipkins, Chris, 240
Hiroshima, 48–49, 51
Hiroshima-Auschwitz Museum, 48
Hirsh, David, 186–87
historical trauma, 238–39
Hitler, Adolf, 93–101, 179, 183–87, 197–98
Hitler's Daughter (French), 225
The Holocaust (miniseries), 149
Holocaust and Antisemitism Foundation Aotearoa New Zealand (HAFANZ), 242–43
The Holocaust and the Literary Imagination (Langer), 49

Holocaust Centre of New Zealand (HCNZ), 242
Holocaust denial and distortion, 22, 51–52, 181–82, 184, 193–94, 199–200, 203, 223, 228, 229
Holocaust education: in Africa, 249–59; in the Arab world, 193–204; in Argentina and Mexico, 65–66; in Australia, 221–30; in Japan, 45–55; and memory, 249–59; in South Africa, 21, 249–59; in South Asia, 179–88
Holocaust Education Center, 47
Holocaust exhibitions, 23–24, 47, 53
Holocaust inversion, 185–87
Holocaust literature, 182, 197–200, 207–16
Holocaust memorials and memorialization, 21, 226–27, 241–43, 252–54
Holocaust memory: in Argentina and Mexico, 59–67; in Chile, 73–83; institutionalization of, 65–66, 241; in South Africa, 17–25
Holocaust survivors, 60–67, 73–83, 92, 148–49, 222–23, 233–35, 241–42, 252, 255–57
Hommes, Rudolf, 212
Horthy, Miklós, 215
Hull, Cordell, 111
humanitarian parole, 127
human rights, 23–24, 62, 64–66, 82, 224, 233, 239–41, 242, 253, 254–56, 258
Hundert, Gershon, 156
Hungarian Jews, 120
Hungary, 214–16
Hyman, Joseph, 111

Idris, Muhammad Jala, 198
Immigration Act of 1917, 106, 108
Immigration Act of 1924, 106, 168
immigration policies, 106–14, 117–28, 131–41, 146–59, 165–74, 233–39, 252
Immigration Restriction Amendment Act, 233
India, 179–88
Indian Express (newspaper), 186–87
"Individual and Mass Behavior in Extreme Situations" (Bettelheim), 49–50
institutionalization of Holocaust memory, 65–66, 241
Intergovernmental Committee on Political Refugees, 234
Intergovernmental Committee on Refugees (IGCR), 110–11
International Holocaust Remembrance Alliance (IHRA), 65, 227, 229, 243

International Holocaust Remembrance Day (UNIHRD), 226, 241
The International Jew (Ford), 197
International Refugee Organization (IRO), 235
International Relief Organization, 173
internment and forced labor camps, 250–51
Inter-Parliamentary Coalition for Combating Antisemitism, 226
Into Exile (Segal), 20
Israel, 60–63, 179, 182, 185–87, 193–200, 228, 235
Israeli Embassy in Buenos Aires, 65
Israelite Central Committee of Mexico. *See* Comité Central Israelita de México (CCIM)
Israelite Press (newspaper), 61

Japan, 1–2, 45–55
Jay, Norman, 120
Jerusalem Post (newspaper), 181
Jewish cemeteries, 32–36, 61, 252. *See also* St. Martin Jewish cemetery
Jewish Cemetery Committee, 32
Jewish deportation to Mauritius, 29–39
Jewish emigration agency (HICEM), 172
Jewish Junior League, 113
Jewish Labor Committee of New York, 173
Jewishness, 132–33
Jewish Refugee Committee (JRC), 107–14
Jewish refugees: in Africa, 251; in Australia, 131–41, 222; in Canada, 146–59; and the Fort Ontario Emergency Refugee Shelter, 117–28; and Guita Blumenthal, 271–79; and Mauritius, 29–39; in Mexico, 165–74; in New Zealand, 233–43; in the Philippines, 105–14; in South Africa, 19. *See also* Evian Conference
Jewish Sports Centre, 61
Jewish Telegraphic Agency, 145
Jewish youth movements, 62–63
The Jews of Islam (Lewis), 202
Johannesburg Holocaust & Genocide Centre (JHGC), 24, 34–35, 254–59
Johnson-Reed Immigration Act, 118
Joint Distribution Committee (JDC), 110, 172
Jones, Harold, 139
Jong, Leo de, 76
Jugnauth, Aneerood, 34

Kathrada, Ahmed, 20, 251
Kaupapa Māori, 238–39

Keller, Arie Leopold, 35–36
Khan, Imran, 181
Kido Kōtarō, 49–50
Kigali Genocide Memorial (KGM), 253–54
King, William Lyon Mackenzie, 152–53, 159
Klass, Irene, 259
Klein, Anna Frank, 36
Klein, Irene, 78
Kluk, Mary, 24, 254
Knafo, Isaac D., 91, 94–95
Korman, Edith, 212–14
Kotsuji Setsuzō, 53
Kria (Wald), 21
Kristallnacht, 118, 168, 241
Kurihara Sadako, 48, 49

LaCapra, Dominik, 75, 76–77
L'Action catholique (newspaper), 154
Landsberg, Michelle, 157–58
Langer, Lawrence, 49
Langsam, Oscar, 35
Lapciuc, Israel, 208–12
Lapointe, Ernest, 152–53
Latin America, 59–67
L'Avenir Illustré (newspaper), 94–95
League of Nations, 234
Lebanon War (1982), 154, 157–58
Le dernier frère (Appanah), 36–37
Leip, Hans, 91
Le Jour (weekly), 154
Lemkin, Raphael, 221
"Les Hitlériques" (Knafo), 94–95
Levi, Primo, 249
Le Voyage de Delcourt (Gordon-Gentil), 37–38
Lévy, Bernard-Henri, 187
Lewis, Bernard, 202
Libertadora, 60
Libya, 250
Lichtner, Giacomo, 242
Life (magazine), 123, 125
Light, Helen, 223
"Lili Marlene" (song), 91–92, 94
Lionnet, Françoise, 37
Litvak, Meir, 181–82
"Lmirkan" (Slaoui), 100
The London Declaration, 226
Long, Breckinridge, 119
Luther, Martin, 198
Lyons, Joseph, 133

Mahraqat al-Naziat (Samra), 198–99
Malan, D. F., 18–19
Malik, Veena, 185
Mandela, Nelson, 20, 23, 249, 251–52
Manila, Philippines, 107–14
Man's Search for Meaning (Frankl), 46
Mansur, Anis, 198
Māori, 238–39
March for the Living, 222
Marco Polo (magazine), 52
"Maréchal, nous voilà" (song), 93, 94
Mariquina Hall, 112–13
"The Mark of the Life Esidimeni Decanting" exhibition, 259
Marrus, Michael, 224–25
Martin, Geoff, 156
martyrs, 184
Maruki Iri, 48
Maruki Toshi, 48
mass resettlement, 111–14
Maurer, Harry, 117
The Mauritian Shekel (Pitot), 36
Mauritian Sub-Committee of the Council for Refugee Settlement, 33
Mauritius, 29–39, 251, 254
McCormack, Gavan, 48
McEwen, John, 135, 140
McNutt, Paul V., 106–14
Medene Sugar Estate Company (MSEC), 32–33
Megilla di Hitler (Hassine), 96–97
Mein Kampf (Hitler), 183, 197–98
memory activism, 249
Mendes, Philip, 228–29
Mendicino, Teresa, 124
Menzies, Robert, 133
Messersmith, George, 109
Mexican *mestizaje* (miscegenation), 167
Mexico, 59–67, 165–74
Miller, Susan Gilson, 94
Milos (ship), 31
Mindanao, Philippines, 111–14
miracle poems, 93–99
modern antisemitism, 194
Modi, Narendra, 187
Mongrel Mob, 241
Morgenthau, Henry, Jr., 126
Moriah College, 223
Morocco, 89–101
Morrison, Scott, 227

Mostny, Marion, 76, 79–80
Motshekga, Angie, 253
Moyn, Samuel, 145
multiculturalism, 138, 147, 150, 155–56
Museum of Memory and Tolerance, 66
museums, 249–59
music, 89–101
Muslims and the Muslim world, 179–86, 193–204, 227–29, 237
"My Congo, My Story" exhibition, 259

Nadeem, Anwar, 182
Nagarkar, Kiran, 186–87
Nagasaki, 48–49, 51
Nakazawa Masao, 49
Nanjing massacre, 53–54
Nanking Incident of 1937, 50–51
Naqba, 194–95, 200, 201, 228, 241
Nash, Walter, 233–34
Nates, Tali, 24
National Action Plan against Racism, 240
National Commission for Truth Clarification of Nazi Activities in Argentina (CEANA), 65
National Holocaust Remembrance Committee, 149
National Refugee Service, 127
national unity, 159
nation building, 22–23, 156
"Nazi Germany and the Holocaust" curriculum, 253
Nazi propaganda, 183, 194
"The Nazis Are in Gaza" (Shukla), 186
Nazi war criminals, 149, 154–55, 235
neo-Nazis, 148–49, 237
Netanyahu, Benjamin, 186
newspapers in India, 186
New York Post (newspaper), 125
New York Times (newspaper), 145
New Zealand, 233–43
New Zealand Human Rights Commission (HRC), 240
Ngabo, Xavier, 256
Ngāi Tahu Research Centre report, 239
Nihon Bunka Channel Sakura (Japanese Culture Channel Sakura), 54
Noguès, Charles, 93
Noma Hiroshi, 50
None Is Too Many (Abella and Troper), 145–59
Non-European Unity Movement, 19

non-survivors, 148–49
No olvidarás (Lapciuc), 208–11
North Africa, 89–101, 119
northern Europeans, 134, 235
Nuwayhed, Hajaj, 197–98
Nuwe Orde (New Order) party, 18

Ontario Chronicle (newspaper), 126
Operation Torch, 94, 97, 119
oral history projects, 64, 65–66
Osrin, Myra, 252
Ossewabrandwag (Oxwagon Sentinel), 18
Oswego NY, 117–28
Otoño dorado (Korman), 212–14
Otsuka Makoto, 47
Ouarzazate, 90

Pacific (ship), 31
Pacific War, 51
Page, Earle, 135
Pākehā, 233, 238
Pakistan, 180–81, 185, 187
Palestine, 31–32, 34–35, 183, 193–99, 228, 234–35
Patria (ship), 31, 35
Pehle, John, 120–22
Perón, Juan Domingo, 60–62
Pétain, Philippe, 92–93
Philippines, 105–14
Pichkaari (comedy series), 181
pilgrimages for peace, 48–49
Pink Triangle (periodical), 240–41
Pinochet dictatorship, 82
Pirow, Oswald, 18
Pitot, Geneviève, 36
pluralism, 156–57
Poirier, Marie, 154
Polillo, Philippines, 112
political asylum, 106, 165–66, 170–71, 173
Popular Unity, 78
Porat, Dina, 182
Portelli, Alessandro, 82, 216
Posel, Deborah, 19
post-conflict societies, 201
prisoners of war, 119
propaganda, 91–93
Pro-Refugee Committee, 171
The Protocols of the Elders of Zion, 194, 197
Public Archives of Canada, 150

public opinion, 65, 133, 138
Purandare, Vaibhav, 183
Purim de los Bombas, 94
Purim de los Christianos, 94
Purim di Hitler, 94
Purim Katan, 93–96

"Qasida di Hitler" (Ben Simhon), 97–98
"Qasida di Hitler the Evil" (Halévi), 98
Quebec, 147, 153–54, 156–57
Quezon City, Philippines, 112–13
Quezon y Molina, Manuel Luis, 105–14
Quota Act of 1930, 18, 252
quota system, 31, 93, 118, 125, 127, 169–70, 236–37

racial refugees, 166
racism, scientific, 167
racism, Zionism as form of, 61, 165
Radical Civic Union, 60
Rashtriya Sahara (newspaper), 182
Rauca, Helmut, 154
Ravi, Srilata, 30, 36
Reconciliation through Truth (Asmal), 23
Refugee Economic Corporation (REC), 108–10
Refugee Resettlement Act, 127
Rein, Jane, 61–62
rescue, 105–14
"Rescue Resolution," 119
Research Commission of Anti-Argentinean Activities, 60
Resolution 80, 65
Rethinking the Holocaust (Bauer), 221–22
Reynolds, Robert, 123
Richler, Mordecai, 157
Robben Island, 20, 23, 251
Rockwell, Lincoln, 149
Roosevelt, Eleanor, 125
Roosevelt, Franklin, 117–26
Rosa Luxemburg Stiftung-Southern Africa, 34
Rothberg, Michael, 83
Royal Commission on Bilingualism and Biculturalism, 147
Rwanda, 24, 221, 241, 249, 253–59

Sack, John, 199
Sadako Sasaki, 45

Sahih Bukhari, 179, 185
Salibi, Kamal, 198
Samra, Mohammed Abu, 198–99
Santander, Silvano, 62
Sargoy, Milton, 123–24
Saron, Gustav, 22
Savarkar, Vinayak Damodar, 183
Sayf al-Samiah (Ahmed), 198
Schorch, Philipp, 229–30
Seager, Frédéric, 154
Segal, Ronald, 20
selection rescue, 109–12
Sendacyeye, Sylvestre, 259
Senegalese soldiers, 90
Serpa Pinto (ship), 172
Shain, Milton, 18
Shalom India Housing Society (David), 180
shame, 155–59
Shanghai, 107–8
Sharaf, Ayman, 199
Sherit Hapleitah (Surviving Remnants), 62–63
Sh'erit ha-Pletah ("the surviving remnants"), 252
Shimizu Ikutarō, 50
Shimoyama Tokuji, 50–51
Shoah through Muslim Eyes (Afridi), 181
Short, Geoffrey, 224
Shukla, Avay, 186
Sides, Krik, 37
Silberhaft, Moshe, 33–34
Silberstein, Viorica, 80–82
silences, 74, 78, 82, 153, 212, 222–23
Sipser, Max, 126
Sivaraman, Satya, 184
Six Million (Wald), 21
Slaoui, Houcine, 91, 100–101
Smart, Joseph, 121, 126
Smith, Mervyn, 34
Smuts, Jan, 19
Snell, David, 159
Society for Culture and Aid, 173
South Africa, 17–25, 249–59
South African Gentile National Socialist Movement, 18
South African Holocaust and Genocide Foundation (SAHGF), 24, 35
South African Jewish Board of Deputies (SAJBD), 21, 32–33

South Asia, 179–88
southern Europeans, 132, 136
Spanish refugees, 166
sponsorship programs in the Philippines, 108–10, 113
Stafford, David, 155
stateless individuals, 106, 117, 169–70, 259
state terrorism, 64–65
Steiner, Jean-François, 145
Stern, Steve, 82
Sternbach, Klara, 77–78
Sternberg, Georg, 124
Sternberg, Helga, 124
St. Louis (ship), 271–79
St. Martin Jewish cemetery, 32–36, 251, 254
Stockholm Declaration, 65
Storfer, Berthold, 31
Stranger to History (Taseer), 180–81
A Study of History (Toynbee), 199
Sugihara Chiune, 1–2, 47, 52–54, 234
Sydney Jewish Museum, 223–24

Takeyama Michio, 46–47
Tamahere, John, 242
Tangier, 94
Tantawi, Muhammad Sayyid, 196
Taranaki Māori, 239
Taranaki Report of 1996, 239
Taseer, Aatish, 180–81
Tel Aviv Review, 195
Tel Aviv University, 35
testimonial accounts about the Holocaust, 60–66, 73–83, 207–17
Thompson, Victor, 135–38, 140
Tibi, Basam, 185
Times of Israel (newspaper), 235
Together for Humanity (T4H), 229
#TogetherWeRemember Coalition, 35
totalitarianism, 49–51
Toynbee, Arnold J., 199
transit visas, 1, 52, 75, 234
trauma, 73–83
Treaty of Waitangi, 238–39
Treblinka (Moyn and Steiner), 145
Troper, Harold, 145–59
Trotter, Sheree (Te Arawa), 242–43
Trudeau, Pierre Elliot, 147
Truman, Harry, 126

Truman Directive, 127
Truth and Reconciliation Commission (TRC), 23
Tunisia, 93
Turia, Tariana, 239
Turkow, Marc, 61

Union of Members of the Resistance, Deported and Victims of World War II, 62
United Nations, 253
United Nations Convention relating to the Status of Refugees, 236
United Nations Resolution 3379, 165
United States, 104–14, 117–28, 148, 150, 168
United States Holocaust Memorial Museum, 224
United States v. Wong Kim Ark, 123–24
Universal Declaration of Human Rights (UDHR), 240, 253
Université des Mascareignes (Mauritius), 35
Uno Masami, 51–52
Urdu literature on the Holocaust, 182
U.S. State Department, 107, 109, 112, 114, 118–19, 125
U.S. Treasury Department, 119
U.S. War Department, 109, 121

vacuum zone, 50
Vajda, Sándor, 215–16
Vallat, Xavier, 92
Vichy France, 90, 92–94, 250–51
Villa Michel, Primo, 169
visas, 1, 52, 75, 106–10, 168–73, 234, 237

Waitangi Tribunal, 239
Waititi, Taika, 240
Wajnryb, Ruth, 222
Wald, Herman, 21, 252
Wallenberg, Raoul, 226
Ward-Harris, E. D., 155, 158–59
War Refugee Board (WRB), 119–22, 125–26
War Relocation Authority (WRA), 121, 126
Warsaw Ghetto Uprising, 61, 62–63, 226, 241
Waseem, Aqdas, 181
Waterbury, Edwin, 125
Weichardt, Louis T., 18
Weinfeld, Morton, 147
Wertheimer, Gila, 156

White, Thomas, 133–34
White Paper of 1939, 34–35
Who Killed Daniel Pearl? (Lévy), 187
Winnipeg General Strike of 1919, 146
Wistrich, Robert S., 182
Wollny, Hans, 173

Yad Vashem, 52–53, 63, 65–66, 223, 242
Yankelevich, Pablo, 167
Yishuv, 182
Yom Ha'Shoah (Holocaust Remembrance Day), 61, 226, 252
Yomiuri Shinbun (newspaper), 46
Yugoslavia, 91, 120, 126

Zachariah, Benjamin, 184
Zahid, Arshiya, 187
Zarb-e-Momin (newspaper), 187
Zindeeq (Abbas), 182
Zionism, 21, 61, 63, 165, 194
Zuroff, Efraim, 235
Zwergbaum, Aaron, 33

In the Contemporary Holocaust Studies series

Unlikely Heroes: The Place of Holocaust Rescuers in Research and Teaching
Edited by Ari Kohen and Gerald J. Steinacher

Antisemitism on the Rise: The 1930s and Today
Edited by Ari Kohen and Gerald J. Steinacher

Global Approaches to the Holocaust: Memory, History, and Representation
Edited by Mark Celinscak and Mehnaz Afridi

To order or obtain more information on these or other
University of Nebraska Press titles, visit nebraskapress.unl.edu.

www.ingramcontent.com/pod-product-compliance
Lightning Source LLC
Chambersburg PA
CBHW030609230426
43661CB00053B/1904